EMPIRICAL POLITICAL ANALYSIS: RESEARCH METHODS IN POLITICAL SCIENCE

Sixth Edition

Jarol B. Manheim
The George Washington University

Richard C. Rich
Virginia Tech

Lars Willnat
The George Washington University

Craig Leonard Brians
Virginia Tech

PEARSON
Longman

New York • San Francisco • Boston
London • Toronto • Sydney • Tokyo • Singapore • Madrid
Mexico City • Munich • Paris • Cape Town • Hong Kong • Montreal

Executive Editor: Eric Stano
Supplements Editor: Kristi Olson
Senior Marketing Manger: Elizabeth Fogarty
Managing Editor: Bob Ginsberg
Project Coordination, Text Design, and Electronic Page Makeup: Thompson Steele, Inc.
Cover Designer/Manager: Wendy Ann Fredericks
Cover Illustration: © Stockbyte
Senior Manufacturing Buyer: Alfred C. Dorsey
Printer and Binder: Hamilton Printing Co.
Cover Printer: The Lehigh Press, Inc.

Library of Congress Cataloging-in-Publication Data

Manheim, Jarol B.
    Empirical political analysis : research methods in political science / Jarol B. Manheim . . . [et al.] . . . 6th ed.
      p. cm.
    Includes bibliographical references and index.
    ISBN 0-321-29860-8 (pbk. : alk. paper)
     1. Political science--Research. I. Title.

JA86.M35 2005
320'.072--dc21

                                        2005008140

Please visit our website at http://www.ablongman.com

ISBN 0-321-29860-8

1 2 3 4 5 6 7 8 9 10—HT—04 03 02 01

Contents

CHAPTER 6

Working from a Plan: Considerations in Research Design   87

CHAPTER 7

Who, What, Where, When: The Problem of Sampling   109

ANALYZING QUANTITATIVE DATA   218

Preface

The Development and Features of This Text

Over the years, the authors of this text have taught research methods at universities on both coasts to students—both undergraduate and graduate—who are planning careers in business, government, and academia. Whether by choice or by administrative requirements, these students found themselves enrolled in courses that examined the nuts and bolts of the research process. Frustration with the lack of an acceptable text that spoke to students both concretely and theoretically led Jarol Manheim and Richard Rich to publish the first edition of this book in 1981.

The years since this book's inception have seen many developments in the research methods used in political science, and *Empirical Political Analysis* has incorporated these new methods into its subsequent editions. The text you are holding is the latest version of this unique political science research methods text. While this volume holds an established position in the discipline, it also embraces the latest developments in the field.

New Features. Each chapter has been fully updated and revised to reflect recent political science research advancements. A few of the new features include:

- **Key Concepts** To sharpen students' focus, key questions are posed at the beginning and main points are summarized at the end of each chapter.
- **Web Research** A new chapter directly addresses Web-based research, alerting students to the benefits and potential pitfalls of electronic resources and offering solutions for each concern.
- **Network Analysis** A new chapter introduces network analysis with numerous examples of specific political science applications and graphical illustrations, making this volume the only major research methods text to address this cutting-edge approach.
- **Ethics** The emphasis on professional and personal ethics is strengthened, with specific guidelines and examples to aid students throughout the text.

Structure and Breadth. This book features a clear and appropriate organizational structure to balance the competing demands placed upon an introductory text. The configuration reflects the various stages of the research process, from conceptualization of the research question to interpretation of the findings. Each chapter has been planned around a series of substantive questions, presented so as to provide examples of the importance or application of the topic, and enhanced with a series of research exercises that give the student practical insights into the issues raised. Each chapter is also rounded out with a bulleted summary, a list of key terms, and an annotated bibliography that suggests more advanced technical discussions of particular methods and sources where these methods have been employed in the literature of political science.

In addition, this book is written at an appropriate level for students. We do not talk down to students, but we do write for them. We try to anticipate the questions a student might raise and to respond to them. We introduce necessary technical terms—which is, after all, a central function of a methods text—but we avoid unnecessary jargon. Specialized terms are defined in the glossary at the end of the book and are shown in **bold print** on their first significant use in context. We do not believe that one must be familiar with every technical term in order to grasp the essentials of the research process. While we present detail and specify procedures, we try to keep sight of the conceptual framework inherent in doing research.

Finally, and perhaps most importantly, this book is *comprehensive*. It introduces a wide variety of techniques, applications, and concerns that are important to political science research; their foci range from survey research to experimental methods, from the difficulties of comparative research to the opportunities of focus groups. And although we do not explore each of our topics in the depth that a specialized text might, we do provide sufficient insights into the workings and applications of an array of key topics so as to meet the needs of the beginning researcher. We believe that after reading this book students will both know and understand a great deal about the research process (not the least of which is how much more there is to learn), and we hope that instructors will find that this is the only text they need to teach a complete methods course.

Acknowledgements

This text represents a collaborative effort of four authors, who hail from a range of political science fields. We publish research on topics ranging from political communications to environmental politics, from international studies to organizational networks, and more. Additionally, we work across the spectrum of methodologies— when we discuss a given research method in this text, we speak from personal experience. For several of us, much of that experience has been gained using data obtained from the Inter-university Consortium for Political and Social Research at the University of Michigan (www.icpsr.umich.edu), and through hands-on exposure to qualitative and quantitative research techniques at the ICPSR Summer Program.

Although we collectively possess broad expertise, this text is for students and has benefited from the useful feedback our own students have offered. We also have benefited from the comments we receive from students who use this text at colleges and universities across the United States and the world—this book has been translated into numerous languages, including Arabic, Chinese, and Russian. Student responses have particularly contributed to the incorporation of on-line research techniques throughout this book.

In preparing this sixth edition, we owe a particular debt to Bruce Pencek, Ph.D., College Librarian for the Social Sciences at Virginia Tech's Newman Library, who directed the thorough rewriting of the bibliographic research techniques contained in Chapter 3. Jessica Folkart, Ph.D., a language professor at Virginia Tech, substantially enhanced the clarity and readability of every part of this text. Also, we wish to thank the following reviewers for their helpful comments:

Matthew M. Shousen, Franklin and Marshall College

Bruce Evans, Susquehanna University

U. K. Heo, University of Wisconsin–Milwaukee

Derrick L. Cogburn, University of Michigan

Stephen A. Borrelli, University of Alabama

Donald R. Raber, Presbyterian College

Lauretta Conklin Frederking, University of Portland

Kenneth Fernandez, University of Nevada, Las Vegas

Cynthia J. Bowling, Auburn University

Thanks, too, to Kara Wylie, Eric Stano, and Nancy Freihofer for helping to make this new edition a reality.

We are grateful to Donna Bahry, whose knowledge of comparative politics and contributions to this text over the years are still reflected in Chapter 12, and to the literary executor of the late Sir Ronald A. Fisher, F.R.S., to Dr. Frank Yates, F.R.S., and to Longman Group, Ltd., London, for permission to reprint Tables IV and VII from its book *Statistical Tables for Biological, Agricultural and Medical Research* (6th ed., 1974).

Finally, we want to thank our families, who, once again, have put up with our undoubtedly intolerable behavior as we came to terms with the fact that signing a publishing contract is not the same as turning in a completed manuscript.

With all of this assistance, the final product is ours. We are responsible for its weaknesses and for its strengths. We think it is still a superb teaching tool, and we hope that you will agree.

JAROL MANHEIM
RICHARD RICH
LARS WILLNAT
CRAIG LEONARD BRIANS

CHAPTER 1

The Research Process

- Why was science developed?
- What are the characteristics of the Political Science research method?
- Are qualitative and quantitative scientific research the only methods available to address political questions?

Curiosity and necessity drive human inquiry. We may seek to understand the world around us for the sake of knowledge, or we seek to understand it so that we may protect or better our lot in it. Whichever is the case, the more we learn about our social and physical environment, the better equipped we are to adapt to our conditions or to manipulate them. This is just as true of our knowledge of politics as it is of other fields. The key to understanding and altering our political environment is, most simply, knowing more about it.

The Quest for Knowledge

But this simple idea of knowing raises two far less simple questions: *How* do we know? *How should we use* what we know? The first is a question of method, the second, one of ethics and preference. In the first instance we are interested in obtaining and structuring knowledge or understanding; in the second we are concerned with the moral obligations that accompany it. Both questions require the exercise of judgment and both draw upon our experience, but each demands its own distinct kind of intellectual effort.

Obtaining Knowledge   To decide how we know, we must set forth certain hard-and-fast rules for defining political reality. For example, we might define political reality as our experience with, and observations of, the political system. That seems straightforward enough. But what is the political system? What kind of observations are we speaking about? Have we witnessed all possible political events, or is our definition unduly limiting? Is political reality a product of the observer, as our definition suggests, or of the system itself? With a definition such as this, different observers, having had different experiences and perspectives, will arrive not only at different understandings of political reality but at different *ways of understanding* as well. The result might be a highly individualized body of knowledge with no mechanism for sharing it. The problem of deciding how we know, then, is a problem of arriving at a generally accepted way of defining reality, at a common language of inquiry, so that anyone who learns the rules or "speaks the language" can communicate on the basis of shared understanding with all others who have been similarly trained. At least in the abstract, if all of us can agree on *how* we know, then eventually we should agree on the higher-order question of *what* we know.

Using Knowledge   Deciding how we should *use* what we know is a different process. Here there is no need for orthodoxy or a common preference, though we still need a common language to permit communication and debate. Ultimately, deciding the best or most desirable application of knowledge is a subjective, individual activity. All of us have certain wants or needs that will lead us to value one outcome of applying our knowledge over another, and it is not necessary—though it may be desirable—that we arrive at some common value judgment. If taxes are lowered, middle-income people will live more comfortably, but social services targeted primarily at the poor, the aged, and the infirm will be reduced. Should taxes be reduced? The answer, clearly, depends not on what we know, but on how that knowledge is related to our own social position and value structure. Ideologies and political systems provide the means for structuring and aggregating the preferences of various individuals, but the decisions themselves are made by individuals, one by one, without resort to a common perspective.

Empirical Versus Normative Analysis   Political scientists distinguish obtaining knowledge and using knowledge. Dealing with how (and what) we know is termed **empirical** analysis. Dealing with how we should use our knowledge is termed **normative** analysis. Empirical analysis is concerned with developing and using a common, objective language to *describe* and *explain* political reality. It can be **quantitative,** based on statistical comparisons of the characteristics of the various objects or cases that are being studied, or it can be **qualitative,** based on the researcher's informed understanding of those same objects or cases. Normative analysis is concerned with developing and examining subjective goals, values, and moral rules to *guide* us in applying what we have learned of that reality.

Thus, although our emphasis in this book is on empirical political analysis, our goal is to develop, in addition to a facility with various aspects of empirical technique, an appreciation of the larger, normative perspective within which knowledge is interpreted. Carried to the extreme, normative analysis without empirical foundation can lead to value judgments that are out of touch with reality. Empirical analysis in the absence of a sensitivity to normative concerns, on the other hand, can lead to the creation of a fact structure in a vacuum, a collection of observations whose significance we are not prepared to understand fully. The object, then, in undertaking political inquiry is to draw upon both types of analysis—empirical and normative—so as to maximize not only our knowledge but also our understanding of political reality.

Scientific Knowledge   In this context, we can see scientific research as a way of knowing and as a common language of inquiry. Scientific research is, to be sure, not the only way of knowing, but it is in many instances and for many purposes the *most effective.* People can know things through experience, but not everyone shares the same experiences. People can know things by keeping their eyes open, but they cannot be sure that through such unstructured observation they will note all or even a representative group of relevant events. Some people can even "know" things by seeing visions or hearing disembodied voices, and others may accept their descriptions and accounts as valid, but not everyone can be trained in visionary methods. Each of these ways of knowing serves a purpose and each has its uses, but none allows for the total sharing both of facts or conclusions and of the knowledge of how those facts or conclusions were obtained. Each allows communication, but none helps us reach a comprehensive, shared understanding.

The Scientific Method   Scientific research is *explicit, systematic,* and *controlled.* It is explicit in that all the rules for defining and examining reality are clearly stated. Nothing is hidden from view and nothing is taken on faith. It is systematic in that each item of evidence is linked by reason or observation to other items of evidence. No ad hoc explanations are tolerated and no carelessness of method is permitted. It is controlled in that the phenomena under analysis are, to the extent possible, observed in as rigorous a manner as the state of the art allows. Generalized conclusions are reached only after the most thorough and painstaking assessment, and caution (in the larger sense of exercising great care and attention to detail) is a watchword. Yet for all its constraints, or, indeed, precisely because of them, scientific research opens for those versed in its ways a whole new level of understanding reality. It is for this reason that the scientific method is applied to the study of politics.

Scientific research, meaning inquiry guided by the scientific method, permits us to know reality and to evaluate the ways in which we know, but—because those ways are commonly understood by those trained in the method—it also permits us to improve upon our means of inquiry. Scientific research is a self-correcting, continuously developing way of knowing.

As a discipline, political science is not always "scientific." The earliest political scientists were trained in philosophy rather than in social science (which did not exist). Much of the earliest empirical work was interpretive and relatively unstructured, and even today there exist differences of opinion over what contemporary practitioners can or should accomplish. In recent years, the political science discipline has seen sharp cleavages between researchers who offer differing answers to the question "is science the best way of knowing?" In an effort to alleviate this conflict, the American Political Science Association in 2003 initiated a new journal "Perspectives on Politics," as an alternative publication source to its flagship *American Political Science Review.* The *Review* is generally regarded as requiring its authors to use scientific methods in their research, while *Perspectives* offers researchers using alternative knowledge systems a widely-distributed publication outlet.

In the discipline as a whole, though, beginning in the 1940s the application of the scientific approach to describing and understanding political phenomena has come to predominate political science. Particularly in the United States, more and more political scientists have become convinced that science yields important insights into the behaviors of individuals, political organizations, and governments, and offers distinct advantages in the replication of results.

Scientific research, or for our purposes *social* scientific research, is a *method of testing theories and hypotheses by applying certain rules of analysis to the observation and interpretation of reality under strictly delineated circumstances.* These are the rules and constraints that we must learn in order to gain and communicate knowledge in the science of politics.

The Research Process   Political science research is best thought of as a *process* of gathering and interpreting information. This research process consists of six distinct but highly interrelated stages: (1) the formulation of theory, (2) the operationalization of that theory, (3) the selection of appropriate research techniques, (4) the observation of behavior, (5) the analysis of data, and (6) the interpretation of the results. These six stages provide the organizing rationale for much of this book and for much of your research.

The Formulation of Theory

The first step in undertaking political science research is the selection of an appropriate *research question,* and here we can readily see the importance of mixing normative with empirical considerations. What criteria make one research question more appropriate than another? While a number of such criteria come to mind, ranging from the personal interests of the researcher to the collective interests of society, most fall into one of two major categories. A question is worthy of research either because it fulfills a scientific need—that is, because its answer will further our theoretical understanding of some phenomenon—or because it fulfills a societal need—that is, because its answer may help us to deal with one or another of the problems faced by our society.

Although these two types of research questions, frequently termed **basic research** and **applied research,** are not mutually exclusive (asking one does not *necessarily* mean you cannot ask the other), they do frequently compete with one another. For example, should we study the hypothetical determinants of aggression under conditions of stress in order to develop a sophisticated predictive model of human behavior, or should we instead focus on the reasons riots occur and on ways to prevent them? Should we examine at length the decision-making processes of national leaders to help us understand leadership, or should we instead concentrate on identifying and avoiding the types of decisions that lead to war? Because too few scientific resources (money, time, and trained personnel) are available to study all potentially interesting or important research questions, there is often a conflict between the need to perform basic research—whose practical payoffs, however great, are almost always felt only indirectly and far in the future—and the need to use our scientific knowledge in the present for the immediate benefit of humanity, even though we may in the process delay or prevent the further development of our science. The choice must be made by individual researchers in accord with their own values.

Once you have identified the problem you wish to tackle and the type of contribution you wish to make, then you need to frame a more specific *research question.* First, you should identify which aspect of the problem interests you most. Since research projects may be lengthy and no research question can be answered adequately without hard work, you should not take on a task in which you have little interest.

Second, you must sift through the various elements or components of the research topic to identify those that may be important to your research. Draw on your powers of observation, reasoning, and on past research to identify the major factors that bear on the behavior you are seeking to understand.

A Research Example   Let us imagine that in the middle of the desert there is a town called Little America that consists of several miles of service stations and restaurants stretching from the exit ramp of an interstate highway to the edge of the horizon. One can do nothing in Little America except eat and buy gas.

Now, suppose we have decided to study the voting behavior of Little Americans in presidential elections so that we may explain why one person votes Democratic while another votes Republican. In this simplified example, the subjects of our analysis (Little Americans) differ from one another in only two ways besides their voting preferences: each is either an owner or a worker, and each is associated with either a service station or a restaurant. Each of these factors, which political scientists term *variables,* represents a characteristic of a particular individual. One citizen of Little America might be (1) an employee of (2) a restaurant who (3) votes Democratic, while another is (1) an owner of (2) a service station who (3) votes Republican. Since we wish to explain differences in voting behavior in terms of other kinds of differences among the voters, we must focus on all factors that might bear on a person's electoral preference. In this instance, we have only two to choose from: employee or owner status and service station or restaurant affiliation. Let us refer to these respectively as *socioeconomic status (SES)*—with ownership representing higher status than employment—and business affiliation. Is there any reason to expect that knowing either characteristic of a particular person will help us to predict his or her voting preference?

To answer that question, we must do two things. First, we must *think*. We must ask ourselves: Is there any *logical reason* to expect either of these factors to influence voting behavior? Second, we must consult the political science literature: Is there, in previous studies of this or related topics, any *empirical evidence* that one or the other of these factors influences voting behavior? In reality, there is little reason to expect the business-affiliation variable to make much difference in voting behavior in this instance. Differences may well exist between those associated with service stations and those with restaurants, but these differences are not likely to have much impact on presidential voting preferences. Few presidential candidates run on a pro-service station, anti-restaurant platform (or vice versa), and, other things being equal, this variable is not likely to help us explain voting behavior. The second variable, SES, however, is a different story. Since the Democratic party is popularly identified as the party of labor and the Republican party as the party of business, and since persons of higher SES are more likely than those of lower SES to vote Republican, we might well expect that employees will be more likely to vote for the Democratic candidate and owners for the Republican. Indeed, the research literature is replete with examples of precisely this kind of relationship. Thus, logical reasoning and empirical evidence both point in the same direction. Our research question might then become, does the SES of a voter in Little America influence voting preference in a presidential election?

In the real world, of course, people differ from one another on more than two or three characteristics, but the problem we face in framing a research question is essentially the same. Because no one has the resources to measure every possible variable, we must choose, from among the thousands of human (or institutional) characteristics, those few that we expect will help us to explain whatever pattern of behavior interests us. With the aid of both logic and literature we try to anticipate and identify the factors that might be related to the behavior of interest. In so doing, we are not prejudging our results, but rather refining our thinking about the research problem to identify those avenues of inquiry most likely to lead to successful explanation. This process of refining our research question through informed selection is what we mean by the term *formulation of theory.*

The Operationalization of Theory

Once we have arrived at one or more research questions and the theory needed to direct our search for answers, we must progress to the next step, that of **operationalization**—the conversion or redefinition of our relatively abstract theoretical notions into concrete terms that will allow us actually to measure whatever it is we are after. It involves moving from the conceptual level (thinking about a problem) to the operational level (deciding how to solve it). It involves learning to think in *practical* terms.

Defining Terms   Suppose, to continue our example, that we have a hypothesis—a statement of the answer we expect to find for our research question—that Little Americans of higher SES (owners) are more likely than those of lower SES (employees) to vote Republican in the next presidential election. This is in line with the findings of countless other voting studies and is a reasonable expectation in the present instance as well. But how do we find out for sure? We cannot simply walk up to a Little American and say, "Good evening. Are you of higher or lower socioeconomic status?" To begin with, the person we are interviewing probably will not understand what we are talking about, since *socioeconomic status* is a technical term with many variations of meaning. And second, even if we get an answer, we will probably not be able to interpret it. Suppose the respondent replied, "Yes, I am of higher socioeconomic status." Higher than whom? How high? How does that person define socioeconomic status? Does it mean the same thing to the respondent as it does to the researcher? Once we have an abstract concept in mind, we must find a way to define more explicitly what we mean by that concept; then we must form our definition into as unambiguous a question or measure as possible.

The problem here is to make intelligent yet arbitrary choices among numerous shades of meaning. When we use the variable SES, are we thinking about respondents' level of income, occupation, or perhaps even subjective notions of which social class they belong to? Each might be a component of SES, but each has a somewhat different meaning, and each must be measured differently: What was the total income of your family last year? What is your occupation? Would you say that you consider yourself to be a member of the working class, the middle class, or the upper class?

In other words, once we arrive at some hypothesis or research question, we have to examine very closely just what it is that we mean by each phrase we use, and we have to translate that more precise definition into measurable indicators. We seek, in effect, the lowest common denominator of meaning. (Although not everyone would, for example, assign the same meaning to the term *socioeconomic status,* almost everyone would mean the same thing by *total annual income in dollars.*) In the process our concepts are narrowed and shades of meaning are lost, but because of this our thinking becomes much more precise, and our ability to communicate in clear, unambiguous terms what we have done is greatly enhanced. This process of translation and simplification, which we term *operationalization,* is *the single most important key to conducting meaningful research.*

The Selection of Appropriate Research Techniques

Once we have decided what we want to measure, we must decide how we will measure it. We must devise a research strategy, a plan of attack. Two considerations are of primary importance here.

First, we must select a technique or a combination of techniques that will enable us to ask the particular questions—to measure the particular variables—that interest us, and we must do so in ways that are consistent with our operationalizations. We cannot, for example, measure the attitudes of individual voters by analyzing the content of newspaper coverage of a given election, because newspaper content may reflect the views of an editor or of those few people whose letters to that editor are published without necessarily reflecting the views of most voters. Moreover, analyzing news or editorial content does not permit us to differentiate among different types of voters, such as those of higher or lower SES. Thus, content analysis would not allow us to answer our research question—that is, to test our hypothesis; survey research would be more useful. On the other hand, suppose that we wish to assess the coverage given by a newspaper to a political campaign. We might simply analyze the content of the newspaper itself, counting references to the candidates and so forth, or we might survey readers of the newspaper to measure what information they remember reading about the campaign. In the first instance, we would have a direct measure of content from which we are forced to infer impact; in the second instance, we would have a direct measure of impact from which we are forced to infer content. Depending on the precise formulation of our research question, one or the other or the combination of both strategies might be useful. The point is that the *appropriateness* of a given research technique is in large part determined by the particular problem we have selected for study.

The second consideration is *feasibility.* This is the stage of the research process at which we prepare to leave our ivory tower and actually go out into the real world. For that reason, we must assure ourselves that whatever method or technique we select can properly be employed under the particular set of conditions we are likely to face. For example, since there is no newspaper in our Little America (only service stations and restaurants), we cannot use content analysis even if we want to. Similarly, the most direct way to measure the level of tension between the leaders of Iraq and those of Turkey might be through a series of personal interviews with those leaders themselves, but such interviews are, to say the least, difficult to arrange. In each instance, we have to find less than ideal ways of measuring the key variables. A feasible technique, then, is one that will be maximally effective given the constraints of the research situation.

To summarize, we must find a way to measure those variables we wish to measure that will be (1) consistent with our working definitions of the variables and (2) practicable. We must be as scientific as possible, but we can be only as scientific as the circumstances allow.

The Observation of Behavior

The fourth stage of the research process involves actually carrying out the research strategy developed in stage 3. Many factors must be taken into account here, but two in particular are worthy of note. The first is the notion of generalizability, the second that of reactivity.

Generalizability refers to the ability to generalize or extend our conclusions with some confidence from the observed behavior of a few cases to the presumed behavior of an entire population. It is a concern we must take into account in selecting the particular cases (people, decisions, organizations, or nations) that we wish to study. The problem here is basically one of scale. If there are only, say, four or five occurrences of an event or subjects in a group we wish to study, we can examine each of those occurrences or subjects individually and make various general statements about them with reasonable confidence that our conclusions apply to all the cases. But if, as is much more frequently the situation, we have so many hundreds or thousands or millions of cases that it is impossible to examine each first-hand, we will have much less confidence that a study of a relative few of these cases, perhaps fewer than 1 in 1,000, will allow us to make accurate statements about the entire group. In such circumstances we must develop a strategy, often termed a *sampling procedure,* by which we can decide which few of those many, many cases we can study to come to conclusions that might apply to the entire population of cases. In doing so, we must decide how many cases to study and how these cases should be selected, and we must try to estimate the representativeness of these few cases. The key to generalizability lies in selecting for observation those cases best likely to represent (be most typical of) the larger population.

Once we have selected our cases for analysis, we must exercise great care in observing them. We must avoid measuring political phenomena or behavior in ways that display **reactivity**—a situation in which either the person who is doing a study or the actual methods of the study somehow interfere with and alter the way those under observation would behave or think in the absence of the researcher. In other words, a danger exists that the act of observation may itself cause those being observed to change their behavior so that the results of the observation are misleading.

Hawthorne Effect   The classic case of reactive observation was a 1939 study of the effects that changes in working conditions at a particular factory had on worker productivity. During the 1920s and early 1930s, such factors as hours of work, rest periods, lighting, and methods of pay were varied for a small group of workers. But regardless of what conditions they worked under, whether long or short hours, few or frequent rest periods, or some other variant, this group of workers continually out-produced all other workers in the same factory. The most influential factor in their productivity, it turned out, was an unusually high level of morale associated with the fact that members of this group knew they were being observed and experimented upon (Roethlisberger and Dickson 1939). This so-called Hawthorne effect, named for the factory where it was first observed, meant that no conclusion could be drawn regarding the relationship between working conditions and productivity because the act of observation created a false reality, a work environment unlike the normal one.

Sometimes in undertaking political science research, we encounter similar, obvious examples of reactivity. An overbearing or unfriendly interviewer, a leading question, or a meddlesome observer can so damage the research situation that no confidence can be vested in its outcomes. As often as not, however, the process is more subtle. We might, for example, properly train the perfect interviewer to ask a perfectly good question, yet still incur reactivity: *Q:* "Do you favor or oppose the president's economic policy?" *A:* "I'm in favor of it. I think it is a good idea." But how do we know for sure that our respondent has really given any thought to the president's economic policy before being interviewed? Is it not possible that the interview itself acted as a catalyst, in effect crystallizing the respondent's thoughts and creating an opinion where none had previously existed? This, too, is reactivity, but of a type that is much more difficult to detect and to avoid.

It is not enough simply to march into the field armed with a few questions and start looking around for answers. We must exercise great care in deciding how and where we shall enter the field and how and whom we shall observe. The best theory and the best plan of attack can be squandered if we are careless in our observation.

The Analysis of Data

The bits of information about each case that we gather during our observations are called **data,** and once we have them in hand, the end is in sight. The object at this point is to ascertain what answers we have found to our research question. This may be done in many instances by answering three questions. First, is there some association between, on the one hand, the behavior we are hoping to explain or to understand better and, on the other hand, the factors we think will help us to do so?

Is There a Relationship?   Suppose, for example, that we expect to find that people who differ in their level of formal education will differ systematically in the likelihood that they will vote. Our first question must be, does this happen? Do people who differ from one another on one of these variables tend to differ consistently on the other as well? Are the more educated people consistently either more or less likely to vote than the less educated people? We might find in examining our data, for instance, that less educated people tend to vote about as often as more educated people and that knowing a person's level of education does not help us to predict or explain the difference between that person's likelihood of voting and someone else's. If this is the case, we say that one's level of education does not influence the likelihood of voting or, alternatively, that there is no association between the two variables. Our expectation is not supported by our analysis. If, on the other hand, we discover that six or seven times out of ten, knowing the level of education does allow us to predict accurately the likelihood of a person's voting, this constitutes evidence supporting our expectation that the two variables are related. It tells us that more educated people are *systematically different* from less educated people when it comes to voting and helps us understand our subjects' voting behavior. The first thing to look for in assessing a hypothesis, then, is whether the two variables are *statistically related.*

What Type of Relationship?   *How* are the two variables related? Are better educated people more likely than less educated people to vote? Alternatively, are they

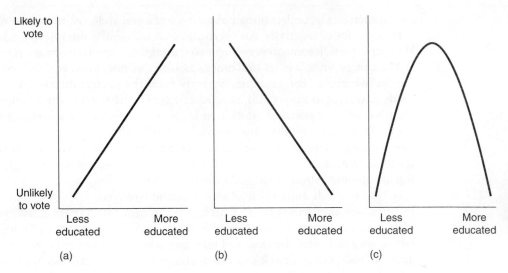

Figure 1.1
The relationship between level of education and likelihood of voting

less likely to vote? Or is the relationship between the variables even more complex? If we have thought through our hypothesis so that we have some reasons to expect the level of education to be related to voting, we probably have one or another of these possibilities in mind.

We might argue, for example, that having more formal education increases the likelihood of one's having the skills and information needed to support an interest in politics. Accordingly, a more educated person is more likely to vote than is a less skilled or less informed person. Thus, we might expect voting to be more frequent or more common among the more educated of the people we study. This type of relationship is illustrated in Figure 1.1(a), where points on the line represent corresponding values on the two variables.

We might also argue, however, that the more educated one becomes, the more one comes to believe that political activity is futile. Education, in this view, gives rise to disillusionment, which in turn reduces the inclination to vote. Here we expect voting to be more frequent among the less educated of our subjects. This type of relationship is illustrated in Figure 1.1(b).

Or we might even argue that education contributes to skills and interests to a point, but that those who are educated beyond that point (for example, those who attend college) become increasingly disillusioned and less interested in politics. Here we expect voting to be most frequent among those of moderate educational attainment, with lower levels of voting at either extreme. This more complex relationship is illustrated in Figure 1.1(c).

In each instance a relationship exists between a person's level of education and likelihood of voting, but clearly the implications of these varying relationships are vastly different. It is possible, then, to find a strong relationship between the two variables and yet fail to substantiate our hypothesis.

Confidence in Findings? How likely is it that any relationship we have found among variables in our study of a small number of cases will also be found if we study the entire population from which those cases have been chosen? This is simply a statistical way of asking how good a job we have done in ensuring that our small sample is representative, or typical, of the larger population. If we have made the proper decisions in selecting the particular cases to be studied, then we can say with confidence that our conclusions, though based on but a few cases, may be applied to all. If we have made errors, we may be less confident. Unfortunately, as will be made clearer in subsequent chapters, when conclusions are based on a sample of the population, we can never be *totally* certain of them.

Interpretation of the Results

Finally, we reach a point where we must put all the pieces together. Have we succeeded in actually asking the research question that we set out to ask? What have we discovered? What is the substantive importance of our findings? How do these results square with our expectations? In essence, we have by this time reduced some aspect of political behavior to a set of numbers, which may or may not reveal statistical relationships. We must decide what any such relationships, as well as other things we have learned along the way, tell us about the answer to our research question. But there is more, for we must also look back with a critical eye on our research itself. Have we made some fundamental error along the way that may invalidate our findings? Have we managed to keep a close relationship between our theory and our research on the one hand and the reality of political activity on the other? Can we credit any of our apparent findings about the real world to the things we have done (or have failed to do) in our research, rather than to actual events? These are difficult questions to answer, but good researchers will always try to do so, because only when they are answered can researchers know how much confidence to place in the product of the research.

Conclusion

This chapter's brief overview of the six stages of the research process will give you a good idea of what scientific research into politics is like and of what this book is about. We shall devote a good many of our pages to learning to perform and to evaluate each of these tasks. We realize, of course, that most who read those pages will never become political science researchers. But we know, too, that the same skills that go into creating good quality research for oneself may also be applied to developing more thorough and more critical skills in reading and evaluating the research done by others, and that is an ability that anyone with an interest in the study of politics will do well to possess. Social scientific research is increasingly used as a basis for both public policy and legal decisions. It is therefore increasingly important that citizens be able to judge the merits of research in order to discharge their responsibilities in a democratic society.

The body of knowledge that we call political science was not handed down on stone tablets in antiquity. It is constantly growing, changing, and being refined. Every piece of research is a potential extension of our knowledge and understanding. But that potential can be met only if the research itself can withstand critical scrutiny, only if it comes up to accepted standards. Those standards are what this book is about, and learning them, whether for research of your own or for critical reading, will provide you with a basis both for understanding the literature of political science and for making a contribution to it.

Summary Points

- Science was developed to search for objective knowledge.
- The Political Science research method is a progression of steps: building a theory, defining terms and operationalization, choosing a research technique, observing behavior, analyzing data, and interpreting results.
- Scientific research, using qualitative or quantitative methods, is but one of many ways to explore politics and explore our political environment.

Suggested Readings and References

Worth a close reading by both experienced and novice researchers, a path-breaking argument against the artificial barriers between qualitative and quantitative empirical political science research is found in *Designing Social Inquiry: Scientific Inference in Qualitative Research* by Gary King, Robert Keohane, and Sidney Verba (Princeton, NJ: Princeton University Press, 1994).

Forming the basis for our modern understanding of study reactivity, the official company report on the experiments done by the Western Electric Company at its Hawthorne assembly plant in Illinois is documented in Fritz Roethlisberger and William Dickson's *Management and the Worker* (Cambridge, MA: Harvard University Press, 1939).

Research Exercises

1. Write a paragraph describing why you think the authors of this book have characterized operationalization as "the single most important key to conducting meaningful research."
2. Use your academic library's online resources to find one example each of basic research and applied research reported in a newspaper or magazine published within the past month. Write a brief summary of each.

Key Terms

empirical
normative
quantitative
qualitative
scientific research
basic research

applied research
operationalization
generalizability
reactivity
data

CHAPTER 2

Theory Building: Concepts and Hypotheses in Political Research

- Why develop a theory before beginning to research a relationship?
- What roles do induction and deduction play in developing theory?
- What are the characteristics of useful theories?
- How do covariation and causation differ?
- How are theories elaborated using hypotheses?

The first chapter highlighted the motivations behind social science research; we want to understand the complex world around us, either for the satisfaction of knowing or because we want to be able to anticipate or even control events. Scientific research, then, begins with something we want to know. This is our **research question.** It is usually quite general. We might want to know, for example, why some people actively support environmental protection while others are opposed or indifferent to it. The most effective way to find an accurate (and therefore useful) answer to this question is to employ established methods of empirical research to investigate the relationships we see in the world. Before we can employ scientific procedures in an attempt to find a generally agreed-upon answer to our question, we have to reduce this highly general question to one or more highly specific ones. Unless we do this, we will not know what to observe in order to seek an answer to the question, and we cannot understand how what we observe is related to our research question.

The Purpose of Theory Transforming our general research question into one or several specific ones requires developing some plausible explanations for what we observe. We might, for instance, reason that people's position on environmental protection is influenced by the nature of their job. Some occupations, for example, benefit from environmental protection measures whereas others are hurt by them (at least in the short run). We might also think that age influences people's attitude toward environmental issues, because younger people have grown up with an awareness of the problems of pollution while older people grew up before these problems were understood.

This reasoning helps us to reduce the complexity of social life and puts us in a position to begin scientific inquiry. We can apply logic and information that we already have about empirical relationships to reason out a set of things we expect to be true if our tentative explanation is valid. Now we can ask questions like these: Do younger people support environmental legislation more often than older people do? Do white-collar and professional people support environmental measures more often than blue-collar people do? We can devise ways to make observations that will allow us to answer these questions and, when we have explored enough small questions, to answer our initial research question.

When we attempt to create possible explanations for events, we are **theorizing** or developing a theory. Theories are created in our effort to gain understanding. They help to direct the research we do to determine if our understanding of events is correct. This is why theory building is the first stage in the research process and why it is essential that we understand the relationship between theory and research.

Theories Aid Interpretation   Without a sound theory we will not be able to tell why our research "findings" provide an answer to the research question. Suppose we begin research with only the general question posed earlier. If we ask a properly selected sample of 2,000 Americans about their position on environmental protection and a series of questions about their personal characteristics, we can use our results to *describe* the kinds of people who support and oppose environmental legislation, but we cannot tell *why* they support or oppose it.

If, on the other hand, we start with a theory that offers an explanation of why people support or oppose environmental protection policies and ask questions to check on the accuracy of the expectations that logically follow from this theory, our results will contribute to our understanding of why people take the positions they do.

To illustrate, say that we theorize that people's first concern is their economic well-being and that their position on environmental protection is determined totally by their perception of how proposed legislation will affect their income. One expectation or prediction that logically follows from this line of reasoning is that people who expect to be financially hurt by environmental protection laws will oppose them while those who expect to be helped by these laws will support them. If our theory is an adequate explanation of how people develop attitudes about environmental protection, then this prediction should be an accurate statement about real-world relationships. We can then get some idea of the usefulness of our theory by checking on the empirical accuracy of the prediction that logically follows from it. For example, we might ask people about their position on environmental protection and their perception of its effect on their income to find out whether the prediction is borne out by what we learn about actual relationships.

Regardless of the outcome, our research can then tell us something about why people feel as they do about this issue. If the research is correctly done and the prediction turns out to be supported, we are encouraged both to believe that we have developed a sound explanation for the behavior in question and to search for further evidence of its utility. If the prediction is shown to be wrong, we at least have reason to believe that this is not likely to be a useful theory for understanding people's position on this matter, and we can begin to explore other possible explanations.

Whether we start our research with a theory or without a theory, it may produce the same facts. But the facts will contribute to our understanding *only* if we can tie them together through a theory. For example, knowing that white-collar people tend to support environmental protection more often than blue-collar people do will provide an explanation of why people take the positions they do only if we can give some reason why occupation and position on ecology should be related. Otherwise, the fact could be a coincidence, and knowing it will add nothing to our ability to explain people's attitudes. Theories provide sets of reasons why facts should be connected in given ways. Therefore, *theories make facts useful by providing us with a framework for interpreting them and seeing their relationships to one another.*

This chapter is designed to help you understand how theories are developed and how they are used to guide research. In it we discuss the nature of social science theorizing, the elements of theories, and the relationship of theory to the rest of the research process. When you have finished the chapter, you should be able to begin thinking about political questions that interest you in ways that will prepare you to undertake systematic empirical research in order to find valid answers to those questions.

The Nature of Social Science Theory

Usefulness of Theories First, theories help simplify reality so that we might understand it in order better to control it or adapt to it. Second, once we have developed such an understanding, theories can guide us in testing its accuracy. Theories do this by providing a logical basis for expectations or predictions about the world that can be compared with reality through research. When our predictions are supported by evidence, the understanding that provides a basis for those predictions is also supported, and our confidence that we have a grasp of the way things work is increased. When our predictions are shown to be inaccurate, we begin to question our understanding of events and to look for ways to improve it.

Theories are *sets of logically related symbols that represent what we think happens in the world.* They are simply intellectual tools. Understanding this is important, because it helps us realize that theories are neither true nor false in any absolute sense, but only more or less *useful.* You cannot expect to discover a theory the way an explorer discovers a new island. Why? Because theories do not exist "out there" to be discovered. They are the products of human imagination, hard work, and sometimes good fortune.

If theories are essential to sound research but cannot be discovered by simply looking at accumulated data, how can we go about building a theory to guide our quest for an understanding of those aspects of political life that interest us? What processes are involved? The answer is not neat or simple, because theories are developed in a variety of ways. We cannot outline a set of procedures to produce a useful theory in the same way as we might describe how to build a table. We can, however, provide an explanation of the major ideas and stages commonly involved in theory construction. The first of these is the *conceptualization of the problem.*

The Logic of Theory Building

Beginning with the event or behavior we want to understand, we must first ask ourselves what we know about the phenomenon that might help us explain it. Insights might be gained from personal experience, casual observation, or creative thinking. More often we will find it useful to investigate systematically what others have found about the subject. Useful theories begin from a thorough knowledge of the events we want to explain. Without such knowledge, we might fail to understand what is to be explained or might not have a clue where to begin looking for relationships that can be used to explain the events. An example might highlight the importance of having a thorough knowledge of the facts to aid our research conceptualization.

An Example   The massive riots that took place in many U.S. cities in the late 1960s deeply worried many Americans. Political scientists and other social scientists were asked to investigate the causes of the riots. When the riots first occurred, many public officials said they were the acts of a group of poor citizens without stable ties to society. If we had accepted this interpretation and sought to understand the riots, we would have defined our task as one of explaining why so many of these "riffraff" were concentrated in our cities at that time and how they were moved to riot. Many public officials turned to the alleged presence of "outside agitators" as an explanation. As social scientists conducted interviews in the riot-torn cities, however, we learned that rioting was not restricted to riffraff. In fact, as a group, rioters differed very little from the general black population of those cities (Fogelson and Hill 1986). This fact presents us with a very different research task from that suggested by the riffraff interpretation. We must now seek to understand how average citizens with jobs, families, and other ties to society were motivated to riot. Subsequent explanations have focused on variables such as African Americans' reaction to white racism rather than "outside agitators."

In this case, an inadequate knowledge of the facts could have fundamentally misdirected our theory-building efforts. This is why **exploratory research,** which is designed to establish the facts in a given case, is important. It is also the reason why we must search the literature for information on the phenomena we seek to explain if we hope to develop sound theories.

But once we have as many facts we can find, how do we construct a theory to explain these observations? We generally begin by searching the facts for patterns that can account for the observed events.

For example, we might want to know what causes political protests on college campuses. Answering this question involves explaining what leads students to take part in protests. Having been or having known protesters might provide us with some insights into their motivation, but to develop an explanation of why large numbers of students participate would require information on a much larger number of people. We would be wise to seek data on the characteristics and motives of student protesters *in general* in order to frame our explanation. If we found among protesters commonalties that set them apart from nonprotesters, we might reason that these characteristics led to their participation in demonstrations. The prominence of these characteristics among college students then becomes part of our explanation of why protests occur.

Induction   The process of generalizing from what we have observed to what we have not or cannot observe is called **induction.** It forms the basis of scientific theory. Theories built through inductions from observations are said to be *empirically grounded*.

In the process of induction, we reason from what we know to be the case in some situations to what might be the case in other, similar situations; we make a logical leap from what we have seen to a prediction about what we have not seen based on the assumption that there is some constant underlying pattern to events in the world. We all use induction in our daily life. If we observe five consecutive times that the ele-

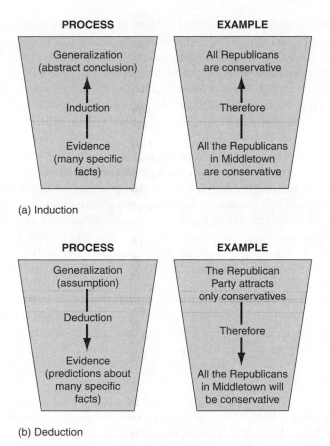

Figure 2.1
Diagrammatic representation of inductive and deductive reasoning

vator door opens after our pushing a button on the wall, we will quickly draw the conclusion that pushing the button causes the door to open. This is an inductive generalization from the few cases we have observed (pushing the button five times) to cases we have not (pushing the button more times or pushing elevator buttons in other buildings). The process of induction is diagrammed in Figure 2.1(a). This diagram suggests how inductively constructed theories are grounded in facts.

There is more to theory building than induction, however, because pointing out facts does not provide an explanation unless we can show *why* those facts have led to the observed results. Let us return to the example of student protest. Suppose we find that protesters tend to be more dissatisfied with public policies than nonprotesters and that protesters also tend to have far less faith in the effectiveness of conventional politics in getting policies changed. Stating this fact constitutes an explanation of protest only if we are able to show why such attitudes should lead to protest behavior. Showing this might involve making some *assumptions* about political behavior. Specifically, it might involve assuming that people will act to change policies they strongly oppose and that they will resort to protest behavior if they feel that conventional political participation (voting, letter writing, etc.) will not alter the policies.

These **assumptions** (sometimes called *axioms* or *postulates*) then become part of our theory. Assumptions describe the conditions under which we expect the tentative explanation we have reached to be supported by evidence. They tell why we expect student protest from what we know about students on college campuses by making general statements about political behavior under certain conditions. We can now explain specific behavior (protest) by showing that it follows logically from a set of theoretical assumptions.

Deduction   This process is the reverse of inductive reasoning. Deductive reasoning moves from abstract statements about general relationships to concrete statements about specific behaviors. This process of reasoning *from the abstract and general to the concrete and specific* is known as **deduction.** We all use deductive logic in everyday life. If we assume that elevators work on a system of wall-mounted buttons and find ourselves confronted with an elevator, we will generally deduce that the way to enter the elevator is to push the appropriate button. We have moved from a generalization to the prediction of a specific event by deduction. This process is diagramed in Figure 2.l(b).

Deduction is the process that enables us to use theories to explain real-world events. If we can show by a process of deduction that some observed event can be logically predicted from the set of assumptions that constitute our theory, then the theory provides an explanation for the observed event. The theory helps us to understand the event by giving a reason why it is as it is. The role of deduction is to provide this link between the theory and our observations.

Theory Construction   The process of theory construction involves the interaction of both inductive and deductive logic in the following stages: (1) we use induction to translate what we have observed into assumptions; (2) we employ deduction to derive predictions; (3) we test these predictions against new observations; and (4) we revise our assumptions to make them consistent with the results of our observations. Then we repeat the process in an effort to make the theory increasingly useful as a tool for understanding events.

Merely devising a theory, however, does not make it valid. We can generally come up with many theories to explain a given event. The question we must ask is, which of these theories is most useful in helping us understand the world? Answering this question will require that we test alternative theories against reality.

Before we can discuss theory testing, however, it is important to understand two things. First, we have to know what features make a theory useful so that we can know how to go about building theories. Second, we must know how the components of a theory are related to each other and to empirical research.

Characteristics of Useful Theories   For a theory to be useful in explaining observations, it must meet several standards:

1. It must be *testable.* Can we reason from the theory to expectations about reality that are concrete and specific enough for us to make observations that either support the expectations or fail to support them? Can the theory be related to the world in systematic ways, or is it only a set of abstractions?

2. It must be *logically sound*. Is the theory internally consistent? Are its assumptions compatible, and the terms it contains unambiguous?

3. It must be *communicable*. Can other, properly trained people understand the theory in ways that allow them to use it to explain events and to test hypotheses derived from it?

4. It must be *general*. Is it possible to use it to explain a variety of events in different times and places? Can we deduce predictions from it that can be tested in different circumstances, or is it tied too closely to one set of observations?

5. It must be *parsimonious*. Is it simple enough to be readily applied and understood, or is it so complex, so filled with conditions and exceptions, that it is difficult to derive explicit expectations about real-world events from it?

Theories can have each of these desirable characteristics in different degrees, and sometimes we have to choose among them in developing a particular theory. We may have to sacrifice some parsimony in order to obtain more generality or testability, for instance. We have to keep all these desirable features in mind when formulating theories if the products of our labors are to be truly useful.

Components of Social Science Theory

Theories are composed of sets of *concepts* that are related by propositions logically derived from a set of *assumptions*. This is the *logical structure* of a theory. It is this structure that allows us to use the theory to explain events, because it allows us to give reasons why we can logically expect things to be as they are.

Defining Concepts   The quest for useful theory begins with the decisions we make about the building blocks of theories: concepts. A **concept** is merely a *word or symbol that represents some idea*. There is nothing mystical about concepts. We use them every day to help us cope with the complexity of reality by categorizing the things we encounter according to some of their properties that are relevant to us. We classify the four-legged creatures we see into cows, cats, dogs, and other species, and that classification alone provides a basis for some important expectations (for example, dogs are not a good source of milk). Assigning a name to something allows us to predict certain things about it, because the name is a symbol for particular combinations of properties.

Social science concepts serve the same purpose. They point to the properties of objects (people, political systems, elections) that are relevant to a particular inquiry. One observer might be interested in a person's personality structure, another is interested in partisan identification, and a third focuses on the person's level of political alienation. The person has all of these properties (a personality, a party identification, and a degree of alienation) and many more, but only certain of the properties are relevant to any given piece of research. All three observers are dealing with the same reality; they simply choose to organize their perceptions of it differently. Concepts help us to decide which of many traits or attributes are important to our research.

Making Concepts Useful   Concepts, like theories, are tools that we create for specific purposes and that cannot be labeled true or false, but only more or less useful. What makes a concept useful? There are three major considerations.

First, since we are involved in *empirical* inquiry the concept must refer to phenomena that are at least potentially *observable*. In medieval times, the concept of divine will played an important role in explanations of events. We cannot verify such explanations, however, because we cannot observe divine will to tell whether it is present or absent in any given case. If it is to have any scientific value, a concept must refer to something that can be measured with our ordinary senses.

This does not mean that all concepts must refer to *directly* observable things. Some of the most useful concepts in the social sciences refer to properties we cannot observe directly. For example, people do not have a class status in the way that they have red hair, but if we know certain things about them (their income or their occupation, for example), we can infer what their class status is. Similarly, nations do not have authoritarian or democratic political systems in the way that they have mountains or deserts, but we can *infer* the degree of democracy that exists in a nation by observing certain things about its political life (the nature of elections and provisions for civil liberties, for instance).

The question is: Can we devise a set of procedures for using our senses to gather information that will allow us to judge the presence or absence or magnitude in the real world of the thing to which the concept refers? If we can do this for a concept, it is said to have **empirical referents**; it refers to something that is directly or indirectly observable.

Second, in addition to having empirical referents, concepts must be *precise*. They must refer to one and only one set of properties of some phenomenon. We must be able to know exactly what we are talking about when we use a concept to describe an object. For instance, is the degree of inequality of distribution of wealth part of what we are referring to when we describe a nation's political system as democratic or authoritarian, or is the nature of the political system determined exclusively by other factors? Precision is important because it tells us what to observe in order to see how a concept is manifested in any given case. Only if we can determine this can we use the concept in empirically grounded explanations.

Precision also helps us identify our empirical referents and make distinctions among observed phenomena. If democracy means *only* the presence or absence of popular elections for public officials, then the former Soviet Union and the United States both were democracies. Do we want to treat these two nations as examples of the same kind of political system for purposes of our research? If not, then we need to refine the concept, making it more precise, so that we can draw a distinction in our study between the two nations.

Finally, useful concepts have **theoretical import**. A concept has *theoretical import* when it is related to enough other concepts in the theory that it plays an essential role in the explanation of observed events.

In our hypothetical explanation of student protest, we employed two concepts. One was *intensity of policy preferences*, and the other was *perception of the effectiveness of conventional political action in changing policies*. These two concepts were tied together by the assumptions that people will act to change policies with which they strongly disagree and that they will turn to protest when they feel that other means of influence will not bring results. Given these assumptions, finding the particular combination of attitudes we have referred to will lead us to expect protest behavior. Each concept is essential to the explanation and is linked both to the theoretical assumptions and to the other concept. Each concept has theoretical import because it plays a necessary role in our explanation.

Relationships in Social Science Theory

Now we can begin to see that theory makes concepts useful by tying them together so that they can be used in formulating explanations. Theory ties concepts to one another by stating relationships between them. These statements take the form of **propositions** derived from our assumptions. Propositions generally posit one of two major types of relationship among concepts. These are *covariation* and *causation*.

Covariational relationships indicate that two or more concepts tend to change together: As one increases (or decreases) the other increases (or decreases). Covariational relationships tell us nothing about what causes the two concepts to change together. For instance, we might predict that level of political information and likelihood of voting covary, so that as one increases so does the other. But are people more likely to vote because they have more information, or do they gain information because they intend to vote and want to make a sound decision, or are both information level and likelihood of voting the products of some third factor, such as interest in politics or perceived civic duty? The covariational proposition does not tell us.

Causal relationships exist when changes in one or more concepts lead to or cause changes in one or more other concepts. For example, the stronger one's party identification, we might argue, the more likely one is to vote. Feeling oneself to be a member of a party can lead one to vote, but the likelihood of voting does not create one's party identification.

We are accustomed to thinking in terms of cause and effect in our everyday life, and we generally use these concepts loosely. In scientific research it is often very difficult to identify the causes or consequences of human behavior; the more important the event, the more difficult isolation of its causes can be. What brings on a war, a social movement, or the creation of a new political party?

Testing Causation   Because of such complexities, we must be careful to postulate causal relationships only when four conditions are simultaneously met. First, the postulated cause and effect must change together, or covary. Second, the cause must precede the effect. Third, we must be able to identify a *causal linkage* between the supposed cause and effect (meaning, we must be able to identify the *process* by which changes in one factor cause changes in another). Fourth, the covariance of the cause-and-effect phenomena must not be due to their simultaneous relationship to some third factor—a condition we discuss next.

Spurious relationships occur when A and B vary together only because they are both caused by C. If they would not covary in the absence of C, the apparent relationship between A and B is termed *spurious*. We must carefully examine the assumptions we are making in an effort to uncover possible spuriousness in relationships before we build them into our theories as though they were the product of causal interaction. A classic instance of spuriousness is the case in which an investigator first finds that the price of imported rum and the salaries of ministers fluctuate together and then reasons that changes in the price of rum cause changes in ministers' salaries. It is more likely that both rum prices and ministers' salaries change in response to changes in general economic conditions and overall price level. The relationship between the first two variables is covariational, but it is not causal.

It is important to recognize two other features of social causation. First, one phenomenon may cause another either directly or indirectly. For example, A may cause B only in that it is the cause of C, which directly causes B. We must be alert to the role of **indirect causation** in attempting to make our theories as complete as possible. Second, we must be sensitive to the fact that human behavior generally has more than one cause. In theorizing, we should avoid oversimplifying and thus recognize the role of **multiple causation** in social life. This simply means that any one event may have several different causes, and that many events sometimes must come together to cause a given occurrence.

To cope with all of these complexities, it is generally a good idea to draw a **causal model** of the theory. This is simply a diagram that clearly specifies all the relationships posited in the theory so that it is easier to see the implications of our arguments. Figure 2.2 presents an example of such a model. Each arrow in the model represents a causal influence, and the direction in which it is pointing indicates which variable is theorized to be dependent and which independent. The theory diagrammed in Figure 2.2 asserts that a variety of factors influence a representative's decision to vote for or against welfare legislation in both direct and indirect ways. For instance, the size of the poor population in the representative's congressional district is depicted as influencing welfare voting both directly (independently) and indirectly through the electoral competitiveness of the district and the seniority level of the representative.

At this point, we should note that although our theories typically specify a causal relationship between our concepts, we rarely encounter social science data that can establish definite causation. Later in this text, we will highlight the exceptional degree of control the experimental setting offers, which helps to identify causal relationships.

Positive and Negative Relationships   Both covariational and causal relationships can be either *positive* or *negative*. This means that the two concepts can change either in the same direction or in opposite directions, respectively. An example of a **positive relationship** is: The *higher* the relative deprivation of minority groups within a society, the higher the likelihood of political violence. A **negative relationship** may be posited as follows: The *higher* the degree of political alienation one feels, the *lower* the likelihood that one will take part in conventional political activities. Our theories must specify whether we expect positive or negative relationships among concepts. This information can be added to causal diagrams by placing a plus (+) or minus (−) sign on each path in order to indicate whether the relationship is thought to be positive or negative.

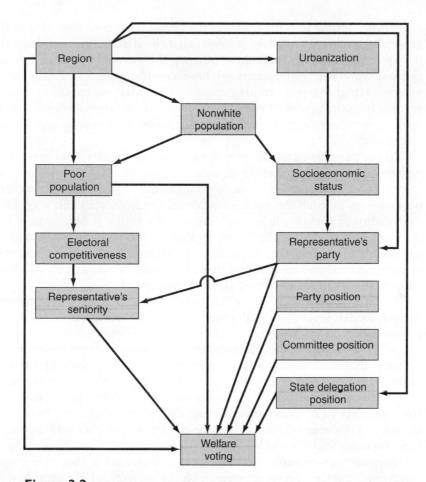

Figure 2.2
Causal model of the determinants of representatives' support for welfare legislation in the U.S. Congress
Source: From Richard C. Rich, "The Representation of the Poor in the Policy Process: Changes in Congressional Support for Welfare," in Robert Eyestone, ed., *Public Policy Formation* (Greenwich. CT: JAI Press, 1984), p. 135. Reprinted with permission.

Theory Testing and Elaboration

Theories must never be regarded as finished products, but always as tools that occasionally need to be inspected and can often be improved. We start with a research question that asks for an explanation of observed events, we select concepts that promise to be useful in explaining those events, and we relate the concepts through propositions logically derived from a set of assumptions we choose to make in order to secure an explanation. Now our backs are against the wall. Is this lovely structure any good? It seems to explain what we want to understand, but can we check it in some way? Can we test its utility so that we can know how much confidence to place in it and persuade others of its value?

Theory testing is at the center of the research process. Because our theories are generally developed from bits of knowledge about actual relationships, the tasks of theory testing are essentially those of using the theory to formulate some expectations about other relationships we have not observed and then checking to see whether actual observations are consistent with what we expect to find. We cannot rely on relationships we have already observed, because showing that the theory leads us to expect the very relationships the theory was built to explain would be no test at all.

In our example of the elevator, after observing the elevators in one building, we will be quite confident that the elevators in that building operate in response to a system of wall-mounted buttons. We might even be willing to generalize from our observations to reach the conclusion that all elevators work this way. We can check the validity of that conclusion only by actually trying it out in other buildings. It does not help to double-check the elevators in the building we started in, because we already know that they respond to the buttons and showing that they do does not make us feel any more secure that other elevators do as well. We have to go to other buildings to see how their elevators operate.

We can never finally prove that our theory of elevator operation is correct because we can never observe all the elevators in the world. As we see more and more elevators that do work this way and we never encounter any that do not, our confidence in the validity of our generalization will increase. If we cannot find any other elevators that work by buttons, however, we will quickly conclude that we have been mistaken in generalizing from the initial observations to all other elevators.

Theory testing in the social sciences works by the same principle. We must move from what we have observed in devising the theory to what we have not observed, in order to discover whether or not the theory provides us with an accurate set of expectations about the world.

Suppose, for example, that we want to construct a theory to explain voting behavior. We review previous research on the subject and discover that, for citizens of the United States, higher education is positively related to the propensity to vote. On the basis of these observations, we include in our theory an assumption that higher educational levels lead to a greater likelihood of voting. We know that these factors are related in the United States, but what about in other nations? Could there be something unique to the educational system in the United States that creates this relationship? The only way we can find out is to observe people in other nations.

From the assumption that education increases the likelihood of voting, we might deduce the prediction that people with some college education will be more likely to vote than people with no more than a high school diploma. We can test this prediction by seeing whether it accurately reflects relationships found in data from a variety of countries. The more often we find evidence consistent with the prediction, the more confident we will feel that our theory is useful in predicting human behavior. We can never be absolutely certain that the theory is "true," because we can neither observe all cases nor be sure how the empirical relationships might change with time. But we can acquire more or less confidence in the utility of the theory by comparing the predictions derived from it with observations. If it allows us to accurately predict things we have not previously observed, then it is useful.

Theories, as sets of concepts, assumptions, and propositions, are never finally proved or disproved. Rather, our confidence in the *usefulness* of a theory builds as we accumulate observations that are consistent with the expectations or hypotheses derived from it. Alternatively, our confidence diminishes as we accumulate observations that are inconsistent with theoretically derived hypotheses.

The Role of Hypotheses

The above section's **theory elaboration** is based largely on a process of comparing hypothesized conditions with reality and, once we have the results, modifying our theory so that the hypotheses that can be derived from it are more and more consistent with what we observe. Now we consider how our research questions are translated into hypotheses that can guide empirical investigations and provide us with clues to the adequacy of our theoretical explanations.

Hypotheses Defined   A **hypothesis** is essentially a statement of what we believe to be factual. It tells what we expect to find when we make properly organized observations of reality. Hypotheses are declarative sentences stating expected relationships between the phenomena to which our concepts refer. They are usually stated in the following general form:

> *The higher (lower, greater, larger, slower, etc.) the ____, the higher (lower, greater, larger, slower, etc.) the ____.*

The blanks are filled in with the names of the phenomena that we expect will change together. For example, working from the theory modeled in Figure 2.2, we might hypothesize the following:

> *The larger the proportion of a district's population that is poor, the more likely that district's representative is to vote in favor of welfare legislation.*

This is a covariational hypothesis. It does not tell us how roll call voting is determined, but it does point us to something that we can observe in an effort to acquire some evidence on the fit between our theory and reality.

Acquiring that evidence through empirical observation requires that we move from the very general level of theory to a more specific level from which to organize observations. In doing this, we have to begin to think in terms of **variables.** A variable may be defined as an empirically observable characteristic of some phenomenon that can take on more than one value. Sex and nationality are two variables that can take on only a limited number of values and can be "measured" only qualitatively by designations such as "male" or "British." Age and gross national product are two variables that can take on a much wider range of values; they can be measured quantitatively by counting.

Concepts into Variables   To facilitate empirical testing, abstract concepts must be translated into statements with more precisely defined variables. For instance, the concept of *pluralism* is important in political science, but its empirical referents are not particularly clear. In order to test the empirical accuracy of any statement relating pluralism to anything else, we have to translate the concept into some variable or set of variables with clear empirical referents. We might want to use the number of organized interest groups in a nation as a variable to represent the concept of pluralism in our research. We can then reason backward from our observation of relationships among variables to evaluate the empirical validity of statements about relationships between concepts. If we are willing to assume that the variable *number of organized groups* captures the essential meaning of the concept *pluralism,* we will be willing to take evidence that this variable is related to some other variable (such as the level of government expenditures) as evidence that pluralism is also related to that other variable or the concept it represents.

Independent and Dependent Variables   Variables have a central place in the research process for two reasons. First, they help us identify what we will have to observe to test our theory by providing more precise empirical referents. Second, we can organize our observations by knowing the role variables play in hypotheses. Variables that are thought to change value in response to changes in the value of other variables are referred to as **dependent variables.** Their value depends on the value of other variables. Variables that influence the value of other variables through changes in their own values are referred to as **independent variables.**

An Example   Whether a variable is dependent or independent is determined by the relationship asserted by the hypotheses containing it. The same variable might be dependent in one study and independent in another. For example, a theorist observing the lobbying efforts of interest groups might reason that the larger the number of organized interest groups in a nation is, the higher the level of government expenditures will be. In this case, the number of groups is the independent variable and the level of expenditure is the dependent variable. This relationship is described in Figure 2.3.

An independent variable's change in value must precede changes in the dependent variable. For example, following the above hypothesized relationship, we might observe an increase in government spending between 1980 and 1990 and also see a positive change in the number of organized groups between 1990 and 2000. Logically, this subsequent surge in interest group formation cannot have been responsible for a level of expenditures that preceded it. In fact, these observed data should prompt a reconsideration and (perhaps) a theoretical reformulation that accounts for this phenomenon.

Intervening Variables   A close look at Figure 2.3 alerts us to another type of variable important in social analysis. In the theory summarized by the diagram in Figure 2.3, lobbying activity is an intervening variable; it comes into play *between* the number of organized interest groups and the level of government spending. **Intervening variables** provide the link between independent and dependent variables. In this case, interest groups would not affect the level of government spending if they did not engage in lobbying to get funds appropriated to their cause.

Intervening variables *condition* the relationships between other variables. This means that the value attained by intervening variables can affect the strength and direction of relationships between other variables. If lobbying activity is slight in Figure 2.3, then the relationship of interest group organization to public spending is

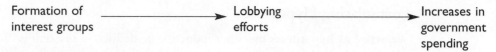

Figure 2.3
Interest group activity (independent variable) leads to higher government spending levels (dependent variable)

weak. If lobbying is extensive, the relationship between the other variables will be strong.

Because intervening variables condition relationships between other variables, our knowledge of the role they play will affect our expectations about relationships between variables. If we are theorizing that lobbying intervenes between group organization and increases in spending, then we can make the following predictions:

> *Interest group organization will be positively related to increases in government spending when lobbying activity is vigorous.*

> *Interest group organization will be related only weakly to increases in government spending when lobbying activity is highly limited.*

We will not be satisfied to predict simply that interest group organization will be related to increases in government spending, because we believe that whether the two variables are related depends on the value of the intervening variable—lobbying. For this reason, we must specify the order of relationships and the role played by each variable in our theories.

Antecedent Variables   Whereas intervening variables come between independent and dependent variables, antecedent variables come into play before the independent variable does. For instance, we know that studies of voting behavior in the United States show that people who identify strongly with a political party are more likely to vote than those who do not. We might then want to theorize that party identification leads to or causes voting frequency. But what causes some people to identify strongly with a party while others do not? We might reason that the strength of their parents' party identification plays an important role in people's development of such party identification. Parents' party identification then is an **antecedent variable** in the causal chain that produces voting frequency.

Using both intervening and antecedent variables in our theories helps to clarify the *causal chains* at work in creating the phenomena we want to explain. It gives us more of a basis for deriving hypotheses through which we can test the utility of our theories, because hypotheses are essentially *statements of relationships between variables.* Hypotheses provide a basis for collecting evidence about the empirical utility of our theoretical structure. The more numerous and the more detailed the relationships we postulate, the more predictions we can make about the world and therefore the more potential tests we have of our theory.

This leads to the question of how we decide what relationships to assert in the form of hypotheses around which to build research projects.

Formulating Hypotheses

We arrive at hypotheses by either inductive or deductive reasoning. Which one we use depends on the stage we have reached in the research process. If we are still using trial and error to construct a theory, we might develop hypotheses by a process of *inductive generalization.* For example, we might observe that among the states in the United States the level of popular political participation varies directly with the extent of industrialization, and we might generalize that this relationship between variables is also found when we compare nations. If we find evidence to support the hypothesis, we will be more confident in including industrialization as a variable in a theory designed to explain political participation. Until we have a theory that shows *why* industrialization and participation are related, however, we cannot use the fact of their relationship as an explanation of political participation.

Hypotheses arrived at inductively can be important in *exploratory research,* which helps us construct theories, but they do not help us explain phenomena. Once we have stated a theory relating our variables in a logically coherent system, we can derive hypotheses from that theory by *deductive reasoning.* Because these hypotheses are predictions about the world that are logically implied by the theory with which we are working, finding support for them does help us explain events, because such findings reflect the validity of the theoretical system from which the hypotheses have been derived.

Deductive reasoning is a highly developed discipline, and we will not attempt to explain its rules here. It is important to note, however, that deductive logic is a process by which the information contained in a set of statements can be made explicit. We cannot learn anything new about relationships from deduction alone. We use it only to tease all the information we can out of what we already assume about relationships. We use deduction to *clarify the implications of our assumptions,* and it is that clarification that produces hypotheses.

The deduction contained in Figure 2.1(b) shows this. If the assumption stated there is correct, that is, if the Republican Party attracts *only* conservatives, then any subset of the members of that party will be conservative also, and since the Republicans in Middletown are members of that party, they too will be conservative. This is the kind of reasoning we refer to when we say that one conclusion "logically follows" from another. The conclusion that all Republicans in Middletown will be conservative is logically implied in the assumption that the Republican Party attracts only conservatives.

The task of hypothesis generation is logically to pull this type of conclusion from the assumptions that form our theories. It is because hypotheses are derived from theories in this way that testing hypotheses provides an indirect test of our theories. If we interview a properly drawn sample of Middletown Republicans and find that not all are conservative, we will have good reason to question the validity of our assumption. Finding liberals among Middletown Republicans shows that the party does not attract *only* conservatives. We will then want to modify our assumption so that the theory can more closely reflect reality. We may want to change it to read, "The Republican Party tends to attract more conservatives than liberals." From this assumption we can derive the hypothesis "There will be more conservatives than liberals among the members of the Middletown Republican Party."

If we find a few liberals and many conservatives among Middletown Republicans, we can say that the evidence is consistent with the hypothesis and the modified assumption from which it has been drawn. We still cannot put much faith in the validity of the assumption until we have seen it supported by evidence about the conservative or liberal character of a larger sample of the national Republican Party. After all, Middletown may be unique in some way. Perhaps, for example, there are only ten liberals in the entire city, and the fact that only a few of the Republican Party's members are liberal is a result of this more than of the relative attractiveness of the party to liberals and conservatives.

Indirect Theory Testing   The important point here is that evidence about the accuracy of hypotheses represents evidence about the accuracy of a theory *only when the hypotheses are linked to the theory by deductive logic.* Only when this is the case can we safely reason backward from evidence of the validity of a hypothesis to any judgment about the parent theory. Theories are developed, expanded, and improved by this process of logically deriving hypotheses, checking them against reality, and evaluating the theory in light of the results.

One type of hypothesis that plays an especially crucial role in this process is the **alternative rival hypothesis.** There are many possible explanations for any event. Some of these explanations are fully consistent with one another; more than one may be correct. In some cases, however, the explanations are opposed to one another: if one is correct, the other cannot be. If we state our explanations as hypotheses, then those which are inconsistent with one another are termed *alternative rival hypotheses.* They are alternatives because they provide different ways of looking at or understanding the event to be explained. They are rivals because they cannot both be valid. If one is accurate, the other has to be inaccurate. We cannot test and compare all possible alternative hypotheses relating to any event, but if we are to have faith in the accuracy of any one hypothesis, we must attempt to test the major rival hypotheses to be sure that we are not being misled by our observations.

One common form of alternative rival hypothesis is that which states that the relationship between any two variables is spurious and that changes in both are in fact due to some third factor. This type of alternative rival hypothesis is especially useful in theory testing because it suggests a research finding that gives us a solid basis for judging which of the two hypotheses in question is more accurate.

Recall, for example, our illustration of inferring a causal relationship between rum prices and ministers' salaries from the finding that the two variables are in fact statistically related. One major alternative rival hypothesis is that fluctuations in both are caused by changes in general economic conditions as represented by the price level. If this hypothesis is correct, then the relationship between rum prices and ministers' salaries will disappear when we "control for" (that is, hold constant) the effect of the price level on each of these variables. Statistical procedures and research designs are available to allow us to determine whether this is the case. If we discover that the statistical relationship between rum prices and ministers' salaries vanishes when we control for general price level, we will have a basis for rejecting the original hypothesis in favor of its rival. If the relationship between rum prices and salaries remains even after our imposition of controls for general price level, we will have more confidence in the hypothesis that they are genuinely related.

Conclusion

Theories gain acceptance as useful intellectual tools as we both find evidence consistent with predictions derived from them and eliminate alternative rival hypotheses. We must keep in mind, however, that no single piece of research provides sufficient evidence for accepting or rejecting any theory or part of a theory that pertains to phenomena beyond those included in the study. There is always the possibility that some future research will produce evidence against the theory's validity. We must always be open to contrary findings and willing to return to induction to build new evidence into more useful theories.

Theory building is a process of constant interaction between conjecture and evidence and between reasoning and research. It calls for both creative ingenuity and hardheaded empiricism. We hope to provide a good dose of the latter in the chapters that follow.

Summary Points

- Theories aid the research process by suggesting explanations of relationships.
- Theories guide testing through simplifying reality.
- Theories may be derived by inducing from specific observations and then tested using deductions.
- Theories may be more or less useful—not true or false.
- Useful theories are testable, logical, communicable, general, and parsimonious.
- Covariates tend to change together, while causal factors lead to changes in other concepts.
- Hypotheses state expected relationships between concepts.
- Hypotheses are deduced from theories and indirectly test the source theory.

Suggested Readings and References

Both newcomers and advanced researchers will find provocative and persuasive arguments on the nature of causation and logical reasoning in the late Wesley Salmon's collection of essays in *Causality and Explanation* (New York: Oxford University Press, 1998). A broad-ranging and highly readable treatment of the role of theory in the research process is *The Elements of Social Scientific Thinking*, 8th ed., by Kenneth Hoover and Todd Donovan (Belmont, CA: Thompson/Wadsworth, 2004).

A book that moves thoughtfully and clearly through the stages of conceptualization, theory building, hypothesis generation, and hypothesis testing is *The Rebirth of Urban Democracy*, by Jeffrey M. Berry, Kent E. Portney, and Ken Thompson (Washington, DC: The Brookings Institution, 1993). Reading it gives a good picture of the links between theory and research.

Referenced work: R. M. Fogelson and R. B. Hill, "Who Riots? A Study of Participation in the 1967 Riots," in *Supplemental Studies for the National Advisory Commission on Civil Disorders* (Washington, DC: U.S. Government Printing Office, 1986).

Research Exercises

1. Several concepts that might be used in political research are given in the following list. List one or more variables that might be used to represent each of them. Indicate how confident you are that the variables you select to represent each concept adequately capture all that you mean when you use the concept. Do you need several variables to capture the meaning of some of the concepts?

   economic development   political representation

   party competition   racial discrimination

   international tensions   liberalism

   political equality   terrorism

2. Select any four of the concepts listed in Exercise 1 and state a hypothesis that predicts a relationship between each of those concepts and some concept *not* on the list. Formulate two of the hypotheses so that they state positive relationships and two so that they state negative relationships.

3. Select a news article about some political trend or event in which you are interested. Devise at least two explanations for the trend or event, and state them as clearly as possible. List the concepts employed in each explanation. Pair each concept with a variable counterpart for it that you could use in a research project, and indicate the status (independent, dependent, intervening, antecedent) of each variable. Diagram the causal chain implied in each of your explanations.

Key Terms

research question
theorizing
theories
exploratory research
induction
assumptions
deduction
concept
empirical referents
theoretical import
propositions
covariational relationships
causal relationships
spurious relationships

indirect causation
multiple causation
causal model
positive relationship
negative relationship
theory testing
theory elaboration
hypothesis
variables
dependent variables
independent variables
intervening variables
antecedent variables
alternative rival hypothesis

CHAPTER 3

Setting the Foundation: Techniques of Systematic Bibliographic Search

- Why should we seek previous research on our topic?
- How can we use the existing literature to help frame our research questions?
- How do we conduct a systematic search of the relevant literature?
- What is the advantage of using the library's resources versus searching the free Web?
- Why do we take notes on the references we find?

One of the most important steps in theory-building is to familiarize yourself with the previous research or writing on your topic. The literature of political science and its subfields is enormous, and even in the best organized and most complete academic library the relevant research may appear to be scattered to three of the four winds. It is to be found in hundreds of scholarly journals and thousands of books. Some of these are available in printed form, some in electronic form, some in microfilm; some are available in most colleges' libraries, some are in very few. This chapter offers a systematic strategy to maximize the effectiveness of your literature searching efforts.

Using the Existing Literature

We may learn a great deal from the successes and failures of those who have already tackled problems similar to our research. This may help us to refine our theories, to avoid pitfalls in our research, and to tighten our thinking. We must realize that our own work can contribute, even if only in a small way, to the intellectual development of the discipline. By placing our work in the context of, and building directly upon, the literature, we increase the potential value of our contribution many times over. Our own work becomes, in effect, part of the literature that researchers may draw upon later.

As with any mature discipline, the body of political science knowledge has incrementally accumulated over a long period through a series of relatively small intellectual advances. Even major theoretical or methodological innovations can be seen, in the longer view, to have been logical next steps that built upon the state of the art. New bits of knowledge become known and these generate new insights. The insights themselves give rise to new research questions, which in turn give rise to still more new bits of knowledge. And so it goes on and on, the insights becoming ever more sophisticated, the bits of knowledge more complete, and the questions more pointed.

It is in the context of this incremental, scientific process of developing our understanding of political reality that the importance of the careful bibliographic grounding of our research becomes clear. Political inquiry has been around in one form or another since the days of Socrates, Plato, and Aristotle. Empirical political science, which focuses on the systematic and objective description of political activity, has developed in large part since the 1940s, but its roots may be traced back as far as Machiavelli. Today, in the United States alone, at least 15,000 people hold advanced degrees in the discipline and work as political scientists of one type or another; worldwide there are many more. Given these facts, it is extremely likely that any research question we might come up with has already been posed or partially explored by someone before us.

Positioning Your Research   The realization that the existing literature may already speak to most questions you might develop does not mean that your research can make no contribution; rather, it means that your contribution will most likely represent an addition to an *existing* body of knowledge instead of the creation of a new one. This fact may cause you to feel that all the really interesting work has already been done, that the field is closed to innovation, and that no individual accomplishment can amount to much. Each of those perceptions is incorrect. The acquisition of knowledge is a cumulative and incremental process, and your knowledge of the existing research allows you to properly position your theory and findings. Contextualizing your work helps others to both locate and utilize your findings.

Thus, rather than erecting constraints, the research process offers opportunities. Familiarity with past political science inquiry suggests the direction for future inquiry, and the value of individual effort is enhanced by the collective context. The value of a piece of research increases as that research builds upon the existing body of political science knowledge.

The Interactive Research Process   Since reading the literature that relates to your theory is an interactive process, you should not be daunted by what you do not know when you begin your research. As you gain familiarity with the extant literature, your literature review plan will also evolve. You will want to read widely the existing literature on topics related to your theory, but also approach this reading intelligently and efficiently. As you are reading, consider: (1) what research questions have already been asked (what theories have been posed), (2) how researchers have gone about answering those questions, and (3) what researchers have found. While gathering this information, keep in mind two specific questions. First, what substantive information about your theory can you glean from the literature? Second, what useful insights have previous researchers developed, what mistakes have they made, and what might they have overlooked in answering their research questions? Or, to put it another way, what methodological lessons can you learn from the literature?

To identify the books and articles that are relevant to your theory, you might just head for the library, locate the political science stacks, and start reading book and article titles until you locate some of interest. Alternatively, you might just search Google or some similar site on the free Web (Internet research will be addressed in Chapter 4). These approaches are inefficient in two ways. First, in undertaking unfocused searches, you waste a great deal of time. In order to find the few titles that might be of interest, you are forced to sift through hundreds of volumes and thousands of journal articles that have nothing whatsoever to do with the topic you are pursuing. Second, an unfocused search simply will not turn up the greater part of the literature you need. This is because political science is so diverse a discipline—it is not at all uncommon to find political science research published in journals of sociology, psychology, communication, geography, and economics, to name only a few. Additionally, the titles of books or articles do not always offer solid guidance to their content, and even if they did, not all of a library's holdings may be on the shelves at a given time. In sum, random searching will yield too much that is somewhat related to your topic, but too little that is directly related to your theory. Clearly, you need a better strategy for identifying the items you are interested in.

Developing a System

Systematic bibliographic search is simply a way of preparing and planning to ensure the most productive use of your institution's library resources. It involves (1) specifying your needs, (2) planning how you will allocate your efforts, (3) maximizing your use of the resources available, and (4) recording what you find for later use. Each of these is explored in turn.

Listing Keywords   The first step is to develop a list of terms from the (at least) three concepts in our theory. An example will best demonstrate this process. Suppose we theorize that *pro-choice voters* with *Republican* partisan identification who favor a *pro-life Republican candidate* are more likely to (incorrectly) think that their preferred candidate shares their abortion policy view, because to think otherwise could cause these voters to experience *cognitive dissonance* (the concepts are italicized).

From the concepts mentioned in our example theory, we brainstorm a list of political terms: pro-choice, voters, Republican, pro-life, candidate, abortion policy, and cognitive dissonance. Then, we can individually list the synonyms or words that are related to these concepts. For example, the term "Republican" may suggest: Republican voter, the Republican Party, Republican partisan identification, a U.S. political party, conservative ideology, right wing, etc. Notice that few of the related words in our list are truly identical in meaning to the initial word. Some are broader (U.S. political party), some are more specific (Republican Party), and some are related but fundamentally differ from the original term (conservative ideology). Additionally, when thinking of related terms, remember the multiple meanings that many words have—Republican Party versus a republican form of government. At this point, an important part of our brainstorming is to develop a fairly wide list of relevant keywords, because we do not know how the existing research may characterize our theory's concepts.

Filling in the Concept Search Grid   A **concept grid** helps us keep track of our potential search terms and their possible relationships. Figure 3.1 illustrates the grid's use with our brainstormed concepts written in. (A printable version of this grid may be downloaded from the Web site of one of the authors: www.psci.vt.edu/cbrians/) The grid in Figure 3.1 is used by simply writing your initial concepts (from your theory) on the upper lines, then listing the brainstormed terms below each concept. These

	Theoretical Concept:		Theoretical Concept:
	REPUBLICAN		ABORTION
Search	Related Terms:	Link (and/or)	Related Terms:
1	REPUBLICAN VOTER		PRO-LIFE
2	REPUBLICAN PARTY		PRO-CHOICE
3	PARTY IDENTIFICATION		ABORTION POLICY
4	CONSERVATIVE		
5	RIGHT-WING		
6			
7			

Figure 3.1
Sample concept search grid
NOTE: Printable copies of this grid may be downloaded from Craig Leonard Brians' Web site:
http://www.psci.vt.edu/cbrians/

"Related Terms" may be synonyms, narrower words, broader words, or subject headings (sometimes called descriptors) from your library's catalog, indexes or databases. The "Link" between the terms is printed in lighter type because it is optional. Initially, you may want to search for your related terms individually, later narrowing your focus by adding (or combining) terms to the search. Since your theory has at least three concepts and you will probably use several different library tools in your search, you will need to use multiple grids to include all of your concepts. Remember, the grid is simply a tool; use it as long as it facilitates your literature search, modifying it as your search progresses.

Developing the initial list of related words should not be too time-consuming, and may provide enough terms to get your keyword search started. Remember, a literature search is interactive; thus, you will be adding words to the grid as your research progresses and crossing off words that you discover to be less useful.

The usefulness of the key terms on the grid is better tested using search tools that more closely represent the text of current research. Thus, we begin our search with periodicals, before moving to books listed in the library catalog.

Periodical Indexes and Databases

Academic libraries typically offer two kinds of tools for article searching: full-text databases and indexes. Full-text databases include complete articles. Oriented around keywords, searching full-text databases is similar to using a search engine (e.g., Google) on the free Web. Indexes describe articles and provide citations. Thus, using indexes is like using the library catalog, and includes the very powerful function of finding related items under a standardized list of subject headings. Online indexes generally include hyperlinks to the journals that your library subscribes to, as well as citations to many articles not available in your library. Print indexes, which are still available, provide citations to articles written before the digital era.

Once you have developed your list of search terms, you need to put these to use discovering what the political science literature has to say about your research topic. An excellent starting point is a **general periodical database,** such as *Infotrac Expanded Academic ASAP* or *EBSCO Academic Search Elite.* Widely available in most academic libraries, these databases include citations—and often the full text—of articles on topics related to a variety of academic disciplines, including the humanities, physical sciences, and social sciences. *Expanded Academic,* for instance, searches articles from more than 2,500 periodicals, spanning the gamut from newspapers to scholarly journals to news magazines. The coverage is wide but seldom deep enough to be the sole source for thorough research.

Starting your search in a general database has two purposes. First, these resources generally offer a good sense of the background information related to your topic, quickly confirming whether or not your theory is plausible. Popular periodicals provide access to information on your topic, since you are not yet an expert on the jargon and techniques of a discipline. Second, while the scholarly content is worth evaluating separately (and we will below), general databases also contain research from many academic journals. Thus, in addition to a popular periodical overview, searching these databases may also give you a taste of the academic research on your topic.

Searching with Keywords   A generic search window is reproduced in Figure 3.2; whether your library subscribes to *Infotrac Expanded Academic ASAP* (*Infotrac*, from now on) or another general periodical database, the **keyword** (the typical default search for library databases) searching process is quite similar. Keyword searches check the available records in the database for articles that (somewhere) contain the search term you enter. The database does not "know" what you or the article's author(s) intend by a word. The search merely matches a string of characters. Therefore, if the author of an article that is relevant to your theory used a different set of words to describe the concepts, or even a different spelling, a keyword search will bypass the article. Keeping records on your search results on the concept grid may assist you in focusing your efforts on the most productive search terms.

Most indexes and databases permit the use of wildcard characters to expand your search; that is, you may substitute a "*" or similar character for several letters (e.g., "Republic*" finds republic, republican, republics, republicans, republicanism, Republican, Republicans, but also republication). Since this type of search expands the terms being searched, wildcard searching yields far more results than any single root word would.

Searching by keywords in *Infotrac* is straightforward. Returning to the words in the grid in Figure 3.1, we type the word "Republican Party" in the *Infotrac* search box. Performing this keyword search in *Infotrac* yields tens of thousands of recent articles that apparently mention the Republican Party. As we begin to read these articles (either online or in hard-copy in the library), we will discover two things. First, many of the articles are only tangentially related to the Republican Party in the U.S. Second, it is exhausting to locate the few articles that even mention abortion policy.

To address these challenges, we need to refine our search and become more efficient searchers. The next section describes a technique to sharpen our focus on articles that are most relevant to our study of the Republican Party. The same prin-

---

Acme Academic Index

Search:

[   ]

Search in: ○ title or abstract   ○ anywhere in record

(Optional limits on search)

     ☐ Only scholarly journal articles
     ☐ Range of dates: [   ] to [   ]

[Search]

[Go to Advanced/Combination search]

Figure 3.2
Typical search window for an online periodical index or database

ciples apply to the abortion policy side of our theory, as well. After mastering these tools, we will be ready to combine searches to locate literature that addresses both aspects of our theory.

Moving from Keywords to Subjects   Once you have located a few relevant (in some respect) articles using the keyword search, you will want to take advantage of librarians' work on your behalf to find related articles. Library indexes, many full-text databases, and library catalogs are designed to get new users past several of the problems associated with keyword searching (e.g., word choice, ambiguity, and spelling). One of the most common and powerful ways is by adding **subject headings** (sometimes called **descriptors**). These standardized headings link articles dealing with related topics by identifying the several fundamental issues or topics that the articles address.

Searching by subject in *Infotrac* is also straightforward. Simply click on the article title in the search results and you will find the *Infotrac* subject links to other articles at the bottom of the article record. Using subject headings benefits your search in two ways. They can help clarify your thinking about your theory. The list of subject headings for a given article can make you aware of connections between concepts in that piece of research; they give you a snapshot of how the discipline categorizes the article. Thus, and second, subject headings help you to locate other articles that fall into those same disciplinary categories.

An Example   An article from the search described above has several subject headings, including "Republican Party (United States)—Demographic Aspects." Clicking on any of these subject heading links will initiate a subject heading search, yielding more articles that are related to the subject. If we carefully choose which subject to search by, these new articles are more likely to have a sharper emphasis on the particular facet of the "Republican Party" that relates to our research.

Our use of the search grid is not finished; as we find these subject headings, we add them to the grid and note which database used them. Unfortunately, the subject headings used in one database will not necessarily be the same as those used in another database, index, or library catalog. In the electronic research environment, there are many ways to get to the same article. Using the grid to trace our search tactics will help us return to useful articles when we need them, as well as giving us potentially productive starting points for further research.

Refining Your Search   Electronic search tools (library catalogs and Web search engines as well as library databases and online indexes) provide a number of ways to refine your searches by combining terms. The most common is by using "Boolean operators," notably *and* and *or*. Connecting your search terms with the *and* operator tells the computer to find items (bibliographic records or articles) that contain both of your search terms. That is, *and* narrows your search. Connecting your terms with *or* tells the computer to find items that contain either your first term or your second (or your third one, etc). Thus, *or* broadens your search.

Working from your concept grid, use *or* searches to combine related terms within each concept column, such as synonyms, variant spellings, and plurals. Once you have found the most effective searches for each concept, use *and* searches to see what, if any, articles covered by your tools deal with more than one concept.

As you have probably noticed in Web searching, Boolean operators are rather imprecise tools. In a general database, especially if it includes newspapers and news magazines, "Republican *and* party" will find articles not only about the Republican Party, but also about New Year's Eve celebrations attended by Republican officials.

Library tools deal with this problem in several ways:

1. By coverage: a specifically political science database like *Worldwide Political Science Abstracts* will include many more articles on political parties as organizations and fewer on festive events. *Infotrac Expanded Academic* and various other databases allow you to restrict your search to scholarly (that is, "peer-reviewed" or "refereed" journals). Full-text databases such as *JSTOR* and *LexisNexis Academic* force you to select specific portions of their content before they will run a search.

2. By the structure of the data: indexes (like library catalogs) break down their descriptions of articles into many pieces (called "fields") to which you can restrict your searches. Author (official writings by the Republican Party), article title (pieces mentioning the Republican Party), abstract (pieces noting the Republican Party, in some context), and subject heading (pieces that catalogers identify as being about the Republican Party) are the most familiar. Other useful fields include date of publication, title of the journal (often, confusingly,

called "source" or "citation" in indexes and databases, but always "title" in the library catalog), and language, among others.

3. By search options: full-text databases usually provide fewer fields to search in; many do not provide subject headings. Explore a database to see if it offers some kind of "proximity" searching: if your search terms occur near one another, it is likely that an article uses them as related terms. Depending on the database, proximity searching allows you to search for words within a given number of words (say, 15 or 25), words in the same sentence, or words occurring in the same paragraph.

Most online library indexes and some full-text databases make it simple to search large swathes of literature and then quickly explore various combinations. Look for a feature called "search history," "previous searches," or "combine," which tracks every search. The terms vary by database. Simply mark checkboxes to tell the database to combine your most effective previous searches.

Experiment with search combinations that use a subject heading for one concept or variable in your theory with keywords for aspects of your other concepts or variables. A caveat: combining subject headings for all of your concepts is not likely to be beneficial to your research. It will either be too narrow to locate much literature, or if this search does produce results, your own research may not be adding much to the universe of political science knowledge.

Often, a database's default search screen is the least useful one. You may want to get in the habit of starting in an advanced search window, even if you seldom use more than one or two of its features in a search session. It will give you more options for selecting fields, combining terms, restricting your searches to particular publication dates or information types, and otherwise making your searching more precise.

Searching Academic Subject Indexes   General periodical databases are broad but not necessarily deep enough for full-fledged literature reviews. **Academic subject indexes,** available for most disciplines, provide depth for specialists. For political science, *Worldwide Political Science Abstracts*, *International Political Science Abstracts*, and *PAIS International* are probably the most comprehensive and widely available. As the titles of these databases suggest, their coverage is not restricted to U.S. politics, the works they identify are not necessarily in English, and your library will probably not subscribe to every periodical or other resource that they cover.

In addition to the tighter scope of their coverage, subject indexes are often easier to search than full-text databases. Indexes are heavily structured descriptions of information sources. They are designed to minimize ambiguities. Thus, you can target your searches more precisely, focusing on words in particular fields—paying particular attention to abstracts—and exploiting their systems of subject headings. Because the index records are shorter than the full text of the articles they describe, they are easier for you to peruse to identify additional search terms, such as authors and technical vocabularies (also known as terms of art or jargon—the consistent shorthand insiders in a discipline use to communicate with one another).

Some examples: when you find a record of the author of one relevant article, look elsewhere in that index, other indexes and databases, the library catalog, and the Web

Figure 3.3
Steps of a systematic literature search

for other articles and books by that author that you could use. Among political scientists, "turnout" denotes specific voting behavior on election day, so it is an effective keyword in a political science index. But in a general database or on the Web, you would need to combine "turnout" with "voter" in order to exclude articles about fashion and firefighting, which use the word "turnout" in a rather different way.

The principles of searching in a subject index like *Worldwide Political Science Abstracts* are very similar to those already described for searching in *Infotrac*: start with keyword searches, look through the results lists for titles that seem relevant to your theory, examine the full records for subject headings (which *WPSA* labels "descriptors") and other potentially useful information, and run further searches with appropriate keywords, descriptors, and combinations.

Summarizing the Literature Search   Figure 3.3 highlights the key steps in searching for literature. These condensed steps apply equally whether you are searching for popular or academic articles, or searching for books.

There is, of course, an additional step in literature searching: finding the articles. Depending on your library's subscriptions, contracts among information providers, and technology, this access may be as simple as clicking on a link in a record to an electronic journal or as complicated as requesting that your library borrow a copy of the article for you from another institution via interlibrary loan. Generally, you will use your library catalog to determine if your library has the journal issues containing the articles your searches identified, what format they are available in, and where you can get them.

Library Catalogs

In the course of your research you will need to physically visit the library for several reasons. First, not all of the relevant articles you have identified are available online. Second, if you limit your bibliography to those articles that are available online, you allow an external source of selection bias to distort your research (Chapter 7 will discuss proper sampling). Third, while doing periodical research, it is likely that your articles will reference books that you will want to review personally.

Library Organization   Once you have a citation for a book or journal from an index or bibliography, you need to locate a physical copy of that work. Finding materials in the library requires knowing something about the way that most libraries are organized, as well as the resources that they make available.

Libraries organize their collections using two different sets of organizing principles that try to put related materials together. One principle has already been described: subject headings are elaborate, standardized sets of labels that describe aspects of the contents of books and the coverage of periodicals. Subject headings make *intellectual connections* among items in the library, even though the items may be physically separated or some of the items are online. The other principle tries to put related items *physically* near each other, so that if you find one relevant book on the shelf, you can easily browse along the shelf to find others that address the same material.

The key tool for this physical arrangement is the call number, which the library affixes to the spines (or sometimes the covers or other containers) of the materials in its collection. Two call number systems are widely used in North America: the Dewey Decimal Classification system, used mainly by schools, small colleges, and public libraries; the other is the Library of Congress Classification system, widely used by universities and large research libraries. If the identifying marks on books (the call number) in your library begin with decimal numbers of the type 320.072, your library uses the Dewey Decimal system. If the identifying marks begin with a combination of letters and numbers, as, for example, JA86.M35, your library uses the Library of Congress system. (Both identifiers, incidentally, designate the same book.)

Under the Library of Congress classification system, each discipline or group of disciplines is assigned a letter of the alphabet. Thus, *H* represents social science in general, *J* political science, *K* law, and so forth. A second letter is assigned in order to designate a subfield. Thus, the *J* classification for political science is further divided as follows:

J	Official documents
JA	General works
JC	Political theory
JF	Constitutional history and administration
JK	United States
JL	British America, Latin America
JN	Europe

JQ	Asia, Africa, Australia, Pacific Islands
JS	Local government
JV	Colonies and colonization
JX	International law and international relations
JZ	International relations

The remainder of the call number organizes the collection by still more specific subjects established by the Library of Congress. The final alphanumeric group in a call number is based on the author's name and is assigned by the library. The net effect of this system is that all books sharing a given topic and all books by a particular author on that topic are shelved together.

Political science researchers should be aware of a third, specialized call number system that may be used in libraries with extensive holdings of U.S. government publications: the Superintendent of Documents Classification—"SuDoc"—system. The U.S. Government Printing Office, the world's largest publisher, distributes studies and reports performed or commissioned by federal agencies and Congress. These publications are rich sources of primary-source information, both narrative and statistical.

Library Catalog Searching   Online catalogs allow us to perform searches by keyword, title, author, subject, or call number. To locate the printed copies of a journal, we *title search* in the library's catalog for the periodical's name—not the article title. Similarly, to find a book that has been cited in your research, search for the book's title. On the other hand, you may use the *author search* feature to locate all of the books written by a given author who does research in your field. For example, perhaps in your search of journal articles you noticed that several articles were written by Ted Jelen. Searching for "Jelen, Ted" in your library's catalog should yield references to several of the books he has written related to abortion policy, as well as others on religion and politics. Subject searches use the official Library of Congress Subject Headings (LCSH). Until you become familiar with the peculiarities of the LCSH and know some by heart, use the subject links in the full bibliographic record for relevant books, just as in the article searching that was discussed previously.

The library catalog is the single best guide to the books, journals, and other works held by a particular library, but from the perspective of the thorough researcher it suffers from two major limitations. First, the catalog lists mainly books, even though much, if not most, of the important empirical research in political science or any other field is to be found not in books, but in articles in scholarly journals. And whereas journals themselves are listed in the catalog, their content is not. Second, most library catalogs list only the holdings of the particular library you happen to be using. Fortunately, neither of these problems is insurmountable. As we have seen, databases and indexes offer access to journal article content. Additionally, union catalogs bring together the catalog records of multiple libraries within a locality, a state, or even around the world, as in the case of *WorldCat* and *RLG Union Catalog* (also called *RLIN*). Increasingly, union catalogs are linked with interlibrary loan systems, whereby your library can borrow materials from other libraries on your behalf.

Organizing Your Findings

Research in the electronic environment, paradoxically, puts a premium on taking thorough notes at each step of the process. Keep revising your concept grid. You want to create a separate grid for each resource: catalog, index, full-text database, Web subject directory, and Web search engine, so you can relocate your information sources easily when you need to; even if you have saved the full text of articles or citations on your computer, your notes will help you locate these resources. Consistent note taking helps to prevent oversights, and including all of the pertinent information at the outset saves return trips to the library databases and catalog.

Recording Literature Research   To facilitate taking thorough notes, you should bring a sizable stack of blank file cards or your laptop computer (with bibliographic or database software) to the library to record your citations' bibliographic information and your comments on each reference. Each time you find a potentially useful source listed, create a separate card or record that includes the complete bibliographic citation, recording—as appropriate—author, title, journal (including volume number, year of publication, and pages), date and place of publication, and publisher. For books, remember to record the call number. Include notes about how you found each article or book, the database you used, your search terms, and the book or articles that cited it. If an article database offers persistent or stable Web links to individual articles, you will want to include these as well. Most article links, though, are specific to your online session, so you should not depend upon them for later access.

Decide in advance the format you will use for reference citations in the research report and remember to record in that format the appropriate information about each source. Check with your instructor to find out the preferred style for references (e.g., APSA, MLA, APA, etc.). Your library should have copies of the preferred style manual. Chapter 22 offers more guidance on the structure of research reports and using political science style manuals.

Your notes should also include all of the main points of the book or article, any especially useful tips or facts, a summary of the method the author used and of the findings if research is reported, and any potentially useful quotations. Make frequent page references to the specific locations of the items you record. Figure 3.4 gives an illustration of a completed bibliography card made with this technique. Alternatively, you might use a separate card for each piece of information, being sure to indicate the author, source, and page number on each card. Individual cards require more preparation and are more cumbersome in a permanent bibliographic file, but they are easier to use when the time comes to actually write the research report, because each substantive point can then be moved around and organized independently of others from the same source.

If you obtain electronic copies of your reference citations and you type your notes on the references, you may be able to begin writing your research report sooner. Still, you should follow the same rules to make entries for each reference in a computer file and take notes on each source right below its bibliographic information. Having the references and notes in electronic form can save time when writing the research

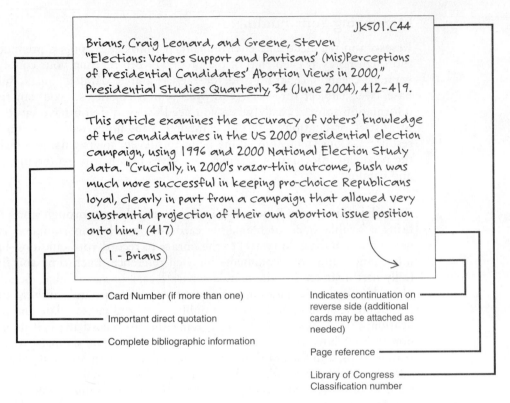

JK501.C44

Brians, Craig Leonard, and Greene, Steven
"Elections: Voters Support and Partisans' (Mis)Perceptions
of Presidential Candidates' Abortion Views in 2000,"
Presidential Studies Quarterly, 34 (June 2004), 412-419.

This article examines the accuracy of voters' knowledge
of the candidatures in the US 2000 presidential election
campaign, using 1996 and 2000 National Election Study
data. "Crucially, in 2000's razor-thin outcome, Bush was
much more successful in keeping pro-choice Republicans
loyal, clearly in part from a campaign that allowed very
substantial projection of their own abortion issue position
onto him." (417)

1 - Brians

Card Number (if more than one)

Important direct quotation

Complete bibliographic information

Indicates continuation on
reverse side (additional
cards may be attached as
needed)

Page reference

Library of Congress
Classification number

Figure 3.4
Sample bibliography card

design or final report. For example, word processing software allows a quick search of the entire file for key words using the "Find" function, making it easier to find all references that address a given issue. You can also copy and paste citations and quotes from your bibliographic notes and insert them directly into the text rather than having to retype them. Whether you obtain direct quotes electronically or paraphrase the reference's text, always include a citation to the original author's work.

Why Keep Notes?   Whether you use note cards or a computer, the physical act of writing notes—which requires thinking about the material that you record—is a more effective way of understanding and applying information than merely highlighting your photocopied or printed articles, or copying and pasting chunks of text. The more you understand of the state of knowledge on your theory, the better able you will be to decide whether any additional piece of information is relevant to your project. Thus, you will want to take notes as you locate your literature resources.

A thorough job of note-taking at each stage of your research saves time in two ways. First, it lets you use, cite, and discuss any of your sources without necessitating a return to the library or rereading the source. Second, if for some reason you must reread a source, the page notations help to pinpoint that portion of the material that is of interest. An investment of a little time and effort to document your literature research carefully pays great dividends.

At the conclusion of this task, you will have accomplished two major objectives. First, you will have compiled a relatively complete listing of the literature in your area of interest. Second, you will have sufficiently familiarized yourself with that literature so that you may better anticipate problems and, thus, improve your own work, properly placing that work in the larger context of which it is a part.

Conclusion

This chapter offers a brief and somewhat generic introduction to the basic procedures associated with using online book and article databases to find literature on your theory. Because this text is used at colleges and universities throughout the U.S. (and in many other countries, as well), it is not possible for us to present a comprehensive primer on the specific resources that your library offers. To complement our general treatment of literature searching, and get the most from your library's resources, you should experiment with searches, utilize your search tool's help functions, and contact a librarian with more involved questions that arise in the course of your research.

Electronic searching looks easier than it is, but with the basic understanding of appropriate literature searching techniques we have provided here and with some perseverance, you can successfully and efficiently apply previous research to your theory. With experience, you will develop a repertoire of preferred resources and search techniques, but never overlook the assistance of your library's reference librarians. Because bibliographical resources vary widely among academic institutions, a reference librarian at your college will be your most authoritative source of information and guidance.

Summary Points

- Identifying previous research findings will help you to position your research within the literature, and help your work to contribute to the cumulative function of scientific learning.
- The existing literature can show us what has been learned and the research methods used, which help to frame our research question.
- A systematic search of the literature includes entering the concepts from our theory into the concept search grid, brainstorming for related terms, searching general periodical databases, searching academic subject indexes, and going to the library.
- The library's resources are preferable to those freely available on the Web, because librarians have filtered this information to enable more efficient searching.
- You begin developing your research report as you gather information from references, making note-taking a crucial part of this process. Additionally, accurate notes enhance searching efficiency.

Suggested Readings and References

For a comprehensive, descriptive listing of journals in political science, see Fenton Martin and Robert Goehlert, *Getting Published in Political Science Journals: A Guide for Authors, Editors, and Librarians*, 5th ed. (Washington, DC: American Political Science Association, 2001).

Summary rankings of the perceived quality of various political science journals are found in James C. Garand and Micheal W. Giles "Journals in the Discipline: A Report on a New Survey of American Political Scientists." *PS: Political Science and Politics* 36(2003), pp. 293–308.

A classic guide to literature reviews is Harris M. Cooper's *Integrating Research*, 2nd ed. (Newbury Park, CA: Sage, 1989).

Scholarly Political Science Journals

This list of some of the major scholarly political science journals is not comprehensive; there are other scholarly journals that have been omitted due to limited space, but the more prominent journals appear here.

American Journal of Political Science

American Political Science Review

American Politics Research

British Journal of Political Science

Comparative Political Studies

Comparative Politics

Foreign Affairs

Foreign Policy

Harvard International Journal of Press/Politics

International Organization

International Political Science Review

International Studies Quarterly

Journal of Conflict Resolution

Journal of Politics

Legislative Studies Quarterly

Perspectives on Politics

Policy Studies Journal/Policy Studies Review

Political Behavior

Political Communication

Political Research Quarterly

Political Science Quarterly

Political Studies

Political Theory

Polity

Presidential Studies Quarterly

Public Administration Review

Public Choice

Public Opinion Quarterly

Publius

Social Science Quarterly

World Politics

Research Exercise

1. a. State a theory.

   b. Develop a keyword list for a search of the literature related to your research question.

   c. Outline a search strategy, both for online and library searching.

   d. Using your search strategy and at least two indexes, develop a bibliography of ten to fifteen items that appear to be of interest. Prepare a file card with all of the necessary information for each item.

   e. Locate at least three items from your bibliography in the stacks of the library. At least one should be a book and one a journal article.

   f. Read each item you have located. Take notes on what you read.

   g. Consider the relationship between what you have read and your research question. How might each item help you to better frame or pursue documents related to your question?

Key Terms

concept search grid

general periodical database

keyword

subject headings (or descriptors)

academic subject index

CHAPTER 4

Internet Research

- What information is available on the Internet?
- What is the best way to search for information on the Internet?
- How do we evaluate information found on the Internet?
- What is the Invisible Web?

The Internet has dramatically changed the way social science research is done. More and more public opinion polls, for example, are conducted with online questionnaires, thus eliminating costly telephone interviews and the need to interrupt respondents' dinners. Millions of informational Web pages, online library catalogs, and online databases allow those who have access to the Internet to conduct research without ever leaving their home or office. The Internet also brings together researchers who have to coordinate national or international projects by allowing them to exchange information quickly and cheaply through e-mail or other Internet-based services.

Most of us who have surfed the Web know that finding useful information online is a big challenge. Answers to simple questions such as "who is the current chancellor of Germany?" usually are found quickly thanks to search engines such as *Yahoo!* or *Google*. More complicated research questions, however, such as "what studies exist about political communication in Great Britain?" require more sophisticated research strategies and some knowledge about where and how information can be found on the Internet.

This chapter provides an introduction to the particular problems of Internet research and finding information online. Special emphasis will be placed on the research tools and the strategies that help to locate useful resources on the Web.

What Is Out There?

The biggest problem with the Internet is how it is organized—not much at all. There are millions of Web pages published by governments, organizations, businesses, academics, and individuals. Most of those pages are scattered and not available through central directories. The trick is to find those pages that might be useful to a particular research project.

It is important to remember that the Internet is a good source of current and frequently updated information, such as news, economic statistics, or polling data for an ongoing election. The Internet also allows easy access to electronic databases and information that otherwise might be difficult or time-consuming to locate. Electronic versions of important public documents, such as political speeches or transcripts of press conferences, are usually accessible though the Internet and can be scanned easily for relevant information with simple text searches.

The Internet is less suited for research on information that might not be available in electronic form, such as older documents that are only available as hard copies. Even primary documents such as books, excerpts, or quotes that are available online might not accurately reflect their original content because they might have changed slightly when they were transcribed or copied from one Web page to another. Thus, it is usually safer to rely on published originals rather than online versions of such documents.

Types of Web Pages   One way of organizing the flood of information from the Internet is to distinguish the various types of Web pages available. According to Alexander and Tate (1999), those pages most useful for research generally fall into four basic categories:

1. **Informational pages** that are created by governments, independent authors, or companies and contain scholarly research, reference sources, or facts. Government Web sites (whose domain names usually end with .gov) usually provide online access to reliable public documents and resources. Informational pages published by individuals should be evaluated more carefully based on the authors' credentials (check the authors' professional background) and the reliability of the provided information (check for sources and references on which the presented information is based). Similarly, informational sites sponsored by companies should be examined for possible biases in the presented information (what might be the reason for a company to provide such information?).

2. **News sources** that are mainly Web sites published by media organizations such as *CNN.com* or *Washingtonpost.com*. Web sites that are maintained by news organizations offer convenient access to current and archived news stories, and are a good starting point to search for background information on a particular issue. Keep in mind that searches on news sites are usually limited to a certain time period or section of the news and therefore cannot offer the same depth and reliability as dedicated news databases such as *LexisNexis*.

3. **Advocacy pages** that are sponsored by non-profit organizations or independent activists and usually focus on a particular issue or cause. In recent years, political and social groups in particular have found the Internet to be a cost-effective way to disseminate information and to promote a particular point of view. While information presented on advocacy Web sites (whose domain names usually end with .org) might provide valuable research information, it should be treated with caution because of possible biases.

4. **Personal home pages** that are mostly published by individual authors and contain résumés, links to favorite sites or publications, or discussions of personal interests. While personal Web sites can contain high-quality information, it is advisable to cross-check information from such sites carefully.

Searching for Information   Now that you are familiar with the various types of Web pages available on the Internet, it is time to think about how to find resources for your research project. As you probably know, simply browsing the Internet might be fun, but it is unlikely to yield much useful information. Because information on the Internet is so spread out and disorganized, you will need to use a set of search tools and strategies in order to find useful information.

There are three basic types of search tools that allow you to explore the Internet: *search engines*, *meta-search engines*, and *subject directories*. Which one of the three tools you should use for your search depends mainly on what kind of information you want to find.

A **search engine** is a searchable database of links to Web pages collected by computer programs called crawlers, robots, or spiders. These programs routinely prowl the Internet and index all Web pages they come across. Users of these search engines are then able to search the index with keywords and are presented with links to those Web pages that contain the particular keywords.

Currently, the two most popular search engines are *Yahoo!* (www.yahoo.com) and *Google* (www.google.com). *Google*'s simple interface and fast keyword searches have a well-deserved reputation for consistently retrieving the most relevant pages by ranking possible returns with a patented algorithm. This algorithm (called "PageRank") ranks the importance of a Web site mainly by the number of external links referring to it. *Google* also offers specialized search services such as *Google Scholar* (www.scholar.google.com), which allows you to search specifically for scholarly literature, including peer-reviewed papers, theses, books, and abstracts from broad areas of research. A similar service called *Google Government* (www.google.com/unclesam) lets you search U.S. government (.gov) and U.S. military (.mil) sites.

Yahoo!, which started in 1994 as a human-compiled Web directory, now offers both a subject directory and an excellent search engine that closely matches *Google*'s performance. Those using *Yahoo!* as their primary search tool should be aware that the directory only provides links to those Web sites that have been reviewed and included by *Yahoo!*'s employees. It therefore represents only a limited view at what is available on the Internet. The regular *Yahoo!* search engine, on the other hand, features comprehensive crawler-based listings of links to Web pages just like *Google*.

The verdict is still out on the new *MSN Search* (search.msn.com). Microsoft is trying to compete in the lucrative search engine market by developing its own search algorithm and offering access to more than five billion pages indexed and updated regularly—a database roughly comparable to *Google*'s and *Yahoo*'s.

Since queries performed on different search engines produce different results, it is usually not a good idea to rely on one search engine only. The easiest way to make sure that you find all relevant Web pages is to use a **meta-search engine** such as *HotBot* or *WebCrawler*. Meta-search engines do not search the Web themselves, but send searches to several search engines at once. The results are then compiled and presented together on one page. *HotBot* (www.hotbot.com), for example, provides access to the Web's three major search engines *Yahoo!*, *Google*, and *Teoma*. *MetaCrawler* (www.metacrawler.com) and *Dogpile* (www.dogpile.com) simultaneously queries *Google*, *Yahoo!*, *Ask Jeeves*, *LookSmart*, *Overture*, and *FindWhat*. Those interested in search returns that differ from the relevance ranking system found in traditional search engines such as *Google* or *Yahoo!* should have a look at *Vivisimo* (vivisimo.com), which automatically organizes Web pages into categories. *WebBrain.com* (www.webbrain.com), on the other hand, displays findings with graphical links to other related issues.

One of the easiest methods of searching for relevant resources is using **subject directories** that have been compiled and organized by commercial, academic, or professional organizations. Subject directories store and present links to Web sites submitted by Web authors or reviewers, and are usually organized into subject or topic categories. Because the categorization is subjective, the contents of even the most popular subject directories differ greatly and cannot be regarded as complete subject classifications. It is therefore a good idea to visit more than one directory in order to obtain a variety of possible subject classifications. The biggest advantage of subject directories is that they make it fairly easy to narrow searches (for example, "government") to a specific topic by simply following links in the directory to selected sub-topics (for example, "political advertising").

Commercial subject directories such as the one offered by *Yahoo!* (dir.yahoo.com) should be used with great caution in research because they cater to the general public and often mix scholarly Internet resources with everything else. Academic and professional directories, on the other hand, are often maintained by subject experts, cater to the specific needs of researchers, and are less dependent on Internet traffic for support. Good examples of academic subject directories are *INFOMINE* (infomine.ucr.edu), a large collection of scholarly Internet resources maintained by several university libraries, and *AllLearn Directory* (www.alllearn.org/er), a guide to more than 12,000 academic Web sites by Oxford, Stanford, and Yale University. One of the most useful professional subject directories is the *Librarians' Index to the Internet* (lii.org), which is a searchable, annotated subject directory of more than 14,000 Internet resources selected and evaluated by librarians for their usefulness to users of public libraries.

Internet Search Strategies

Finding information on the Internet usually requires more than simply inserting a few keywords into a search engine and then sifting through hundreds of hits. While many of us probably do just that, a carefully planned search on the Internet can yield more reliable information in a fraction of the time it takes to conduct a series of more or less random searches. Because information on the Internet is highly decentralized, successful searches generally require a carefully planned search strategy. Depending on the complexity of your search, you should consider the following steps as part of your search strategy.

Determine what kind of information you need   Before you start a search, consider whether the Internet is really the best place to find what you are looking for. Not all information is available on the Internet (listings of older books, for example), which means that it is sometimes necessary to search other resources as well (such as your library's electronic catalog). Next, think about what *type* of information you are looking for—this will allow you to narrow your search and focus on specific sources. If you are looking for a general news story, for example, you should start with searching news sites such as *CNN.com* or *Washingtonpost .com*. To find books, it is usually best to search the catalogs of online libraries rather than the Web in general. If you are looking for information that originated within the government, on the other hand, you might want to limit your search to government Web pages (those ending with .gov). You also might focus your search on specific *forms* of information such as images, videos, or audio files. Most search engines allow you to search for these data separately.

Develop keywords for your search   This is probably the most crucial step and usually requires a bit of intuition. Before you start a search, try to develop a list of keywords that might produce the most relevant search results. Enter these keywords into a search engine and check the results. In most cases, you probably have to adjust or change the keywords in order to focus your search. Consider related terms, concepts, synonyms, or other keywords that might be associated with the information you are searching for. If you have trouble coming up with new terms, it is often helpful to search for related keywords on Web pages that come very close to what you are seeking.

Use more than one search engine   Remember that queries performed on different search engines usually produce different results. It is therefore not a good idea to rely on one search engine only—try the same search on different search engines or use meta-search engines such *WebCrawler* or *Dogpile*.

Learn about the advanced search functions   While many of the advanced functions found in search engines such as *Yahoo!* or *Google* are similar, there are some crucial differences that are important to know. Searches in *Google*, for example, are not case sensitive (this means that a search for "United States" and "uNiTeD StAtEs" will yield the same results), while queries in other search engines are. Thus, if you are interested in more efficient and precise searches, it usually pays to spend a few minutes learning the advanced search functions of one or two major search engines.

Consider using a subject directory   Sometimes it might be better to start your search with a subject directory instead of a keyword search. Subject directories can be useful, for example, when you are not very familiar with a particular topic and cannot think of good keywords to describe it. In such cases, you will be able to start with a broad topic like "government," and scan the sub-categories until you find what you are looking for. Subject directories are also helpful when keyword searches alone yield too many false hits (records that match the search criteria but aren't relevant to your project). Under such circumstances, a combination of keyword and subject directory searches is likely to result in a more focused search.

Narrow your search results   Search engines use a number of different mechanisms to search for or limit information. The most common search mechanism is called **Boolean logic.** Boolean logic uses three primary search operators: AND, OR, and NOT. The operator AND will narrow a search. For example, a search for "public" AND "opinion" will return only links to Web pages that contain both keywords. Note that some search engines (such as *Google* and *Yahoo!*) automatically return results that contain all keywords (thus assuming the operator AND between all keywords). In most cases, adding keywords to a search is a very simple and effective way for narrowing searches. The operator OR, on the other hand, will broaden a search. For example, using the terms "Spain" OR "France" will return links to Web pages that contain any or both keywords. Since only one of the two keywords needs to be found on a Web page to be recognized as relevant, you will get many more hits compared to using the AND operator. The operator NOT, on the other hand, will narrow a search by dropping any links to Web pages that contain the excluded keyword. For example, a search for "virus" NOT "computer" will exclude links to Web pages that contain discussions of a computer virus—but it will be more likely to retrieve links to pages with discussions of a biological virus.

One of the most effective ways to narrow a search is to use entire phrases rather than keywords. For example, a search for "political effects of the Internet" will retrieve only links to Web pages that contain this particular phrase (97 *Google* hits). Obviously, a search using the separate keywords "political" "effects" and "Internet" would result in many more hits compared to the phrase search (4.4 million *Google* hits). Almost all search engines have additional "advanced" search functions, which allow you, for example, to search for keywords in the title or in the text of Web pages only. Make sure you are familiar with these functions, as they make searching for information much easier and more precise.

Maximize your search results   There are a variety of strategies to improve searches that do not retrieve the desired information. One way to maximize the number of possible search hits for a particular term is to use the **stem** of a word rather than the entire word. For example, a search for politic* will result in links to Web pages containing the keywords politics, political, politician, etc. (The wildcard symbol depends on the search engine. Some search engines, such as *Google* and *Yahoo!*, automatically use stems in keyword searches.) In cases where your search results in only a few but very relevant links, you might be able to find more information by tracing the URL of a relevant Web site to the root URL, which usually links to the home page of Web sites (for example, www.gwu.edu/~smpa can be reduced to www.gwu.edu). Another trick is to pursue the links to "similar pages" (*Google*) or "more from this site" (*Yahoo!*) that are offered as alternatives to the displayed results in most search engines.

Search the Invisible Web   Since not all information available on the Internet can be retrieved with regular search engines (for example, password protected databases), for some projects it might be useful to search *database directories* that list those "hidden" resources. The information available in databases and other resources that cannot be easily retrieved with search engines might be extremely valuable and should not be ignored in any research project. For information on how to find these directories, see the section on the "Invisible Web" (page 53).

Evaluate your search results   It is always important to check the quality of the information you find on the Web. Remember that anybody can "publish" on the Internet and that there is no guarantee that the information you find is indeed accurate or important. According to Alexander and Tate (1999), information obtained from Web sites should always be checked for its authority, objectivity, accuracy, currency, and coverage. To do so, simply try to answer the following questions when encountering doubtful material on the Internet:

- *Who made the information available? (Authority)* To answer this question, check the publisher or author of the Web site from which you obtained the information. In general, information published by academic and government institutions is more reliable than information from interest groups, businesses, or individuals. Make sure you check the original source of the information you found, even if it is published on a Web site of a reputable organization. Verify the legitimacy of any source you are not familiar with.

- *What was the reason for making the information available? (Objectivity)* Always ask yourself whether the objectivity or quality of information you found on the Internet might have been influenced by the goals or interests of the source. Make sure you understand potential ideological, political, or other biases of any Web site you use in your research. The National Rifle Association, for example, is unlikely to publish data showing the negative consequences of gun ownership. Clues about the goals of such interest groups or other organizations usually can be found in the "About Us" section of their home pages.

- *How accurate is the information? (Accuracy)* As in any other research, you have to evaluate the quality and reliability of information you gather on the Internet. Check whether the sources for any factual information are clearly listed and referenced. For example, if you read about the findings of a public opinion poll on the Web site of a political party, you should be able to find information about who conducted the poll on the same site. If you are not absolutely sure about the quality of the information you find, try to verify it by searching for the same information on other Web sites, or in books, journals, etc.

- *How old is the information? (Currency)* While it is true that the Internet is a great source for up-to-date information such as news or business data, many Web sites contain information that is not regularly maintained or updated. This might not be a problem with information that does not need frequent updating (historical reviews, for example). Other data, such as Internet user statistics, on the other hand, have to be as recent as possible. If you need current information, check if there are any dates which might indicate when the information was compiled or when the source page was last revised. You also might want to verify whether there is any more recent information than the one you found by searching for similar data in other resources.

- *How complete is the information? (Coverage)* One of the most important steps in evaluating information gathered from the Internet is to find out how complete or detailed it is. The best way to assess the potential breadth and depth of information found on the Internet is to check the purpose of the source and what audience might be the target. If there is any indication that the information you found on a particular Web page is incomplete or simplified, track down the original source. In addition, ask yourself whether it is reasonable to assume that all information is available online. It is, for example, quite likely that some materials are excluded because they are copyrighted or simply not available in digital format.

Save and organize your search results   If you do a lot of online research, keeping track of what you find can be difficult. The simplest way to save your search results is to bookmark each site you have visited or to save individual Web pages from within your browser (*Internet Explorer*, for example, lets you save complete Web pages and stores them on your computer). However, you will quickly learn that bookmarking or saving entire Web pages is not the most efficient way to keep track of bits and pieces of information found on the Internet. Too often the content of Web pages disappears or changes and is therefore impossible to retrieve at a later point. Information on Web pages that have been saved on your computer, on the other hand, might be difficult to locate later.

Fortunately, there are now a number of commercially available computer programs that make Web research more efficient. One of the best tools for collecting and organizing the data you find online is called *Onfolio* (about $30 for the standard edition available at www.onfolio.com). The program works together with *Internet Explorer* and displays a separate window, where you can create and save research folders. Within each folder, you can collect and sort different types of data you gather from the Web: entire Web sites, URLs of Web sites you visited, images, snippets of text, etc. The program will save the gathered information on your computer together with automatically collected information about where and when you found each item. The biggest advantage of this research tool is that it allows you to gather and organize a lot of different pieces of information in a central location on your computer without the need to find and retrieve it later from the Internet.

Cite your search results   While it easy to obtain and copy information from the Internet, it is important that you quote and cite your sources accurately and honestly. The most common citation styles are the *Modern Languages Association* (MLA) style and the *American Psychological Association* (APA) style. Because there is a large variety of Web sources you might be dealing with, it is best to check the Web sites of these organizations for the most recent style information (details are available at www.mla.org and www.apa.org). In general, though, references to documents found on the Internet are formatted as follows: **MLA style:** Author, A. A. (2005). *Title of work.* Date of Internet publication (if available). Retrieved day, month, year, <source URL>. **APA style:** Author, A. A. (2005). *Title of work.* Retrieved month day, year, from source URL.

The Invisible Web

A large part of the most valuable information that is accessible through the Internet is hidden from regular search engines like *Google* or *Yahoo!* This information is located on the **Invisible Web,** which consists of databases from businesses, government agencies, universities, libraries, and other organizations around the world. Invisible Web sources usually offer access to real-time information (such as news or airline schedules), specialized databases (such as phone books, job postings, or business directories), or other data sources not available on the regular Internet. Since most of these databases are only accessible through direct user queries (often requiring special logons or passwords), crawler-based search engines typically do not index the content of the Invisible Web.

Recent studies suggest that the size and growth rate of the Invisible Web greatly exceeds that of the regular Internet, and that more and more of the most valuable information is available only in these hidden databases. A good example for such an "invisible" source is the Web site of the *Library of Congress* (www.loc.gov) with its invaluable reference databases and the congressional online site *THOMAS* (thomas.loc.gov). Similarly, thousands of federal government databases are accessible through Web-based queries from users who are aware of these resources.

Even though most search engines cannot index the data available on the Invisible Web, there are numerous **database directories** that specialize in collecting links to the most important and publicly accessible Web databases. One such directory is *ProFusion* (www.profusion.com), which lists over 70,000 searchable databases and has links to various specialty search engines. Another well-known directory is *Complete Planet* (www.completeplanet.com), which also lists thousands of databases by category. Publicly accessible databases maintained by the federal government are available through directories such as *FedWorld Information Network* (www .fedworld.gov) or *FirstGov* (www.firstgov.gov), which provide links to millions of federal, state, and local government pages, and databases. Similarly, *GPO Access* (www.gpoaccess.gov), a service by the U.S. Government Printing Office, provides direct online access to over 1,500 federal databases.

Another large section of the Internet that is mostly invisible to search engines is the thousands of *newsgroups, mailing lists,* and *weblogs* (or *blogs*). While none of these information networks is particularly new, they have gained importance in recent years as alternative sources of news and information. The importance of these networks is based on the fact that they are free and easily accessible to every Internet user—which means that they can link a large number of users with similar interests and provide them with the most recent information.

The various types of networks available on the Internet can be good sources for information on issues that are difficult to research. **Newsgroups,** for example, offer public discussions of topics that might be difficult to find in more traditional resources. The origin of newsgroups can be traced back to a collection of e-mail-based bulletin boards (also called *Usenet*) that started in 1981. Since then, the popularity of newsgroups has increased enormously, and they now cover even the most obscure topics imaginable (in early 2005, *Google* listed more than 47,000 newsgroups and more than 500 newsgroups related to "politics"). It is possible to read and post messages in newsgroups with so-called newsreaders, which are included in most browsers and in Web-based e-mail programs such as *Outlook*. The easiest way to access and search newsgroups, however, is through *Google Groups*, which provides a searchable list of all *Usenet* and *Google* discussion groups and an archive of more than one billion newsgroup postings that date back to 1981.

Mailing lists are another good way to keep up with new developments on issues of interest to you. Mailing lists will connect you with people who share your interests and might be able to provide you with new insights or answers to any questions you may have. The main difference between newsgroups and mailing lists is that you can read the discussions in a newsgroup whenever you want, while discussions in a mailing list are sent to you via e-mail. To subscribe to a mailing list, usually all you have to do is send a "subscribe" message to the mailing list program address. Since some of the more popular mailing lists might generate a large number of e-mails, you should carefully select the lists to which you subscribe—otherwise, you will end up with thousands of e-mails in your mailbox every day. To find interesting mailing lists, check the Web sites of organizations that you belong to or are interested in. The *American Political Science Association*, for example, offers a good selection of mailing lists related to political science at www.apsanet.org.

The surge in the number of Internet users in recent years also has led to a proliferation of **blogs** (short for **weblogs**). A blog is a personal journal that is frequently updated and intended for general public consumption. The content and purposes of blogs vary greatly—from personal diaries to news about sports, celebrities, or political commentary. Many blogs also contain links and commentary about other Web sites the author favors. Similar to newsgroups and mailing lists, blogs bring together people of similar interests to share information, ideas, and questions about those interests. While it is difficult to determine the exact number of blogs that exist on the Internet (not all are visible to search engines), there were an estimated 5.5 million blogs worldwide in early 2005 (see *Technocrati* at www.technocrati.com for the most recent estimates and a list of the top 100 blogs).

As the popularity of blogs has grown in recent years, various institutions have adopted them as a new form of communication. Media organizations such as *The New York Times* or *ABC News*, for example, make their news stories available to blogs through automatic feeds or offer blogs of their own. The political importance of blogs has been demonstrated by the fact that all major contenders for the 2004 Democratic presidential nomination established official campaign blogs, thus creating a new channel of communication between candidate and voter, and among voters themselves. If you are interested in starting your own blog, go to www.blogger.com and follow the simple instructions. Those interested in reading political blogs can find a comprehensive list at the Web site of the *Campaigns & Elections Magazine* (www.campaignline.com/blogs).

Political Sources on the Internet

The following list of selected Web sites offers information that might be of interest to students of political science and other social sciences. This list is by no means complete and should be seen only as a starting point for further searches.

- **American FactFinder** (factfinder.census.gov) allows quick and easy access to basic U.S. Census facts.
- **Center for Responsive Politics** (www.opensecrets.org) is a non-partisan and non-profit group that tracks money in politics, and its effect on elections and public policy.
- **CIA World Factbook** (www.cia.gov/cia/publications/factbook) provides reliable international statistics and background information about foreign nations compiled by the Central Intelligence Agency (CIA).
- **Congressional Quarterly** (CQ) (www.cq.com) is a well-known magazine that covers the U.S. Congress. It has news about Capitol Hill and provides online access to information about pending bills and political candidates at federal and state levels (subscribers only).

- **DefenseLINK** (www.defenselink.mil) is the official Web site for the U.S. Department of Defense and a good starting point for finding U.S. military information online.

- **Documents Center** (www.lib.umich.edu/govdocs) is a central reference and referral point for U.S. and foreign government information.

- **ElectionGuide.Org** (www.electionguide.org) provides information on all national-level presidential, parliamentary, and legislative elections in other countries. It also has links to each country's election authorities, summaries of election results, and data on voter turnout.

- **Elections Around the World** (www.electionworld.org) is a comprehensive (but unofficial) guide to elections in every independent country and overseas dependency.

- **FedStats** (www.fedstats.gov) is a gateway to statistics from over 100 U.S. federal agencies.

- **FedWorld Information Network** (www.fedworld.gov) provides online access to millions of U.S. government pages, files, and databases.

- **FirstGov** (www.firstgov.gov) provides the most comprehensive search of government information on the Internet. It has links to every federal agency and state government.

- **GovSpot.com** (www.govspot.com) is a non-partisan government information portal designed to simplify the search for the best and most relevant government information online.

- **GPO Access** (www.gpoaccess.gov) is a service of the U.S. Government Printing Office and provides online access to many of the government's best information products, including the Federal Register, the Commerce Business Daily, the Code of Federal Regulations, the Congressional Record, and the United States Code.

- **Library of Congress** (www.loc.gov) contains the holdings of the U.S. National library, which includes all items holding a U.S. copyright. It also provides online access to the Copyright database, the American Memory site, and a link to **THOMAS**, the library's congressional online site (thomas.loc.gov).

- **National Archives and Records Administration** (http://www.nara.gov) is a huge collection of official records from the executive, legislative, and judicial branches of the federal government. It also has links to all presidential archives.

- **National Journal** (www.nationaljournal.com) is a magazine that covers the U.S. Congress. It offers online access to polling data and House and Senate races (subscribers only).

- **Political Information** (www.politicalinformation.com) is a searchable collection of more than 5,000 Web sites on U.S. politics, policy, and political news.

- **Political Resources on the Net** (www.politicalresources.net) is a searchable directory of international political Web sites with links to parties, organizations, governments, and the media in each country.

- **Project Vote Smart** (www.vote-smart.org) provides non-partisan information about political candidates and elected officials in five basic categories: biographical information, issue positions, voting records, campaign finances, and interest group ratings.
- **Public Agenda** (www.publicagenda.org) provides non-partisan information and academic research on what the public thinks about important U.S. policy issues.
- **Public Register's Annual Report Service** (www.prars.com), the **Annual Report Service** (www.annualreportservice.com), and **AnnualReports.Com** (www .reportgallery.com) provide access to annual reports of publicly traded companies.
- **U.S. Securities and Exchange Commission (SEC)** (www.sec.gov) provides reliable information about companies and industry trends. The SEC's EDGAR (Electronic Data Gathering, Analysis, and Retrieval) Web site provides online access to officially required statements by publicly traded U.S. companies.
- **U.S. Census Bureau** (www.census.gov) provides online access to the official U.S. Census data and statistical information on U.S. businesses.
- **White House** (www.whitehouse.gov) provides online access to transcripts of presidential speeches, press briefings, proclamations, and executive orders.

Conclusion

It should be obvious by now that Internet research requires much more than simply plugging a few keywords into a search engine. While it is true that more and more information is available online, the rapid growth of the Internet also makes it more difficult to find useful and reliable facts. Moreover, search engines such as *Google* or *Yahoo!* encourage somewhat random searches because of the way they index and display information. Thus, in order to become "good" Internet researchers, we need to learn how to use appropriate search tools and strategies that will efficiently retrieve the information we are looking for.

Summary Points

- Most of the important research information available on the Internet can be found on informational pages, pages maintained by news sources, advocacy pages, and personal home pages.
- The best way to search the Internet is to develop a search strategy that will allow you to do a systematic search for relevant and high-quality information. It is generally useful to rely on more than one search engine and to be familiar with the advanced search functions these tools offer.
- The quality of information gathered from the Internet should be evaluated by assessing its authority, objectivity, accuracy, currency, and coverage.
- The Invisible Web consists of databases from businesses, government agencies, universities, libraries, and organizations around the world that are mostly hidden from regular search engines. To find these databases, you must use special search engines and database directories.

Suggested Readings and References

Good introductions to Internet-based research can be found in (listed by year of publication): Heather Dawson, *Using the Internet for Political Research* (Oxford: Chandos Publishing, 2004); Maureen Henninger, *The Hidden Web: Finding Quality Information on the Net* (Sydney, NSW: University of New South Wales Press, 2004); Don Barker and Carol D. Terry, *Internet Research*, 2nd ed. (Boston, MA: Thomson Course Technology, 2004); Claire Hewson, Peter Yule, Dianna Laurent, and Carl Vogel, *Internet Research Methods: A Practical Guide for the Social and Behavioral Sciences* (Thousand Oaks, CA: Sage, 2002); and Niall O'Dochartaigh, *The Internet Research Handbook: A Practical Guide for Students and Researchers in the Social Sciences* (Thousand Oaks, CA: Sage, 2001). An excellent introduction to searching with *Google* is Nancy Blanchman's *Google Guide*, which is available online at www.googleguide.com.

Reference: Janet E. Alexander and Marsha A. Tate, *Web Wisdom: How to Evaluate and Create Information Quality on the Web* (Mahwah, NJ: Laurence Erlbaum, 1999).

Research Exercises

1. a. Use at least two different search engines to search for information about "Political Action Committees." Compare the results you retrieve from each search engine. When comparing your results, consider the following points: How many results did you retrieve in each search engine? What proportion of these results did you consider relevant to your search?

   b. Next, use a multi-search engine such as *Dogpile* to search again for information about "Political Action Committees." Compare your results with those you retrieved with individual search engines. Consider the same points as you did above.

2. Browse the *Yahoo!* subject categories to find information about the topic of "Political Action Committees." Consider the following points: Which of the two methods—search engines or subject directories—do you consider more successful or more appropriate? Why? What are the advantages and disadvantages of each method?

3. Use a specialized search engine such as *ProFusion* to search the Invisible Web for information on "Political Action Committees." Consider the following questions: Do the results from these Invisible Web searches differ from what you found in the previous searches? Do you consider the results from them useful?

Key Terms

search engine	APA style
meta-search engines	Invisible Web
subject directories	database directories
Boolean logic	newsgroups
stem	mailing lists
MLA style	Weblogs (blogs)

CHAPTER 5

From Abstract to Concrete: Operationalization and Measurement

- How are theories operationalized?
- What are the levels of measurement?
- How might error creep into measurements?
- Of what importance to accurate measurement is internal validity? External validity? Reliability?

Empirical research is a means of obtaining answers to questions about our observable reality. Our questions may be primarily practical, or they may be principally of academic interest. In either case, they will probably be stated in abstract terms. Yet the answers we want are usually concrete and specific. One of the first challenges in research is to devise ways of getting from the abstract level of our questions to some concrete observation that will allow us to answer them.

To take a nonpolitical example, suppose we want to resolve a debate between roommates about which of the grocery stores in their neighborhood is preferable. Obviously we will need to compare the two in some way to settle the argument. But on what grounds shall we compare them? We want to determine which one exhibits more of the qualities of a great store, but *grocery store excellence* is an abstract concept. In order to evaluate each store in terms of this quality, we may choose to *quantify* the concept of grocery store excellence. We might agree to compare their prices on a fixed set of items, and to let the resulting quantity stand for grocery store excellence. Or, more likely, we might perform several such operations on different aspects of the stores' performance so that we can get a more complete picture of how well they perform, and then combine them in some way. Once we have these numbers, we will be ready to make concrete comparisons and attempt to resolve the dispute.

What we have just described is essentially the process by which we proceed from abstract concept to concrete observation in quantitative social science research. It is a crucial phase in the research process, for only if it is done correctly will the information we gather represent evidence about the utility of our theories or provide answers to our questions. The process of selecting observable phenomena to represent abstract concepts is known as **operationalization,** and the specification of steps to take in making observations is called **instrumentation.** The application of an instrument to assign numerical values to cases results in a **measurement,** and it is this measurement that we finally use as evidence in making decisions and answering questions.

In this chapter we describe these processes in detail and discuss the problems you may encounter in attempting to operationalize and measure concepts. When you complete this chapter, you will be ready to state the explanations you have devised from your search of the literature in a form that will allow you to test them through actual observations.

It should be noted that this chapter primarily focuses on answering research questions using *quantitative* data rather than employing *qualitative* methods; this focus is intentional, but is not intended to exclude qualitative research. It is likely that you have been using quantitative data to address a science fair project or other physical science research questions since you were in grade school, and this chapter draws on your familiarity with these methods. Techniques for qualitative operationalization are integrated directly into the chapters on interviewing, direct observations, and focus groups, applying the distinct approaches to each method.

Operationalization: The Link Between Theory and Observation

In Chapter 2 we stressed the importance of having a theory to guide observation. We described the research process principally as a matter of comparing actual observations with the expectations about reality that we derive from our theories in order to judge how much we can rely on the theories as explanations of political phenomena. These expectations are stated in the form of hypotheses, which predict relationships between variables that represent the concepts in the theory. The object of this chapter is to describe how we can devise observations that will make these comparisons possible. The question is how we can quantify our concepts in order to make precise statements about whether or not our theoretically derived expectations are supported by what we observe. The problems encountered in doing this in the social sciences are basically the same as those encountered in the physical sciences. A simple example will help make some of the issues clear.

An Example   Let us say that we want to test experimentally the hypothesis that a chemical fertilizer spread in one cornfield will stimulate more growth than the natural nutrients found in another field. Growth is an abstract concept. We cannot see it directly. We need to translate *growth* into an empirically observable variable so that we can determine when one plant has shown more of it than another.

We can let the variable *height attained* represent the concept *growth* because relative heights are empirically observable. But corn plants don't wear signs telling their height; we have to ascertain it for ourselves. How? We could use human judgment and have observers rate plants in the two fields as tall or short. Such a procedure would allow only crude comparisons between plants and would be subject to all kinds of errors, because people differ in their perceptions. We need a more precise and dependable means of determining heights if we are to make meaningful comparisons.

Implementing Instruments   To quantify our measurements, we must translate the variable height into terms of *an instrument* that can be used to yield precise, standardized indications of the extent to which the characteristic is embodied in individual corn plants. We can let height be represented by an **indicator,** such as *length in inches,* and measure the plants with a tape measure. The readings from the tape measure then become the **values** we assign to plants on the variable *height,* and these values are what we actually compare in attempting to assess the accuracy of our theoretical prediction of greater growth in one field than in another.

We have moved, then, from the abstract concept *growth* to the variable *height*, and then to the indicator *length in inches*. This transformation is known as *operationalization*, because we have reduced an abstract concept to a set of values that can be obtained through specifiable operations.

Observing Indicators   We finally make the comparisons on which we will judge the accuracy of our hypothesis about relative growth by comparing the values that result from the measurement process (in this example, the readings from the tape measure). When we speak of **observation** in research, we are referring to *the process of applying a measuring instrument in order to assign values for some characteristic or property of the phenomenon in question to the cases being studied.* In other words, observation means using an instrument to measure a trait or behavior.

This is an important point to understand. It makes clear the significance of operationalization and measurement in the research process. We can never actually compare concepts, even though our theories and our research questions will be stated in concepts. What we compare are *indicators of concepts*. In our example, we cannot compare the growth of plants in the two cornfields in our example. We can compare only the readings we get from the tape measures—the measures produced by the indicator that we have decided to let represent the concept.

This means that our *comparisons can be accurate only to the extent that the indicators selected mirror the concept we intend them to measure.* If we have improperly operationalized our concepts, the relationship between our indicators may not be an accurate reflection of the relationship between the concepts they are supposed to represent. As a result, any conclusions we draw from our observations about the concepts or the theory of which they are a part will be faulty.

Figure 5.1 illustrates this situation. Our theory posits a relationship between two abstract concepts. Our hypothesis predicts a relationship between two empirically observable variables, which we reduce to measurable indicators, and our observations reveal a relationship (or lack of relationship) between two sets of values on these indicators. Obviously we can infer something about the reality of the theoretical relationship only if the variables accurately represent the concepts *and* the indicators accurately represent the variables. (Note: for simplicity, Figure 5.1 omits the theory's explanatory component.)

Operationalization almost inevitably involves some simplification or loss of meaning, since indicators seldom reflect all that we mean by a concept. Since we almost always have to accept some loss of meaning, we need to operationalize so as to minimize that loss. We have to seek indicators that capture as much of the meaning of the concept as possible and that represent at least some aspects of our concepts as accurately as possible.

Using Multiple Indicators   Often a single indicator fails to capture fully our concept. We can see the implications of this in our agricultural example. Once we have begun the research, we may realize that there is more to the concept *growth* than height and that the indicator *length in inches* does not fully capture what we want to measure. For instance, it may be that the amount of growth in the two fields is

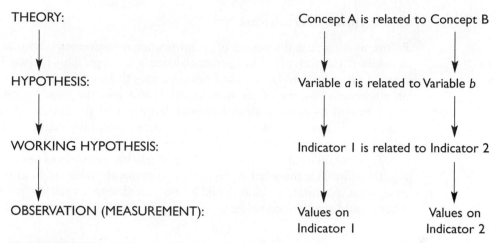

THEORY: Concept A is related to Concept B

HYPOTHESIS: Variable *a* is related to Variable *b*

WORKING HYPOTHESIS: Indicator 1 is related to Indicator 2

OBSERVATION (MEASUREMENT):   Values on   Values on
                                    Indicator 1   Indicator 2

Figure 5.1
Operationalization: The relationships of concept, variable, and measure
(NOTE: This simplified example omits the theory's explanatory component.)

substantially different, but all the difference is in stalk diameter, width of leaves, and weight of corn ears; the height of the plants in the two fields may not be noticeably different. In that case, if we look only at height in evaluating the effects of the fertilizer, we will be seriously misled, because the link between the concept (growth) and the variable that represents it (height) is imperfect. The variable used here does not *fully operationalize* the concept it represents. It does not capture all the meaning in the concept, and using it misleads us about the relationship that exists in the real world.

This is an especially common situation in the social sciences since most important social science concepts are **multidimensional** in that they have more than one aspect or component. Our measures of these concepts must reflect their diversity if they are to be useful indicators of the concepts. For example, if we operationalized the concept democracy only in terms of the holding of regular elections, we might classify dictatorial regimes that hold elections with only one candidate per office and do not allow freedom of expression as being just as democratic as the nations of Western Europe. To obtain an accurate measure of the degree to which nations are democratic, we obviously need indicators that reflect the various dimensions of the concept.

The fact that even Iraq under Saddam Hussein held regular elections should help to clarify why operationalization is crucial to theory testing and the research process in general. It is not as easy to explain how to ensure proper operationalization. This is because selecting variables to represent concepts and devising indicators for the variables both involve a good deal of creativity and cannot be reduced to a set of standardized steps that will unerringly produce good measures. What we do here is to point out some of the pitfalls to be avoided in the process and to describe ways of evaluating the adequacy of operationalizations once they have been selected. We do this in the sections on measurement in this chapter.

Operational Definitions

Before moving to a discussion of social science measurement, however, we should consider what is involved in operationalizing a concept. This is done by specifying a set of procedures to be followed or operations to be performed in order to obtain an empirical indicator of the manifestation of a concept in any given case. These procedures then provide an **operational definition** of the concept and its variable counterpart. The process of operationalization essentially reduces to a matter of selecting operational definitions for concepts.

To be useful (that is, to provide valid and reliable measures of our concepts), operational definitions must tell us precisely and explicitly what to do in order to determine what quantitative value should be associated with a variable in any given case. They should specify a complete set of steps to take in the process of measurement.

Importance of Precise Definitions   We need precise definitions for at least three reasons. First, we want to be able to tell others exactly what we have done to obtain our measures, so that they can evaluate our work and possibly repeat our study to verify its results in another setting. Second, if we have assistants actually gathering the information, we will want our instructions to them to be detailed and precise enough to ensure that each one takes the measurements in exactly the same way as the others do. If our instructions are vague and our assistants go through slightly different sets of steps in obtaining measures, their results will not be comparable and we will be unable to draw valid conclusions from them. Finally, precise and detailed statements of how to operationalize a variable will help us in evaluating the results we obtain and in eliminating rival explanations of those results that essentially claim that the "findings" have been produced by flaws in the measurement process. (We will have more to say about this in subsequent sections of this chapter.)

When devising operational definitions for variables, you should routinely write out a description of the procedures you will use to obtain measurements. Every step should be detailed. This not only provides a record of your research and ensures standardization of measuring procedures but also gives you an opportunity to think through the act of obtaining a measurement in order to discover possible errors that can damage the reliability of the results.

An Example   Suppose we want to measure the degree to which members of the two main parties support their own party in a state legislature. We can operationalize the concept *party unity* as *voting together on roll call votes* and then use the percentage of the average member's votes that agree with those of the majority of his or her party as our indicator of *voting together*. Having decided to do this, however, we face a number of critical choices in actually operationalizing our variable.

Before doing anything else, we must initially define both voting and unity. We might get information on how each legislator votes from the records of the legislature, but we will then have to decide which of the many recorded votes to include in our count. Some votes are unanimous (such as a vote to issue a proclamation of praise for some national hero) and do not reflect party unity because they do not involve partisan issues. Thus, including all votes reduces the extent to which our measure reflects our concept. We have to state criteria for selecting votes to include.

In order to focus only on controversial issues, therefore, we might, for instance, choose to include only those roll calls in which at least two-thirds of the legislators vote and in which the losing position gets no less than 30 percent of the vote.

We also have to decide how to devise a procedure for determining how a majority of the party has voted in order to classify each member's votes as consistent or inconsistent with that majority position. We need to decide how to treat abstentions. Do they count as a failure to support the party, or do we exclude them from our count? In addition, we have to specify a procedure for first computing and then averaging the percentages of agreeing votes for each legislator.

With every operationalization, we face similar decisions about exact procedures to follow in obtaining measures. A well-constructed, complete operational definition reveals how we have decided to handle such problems and leaves no ambiguity about what we actually did in taking our measures.

Developing Instruments   Building an operational definition results in the development of an **instrument** for taking measurements. In the physical sciences, such instruments as scales, light meters, and micrometers are used to obtain indicators of the degree to which things exhibit some property. In the social sciences, measuring instruments take different forms. Typical social science instruments include a series of questions on a survey form, instructions on how to make and record observations of certain events (such as a debate on the floor of the United Nations), and sets of numbers to be taken from some sourcebook and the rules for combining them into a measure.

Proper instrumentation is as important in the social sciences as it is in the physical sciences. Just as we would not attempt to measure weight with a ruler, we would hesitate to measure *political alienation* solely using demographic questions, such as age or family size. In discussing the validity and reliability of measures in the next section, we also suggest some ways to test the instruments developed in the process of operationalization in order to increase our confidence that they measure what we want.

Measurement

We operationalize variables in order to have a way to concretize abstract concepts so that we can make meaningful comparisons between real-world phenomena in terms of the properties suggested by those concepts. This assigning of numerals to represent properties is known as measurement. The result of measuring is that we have a *value* to associate with some variable for a given case.[1]

This means simply that we can speak with more precision about the extent to which a given unit of observation (for example, a person, a city, a nation, or an organization) exhibits the property represented by the variable being measured.

---

[1] It is crucial that we appreciate the difference between a variable and its *values*. We recognize a variable because of its capacity to take on different values. The variable is a concept translated into empirical terms. A value is some magnitude or quality of the variable that individual cases can reflect. For example, Lutheran is a value for the variable *religious denomination*; upper class is a value for the variable *socioeconomic status*; and 23 years is a value for the variable *age*.

Rather than say that a city has a "bad crime problem," we can speak of specific crime rates. Rather than say that a person is a "devoted Republican," we can say that one has scored a 7 out of 7 on our *strength of party identification* measure.

Levels of Measurement

Measuring procedures provide a means of categorizing and ordering phenomena. Some procedures, however, produce more precise and detailed distinctions between events than do others. When we say a procedure produces a given **level of measurement**, we are classifying it according to how much information it gives us about the phenomena being measured and their relationship to one another. The levels of measurement are referred to as *nominal, ordinal,* and *interval/ratio.* These terms may be more easily remembered in order using the acronym NOIR (the French word for "black").

Nominal measurement provides the least information about phenomena. It gives us only a set of discrete categories to use in distinguishing between cases. Nominal measurement is obtained by simply naming cases by some predetermined scheme of classification. Nationality is generally "measured" at the nominal level by classifying people as Swiss, Brazilian, and so on. However, that "measurement" neither tells us how *much* of the characteristic "nationality" different individuals have nor allows us to rank-order them. Using nominal measurement simply gives us a way of sorting cases into groups designated by the names used in a classificatory scheme.

To be useful, nominal measurement schemes must be based on sets of categories that are **mutually exclusive** and **collectively exhaustive.** This means (1) it must not be possible to assign any single case to more than one category and (2) the categories should be set up so that *all* cases can be assigned to some category. If we want to classify voters in the United States by use of a nominal measuring scheme, we cannot use the categories *Democrat, Republican, liberal,* and *conservative* successfully, because these categories are not mutually exclusive. Since each U.S. political party appeals to a broad spectrum of voters, it is possible for a person to be both a Democrat and a conservative or liberal, or both a Republican and a conservative or liberal. The categories do not allow us to differentiate among voters in all cases. Similarly, if we try to categorize voters by party affiliation using only two categories—*Republican* and *Democrat*—we will find that our categories are not collectively exhaustive, because some voters consider themselves independents or members of other parties.

In order to facilitate analysis, we will probably want to substitute a number for each category in a scheme of nominal measurement. It is important to recognize, however, that such numbers have no real meaning in this context; they are simply symbols. Just because we choose to substitute a 5 for the *Republican* category and a 1 for the *Democrat* category, we *cannot* assume that Republicans have five times as much party affiliation as Democrats. Any number can be substituted for any category of a nominal measurement so long as each category has a unique number associated with it.

Ordinal measurement provides more information because it allows us both to categorize and to order, or rank, phenomena. Ordinal measurement allows us to associate a number with each case. That number tells us not only that the case is different from some other cases, and similar to still others, with respect to the variable being measured, but also how it relates to those other cases in terms of how much of a particular property it exhibits. With ordinal measurement we can say which cases have more (or less) of the measured quality than other cases, and we can rank cases in the order of *how much* of the quality they exhibit. That ranking gives us more detailed and precise information about the cases than we would get from a nominal measurement. The concept *social class* is often measured at the ordinal level, with individuals being ranked as lower-, middle-, or upper-class.

Interval/Ratio measurement provides even more information. Not only can we classify and rank-order cases when they have been measured at the interval level, but we can also tell *how much* more (or less) of the measured property they contain than other cases. Ordinal measurement is not based on any standardized unit of the variable in question and does not allow us to tell how far cases are from one another in terms of that variable. It allows us only to say that some have more or less of it than others. Interval/Ratio measurement is based on the idea that *there is some standard unit of the property being measured.*

Whereas ordinal measures give us only a rough idea of the relationship between cases with respect to a variable, interval measures provide information on the "distance" between cases. The variable *income* is a clear example. Income is usually measured in units of currency (for instance, dollars in the United States). Because we can use *standard units* in our measurement, we can say that the difference in income between $10,000 and $11,000 a year is exactly the same as the difference in income between $50,000 and $51,000 a year (i.e., $1,000). We cannot do that with ordinal measurement. If we measure income ordinally by dividing people into such income categories as *under $10,000* and *$10,000 to $19,999,* we can say that one person has more or less income than another, but we cannot say exactly how far apart they are in income because we cannot tell where an individual falls within the category. The income difference between a person in category 1 (under $10,000) and a person in category 2 ($10,000 to $19,999) can be as little as one dollar ($10,000 minus $9,999) or as much as $10,000 ($19,999 minus $9,999), depending on their exact incomes, but we cannot make this distinction from an ordinal measure.

In addition to giving us precise information on the absolute differences between cases, interval measurement lets us make accurate statements about the *relative* differences between concepts. We can, for instance, agree that 50,000 people is twice as large a population as 25,000 people because we can speak meaningfully of a place that has no population. There is a *zero point* in true interval/ratio measures and it is at least conceivably possible for a case to score zero on such measures. Because there is no meaningful zero point on an ordinal scale, we cannot say, for example, that upper-class people have twice as much "class" as lower-class people, because we don't know what it means to completely lack any standing in social class.

It should be noted that we have merged interval and ratio as a single level of measurement. They actually differ based upon the meaning of a variable's zero point, but this distinction is rarely a factor in political science.

Increased Precision is Advantageous   The benefit of increasing precision suggests an important point about levels of measurement. Nominal-level measurement is the least useful form of measurement when we have to compare phenomena. If we use it when we can use a "higher" (more precise) level of measurement, we may be wasting potentially valuable information. If, in a study of voting behavior, we categorize people only as Republicans, Independents, and Democrats when we can ask a different set of questions and produce a rank ordering of them as strong to weak party identifiers, we may be giving up information that will help us understand the relationships we observe. Ordinal-level measurement is more useful than nominal, but it too has limitations. Interval-level measurement is the most desirable form of measurement both because of the amount of detail in the information it provides and because of the mathematical procedures it allows us to perform on our data.

The point is that we should strive for operationalizations that allow interval level measurement whenever possible and appropriate. But how do we decide which level of measurement is appropriate for the particular concepts we want to operationalize? This is a matter of both conceptualization and measurement technology.

In the theory-building stage of research, we must first ask ourselves if there is some continuum underlying the differences we see in cases. If there is, we can devise ordinal and even interval measurements for a concept that might otherwise be measured only by nominal classification. An historical example will help clarify the significance of this.

An Example   Suppose we are studying the effects of immigrants' nationality on the degree of their support for big-city political machines in the early twentieth century in the United States. If we operationalize nationality at the nominal level and categorize city voting precincts' support for the machine, we might get a picture like that presented in Figure 5.2(a). There is no apparent relationship between nationality and voting behavior, because knowing a precinct's dominant nationality does not help us rank it relative to the others.

If we examine our reasoning, however, we might conclude that the reason we expect nationality to be related to support for the machine is that countries of origin differ in the opportunities they allow their citizens for political participation. When people have had little experience with democratic politics in their native land, we might reason, they will be more willing to give up to a political boss their right to self-government. If we can follow this reasoning and rank-order the nations of origin by the extent of political participation they allow their citizens, we can construct a graph like that shown in Figure 5.2(b). In that graph, a relationship between nationality and support for the machine is apparent. The ordering of categories on our independent variable helps us discover a pattern in its relationship to the dependent variable.

If we are bold enough, we may even upgrade our measurement of the independent variable to an interval level. For example, we might count the number of legal provisions for political participation in the statutes of each country in question for the years just prior to the beginning of significant immigration to the United States. We can use the resulting numbers to rank nationalities along an interval scale and make even more precise comparisons of independent and dependent variables.

Whether or not we can achieve this upgrading of variables from the nominal to the ordinal or interval level depends both on developing a theoretical rationale for doing so and on the technical possibility of applying the operational procedures that produce the higher-level measurements. Even if we can conceptualize *nationality* in

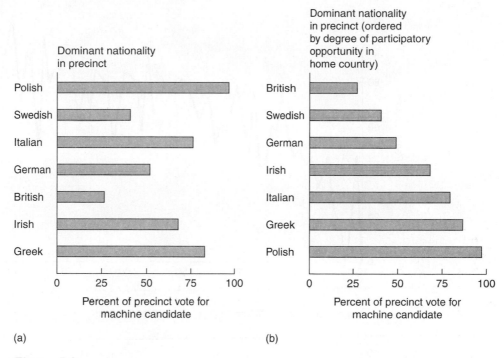

Figure 5.2
An example of how level of measurement can affect the interpretation of data

interval terms in our example, we may not have access to the legal records necessary to place countries along the interval scale. In that case, *measurement technology* limits what we can do to strengthen our measures.

These situational factors make it difficult to set down rules about operationalizing concepts to achieve certain levels of measurement. We can, however, suggest that you use measures as precise as possible given the subject you are studying. This generally means upgrading measurement procedures so that they yield higher levels of measurement whenever possible. Do not settle for an operationalization that produces nominal measurement when ordinal or interval measurement is theoretically defensible and technically possible.

Excessive Precision is Disadvantageous   At this point, we need to add a qualification to our general interest in greater precision. There are cases in which too much precision in measurement is actually undesirable. In Figure 5.3 we see data on the relationship between age and presidential election voting is presented in two different ways. In Figure 5.3(a), age is measured in single years. Because there is greater volatility due to the few people in each age group (for example, 21–22, 35–36, 50–51), the chart reveals no clear pattern in the relationship between the two variables. In Figure 5.3(b), age is measured less precisely, in five-year groupings. With more cases in each group, we can see that there is a broad pattern to the relationship, with voting likelihood increasing to age 75 and then generally declining.

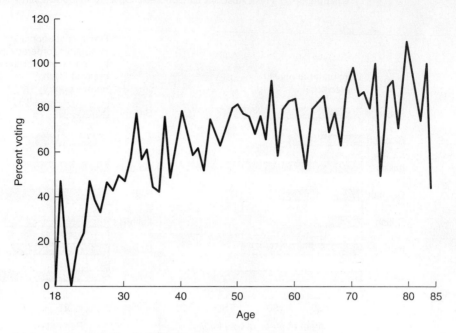

(a) Age and participation in 2002 election: age measured by years

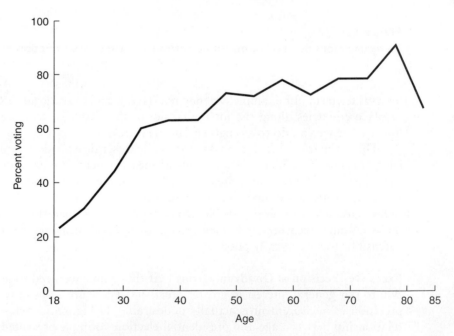

(b) Age and participation in 2002 election: age measured by half-decades

Figure 5.3

An example of the effect of grouping data on interpretation

SOURCE: W. Philips Shively, *The Craft of Political Research*, 6th ed. Upper Saddle River, NJ: Pearson Prentice Hall, 2004, pp. 59–60. Reprinted with permission.

Giving up some precision in our measurements may provide clearer results, but if taken too far we may lose sight of relationships. If we use twenty-year groupings to measure age, we will see little difference in the percentage of each age group that votes and might falsely conclude that age is unrelated to the likelihood of voting. Because we generally do not know in advance of actual data analysis how much precision will be needed to allow us to discover relationships, we should follow the rule of operationalizing our concepts as precisely as possible. We can always discard unnecessary precision by "collapsing categories" (moving to larger units of differentiation) if we find it necessary. But if we do not collect the information in the first place, we cannot draw on it later.

Working Hypotheses

Measurement assigns values to cases with respect to given variables. These values are what we use to represent concepts when we compare observations. Before we can understand the implications our observations have for our theories, we have to translate our hypotheses concerning relations between variables into working hypotheses, which state the expected relationships between measures or indicators. The next-to-last line in Figure 5.1 suggests the form that **working hypotheses** take. These hypotheses force us to state explicitly the linkages between indicators and variables that are implied by the operationalization of our theory.

Consider an example from the study of international relations. Suppose we are interested in a theory of dominance in the international sphere. We start with the theoretical proposition that *the more dominated a nation is, the more conformist its foreign policy will be because the nation economically depends upon its patron state.* From this theory we can hypothesize: *As a nation's economic dependency increases, its support for the international policies of its patron state will increase.* We can operationalize *economic dependency* as the percentage of the nation's exports that go to the patron country. The percentage of exports becomes our indicator of the independent variable *dependency. Support* can be measured by the percentage of votes in the United Nations General Assembly in which the client nation's vote differs from that of the patron state. A percentage of votes in the United Nations becomes our indicator of the dependent variable *support for the patron state's policies.* We can now set out a working hypothesis that states the positive relationship we expect between indicators: *The higher the percentage of exports going to the patron state, the higher the percentage of votes in the United Nations that agree with the votes of the patron state.*

This working hypothesis tells us what observations are consistent with our hypothesis and our theory. It also suggests the relationship we envision between our variables and our indicators. That relationship is diagrammed in Figure 5.4.

When doing research, in addition to your theory about political phenomena, you should be able to state a **measurement theory** that sets out *why you expect your indicators to be related to your concepts.* In this example, why should we expect economic dependency to be related to concentration of exports? What is there about the distribution of exports that makes it a reflection of what we mean when we refer to dependency? These are the types of questions a well-developed measurement

Figure 5.4
Specification of the relationships of concepts, variables, and indicators

theory helps us answer. A measurement theory consists of the assumptions that explain why our indicators should change values as the degree to which cases manifest our concepts changes.

Indicators cannot be casually selected but must be chosen as a result of careful reasoning about the way things are related in the world. That reasoning is much like what we go through in constructing theories about political phenomena. This issue of whether or not there is any correspondence between our concept and variables on the one hand and our indicators or measures on the other is the central problem of measurement in science. The question of whether changes in our indicators are actually the result of changes in the concepts they represent gives rise to the problems of reliability and validity that we discuss in subsequent sections of this chapter.

Measurement Error: The Enemy

The process of measurement determines the values of cases depending upon how they score on our indicators. The differences in the scores can all be attributed to two basic sources. One source is the extent to which the cases really exhibit different degrees of the property in which we are interested. Different scores occur when our measures actually pick up those differences. In this case, *real* differences in the concept are reflected in our measures. The other source of differences in the scores is the extent to which something about the measure itself or the setting in which it is applied causes different cases to get different scores. In that instance, our measures are showing differences between cases that are *not* real—in the sense that they do not reflect authentic differences in the concept we want to measure. The differences we observe when this happens result from inconsistencies in the procedure for measurement.

If our measures were perfect, they would reveal only the first kind of differences between cases. But our measures are rarely flawless. Differences in the values assigned to cases inevitably reflect not only real differences in the degree to which those cases manifest the concept, but also "artificial" differences created by the measurement process. Any differences in the values assigned to cases that are attributable to anything other than real differences are known as **measurement error.** They are not real differences between cases, but differences that are erroneously recorded because of flaws in the measuring process.

An Example   This distinction between true variations in scores and variations due to measurement error is similar to the distinction between differences in objects we view directly and differences we see when we look only at their reflection in a mirror. To the extent that the mirror distorts the images, it either masks differences we would see when viewing the images directly or creates an impression of differences we would not otherwise perceive. In the social sciences, we can rarely see our key concepts directly and must rely on measurement procedures analogous to the mirror to reflect these concepts in any given case. Consequently, the accuracy of our impressions of the two depends on the precision with which our measures reflect reality.

What are some of the sources of distortion in the images our measures provide? We need to know the answer to this question if we are to control measurement error or recognize it when it is present in our data. We can list several of the primary sources of measurement error by identifying common sources of differences in the scores assigned to cases *other than true differences in the characteristics we want to measure.*

1. *Differences in the distribution of other, relatively stable characteristics among the cases that are unintentionally revealed by our measures:* For example, the questions representing our measure of political ideology may require a given level of intelligence to interpret and answer. If this is the case, responses will reflect not only differences in people's political ideology, but also differences in their intelligence. When we look at the resulting data, the effects of intelligence and political ideology will be confused, and we will be unable to distinguish differences in scores that reflect ideological difference from those that reflect differences in intelligence. Similarly, other characteristics of our units of analysis (such as the regional location of cities, the cultural traits of nations, or the sources of documents) can be inadvertently reflected in our measures and

distort our perceptions of the manifestation of the target concepts. When we can identify and measure these "contaminating" influences, we should check to see whether holding their values constant wipes out, reduces, or increases differences in the scores that cases receive on our measures.

2. *Differences in the distribution of temporary characteristics among the cases that are reflected in our measures:* A person's mood or state of health can affect the way one responds to items on a questionnaire. The recent political history of cities (the revelation of corruption among public officials, for instance) can create systematic but temporary differences in the way those cities' citizens answer survey questions. A massive natural disaster can produce a drastic but temporary change in the statistics we are relying on to indicate the level of economic development. The effects of such temporary "abnormalities" are more difficult to identify and control than the effects of the stable characteristics in our cases. The only approaches for guarding against them are being alert to signs that individual cases are subject to such transient influences (for example, studying the recent political history of the cities included in our sample or advising our interviewers not to attempt to interview a person who is temporarily bedridden) and following the procedures for checking the reliability of measures described in the section of this chapter discussing reliability.

3. *Differences in subjects' interpretation of the measuring instrument:* This is a problem only when people must respond directly to questions, as opposed to when the researcher constructs measures by observing behavior. If our questions are ambiguously worded, the different interpretations our respondents place on them can produce differences in their scores on the measures composed of those questions. Suppose, for instance, we are careless enough to ask the question *Did you vote in the last election?* in a study of voting behavior. If some of the interviewees do not know that a city election has been held the prior week, they may answer that they *have* voted because they think the question refers to the last national election, even though they have not voted in the election to which we intend our questions to refer. We can guard against this source of unintended differences in scores by pretesting questions and testing our measures for reliability.

4. *Differences in the setting in which the measure is applied:* This is a source of measurement error principally in research that relies on individuals' responses to questions as its measures. One well-established fact in survey research, for example, is that the race, sex, and age of interviewers can affect responses. Answers (and therefore scores on measures) can differ from interview to interview on the basis of the characteristics of the interviewer alone. Similar problems can arise outside survey research. We may, for instance, make the mistake of doing a content analysis of one country's domestic newscasts and another's newscasts intended only for foreign nations. We will then be applying the same instrument in very different settings and can expect some differences in scores from this fact alone. We can avoid this source of measurement error only by making every effort to see that the situations in which our measures are applied are standardized.

5. *Differences in the administration of the measuring instrument:* The scores assigned to cases can differ as a result of a variety of errors that occur in col-

lecting and recording information. Interviewers may misunderstand instructions and ask questions in ways the researcher might not intend. Poor lighting may cause a respondent to mismark a questionnaire. Pencils can break and pens run out of ink at crucial moments so that observers fail to record key events in a group interaction. These kinds of variation in the administration of measuring instruments cause differences in scores independent of any differences in real values for the variable under investigation. Beyond employing only dependable assistants, the primary way to guard against such sources of measurement error is through *pretesting* our instruments. A trial run will help us discover potential "mechanical" problems with the instrument (such as insufficient space for recording typical answers on a coding form) and human factors that may affect results (such as length of time observers can work without fatigue).

6. *Differences in the processing and analysis of data:* Information has to undergo a great deal of handling before it can be analyzed. It often changes form several times. For example, interviewers may record responses by writing down every word an interviewee says in answer to a question. Those written passages may subsequently be reduced to a single number as responses get coded. The written number may be transferred to a computer file as an entry in the appropriate column of a spreadsheet. In each of these steps, data analysis has been made simpler, but with each step there is a chance of errors that can cause cases to appear to differ on a variable when they do not. The possibility of such errors makes it a good idea to always double- and triple-check each transformation of data and to keep the original form for future reference.

7. *Differences in the way individuals respond to the form of the measuring instrument:* This is especially a problem when our units of analysis are people. Measuring instruments can take such different forms as oral interviews, questionnaires to be filled out by the respondent, and observation by a trained researcher. The different forms place different demands on the people under study. An interview requires ease of speaking, and a questionnaire requires an ability to read and write, for example. If people differ in these abilities, their scores may differ even when the people are actually alike on the variable being operationalized. The best guard against this source of measurement error is the use of more than one form of measure meant to operationalize each concept. We say more about this in the next section of this chapter, which discusses validity.

All of these factors can introduce measurement error into our research. The various errors that arise from these seven sources are generally categorized as either *systematic* or *random* errors.

Systematic errors are those that arise from a confusion of variables in the world (as discussed in item 1 in the preceding list) or from the nature of the instrument itself. They appear in each use of the instrument and are constant among cases and studies in which the same measure is used. Constant errors cause our results to be *invalid,* in that the differences (or similarities) our measures seem to reveal are not accurate reflections of the differences we think we are measuring.

Random errors affect each application of the instrument differently. They occur as a matter of chance and are due to transient characteristics in our cases, situational variations in application of the instrument, mistakes in administration and processing, and other factors that vary from one use of the instrument to the next. They make our measures invalid in much the same way that systematic errors do. Random errors also make our measures *unreliable,* in that we cannot consistently get the same results when we use the measure if random errors are occurring.

How do we avoid having measurement error distort our results and render our research useless or misleading? To answer that question we must give careful attention to the issues of validity and reliability.

Validity

We can seldom obtain direct measures of the concepts used in social science theories. Such concepts as power, democracy, and representation cannot be quantified as simply as such concepts as length and weight. We have to use indicators that correspond only indirectly to the concepts they represent. There is always a chance then that the indicators we choose will not adequately reflect the concepts we want to measure. **Validity** is the term we use to refer to *the extent to which our measures correspond to the concepts they are intended to reflect.* To ask about a measure's validity is to ask if we are in fact measuring what we think we are measuring when we use it. Achieving validity is often viewed as the basic problem of measurement in the social sciences.

To be valid, a measure must be both *appropriate* and *complete.* If, for example, we are interested in comparing the quality of public education in different cities, we may be tempted to use the number of teachers in those cities' schools as an indicator of the quality of educational services. This measure is *inappropriate,* because the number of personnel in a school system is determined largely by the number of students and the size of the city and may have little to do with the quality of education. If we use the ratio of students to teachers as our indicator of educational services, we will have a more appropriate measure, in that differences caused by city size will be reduced or eliminated. The measure, however, will still be *incomplete.* Education involves more than teachers. It also involves school buildings, films, books, labs, and a variety of other factors. Looking at any one of these factors by itself might leave us with a false impression of the total quality of educational services. A school system may have a highly desirable student-teacher ratio but inadequate facilities and learning materials. It is a mistake to say that such a school system is equal to one with an identical student-teacher ratio *and* excellent facilities and learning materials. If we are to achieve validity, we must strive to construct measures that are both appropriate and complete.

This raises two questions: How can we create measures that are complete and appropriate, and how can we tell whether we have succeeded in doing so?

The answer to the first question begins with the operationalization process. We can define *validity* as the extent to which differences in scores on a measure reflect *only* differences in the distribution of values on the variable we intend to measure. Since we can probably never achieve complete and total validity, our goal should be to select measures that are susceptible to as few influences as possible other than differences in our target variable. This requires that we carefully think through the processes that surround our measures in search of possible causes of variations in scores. We are essentially concerned at this point with guarding against the effects of systematic error.

Table 5.1
Types of validation

Pragmatic Validation	Construct Validation	Discriminant Validation	Face Validation
Check results obtained from use of the indicator against results obtained from use of another indicator that is known to be a valid measure of the concept, or test the *predictive validity* of the indicator by using it to predict events that reflect the concept being measured.	*Internal (convergent) validation:* Infer validity of the indicator from its relationship to other indicators of the same concept using *multiple indicators*. *External validation:* Infer validity of the indicator from its relationship to indicators of *other* concepts to which the concept being measured should *theoretically* be related.	Infer validity of the indicator from the degree to which it is *unrelated* to indicators of other concepts that are theoretically distinct from the concept being measured.	Assume validity from the self-evident character of the indicator. (Can knowledgeable persons be persuaded that this is a valid indicator of the concept?)

Types of Validation   Achieving appropriate and relatively complete operationalizations depends both on knowing a good deal about the subject of our study and on conducting a careful, logical analysis of alternative operationalizations. Unfortunately, we can check the validity of our measures in order to determine whether or not we have developed sound measures only *after* we have collected data. The process of evaluating the validity of our measures is referred to as **validation.**

There are four basic approaches to validation summarized in Table 5.1. The first is often called **pragmatic validation,** because it involves assessing the validity of a measure from evidence of how well it works in allowing us to predict behaviors and events. For example, say that we devise a measure of how appealing candidates for public office are to voters. We can get some indication of the validity of this measure by applying it to all the candidates for seats in the U.S. Senate in a given election year and predicting their chances of being elected on the basis of their relative scores on our "voter appeal" measure. The more successful we are at predicting the candidates' electoral fate, the more confident we become that we have a valid measure, one that accurately reflects the intended concept. Measures that allow us to predict future events accurately are said to have **predictive validity.**

Pragmatic validation requires that there be some alternative indicator of variables that we feel fairly certain is a valid reflection of them. We check our measures against this alternative as we might check the accuracy of verbal reports of age against birth certificates. Unfortunately, there are seldom any clearly valid alternative indicators for the concepts used in social science research. As a result, we generally have to rely on the second type of validation—*construct validation.*

Construct validation is achieved by *inferring* the validity of a measure from evidence of the extent to which actual relationships between scores of various measures are consistent with what we expect from the theory that has led us to use a given indicator. This involves two lines of reasoning.

First, we might say to ourselves, "If concept X has a positive relationship to concept Y and a negative relationship to concept Z (as our theory says it does), then it will also be true that scores on a valid measure of X will have a positive relationship to scores on a valid measure of Y and a negative relationship to scores on a valid measure of Z." We cannot validate the measure by comparing scores on it to scores on some other measure of the same variable that we know to be valid (as in the case of the birth certificate). We can, however, judge its validity by the extent to which using it as an indicator of our variable produces the kinds of relationships that our theory leads us to expect between that variable and other variables.

An Example   To study international alliances, we might create a measure of the strength of an alliance based on a content analysis of newspaper articles from the countries involved. Is what the newspapers of one nation say about another nation a valid indicator of the strength of the alliance between the two countries? We might get an idea of whether it is by reasoning as follows: "Our theory tells us that the stronger an alliance between two nations is, the more often they will vote together in the United Nations and the fewer restrictions they will place on trade with each other. Therefore, scores on a valid measure of *strength of alliance* will be positively related to scores on measures of *voting together in the United Nations* and negatively related to scores on measures of *number of trade barriers*." We then proceed to do the data analysis necessary to see whether this expectation is supported by our observations. If the relationships are as expected, we will have greater confidence in the validity of our measure of *strength of alliance*. If they are not as we have expected, we will question whether we have a sound measure of this concept.

What we have just described is often referred to as **external validation**. It involves comparing scores on the measure being validated with scores on measures of *other* variables. To use this method of validation, of course, we have to include measures of the other variables in our research. This means that *we have to begin thinking about ways to validate our measures early in the research process.* Certainly by the time we are ready to develop a research design, we have to know how we will want to check the validity of our measures so that we can be certain to gather any information we will need.

Our efforts at external validation will produce convincing evidence about the validity of our measure of one variable only if we can have a high degree of confidence in the validity of the measures we use for the other variables. In the previous example, for instance, we could not conclude anything about the validity of our measure of *strength of alliance* from the relationships between scores on it and scores on the other two variables if we did not believe that our indicators of *voting together* and *trade barriers* were valid.

Because it is often difficult to find clearly valid indicators of variables to which our key variable should be related, external validation procedures must be used with caution. This is very much like testing a hypothesis. No single result guarantees the validity (or invalidity) of the measure. Rather, as instances of successful validation attempts accumulate, our confidence in the validity of our measure grows. For that reason, it is wise to seek out as many theoretically predictable relationships as possible to use in external validation. The more different tests of validity we have, the stronger our case will be.

This same logic applies to the second type of construct validation—**internal** or **convergent validation.** This type of validation involves devising several measures of the *same* variable and comparing scores on these various measures. We reason that if each of the indicators provides a valid measure of the concept in question, the scores individual cases receive on the measures should be closely related. If A, B, and C are all valid measures of X, then any individual's scores on A, B, and C should be highly similar.

An Example   Suppose that we want an indicator of the quality of street lighting in residential neighborhoods as part of a study of the distribution of public services. We might want to use citizens' perceptions of the adequacy of street lighting (as revealed in survey interviews) as that indicator. We can ask a sample of citizens in a neighborhood how adequate they think the streetlights in their area are and take the average evaluation as our measure of *quality of street lighting*. In order to perform an internal validation, we may also measure street lighting quality (1) by using a light meter to get a physical measure of the brightness and distribution of lighting, (2) by having trained observers rate the lighting, and (3) by having citizens compare their street lighting with that pictured in a series of photos showing streets with different qualities of lighting and then averaging their rankings to get a measure for the neighborhood. This gives us four measures of the variable. If each is valid, all should be strongly related.

We can check this with appropriate statistics. If we find that scores on the measure based on responses to interview questions are weakly related to scores on the other three measures *and* that scores on those other measures are strongly related to one another, we will have reason to suspect that our first measure is not valid.

This is much like weighing the same object on three different scales. If each of the scales gives an accurate weight and we have no reason to assume that the object has changed weight in the course of the test, we expect the weights obtained from the three scales to be identical. If one gives a different weight, we suspect it of being out of adjustment.

Figure 5.5 suggests the differences between internal and external forms of construct validation. In Figure 5.5(a), we see that internal validation is achieved by checking the correspondence of scores on several different measures of the *same* concept. The more closely they correspond, the more justified we feel in claiming that any of the measures is valid. In Figure 5.5(b), we see that external validation involves determining whether our measure of one variable shows it to be related to *other* variables as we expect it to be from our theory. If the expected relationships do not appear, we have reason to suspect that the indicator we have selected does not provide valid measures of the concept.

The same caution that applies to the use of external validation procedures applies to the use of internal validation. We cannot always be certain that our measures of the key concept are valid, and we should therefore always be careful about concluding that a measure is valid or invalid from any one test of validity. We can significantly increase our confidence in the results of an internal validation if we follow a simple rule: *The alternative measures of the concept should be based on as many different types of operationalization as possible.*

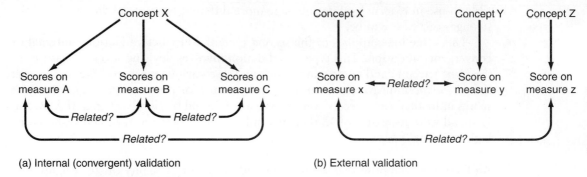

(a) Internal (convergent) validation   (b) External validation

Figure 5.5
Forms of construct validation

In the street lighting example, our measures come from four distinct types of operationalization: citizens' verbal ratings, physical measurements, observers' judgments, and citizens' selection of photographs. Each of these represents a different *mode of operationalization*. The more different modes we can use and the more independent they are of each other, the more confidence we can place in our validation. Why? The logic is as follows:

The principal source of invalidity is systematic and random measurement error. Different measures are subject to different kinds of measurement error. The more indicators we have for any variable and the more they differ from one another, the less likely it is that all the indicators will be affected by the same measurement error. If this is true, we will have a better chance of both recognizing measurement error as a source of differences in the scores on any one of our measures and getting an accurate measure of our variable if we use **multiple indicators.**

An Example   The factors that may invalidate our physical measure of street lighting quality (such as a faulty light meter) are likely to be quite unrelated to any factors that might introduce systematic errors into the measure based on citizens' evaluations (such as a tendency for people to claim, out of a sense of community pride, that public services in their neighborhood are as good as those in other areas). If we use only one mode of measurement, any source of measurement error may affect the scores on each measure, giving us a consistently invalid indicator and not allowing meaningful comparisons among measures. If, for example, we rely only on the physical measure of lighting but take readings in several different ways (say, on the sidewalk, on the curb, and in the street), then any flaw in the measuring instrument (the light meter, in this case) will affect all measures and none can be used to check another.

This logic suggests the great value of having multiple indicators for our variables. The availability of multiple measures not only gives us an opportunity to *test* the validity of our indicators, but also *improves our chances of obtaining a valid measure* of our variables in the first place. Multiple measures can actually increase the validity of measurement by allowing us to combine the results of several different measurement procedures so as to produce a *composite score* that is more likely to be a valid reflection of the actual value of our variable than is any of the measures taken alone. This is because there is a chance that the errors that cause each measure to be invalid will cancel out when the results of several measurement procedures are combined. (In Chapter 9, the sections on scaling describe some possible methods of combining scores to produce a composite measure.)

A third approach to validation is referred to as **discriminant validation.** When we ask whether a measure exhibits *discriminant validity,* we are essentially asking whether using it as an indicator of a given concept allows us to distinguish that concept from other concepts. For example, we might want to measure the concept *trust in political officials* through a series of questions in a survey. If we also have on the questionnaire a series of questions designed to measure *trust in people* (in general), we can compare the scores on the two measures to ask whether our first set of questions actually reflects simply another way of measuring trust in people. If scores are highly similar, we say that the political trust measure does not have discriminant validity because it does not permit us to distinguish the concept of *trust in political officials* from the concept of *trust in people.*

A final approach to validation relies on the concept of **face validity.** Some measures are based on such direct observation of the behavior in question that there seems to be no reason to question their validity; such a measure seems valid "on the face of it." For example, suppose we want to measure compliance with a state law requiring each business establishment to display its operating license on its front door. Having trained observers simply note the presence or absence of such licenses seems to provide an obviously valid measure of compliance. Though we should always ask ourselves if the measures we have selected appear valid on their face, it is generally a mistake to rely on face validity alone to ensure accurate results from our research. We should attempt to ascertain the validity of our measures through established procedures, such as those already described.

Reliability

When we ask about the validity of a measure, we are asking how closely the values it yields correspond to the true values of the variable being measured. When we ask about the **reliability** of a measure, we are asking how *stable* the values it yields are. Can we get the same value for any given case when we apply the measure several different times, or does each application result in the assignment of a different value to each case? If we do not get substantially the same value for any given case from successive applications of a measure, that measure is *unreliable* as an indicator of the concept. Rulers are made of inelastic materials in order to ensure reliability. If they were made of elastic materials, they might very well show different lengths for the same object—even when the object's true length has not changed—simply because the ruler stretches and contracts.

Reliability Versus Validity   If a measure is unreliable, it cannot be valid because at least some of the differences in the scores assigned to cases result from measurement errors rather than from true differences between cases. Recall our example of the study of street lighting. What if the light meter we use is so sensitive that in addition to recording the light from the streetlights, it picks up light from the moon? Then the values assigned to each street on the variable *quality of street lighting* will depend both on the brightness of the street lights and on such random factors as the fullness of the moon and the density of the cloud cover. To the extent that these random factors influence our results, the measure will not be a valid reflection of actual differences in the quality of street lighting. In this case, unreliability produces invalidity.

A measure may be quite reliable and yet invalid. Recall our example of the study of the extent to which people in different nations agree with the policies of their government. We said that survey questions may give invalid measures because people in authoritarian countries are afraid to tell the truth about their opinions. Because this factor produces a systematic rather than a random error, the questions might produce very stable results. No matter how many times they are asked, people might give the same "safe" responses. This does not, however, make the measure valid.

Thus, a measure may *be reliable without being valid, but it cannot be valid without being reliable.* Whereas validity is challenged by both systematic and random error, reliability is jeopardized only by random error. This means that if a measure has been convincingly validated in prior studies we can use it without being worried about its reliability; it has to be reliable if it is valid. But demonstrating reliability does not guarantee validity.

Testing Reliability   How do we guard against unreliability? How do we determine whether or not a given measure is reliable? Preventing unreliability depends on our being aware of the various sources of random measurement error described earlier in this chapter and doing what we can to control them. This involves thinking through the actual measurement process and pretesting our measuring instruments to discover previously unrecognized causes of random error.

It is often quite difficult to determine whether or not we have devised a reliable measure in the social sciences. This is because the true value of the variables with which we are concerned can change dramatically with time and circumstance—people change their opinions in response to experience, nations alter the way they allocate resources between social services and defense efforts in response to perceived military threats, and so on. When real values are changing, it is hard to distinguish the effects of random measurement error from genuine fluctuations in the concepts being measured. This means that tests of reliability should be conducted over as short a time span as possible.

There are essentially three broad methods of assessing the reliability of measures in the social sciences. The first is the *test-retest method*. Here the same measure is applied to the same set of cases again and again, over time. To the extent that cases get the same score each time, the measure is considered reliable. A difficulty with this technique arises when our measure involves interviewing people (as opposed to measuring inanimate objects or making concealed observations of people). If we repeat questions in a short time, interviewees may remember their first answer and, in an effort to be consistent, repeat that answer rather than respond truthfully in answering the question. If this happens, we cannot get an accurate picture of the questions' reliability as an indicator of the concept. In an effort to avoid this test effect, we might let a good deal of time pass before asking the questions a second time. If we do that, however, we will run into another problem: true values on the variable may have changed with the passage of time, and we may be unable to distinguish differences in scores caused by unreliability in the measure from actual changes in the variable.

Because of that difficulty, a second type of reliability test has been developed: the *alternative form method*. Different forms of the measure are applied to the same group of cases, or the same measure is applied to different groups *at the same time*. In this way there can be no reaction to being measured because no case will be measured more than once and, because no time lapses between applications of the measure, actual changes in the variables under study cannot affect the results. The success of this strategy, however, depends on the alternative forms of the measure being perfectly comparable to each other as a measure of the concept, or on the two groups being virtually equivalent with respect to the distribution of the variable being measured. If we can assume that these conditions are met, the more the scores on the two measures, or the scores of the two groups, are alike, the more confidence we have in the reliability of our measure. If we cannot come up with comparable measures or groups, however, we cannot use the method properly.

The final basic approach to testing the reliability of a measure is known as the *subsample method*. In it we draw one sample of cases and divide it into several subsamples in such a way that each is highly similar to the others in composition. We then apply the same measure to all subsamples and use the similarity or difference of responses from subsample to subsample as an indicator of the reliability of the measure. Because we use the same measure, we do not have to be concerned about comparability as in the alternative form method and, because we can rely on sampling theory to ensure the equivalence of our subsamples, we do not have to worry that the groups selected for measurement will not be sufficiently alike. Because no case is measured twice, we can discount reaction to testing as a threat to the accuracy of our reliability test, and because the measures are administered simultaneously, actual changes in the variable cannot create problems for this method as they can for the test-retest method. However, use of the subsample method depends on our being able to draw a large enough sample that we can divide it and still have subsamples large enough for our statistical tests to be meaningful. This is not always possible and can represent a barrier to the use of the subsample method in testing reliability.

There are many variations on these methods. Which one is most appropriate for any given research project will depend both on the time and resources available to complete the research and on the nature of the study. For instance, if we want to measure street lighting by having trained observers rate the lighting on various blocks, we can easily use the test-retest method without concern about a test effect. Street lighting will not change simply because it is measured by someone, and so we can have different observers independently rate the same street on the same night. We cannot have the same confidence in this method if our measure of street lighting quality is based on citizens' responses to interview questions.

Regardless of the reliability test we choose to use, it is important to establish the reliability of our measures *before* actually beginning research. This involves pretesting the measure by collecting the data necessary for the purpose of assessing the instruments we will use in the final study. If we fail to do this, we may find only *after* the study is complete that our measures of key variables are unreliable (and therefore invalid). This means that we will not be able to place any faith in the results of

Figure 5.6
A model of the research process

the research and that our energies will have been partially or totally wasted. *Pretests of the validity and reliability of measures should be part of any research project that either uses measures that have not been convincingly validated elsewhere or relies on measures that have been validated only in settings very different from those in which they will be used.*

Conclusion

At this point we have introduced all the basic elements of the research process. Figure 5.6 depicts their relationships to one another. The operationalization of our concepts through the development of measurable indicators prepares us to enter the field to make the observations on which we will base our conclusions. Before we can make those observations, however, we need a "plan of attack"—a scheme for making the observations in a way that will maximize the number of conclusions we can confidently draw from them. This plan, or *research design,* is the subject of the next chapter.

Summary Points

• Theories are operationalized with instruments to measure their concepts.
• The levels of measurement are: nominal, ordinal, and interval/ratio. These may be easily remembered using the acronym NOIR.
• Sources of measurement error include: instrument weakness, subjective interpretation, and inaccurate or incomplete interpretation of results.
• Internal validity is strengthened if your measurements are appropriate and complete.
• Stronger external validity increases the generalizability of your results.
• Reliable measures enhance replication of your research.

Suggested Readings and References

Most explanations of measurement in the social sciences are found in literature that reports research results or develops sophisticated measurement techniques. General introductions to the subject are rare. However, one of the best introductions to measurement strategies is W. Philips Shively, *The Craft of Political Research*, 6th ed. (Upper Saddle River, NJ: Pearson Prentice Hall, 2004). Some advanced approaches to measurement can be found in an earlier work by Hubert M. Blalock, Jr., *Conceptualization and Measurement in the Social Sciences* (Beverly Hills, CA: Sage, 1982).

A more detailed discussion of measurement error, from the psychology research tradition, is found in Rick H. Hoyle, Monica J. Harris, and Charles M. Judd, *Research Methods in Social Relations*, 7th ed. (Pacific Grove, CA: Thompson Wadsworth, 2002).

Research Exercises

1. Using one of the political science periodicals given in Chapter 3, locate an article that reports the results of an empirical investigation. Identify at least two principal concepts from the article, and write down how each concept was operationalized. If the article uses only one operationalization for each concept, describe at least two more for each concept. If more than one operationalization is used for each concept in the article, describe at least one alternative operationalization for each. If possible, your operationalizations should rely on indicators that are in a different form from those used in the article.

2. Select another scholarly article reporting the results of empirical research. Identify at least two of the major concepts employed and describe how they were operationalized. Then state a line of reasoning that will lead us to expect the indicator selected for each variable to change when values of the variable change. In other words, state a *measurement theory* justifying the use of that indicator.

3. Using the variables from the article selected for Exercise 2, devise at least two alternative measurement theories showing how changes in each indicator employed in the article can result from changes in some variable *other* than the one it is used to represent. In other words, identify at least two possible sources of invalidity for each indicator.

Key Terms

operationalization
instrumentation
measurement
indicator
values
observation
multidimensional
operational definition
instrument
level of measurement
nominal measurement
mutually exclusive
collectively exhaustive
ordinal measurement
interval/ratio measurement
working hypotheses

measurement theory
measurement error
systematic errors
random errors
validity
validation
pragmatic validation
predictive validity
construct validation
external validation
internal (convergent) validation
multiple indicators
discriminant validation
face validity
reliability

CHAPTER 6

Working from a Plan: Considerations in Research Design

- Why is a research plan fundamental to a successful project?
- In explanatory research, what components comprise the research plan?
- What design technique do experiments utilize to permit comparison and manipulation?

Just as experienced mountaineers would not attempt to climb Mount Everest without a great deal of planning designed to ensure that they had the right equipment, took the best route, and knew what to do if certain things went wrong, social scientists would not undertake a research project without carefully planning the steps that they would take. This plan of attack is referred to as a *research design*.

"A **research design** is the scheme that guides the process of collecting, analyzing, and interpreting data. It is a logical model of proof that allows the making of valid causal inferences" (Nachmias 1979, p. 21, emphasis added). Without an adequate and appropriate design for research, the best of measures will be useless, since their meaning cannot be determined. Before undertaking any serious study, you should write out a research design that not only tells exactly what you intend to do in the research process and how you intend to do it, but also tells *why* you are taking each step and why you are taking it in the way that you are rather than in some other way.

Research Ethics Before planning a research project, the single overarching consideration in designing research is whether a given project will require a breach of personal or professional ethics. Will the research harm anyone in any sense? If so, how severely? Do the benefits to society outweigh those costs? These are questions each professional must answer according to his or her values and the prevailing standards of the profession. Appendix B presents the recommended standards of research ethics endorsed by the leading professional associations in political science and sociology. Your institution may have established its own ethical research standards. Research review boards, required by federal regulations at all institutions receiving grant funding, are used to standardize the application of ethical rules to all research projects.

Formal limitations on the types of research that may be conducted on humans and protections for those research subjects stem from perceived past abuses by researchers. The best-known cases in the social sciences are Zimbardo's Stanford (University) Prison Experiment and Stanley Milgram's work in *Obedience to Authority* (1974). Concerns about long-term harm to people involved with both of these experiments have made them emblematic of some of the potential dangers inherent in conducting social research. A film and a very informative Web site (www.prisonexp.org) document the former study, and the latter is described in a book of the same name. Returning to the question of protecting research subjects, the only general guide that we can offer for making ethical choices is to remember that science is a tool to be used in the service of humanity; it is not an end in itself.

Research Purpose and Research Design

We have largely discussed political science research as if it were all intended to test hypotheses through the process summarized in Figure 5.6. Though hypothesis-testing studies are generally recognized as the most crucial of social science undertakings, research can have a variety of purposes, and the research design that is most appropriate for any given project depends on the project's purpose.

Types of Research   Some research projects consist of **exploratory research.** They are intended only to provide greater familiarity with the phenomena we want to investigate so that we can formulate more precise research questions and perhaps develop hypotheses. Such studies can be essential when we are investigating new phenomena or old phenomena that have not been studied before. Some projects involve **descriptive research.** They are intended to provide an accurate representation of some phenomenon so that we can better formulate research questions and hypotheses. We may, for example, need to know the frequency, geographic distribution, and sequence of events of some phenomenon or need to know what other phenomena it tends to be associated with before we can begin to theorize about what might have caused it. Finally, research can be intended to test causal hypotheses. If we can use the results of a study to argue that one thing causes another, we can begin to develop explanations of the second event. For that reason, hypothesis-testing research may be described as **explanatory research.** Such research is appropriate when we have enough knowledge about a phenomenon to begin to seek explanations for it.

The significance of this rough typology of research purposes is that research of each type requires different things of a research design. Exploratory research requires flexibility more than precision, because its purpose is to discover possible explanations rather than to test hypothetical explanations. Exploratory research designs need only provide an opportunity to observe the phenomenon in question. Descriptive research, however, requires accurate measurement of phenomena. In descriptive studies, the research design must ensure unbiased and reliable observations if the studies are to produce accurate pictures of the events of interest. Explanatory research designs must ensure both unbiased and reliable observation and provide a basis for inferring the causal influence of one or more variables on others. A research design provides a basis for causal inferences when it allows us to rule out any plausible explanations for observed results that represent alternatives to the causal hypothesis being tested.

Regardless of the specific purpose of a study, its research design should include the following *basic elements:*

1. A statement of the purpose of the research
2. A statement of the hypothesis to be tested (if any)

3. A specification of the variables to be employed

4. A statement of how each variable is to be operationalized and measured

5. A detailed statement of how observations are to be organized and conducted

6. A general discussion of how the data collected will be analyzed

Chapters 2 and 5 provide the background you need to prepare sections 1 through 4 of a research design, and Chapters 14 to 18 present an introduction to data analysis. Chapters 6 and 7 are devoted to the organization of observations. It is this aspect of research design that provides a basis for ruling out alternative rival hypotheses and that most scholars have in mind when they refer to a research design.

Coping with Alternative Rival Hypotheses Through Research Design

We can demonstrate the impact of the way we structure or organize our observations on how useful the results of research are by considering a hypothetical research project.

An Example   Imagine that the justice department in your state has implemented a new program designed to reduce juvenile delinquency. The program involves taking juvenile offenders, as well as potential offenders who volunteer or are volunteered by their parents, into prisons for one-day visits. The program is founded on the theory that glimpsing the horrors of prison life will discourage juveniles from committing crimes that might result in their being sent to prison, because the youths' exposure to incarceration will cause them to fear prison. Let us say that after the program has been in operation for some months, the state government wants to know whether it is having the desired effect, and it hires you, a skilled political scientist, to evaluate its results. How will you go about this?

Because the program, known as Operation Fright, is intended to reduce juvenile delinquency, delinquency will be your dependent variable. You might operationalize it as *being arrested for a criminal offense* and then, one year after their prison visit, simply check on the criminal records of the youths who went through Operation Fright. If they have been arrested during this time, you label them delinquent. If they have not been arrested during this time, you label them nondelinquent.[1]

Let us say that you find that 70 percent of those who have been in the program have *not* been arrested during the following year. Can you then conclude that the program has been 70 percent effective in preventing delinquency? To do so with any confidence, you need to rule out other explanations of why 70 percent of those youths have not been arrested.

---

[1] This operationalization of delinquency treats it as a dichotomous, nominal variable. In practice, you would probably want to use an operationalization that provided more information and was more sensitive to differences between individuals. You might, for example, want to develop a "delinquency index" that combined the number of arrests in a year with some measure of the severity of the crimes for which the subjects were arrested in order to have an indicator of the *degree* of delinquency.

Evaluating Alternative Rival Hypotheses Your *operating hypothesis* is that the Operation Fright experience prevents delinquent behavior. Some possible alternative rival hypotheses that may explain your findings include the following:

1. No more than 30 percent of the youths would have been arrested, even if they had not gone through Operation Fright.

2. The family background of those who were volunteered for Operation Fright is different from that of those who were not, and it is that background that has prevented their delinquency, not the state program.

3. Many of the youths have committed crimes but have not been caught.

4. Though there may be temporary effects from Operation Fright, they will wear off and the youths will revert to criminal behavior. (The program delays delinquency rather than prevents it.)

5. The youths involved in the program have been arrested more often than they would have been had they not taken part in Operation Fright, because participation labels them as potential criminals and subjects them to greater police scrutiny. (The program causes more frequent arrests regardless of its effect on behavior.)

Alternative rival hypothesis 1 essentially asserts that the program has had no impact. With a single observation you cannot demonstrate that this is or is not true. You can never know how those who have gone through the program would have acted if they had not taken part in Operation Fright, but you can include in your research design a check of the criminal records of a group of youths who have *not* gone through Operation Fright but who are otherwise similar in as many respects as possible to those who have. You can then compare the delinquency rate of those who have been in the program with that of those who have not and argue that any difference in the two rates can be attributed to the program, since we can assume that those in the program would have acted essentially the same way as their peers in the absence of Operation Fright. Observing the control group (those not participating in the program) allows us to assert a causal link between the program and delinquent behavior.

Rival hypothesis 2 is a claim that any apparent relationship between program participation and delinquent behavior is spurious. It holds that family background causes both program involvement and subsequent nondelinquency. This reasoning suggests that there is a selection process in which those who have the family support to help them avoid criminal behavior are also the ones most likely to have gone through the program and that this creates an *apparent* relationship between Operation Fright and nondelinquency.

A single observation will not allow you to rule out this possibility, but having a control group including youths with family backgrounds similar to those who have gone through Operation Fright does, as in the case of rival hypothesis 1, allow you to determine whether this is the case. You can check to see whether program participants and nonparticipants do in fact tend to have different family backgrounds, and whether those with similar family backgrounds tend to have the same delinquency rate regardless of participation in Operation Fright.

Ruling out rival hypothesis 2, like dealing with hypothesis 1, requires that you make a second observation (checking the criminal records of some youths not involved in the program). In addition, however, coping with hypothesis 2 requires that you make a third observation, in which you collect data on the subjects' family backgrounds. You may be able to obtain some objective indicators of this variable (for example, presence of both parents, parents' educational level and occupation, and family income) from public records, but you may also have to conduct interviews with family members or the youths themselves. If you operationalize family background to include attitudes and the character of personal interactions, such interviews will be necessary. You will therefore not only increase the amount of data you collect but also adopt another method of data collection—the personal interview.

Rival hypothesis 3 reinforces the need for this additional data collection method. It poses the possibility that Operation Fright has made its participants more cautious and perhaps even more clever criminals rather than reducing the number of crimes they commit. It questions the adequacy of the operationalization of the dependent variable. As long as official arrest records are your only measure of delinquency, you cannot have any confidence that this is not the case.

One way to cope with rival hypothesis 3 is to operationalize delinquency so as to include reports of criminal actions from the youths themselves and to conduct interviews both before and after they go through the program. You will have to interview both participants and nonparticipants and include information on family background for each group to be sure that your results cannot be explained by hypotheses such as 1 and 2 phrased in terms of this new indicator of delinquency. With this action you have added not only another **observation point** (the preprogram interview) but also another mode of operationalization for the dependent variable.

Rival hypothesis 4 adds a time dimension to the study. If you are to discount it, you will have to interview and check on the criminal records of both program participants and the control group not only one year after the prison visit but also two and perhaps three years after as well. The reason for making subsequent observations of program participants should be clear, since hypothesis 4 contends that participants will eventually become delinquent. You will also need to observe the control group in order to ensure that changes in delinquency rates for program participants in later years are not the result of other factors, such as maturation, changes in family situation, or worsening economic conditions. Only if program participants have a subsequent delinquency rate similar to (or worse than) the delinquency rate for nonparticipants *at the same time* can you conclude that the program has been ineffective (or that it has had a negative effect).

Unlike the others, rival hypothesis 5 argues that Operation Fright has been *more* effective than your results suggest. It raises the possibility that by using arrests as the measure of delinquency, you have introduced an additional independent variable (selective treatment from authorities) whose effects cover up the actual influence of Operation Fright on delinquent behavior.

One way to cope with this possibility is to include yet another operationalization of the dependent variable. If you look at *convictions* as well as arrests for both participants and nonparticipants, you will have some evidence of whether the cases brought against program participants are any less valid than those brought against youths who have never gone through Operation Fright, and you may infer from this whether or not the police are any more likely to arrest those who volunteered for Operation Fright. If participants are arrested without ultimately being indicted or convicted significantly more often than are nonparticipants, you will have reason to believe that rival hypothesis 5 is correct.

This brief examination of a few of the possible rival hypotheses that can challenge the value of your results has provided the basis for developing a much more elaborate research design than that first suggested. If you want to be able to rule out these five alternative interpretations (and you must do so if your study is to be of any value), you will have to move from a single operationalization of the dependent variable and a single observation to a research design involving multiple modes of operationalization, multiple methods of data collection, and several observation points. The new research design might involve the following major steps:

1. Select a sample of youths who have been designated to take part in Operation Fright and a sample of youths who have the same mix of characteristics relevant to delinquency (for example, sex; age; race; education; parents' occupation, education, and income; living situation; and place of residence) but who are not to participate in the program.

2. Interview those subjects designated to participate in the program before they take part in Operation Fright, and at the same time interview the control group to obtain self-reports of delinquent activity and information on family background.

3. Interview members of all subjects' families to obtain information on family background.

4. One year after the subjects have visited the prison, interview both participants and nonparticipants to obtain self-reports of delinquent activity and to find out whether family circumstances have changed.

5. At the time you perform step 4, check the arrest and conviction records of both program participants and nonparticipants.

6. Two years after the subjects have taken part in Operation Fright, repeat steps 4 and 5.

7. Three years after Operation Fright, repeat steps 4 and 5.

In analyzing the data, you will want to compare the arrest rates, the conviction rates, and the differences between arrest and conviction rates for the program participants and the control group, being careful to eliminate any members of the control group who have taken part in Operation Fright after their initial selection for the study. By employing appropriate statistical procedures in the analysis of the data produced by these observations, you should be able to reach highly defensible conclusions about the value of Operation Fright as a deterrent to juvenile delinquency. Because of your ability to rule out major rival hypotheses, the state's justice department may place a good deal of confidence in your conclusions—a confidence they could not have if those conclusions were based on the first research design.

Adequacy of Design   The purpose of this exercise is not to argue that complex research designs are preferable to simple ones. The important consideration is the *adequacy* of the design, not its complexity. If a research design provides a logical basis for the kinds of inferences the researcher wants to make, it is adequate.

The discussion of this hypothetical study provides an example of how adequate research designs are developed. In planning a research project, you will go through the same kind of reasoning that we have just laid out. *Research design is a process of formulating alternative rival hypotheses and reasoning through the kinds of observations that are needed to test those hypotheses so that they can be ruled out as explanations for potential findings.*

Alternative rival hypotheses are arrived at in the same manner as operating hypotheses. They result from logical analysis of our theories and from thorough knowledge of the facts that surround the events we are trying to explain. A true alternative rival hypothesis predicts the *same relationship* as our main hypothesis but explains it in terms of a different causal process.

Alternative Rival Versus Other Hypotheses   It is important not to confuse true alternative rival hypotheses with what we can call *other hypotheses*. Due to the existence of multiple causation in social phenomena, it is usually possible to come up with a variety of equally valid explanations of any given event. Identifying another cause of the observed relationship produces simply another hypothesis that may in no way be a rival to the original. *A hypothesis is an alternative rival hypothesis only if it is logically impossible for both that hypothesis and the original hypothesis to be true at the same time.*

Identifying crucial rival hypotheses is principally a creative activity. There are no hard-and-fast rules to ensure that you will identify all the rival hypotheses that can challenge the value of your research. The process of designing a research project will differ with each study. You cannot simply select an appropriate research design from a limited set of alternatives as you might choose a pair of shoes from those that are your size in a shoe store. There are, however, several general types of research designs, each of which is suited for dealing with particular types of problems. The next section provides an overview of the major types of research design and an introduction to the logic of research design.

Experimental Research Designs

The purpose of a sound research design is to allow us to identify the effects of one variable on another with as much confidence as possible. Research designs allow us to do this by providing an element of **control** over the conditions under which variables interact. This control is the key to research design.

Control: An Example   If several animals on a farm contract a disease after a new kind of feed is added to their diet, the farmer cannot feel sure that the new feed is the cause of the illness, because the animals may have been exposed to a variety of new substances (for example, insecticides in their water supply) at the same time. On the other hand, if an unusually large proportion of the test animals in a medical research laboratory contracts a disease after a new substance is added to their diet, the researcher is more likely to feel sure that the substance is the cause of the disease, because here it is possible to control the environment of the test animals and ensure that they are *not* exposed to any other new substances during the observations. The setting in which the researcher works permits an element of control, whereas the farm does not.

Table 6.1
The classic experimental design

Group	Time 1	Time 2	Time 3	Effect Formula
Experimental	Pretest	Stimulus	Posttest	Effect (of experimental variable) = $(posttest_E - pretest_E) - (posttest_C - pretest_C)$ where E refers to the
Control	Pretest	—	Posttest	experimental group and C to the control group

Research designs can be classified by the degree of control they allow. The basic distinction that is of interest to political scientists is that between *experimental* and *quasi-experimental designs*.

The *experiment* is the classic model of scientific proof. It is based on an assumption that changes in the value of one variable cause changes in the value of another variable (for example, *changes in temperature result in changes in the viscosity of oil*). The experiment allows us to test this assumption by exposing those cases or **subjects** manifesting the dependent variable to the independent variable under conditions that allow us to be relatively sure that any observed change in the dependent variable is a result of changes in the independent variable.

The basic **experimental design** involves an **experimental group** composed of subjects who will be exposed to the independent variable, or **stimulus**, and a **control group** of subjects, who are like the experimental group in all relevant respects but will not be exposed to the stimulus. The value of the dependent variable in each group is measured prior to introduction of the stimulus in what is called a **pretest**, and again after the experimental group has been exposed to the stimulus in what is called a **posttest**. The impact of the stimulus (independent variable) is inferred from a comparison of the pretest and posttest scores for each group. The greater the difference in values between pretest and posttest in each group, the greater the effect attributed to the independent variable. Table 6.1 shows the logic of the experimental research design. The advantage of this research design is that it allows us to achieve two conditions that facilitate valid causal inferences: *comparison* and *manipulation*.

The assertion that one thing has caused another is based on the concept of change. We must be able to show that some change has occurred before we can claim that causal forces have been at work, and the idea of change implies comparisons. We must be able to compare values of the dependent variable before the subjects have been exposed to the independent or causal variable with values of the dependent variable after such exposure, and if possible we should compare values of the dependent variable after exposure with some indicator of what those values might be if exposure had never occurred. The experimental design, with its pretest-posttest procedure and its test and control groups, provides an opportunity for both types of comparison.

In order to feel confident that one variable has a causal influence on another, we must be able to know which subjects have been exposed to the independent variable and which have not so that we can make the appropriate comparisons. The

Table 6.2
The Solomon two-control-group research design

Group	Time 1	Time 2	Time 3	Effect Formula
Experimental	Pretest	Stimulus	Posttest	Effect = [(posttest$_E$ − pretest$_E$)
				− (posttest$_{C1}$ − pretest$_{C1}$)] −
Control 1	Pretest	—	Posttest	(posttest$_E$ − posttest$_{C2}$)
Control 2	—	Stimulus	Posttest	

classic experiment provides this knowledge because it is the researcher who introduces the independent variable. The scientist manipulates the subjects' environment so that their exposure to the causal influence is not left to chance. In addition, the researcher manipulates the subjects' environment to ensure that all other possible causes of a change in the dependent variable are removed from the experiment at the time of the subjects' exposure to the independent variable.

A variety of other research designs build on the logic of the classic experiment but add modifications that are especially relevant to social scientists. Social scientists' need for more elaborate research designs is largely due to the facts that (1) the objects of their research are often affected by the very act of studying them (for example, people's behavior may change if they know they are being watched) and (2) the objects of their research are not static but ever changing (for example, people's values may change as new situations arise). Two experimental designs developed by R. L. Solomon (1949) illustrate ways of dealing with these facts.

Illustrated in Table 6.2, Solomon's first design addresses a type of reactivity known as the **test effect.** When experimental subjects are pretested, it is always possible that their score on the posttest will be a result of both their reaction to the stimulus *and* a reaction to the pretest itself. Any difference between pretest and posttest scores that is due solely to reactions to the pretest is known as a test effect. If we are to get an accurate picture of the impact of the stimulus on behavior, we must be able to remove this test effect from the scores. The **Solomon two-control-group research design** in Table 6.2 allows us to do this.

This design is just like the classic experiment except that a third group is added. The third group (Control 2) receives the stimulus and posttest, but no pretest. Though changes from pretest scores to posttest scores in the experimental group can be due to both the pretest and the stimulus, changes from pretest scores to posttest scores in Control 1 can be due only to the pretest and in Control 2 only to the stimulus. If we can assume that all groups have had essentially the same value on the dependent variable initially and have reacted to the stimulus in the same way, then the difference in the posttest scores of the experimental group and Control 2 represents the test effect. The effect of the independent variable (stimulus) alone can then be gauged by subtracting this test effect from the total effect of the experiment, which is computed by the same formula used to evaluate the results of the classic experimental design. The effect formula in Table 6.2 summarizes this logic algebraically.

In addition to the test effect as an alternative explanation of observed changes in subjects' scores, there are, however, other possible causes of change in the groups'

Table 6.3

The Solomon three-control-group research design

Group	Time 1	Time 2	Time 3	Effect Formula
Experimental	Pretest	Stimulus	Posttest	Effect = [(posttest$_E$ − pretest$_E$)
				− (posttest$_{C1}$ − pretest$_{C1}$)] −
Control 1	Pretest	—	Posttest	[(posttest$_E$ − posttest$_{C2}$) +
				(posttest$_{C3}$ − pretest$_E$)]
Control 2	—	Stimulus	Posttest	
Control 3	—	—	Posttest	

scores on the dependent variable (DV) from pretest to posttest. One is the influence of *external factors* not under the control of the experimenter. Another is natural changes in the subjects that proceed independently of the experiment (such as aging—in long-term experiments—or mental fatigue). The impact of such erroneous factors can be judged (and therefore ruled out as a rival explanation of the experiment's results) by use of the **Solomon three-control-group research design,** depicted in Table 6.3.

This design adds a third control group, which receives neither pretest nor stimulus. Any difference in pretest and posttest scores in this group can be due only to the influence of extraneous factors. If we can subtract this change from the effect of the experiment, we can remove from our results the effects of extraneous factors and changes in the respondents, and we can hope to rule out the alternative hypothesis that it is these influences rather than the independent variable that have caused the change in the experimental group's score from Time 1 to Time 3.

The difficulty is that Control 3 is not pretested. How can we determine how much these subjects' scores have changed from Time 1 to Time 3? If all of our groups are essentially alike, we can assume that their pretest scores will have been highly similar and simply assign Control 3 a pretest score equal to the average of the scores for the experimental and first two control groups. We can then subtract this score from Control 3's posttest to obtain a measure of the change due to extraneous factors and natural changes in the subjects. With this change removed, we can see more clearly the effects of the independent variable on the dependent variable.

Assigning Cases to Groups

Each of the experimental designs just described is intended to provide a sound, logical basis for conclusions about the effects of one variable on another. To be successful in this, each design fundamentally depends on the assumption that all groups in the study are essentially the same with respect to those factors that might influence their response to the experiment. If we cannot assume that the groups are essentially the same, we have no logical basis for inferring that observed differences in their scores are the result of differences in the way they have been treated in the experiment (for example, whether or not they have been pretested), and we cannot make sound arguments about the causal influence of our independent variable.

Assigning Groups by Characteristics   How can we ensure that members of the various groups will be essentially the same? There are three approaches to assigning members to groups. The first is by way of **precision matching.** After deciding what characteristics might influence subjects' response to the independent variable, we select a set of subjects for the experiment. For each subject selected, we locate for the control group another subject who has exactly the same combination of relevant characteristics. The result is two groups that are identical in the characteristics that might influence their response to the experiment. Ideally, their pretest scores will be highly similar, and we can use the degree of similarity we actually find when we pretest them to judge how well our matching efforts have worked.

There are several problems with this procedure. First, if we need to control for a large number of characteristics, we may find it extremely difficult to find subjects who are matched in all the characteristics, as they must be in precision matching. We might, for instance, be able to find people of the same sex, age, and race but have difficulty finding people who share those characteristics *and* have the same occupation, educational background, and length of residence in the community. In addition, if we want to use a research design calling for more than two groups, we may find it most difficult to locate three or four subjects with identical characteristics. Unless we have an extremely large pool of potential subjects or a very simple experiment, matching may be impracticable as a means of assigning subjects to experimental groups.

A second method of obtaining similar groups is **frequency distribution control.** Here we do not match each subject with another on all characteristics. Rather, we assign subjects to groups in such a way as to ensure that the groups have the same average characteristics and the same distribution of each characteristic. There may be no two subjects with the same combination of sex, age, race, and occupation, but each group will have the same proportion of males and females, the same average age, and so on. Moreover, the groups will have highly similar distributions of these characteristics among their members.

Frequency distribution control is more often practicable than precision matching, but it has two significant defects. First, it allows us to control for only one variable at a time. Frequency distribution assignment may produce, for example, two groups with equal numbers of subjects over forty years of age and equal numbers of women, but there is no guarantee that all the over-forty subjects will not be men in one group and women in the other. If it works out this way, the two groups will not be truly similar. Second, the method offers no control over any factors that influence subjects' reactions but have not been identified by the researcher. If our theory of the phenomenon under study is incomplete (and it almost *always* is), we may have failed to control the frequency distribution of some important variable. If the control and experimental groups happen to differ systematically on this uncontrolled variable, our results may be distorted.

Randomly Assigning Groups   The third method of assigning subjects to groups is more flexible than precision matching and avoids both of the problems associated with frequency distribution control. It is **randomization.** A subject selected from a list of all eligible subjects is assigned to a group by some random process, such as use of a table of random numbers. True randomization is *not* achieved by chance procedures (such as taking the first thirty people who apply for the experiment as the test group and the next thirty as the control group).

Randomization has the great advantage of allowing us to feel quite confident that all of our groups are highly similar in *all* respects, not just in terms of the variables we identify as relevant to the experiment, because random assignment ensures that differences in subjects will cancel out *when large numbers of subjects are chosen*. Randomization, then, allows us to rule out any alternative rival hypothesis that contends that some systematic difference in the groups has produced the observed results. It is *the key to successful laboratory experiments*. In Chapter 7 we discuss detailed procedures for the random selection of cases.

Political Communications Experiments   Political communications researchers are particularly likely to utilize laboratory experiments to study perceptions and effects of media messages. In these experiments subject treatments may include viewing or reading political content ranging from press releases to campaign ads to news broadcasts. The laboratory environment permits controlling exposure, as well as manipulating content message and formatting. Researchers may evaluate major content effects by varying specific text in ads, making the same advertisement carry a positive or negative tone, for example. Production effects may include controlling for male or female ad voice-overs, evaluating the type of photos or colors of circulars. All of this research assumes that certain types of images or messages may differentially influence citizens.

Field Experiments and Nonexperimental Designs

Political scientists seldom work in laboratories, due to the nature of their subject matter. Rather, these researchers often observe events in natural settings, where they can exercise less control over the factors that might influence the results of the study. In cases when researchers can manipulate the independent variable and control subjects' exposure but cannot control other aspects of the situation, they may conduct **field experiments.**

Field Experiments   In recent years, interest in political science field experiments has grown, largely driven by community political mobilization experiments. Campaigns are increasingly depending upon electronic communications (i.e., televised ads) and direct mail circulars, but little research has compared the relative effectiveness of various media. Others are more concerned with attempting to halt the widely-noted decline in U.S. voter turnout since the 1960s, using voter mobilization. Field experiments are a logical means to assess the general turnout or persuasive effects of mail, e-mail, phone, and door-to-door canvassing. In a number of path-breaking experiments conducted by Gerber and Green (2004), cities and communities were divided into quadrants, and citizens in each area were contacted using different methods (or no method, in the control condition). Not surprisingly, the researchers found that personal contact carried the strongest mobilization or (candidate-specific) persuasive message.

The field setting makes it more difficult to isolate the effects of the treatment (contact) from other possible causes of changes in subjects' behavior, but it has the distinct advantage of giving a realistic test of how mobilization efforts would work in practice. A laboratory experiment, even if it could have been arranged, would not have been as satisfactory, because we cannot be sure that the results obtained in such an artificial environment accurately represent what happens in the outside world. This is a general advantage of field experiments over laboratory studies.

In field experiments, researchers use careful selection of the subjects and random assignment of subjects to the test and control groups to gain some control over background characteristics that may influence results. They also keep a close check on subjects' circumstances throughout the experiment to rule out alternative hypotheses that attribute observed results to outside events that occur during the experiment.

In many cases, political scientists cannot even manipulate the independent variable. You can imagine the difficulty of persuading some nations to have revolutions and others to postpone them in order to conduct a field experiment on the effects of revolutions on political development! The more important the subject under investigation, the less likely it is that we can control it. Under these circumstances, researchers must attempt to approximate an experimental design, as we describe in the next section, or they resort to the use of a nonexperimental design.

Nonexperimental Research   In **nonexperimental designs,** the scientists can control neither the assignment of subjects to experimental groups nor the occurrence of the independent variable, and they cannot obtain pretest scores on the dependent variable. They may be forced to use what is referred to as an *after-only* design, in which a single observation is made after the occurrence of the presumed causal event. Sometimes a "control group" of similar subjects not exposed to the independent variable (IV) can be added and differences in the scores of the two groups attributed to the IV. Such designs, however, provide no basis for sound inferences about the effect of the IV, since they do not allow us to rule out even the most simple of alternative hypotheses. We cannot, for instance, even be sure that the value of the DV we observe after exposure to the IV is any different from the value of the DV before that exposure. Thus, nonexperimental designs are suited only for descriptive or exploratory research, not for explanatory studies.

Quasi-Experimental Designs

Most of the research schemes employed by political scientists can be classified as **quasi-experimental designs.** In these studies, researchers cannot control exposure to the independent variable or the conditions under which it occurs, but they attempt to simulate an experimental design either by gathering additional data or by data analysis techniques. Properly constructed quasi-experimental designs allow us to proceed *as if* we had exercised all the control characteristic of a true experiment, and they provide a sound, logical basis for causal inferences.

Perhaps the most common type of quasi-experimental design in political science is the **ex post facto experiment.** In it researchers make a single observation and collect data about the independent and dependent variables and any other variables they feel they should control for. If we want to investigate the effects of college education on voting behavior, for instance, we may conduct a survey of randomly selected subjects. Then we analyze our data in such a way as to determine whether people who are similar in other regards (for example, race, sex, age, and region of residence) but have different educational backgrounds vote differently. There are sophisticated statistical techniques for doing this, but at the simplest level we may sort out our respondents in contingency tables so that we can examine the relationship between education and voting in different categories of other variables, looking, for example, only at women who have and have not gone to college or only at men who have and have not gone to college.

This procedure allows us to act *as if* we had set up an experiment years ago in which we had assigned people to experimental groups, had exposed some to college education (the independent variable), and were now testing them to see what impact this had had on their voting.

The members of our sample who have had less than a college education but are similar in other respects to those in our sample who have had a college education serve as a "control group." Because we have not had a pretest, we cannot be sure that it is the college education that has created any observed differences in voting, but we can use the additional data we have gathered in the survey to rule out some plausible rival hypotheses, and we can rely on random selection of the sample to cancel out the effects of variables we cannot control for in data analysis.

There are some situations in which we cannot use random sampling and cannot select comparable control groups. We will find this to be the case if our units of analysis are few in number or unique in many relevant regards. An example is the situation in which a city government wants to know what effect an administrative reorganization has had on the costs of city services. To fulfill the request, political scientists might use another common research design known as a *time-series design*.

In **time-series designs,** the researcher makes several observations both before and after the introduction of some causal phenomenon and compares values on the dependent variable before and after. In our example, political scientists might use city records to compare the per capita costs of municipal services before and after the administrative reorganization. (They will have to use per capita costs and control for inflation in order to rule out the possibility that either an increasing city population or rising prices have affected the costs of public services independently of the impact of the reorganization.) Figures 6.1 through 6.3 illustrate some possible results of this study.

In a sense, time-series designs use as a control group the *same* subject or set of subjects but at an earlier time. If there is a clear trend in the values of the dependent variable prior to introduction of the independent variable, we assume that the trend would continue were it not for the independent variable, and as an indicator of the effect of the IV, we use the difference between observed values of the DV and the values that it would have if the trend were continuing.

Figure 6.1 illustrates this logic. If the data come out as presented in that figure, city officials will be delighted to learn that the reorganization not only has reduced the cost of services but also has reversed the trend toward steadily increasing costs. The effect of the reorganization in any given year can be measured *by the difference between the value predicted for that year from the original trend line and the observed value.*

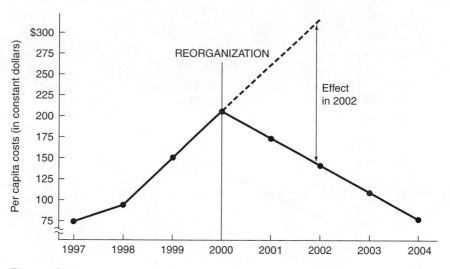

Figure 6.1
Hypothetical trend in public service costs showing that reorganization has reversed the original trend

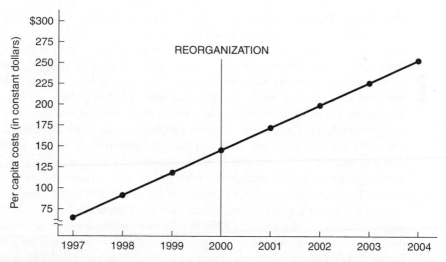

Figure 6.2
Hypothetical trend in public service costs showing no effect from reorganization

If the data come out as in Figure 6.2, the predicted and observed values will be the same, and reorganization will be judged to have had no effect on costs. Figure 6.3 illustrates a case in which the reorganization has initially reduced costs but has had no effect on the trend.

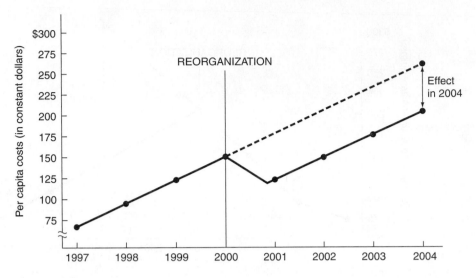

Figure 6.3
Hypothetical trend in public service costs showing that reorganization has changed the
level of costs but has not interrupted the trend

Fluctuating Trends: An Example   In most instances, the trend we are dealing with
is not as clear and steady as in this example. For instance, let us say that state prosecutors, alarmed by a rise in delinquent court-ordered child support payments to
single parents, institute a crackdown to collect the owed money from these dead-
beats and subsequently want to know how successful it has been. Figure 6.4 shows
the kind of data that might be collected over a ten-year period. The values of the
dependent variable (delinquent child support payments) rise and fall from year to
year throughout the period. The researcher's task is to determine whether the
general postcrackdown trend is significantly different from the general precrackdown trend. One way to do this is to compare the average annual delinquent payment rate prior to the crackdown with the average annual rate in postcrackdown
years. (Both are nine in this example.) If we assume that the original trend would
continue without a crackdown, we can use any difference between the two averages
as an indicator of the impact of the crackdown on the *level* of delinquent child support. Another approach is to compare trend lines (represented by a dashed line in
Figure 6.4) passed through the precrackdown and postcrackdown scattering of values for the DV to determine whether the general trend differs.

    This example illustrates one of the important advantages of time-series designs.
If we observe delinquent child support payment rates only in 1997 and 1999, as in
a typical before-after study, we may conclude that the prosecutor's crackdown has
reduced nonpayment of child support. The time-series data, however, allow us to see
the 1997–1999 drop in deliquencies as *a normal fluctuation around a general trend*
(represented by a dashed line), which remains unaffected by the government action.

    Despite this strength, time-series designs have a weakness. In many instances,
we have no control group and therefore cannot be sure what the effects of the IV
are because we cannot be sure what the value of the DV would be without the IV;

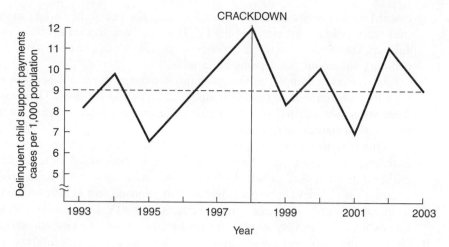

Figure 6.4
Hypothetical trend of delinquent child support payments to single parents, showing no effect from the crackdown

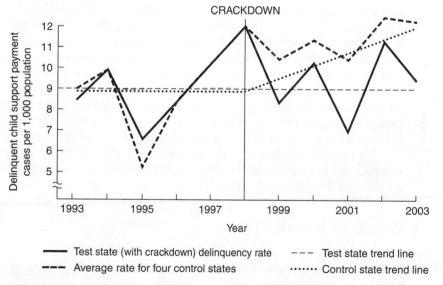

Figure 6.5
Hypothetical trend of delinquent child support payments in a test city and a group of control states

we can only guess that the original trend would continue. There are many reasons why this can be a mistake. One of the most important is *regression toward the mean*. This is a phenomenon that poses a challenge to the validity of conclusions drawn from a variety of research designs.

Regression toward the mean is basically a process by which subjects who have extreme values on a dependent variable at any one time tend naturally to return to a more nearly average value on that variable in subsequent measurements *regardless of any exposure to some hypothesized independent variable*. If this regression toward the mean occurs at the time of a study, the researcher might mistake the natural regression for an effect of the IV. This can be a special problem in cases when subjects are exposed to the independent variable precisely because they have extraordinary values on the dependent variable.

In our last example, prosecutors instituted a crackdown because of an exceptionally high number of case of nonpayment of child support. This was a deviation from what was normal for the state, and it might have corrected itself even if the government had done nothing.

One way to rule out regression toward the mean as an alternative explanation is to employ a *controlled time-series design*. In **controlled time-series designs**, we gather data on a case or set of cases that are as similar as possible to our test case or group in all relevant respects but are not exposed to the IV, and we use that case or group as a control in assessing the effects of the IV. In our example, we can select one or more states very similar to the one conducting the crackdown that have not changed their policies toward collecting child support payments and observe their delinquency rates in the same years. Figure 6.5 shows some possible results.

By comparing the test (crackdown) state with a group of similar states, we can see that while the pre-1998 trend in child support delinquency continues unchanged in the test state, the average delinquency rate rises dramatically in the control states. This suggests that while the crackdown has failed to change the trend in the test state, it may be preventing it from being changed by the same events that are driving child support nonpayment rates up in other, similar states. In this case, we use the difference between the test state's postcrackdown rates and those of the control states in the same year as a measure of the effect of the IV, on the assumption that the test state would follow the trend of its companion states were it not for the crackdown. In 2003, for example, the effect of the crackdown is assessed as three child support delinquencies per 1,000 population (i.e., subtract the trendlines: $12 - 9 = 3$).

Adopting a stronger research design would prevent us, in this example, from reaching the apparently incorrect conclusion that a program that actually served as an effective deterrent had no impact.

Creating a Research Design

There are a number of both experimental and quasi-experimental designs that we have not discussed here. The number of variations on these basic designs is limited only by human ingenuity, and the research design for any study will reflect its particular purpose. We do not *choose* a research design so much as we create one suited to the particular study at hand, though we generally build on one of the basic design types. The three principal considerations that guide researchers in developing research designs are the need for validity, the availability of resources, and professional ethics.

The purpose of research design in explanatory studies is to allow us to draw valid inferences about the causal relationships between variables from observed changes in our measures of those variables. Consequently, ensuring the validity of our results ought to be a central consideration in devising a research design. There are two primary types of validity associated with empirical research: internal and external.

Internal validity involves whether we are accurately measuring the theory. In other words, does the design provide a *sound, logical basis* for inferring that the independent variable does or does not cause a given change in the dependent variable? To ask about internal validity is to ask whether there is anything about the research design that will lead us to attribute a causal influence to the IV when it does not have such influence, or to fail to recognize any causal influence the IV does have. For example, if there is a strong test effect associated with the use of some particular measure, any research design that does not provide a way to control for the test effect will lack internal validity because it can lead us to misinterpret changes due to the test effect as evidence of the independent variable's causal impact.

External validity pertains to the *generalizability of our results.* Can we reasonably expect to find the same causal influences at work in other settings? Does this study tell us anything about the part of reality *not* included in it? A field experiment on the effects on the public's driving habits of adding a dollar-a-gallon surcharge to the price of gasoline, for example, has little external validity if it is conducted in a community where the average family's annual income is above $100,000, because we cannot expect middle- and low-income people to behave in the same way as these upper-class people would.

Factors That Threaten Validity

The major categories of threats to both internal and external validity include the following (Campbell 1969, 407–429):

Factors That Threaten Internal Validity

1. *History:* Events other than the IV that can alter posttest scores and that occur between the pretest and posttest. For example, a well-publicized statement by a political leader can alter subjects' attitudes independently of some long-term experimental treatment they are undergoing.

2. *Maturation:* Natural changes in the subjects that alter scores on the DV over time independently of the IV (for example, human fatigue, population growth in geographically defined units of analysis, aging of physical facilities).

3. *Instability:* Random changes in recorded values due to unreliable measures, inconsistent sampling of subjects, or other causes.

4. *Testing:* The test effect described in this chapter.

5. *Instrumentation:* Differences in the measuring devices used that produce differences in scores independently of the effects of the IV (for example, different biases among interviewers, an improperly calibrated machine, or inconsistent precision among coders).

6. *Regression artifacts:* Changes due to regression toward the mean, discussed in this chapter

7. *Selection:* Differences in scores resulting from differential recruitment of test and control groups (for example, when members of a test group are forced by law to be exposed to the IV, whereas members of one of the control groups volunteer to be exposed).

8. *Experimental mortality:* Different rates of loss of subjects from test and control groups (for example, those cases that can make the control group as a whole respond to the IV in the same way as the test group may drop out of the experiment before posttest).

9. *Selection-maturation interaction:* Biases in selection processes that lead to different rates of maturation in test and control groups (for example, in the Operation Fright study, test subjects may be older because they have volunteered for the program only after a series of juvenile arrests, and they may thus outgrow juvenile delinquency faster than the younger control group).

Factors That Threaten External Validity

1. *Interaction effects of testing:* Posttest scores of the pretested subjects may be rendered unrepresentative of the unpretested population because of the way in which the pretest has sensitized the subjects to the IV.

2. *Interaction of selection and experimental treatment:* Biased selection processes may produce a test group that responds to the IV in ways atypical of the larger population.

3. *Reactive effects of experimental arrangements:* Conditions of the experimental setting may be unrepresentative of real-world conditions.

4. *Multiple-treatment interference:* The simultaneous application of more than one treatment may create changes that are different from what would occur if any one treatment or IV were used alone.

5. *Irrelevant responsiveness of measures:* All measures pick up multiple aspects of the environment, and some may include irrelevant components that give the appearance of change when none has occurred or that obscure actual changes.

6. *Irrelevant replicability of treatments:* When IVs are complex events (as are the visit to the prison in the Operation Fright example and college education), researchers may not be aware of what aspect of them causes the change in subjects, and they may fail to include the relevant aspect of the IV in all experimental exposures to it.

Ideally, research should employ a design that avoids as many of these threats to validity as possible. Even a perfect design, however, is useless unless we have the resources necessary to execute it. The availability of time, money, skilled personnel, facilities, and necessary data sources will always constrain the choice of research design. If researchers are not confident that the major threats to validity likely to apply to their particular study can be controlled by a design that is practical given the existing resource constraints, they should consider abandoning the project until adequate resources are available. *No research is preferable to bad research that can lead to inaccurate conclusions.*

Summary Points

• A clearly constructed research plan enables you to evaluate your project's feasibility and its measurement qualities.

• An explanatory research plan clearly states your theory, hypotheses, relevant literature, variable operationalization and measurement, data source(s), and data analysis techniques.

• Laboratory experiments allow direct control of extraneous factors, by comparing groups that are exposed to a treatment to those that are not.

Suggested Readings and References

A general introduction to social science research that contains useful discussions of research design is Earl Babbie, *The Practice of Social Research,* 10th ed. (Belmont, CA: Wadsworth Thompson Learning, 2004). A now dated, but still widely used text devoted entirely to research design issues is Thomas D. Cook and Donald T. Campbell, *Quasi-experimentation* (Chicago: Rand McNally, 1979).

A wide variety of experimental and quasi-experimental designs is described in Delbert C. Miller and Neil J. Salkind, *Handbook of Research Design and Social Measurement,* 6th ed. (Thousand Oaks, CA: Sage, 2002). Many applications of experimental designs in political science can be found in Donald R. Kinder and Thomas R. Palfrey, *Experimental Foundations of Political Science* (Ann Arbor: University of Michigan Press, 1993). Examples of field experiments comparing the effectiveness of voter mobilization by mail, e-mail, phone, and door-to-door canvassing are contained in Donald P. Green and Alan S. Gerber, *Get Out the Vote! How to Increase Voter Turnout* (Washington, DC: Brookings Institution Press, 2004).

A memorable and concise statement of the characteristics and purpose of a research design is offered by David Nachmias in *Public Policy Evaluation* (New York: St. Martin's Press, 1979). Richard L. Solomon contributed two of the most important and frequently used experimental designs in "Extension of Control Group Design," *Psychological Bulletin,* 46 (January 1949), pp. 137–150. Donald T. Campbell offers a detailed list of threats to research validity in "Reforms as Experiments," *American Psychologist,* 24 (April 1969), pp. 407–29.

Documenting his research, which convinced many participants that they had physically harmed other people or even killed them, Stanley Milgram wrote *Obedience to Authority: An Experimental View* (New York: Harper & Row, 1983, 1974). The 1971 Stanford Prison Experiment, which explored people's situational and group behavior in detention settings, is described at www.prisonexp.org.

Research Exercises

1. Refer to the example of Operation Fright, used early in the chapter, and state one additional, plausible alternative explanation of why so few of those going through the program are subsequently arrested. Explain in detail what modifications of the original research design described in that example would be needed to evaluate the accuracy of this hypothesized explanation.

2. You are studying the relationship between inequality in the distribution of wealth and internal political violence in the nations of the world. You have operationalized inequality as the difference in the proportion of national income that goes to the top 20 percent of income earners and the proportion that goes to the bottom 20 percent of income earners. Political violence is operationalized as the number of incidents of politically motivated violence reported by the domestic press each year in each nation. Your operating hypothesis is: *The greater the inequality in the distribution of income, the larger the number of incidents of political violence.*

  List at least three hypotheses that represent rivals to this operating hypothesis. For each alternative you suggest, list each variable you will have to control in order to be able to rule it out as a valid explanation of observed events.

3. You want to evaluate the effects of a film about race relations on the levels of racial prejudice held by the film's viewers. Assume that you can select subjects from a pool of 300 college students who have volunteered to take part in scientific experiments. Describe the research design you would use to determine the film's effects on racial prejudice if you wanted to maximize your confidence in the validity of your results.

Key Terms

research design
exploratory research
descriptive research
explanatory research
observation point
control
subjects
experimental design
experimental group
stimulus
control group
pretest
posttest
test effect

Solomon two-control-group research design
Solomon three-control-group research design
precision matching
frequency distribution control
randomization
field experiments
nonexperimental designs
quasi-experimental designs
ex post facto experiment
time-series designs
regression toward the mean
controlled time-series designs
internal validity
external validity

CHAPTER 7

Who, What, Where, When: The Problem of Sampling

- What is a sample?
- What constitutes a representative sample?
- How is a representative sample selected?
- How many cases must be selected before a sample is representative?

Once every ten years, the Census Bureau, a part of the U.S. Department of Commerce, conducts a census in an attempt to identify, count, and measure certain characteristics of every individual living in the country at a given time. In the 2000 census, it is estimated that the federal government employed 970,000 clerks, interviewers, and others over a period of five months to obtain the information. In all, approximately 283,000,000 residents of the United States were located and studied. Over the ten-year cycle, the total cost of the 2000 count was approximately $6.5 billion.

Needless to say, few political scientists are able to marshal such vast resources in pursuing their own research interests. Yet the objects of those interests may be, for all practical purposes, equally numerous: 100,000,000 voters, 500,000,000 residents of Western democracies, 100,000 documents—each might be the focus of political science research, yet each consists of far too many individual cases to permit a comprehensive analysis. Even the Census Bureau, with all its thousands of workers and millions of dollars, found it impossible to ask every one of its questions of each person it located. Instead, it developed a short questionnaire for most people and a longer one for a *select few*. Like political scientists and many other researchers, the bureau found it necessary to employ a *sample*.

In this chapter, we examine the uses and the mechanics of sampling—of choosing a relatively small number of cases that may tell us much about the larger population from which they have been selected. In doing so, we are concerned with **generalizability**—the ability to draw general conclusions based on an analysis of only a few cases.

Defining a Representative Sample

We begin with three questions: What is a sample? When is it representative? What does it represent?

A **population** is any group of people, organizations, objects, or events about which we want to draw conclusions; a *case* is any member of such a population. We should emphasize here that populations may consist not only of people but of anything we wish to study. Thus, we may speak of a population of governments, of decisions, or of court documents as readily as of a population of unemployed males living in Massachusetts. Whenever we refer to a population of any kind, however, all identifying characteristics of that population must be stated, and all members of that population must share them.

A **sample** is any *subgroup* of a population of cases that is identified for analysis. If we want to study and reach conclusions about the decision-making behavior of state legislatures, for instance, we might do so by examining such behavior in the legislatures of Wyoming and Montana rather than in those of all fifty states, and from these we might *generalize* our findings to the larger population from which the two have been selected. If we wish to study the issue preferences of voters in, say, Pennsylvania, we might do so by asking questions of fifty mill-workers in Pittsburgh and we might generalize these results to all voters in the state. Similarly, if we wish to measure the intelligence of college students, we might test all defensive linemen enrolled at Ohio State University during a given football season and then generalize our findings to all U.S. college students. In each instance, our procedure is to identify a subgroup of a larger population; to study that subgroup, or sample, in some detail; and to generalize our results to the population as a whole. These are the basic steps involved in sampling.

It should be quite obvious, however, that each of these samples has a fundamental weakness. Although the legislatures of Wyoming and Montana are, for example, indeed part of the population of state legislatures, they are, for reasons of history, region, and political culture, quite likely to operate in a manner very similar to one another and very different from the legislatures of such diverse states as New York and Texas. Although the fifty mill-workers in Pittsburgh may indeed be Pennsylvania voters, they are, for reasons of socioeconomic status, education, and life experience, quite likely to have different views from those of many other such voters. And in like manner, although Ohio State's football players are indeed college students, they are, for a variety of reasons, likely to be different from other college students. In other words, even though each of these subgroups is, in fact, a sample, the members of each are systematically different from most other members of the population from which they are drawn. As a group, none of these is typical of the distribution of attributes (opinions, behaviors, characteristics) in the larger population with which it is associated. Accordingly, political scientists would say that none of these samples is *representative*.

A **representative sample** is one in which every major attribute of the larger population from which the sample is drawn is present in roughly the proportion or frequency with which those attributes occur in that larger population. Thus, if 50 percent of all state legislatures meet only once every two years, roughly half the bodies in a representative sample of state legislatures should be of this variety. If 30 percent of the voters in Pennsylvania are blue-collar workers, then about 30 percent of a representative sample of those voters should be blue-collar workers. And if 2 percent of all college students are athletes, roughly the same proportion of a representative sample of college students should be athletes.

In other words, a truly representative sample is a microcosm—a smaller, but accurate, model—of the larger population from which it is taken. To the extent that a sample is truly representative, conclusions based on a study of that sample may be

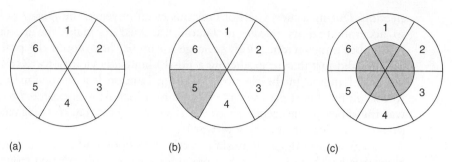

Figure 7.1
Sampling from a population with six population types

safely regarded as applying to the original population. This extension of findings is what we mean by *generalizability*.

An Example   Suppose we want to study patterns of membership in political groups among adults in the United States. Figure 7.1 shows three circles, each of which has been divided into six equal segments. Figure 7.l(a) represents the population in question. Members of the population have been classified according to the number of political groups (such as parties and interest groups) they belong to. In the example, every adult is assumed to belong to at least one and not more than six groups, and these six levels of membership are equally distributed throughout the population. Suppose that we wish to study people's motivations for membership, choices of groups, and patterns of participation, but because of limited resources, we are able to examine only one of every six members of the population. Which individuals should we select for analysis?

The shaded area in Figure 7.l(b) illustrates one possible sample of the size we have specified, but one that is clearly atypical of the population. Were we to generalize from such a sample, we would conclude (1) that all American adults belong to five political groups and (2) that all group-related behavior of Americans is like that of those who belong to precisely five groups. Yet we know that the first conclusion is not accurate, and we may hold suspect the validity of the second as well. The sample illustrated in Figure 7.l(b), then, is not representative, because it does not reflect the distribution of this *population attribute* (often called a **parameter**) roughly in proportion to its actual incidence. Such a sample is said to be *biased toward* members of five groups or *biased against* all other patterns of group membership. Reliance upon such a biased sample will usually lead us to draw erroneous conclusions about the larger population.

The *Literary Digest* Fiasco   The potential problems of biased samples were clearly illustrated in a public opinion polling disaster that befell a magazine called the *Literary Digest* in the 1930s. The *Literary Digest* was a periodical compilation of newspaper editorials and other opinion pieces that enjoyed a wide readership in the early years of this century. Beginning in 1920, the magazine conducted a large-scale, nationwide straw poll in which postcard ballots were sent to more than a million persons asking them to state their candidate preference in the coming presidential election. During a succession of previous election years, the *Digest* poll had proved so accurate that its release in October seemed to make the actual election in November anticlimactic. With so large a sample, how could the poll miss? Yet in 1936, it did just that in predicting a 60–40 landslide victory for Republican candidate Alf Landon. In the election, however, Landon lost to incumbent Franklin D. Roosevelt by almost precisely the margin by which he was expected to win. So great was the shock to the credibility of the *Literary Digest* that the magazine was forced to cease publication shortly afterward.

What went wrong? Quite simply, the *Digest* poll had used a biased sample. The postcards had been issued to persons whose names were drawn from two sources: telephone directories and automobile registration lists. And whereas this method of selection hadn't made much difference earlier, it did in the Depression year of 1936, when less affluent voters—those most likely to support Roosevelt—could not afford telephones, let alone automobiles. In effect, then, the sample used by the *Digest* poll was biased toward those most likely to be Republicans.

Avoiding Bias   Returning to our illustration, compare the sample in Figure 7.l(b) with that in Figure 7.l(c). In the latter, one-sixth of the population is again selected for analysis, but each of the major population types is present in the sample in the same proportion in which it is present in the entire population. Such a sample tells us that one in six American adults belongs to one political group, one in six to two, and so forth. It will also permit us to recognize other differences among members of our sample that might correspond with their varying numbers of affiliations. The sample illustrated in Figure 7.l(c), then, is a representative sample of the population in question.

This example is, of course, simplified in at least two very important ways. First, most of the populations that political scientists wish to study are more diverse than the one in the illustration. People, documents, governments, organizations, decisions, and the like differ from one another on many more than just one attribute. Thus, a representative sample must be one that provides for *each* of the principal areas of difference to be represented in proportion to its share of the population. Second, more often than not the true distribution of the variables or attributes we wish to measure is not known in advance; it may not have been measured previously by a census of the population. Thus, a representative sample must be drawn in such a way that we have confidence in its ability to reflect accurately this distribution even under circumstances when we cannot directly assess its validity. A sampling procedure must have an internal logic that assures us that if we *were* able to check the sample against a census, the sample would prove to be representative.

In order to provide both the capability to reflect accurately the complexities of a given population and some measure of confidence in their procedures for doing so, researchers draw upon certain techniques developed by statisticians. They do so in two ways. First, they follow certain rules in deciding which specific cases to study, meaning, which to include in a particular sample. Second, they follow still other rules in deciding how many such cases to select. Though we do not examine these various rules in detail here, we do consider their practical implications for political science research. Let us begin by looking at strategies for selecting the cases that make up a representative sample.

Procedures for Selecting a Representative Sample

As we can see from the examples in the preceding section, not all samples are equally representative. Straw polls, in which individuals select themselves as participants and may vote for a favored position or candidate more than once; street corner interviews, in which selection of location and lack of control over passers-by may strongly influence the findings; legislators' questionnaires, the results of which depend heavily on the views of the more articulate and more politically interested few who are most likely to respond; analysis of the foreign press, of propaganda messages, or of some variety of published materials that is restricted to sources available in English, which may be systematically different from other sources of the same type; and blind sampling, in which a researcher simply leaves a stack of questionnaires at a given location with instructions for their completion and surrenders all control over the selection of respondents, all provide common examples of sampling bias. In part, these difficulties may be resolved by a careful definition of the population to which we intend to generalize. In the case of street corner interviews, for instance, we might want to generalize only to all persons passing a particular location between 10 A.M. and 11:15 A.M. on March 4. But in far larger measure, these difficulties may be resolved only by developing a systematic and relatively more sophisticated procedure for selecting the cases to be analyzed.

Random Samples   The guiding principle underlying such a procedure is that of *randomization*. A sample is said to be a **random sample** (sometimes referred to as *simple random sample*) if two conditions are met. First, the sample must be chosen in such a manner that each and every individual or case in the entire population has an equal opportunity to be selected for analysis. Second, the sample must be chosen in such a manner that each and every possible combination of n cases, where n is simply the number of cases in the sample, has an equal opportunity to be selected for analysis.

It sounds a bit complicated and is in fact a more rigorous definition of randomness than we use in everyday conversation, but it is at heart a rather simple and straightforward notion. Random selection amounts to little more than selection by lottery. If we have a population of 1,000 persons whose behavior we wish to examine by studying a representative sample of 100, we might write the names of all 1,000 members of the population on equal-sized pieces of paper, place them in a hopper, mix them well, and draw the names of the 100 persons in our sample. Through such a procedure, each individual has an equal chance of being selected (100 chances in 1,000, or 1 chance in 10), and every possible combination of 100 individuals has an equal chance of selection as well. It is this dual equality that makes the sample a random one.

Often, random samples are employed in studying populations that are too large to permit such a physical lottery procedure. Writing out the names of several hundred thousand cases, entering them in a hopper, and drawing out several thousand, after all, would be a very cumbersome process. In these instances, an alternative, but equally valid, approach is employed. Each case in the population is assigned a number. The numbers of the particular cases to be included in the sample are then

10097	32533	76520
37542	04805	64894
08422	68953	19645
99019	02529	09376
12807	99970	80157

Figure 7.2
Portion of a random number table

identified using a *random number table,* such as Table A.1 in Appendix A, a portion of which is reproduced in Figure 7.2. The arrangement of numbers in such tables is usually created by a computer program called a *random number generator,* which, in effect, places a great many numbers in a hopper, draws them randomly, and prints them in the order in which they were drawn. In other words, the lottery process still takes place, but the computer, using numbers rather than names, conducts an all-purpose drawing. We are able to make use of this drawing simply by numbering each of our cases.

A random number table such as that illustrated in Figure 7.2 may be used in several different ways, each of which involves the combination of three decisions. First, we must decide how many digits we shall use; second, we must develop a decision rule for using them; and third, we must select a starting point and a system for proceeding through the table.

The first decision is simply a function of the number of cases in our population. If the population consists of fewer than 10 cases, we use single digits; 10 to 99 cases, double digits; 100 to 999 cases, three-digit combinations; and so forth. In each instance, we must take care to allow each of our numbered cases a chance to be selected.

Once this has been accomplished, we must devise a rule to relate the numbers in the table to the numbers of our cases. Two choices are available here. The easiest and most straightforward approach, though not necessarily the most correct, is to use only those numbers that fall within the range of our number of cases. Thus, if we have a population of 250 and choose to begin at the top left of the table and work down each column, we will include in our sample those cases numbered, say, 100, 084, and 128, and we will ignore cases numbered, say, 375 and 990, neither of which corresponds to any of our cases. We will continue this procedure until we have identified the number of cases needed for our sample.

A more cumbersome, but technically more correct, procedure arises from the argument that *every* number of a given magnitude (for example, every three-digit number) in the table must be used to preserve the underlying randomness of the table. Following this logic, and again assuming a population of 250, we must break the range of three-digit numbers from 000 to 999 into 250 equal parts. Because there are 1,000 such numbers, we divide 1,000 by 250 and find that each equal part comprises four numbers. Thus table entries 000 to 003 correspond to case 1, entries 004 to 007 to case 2, and so forth. In order to identify the case number that corresponds to an entry in the table, then, we divide a three-digit table entry by 4 and round to the lower integer. When we use this method, the same portion of the table that we used earlier leads us to include in our sample cases 025 (100 ÷ 4), 093 (375 ÷ 4, rounded down), 021 (084 ÷ 4), 247 (990 ÷ 4, rounded down), and 032 (128 ÷ 4) and to ignore none of the entries in the table.

Finally, we must select a point of entry into the table and a system of use. The point of entry might be the upper left-hand corner (as in the previous example), the lower right-hand corner, the left end of the second row, or *any* other location. This decision is strictly arbitrary. Once in the table, however, we must proceed systematically. We might select the first three digits of each five-digit set, as in the previous examples; the middle three digits; the last three digits; or even the first, second, and fourth digits. (In the first five-digit set, these various procedures yield, respectively, the numbers 100, 009, 097, and 109.) We might work these procedures backward getting 790, 900, 001, and 791. We might work across rows, taking each digit in turn and ignoring the groupings of five (getting 100, 973, 253, 376, and 520 for the first row). The possibilities are many and varied, and each is equally appropriate. Once we have decided upon a pattern of use, however, we must follow it systematically so as to maximize the randomness of the entries in the table.

Variations on Random Sampling

As you can see from even this brief discussion, the drawing of a simple random sample may be no simple matter. In addition to other problems, which we will discuss, the technique involves a great deal of clerical work, especially when it is employed on a large scale. For this reason, random sampling procedures are often modified to enhance their manageability.

Systematic Random Samples   One common variation is called the **systematic random sample** and is used when we wish to study a relatively large population whose members are individually listed in some central location, such as a telephone book, a student directory, a list of registered voters, an index or a table of contents, an agenda, or a membership roster. The procedure is as follows:

Count (or estimate) the number of cases in the population, and divide this by the desired number of cases in the sample. If we label the result k, we are saying, in effect, that we wish to select one case out of every k, or to put it another way, we wish to select every kth case. A concrete example should help to make this clear. Suppose that from a population of 10,000 public statements issued by the Department of Defense we wish to draw a sample of 500, and suppose further that we have a chronological listing that includes all 10,000 documents. To select a systematic random sample:

1. We divide the number of cases in the population by the desired sample size to determine k (in this case, $k = 10,000 + 500 = 20$).
2. With the assistance of a random number table, we select a case number in the range 1 to k (in the example, 1 to 20) to be included in our sample.
3. We proceed through the listing of documents, selecting every kth (20th) case.

Thus, if k is equal to 20 and we use the portion of the random number table illustrated in Figure 7.2, entering at the top left, seeking two-digit numbers (k here lies between 10 and 99), and using only table entries that correspond to actual case numbers (that is, only those in the range from 01 to 20), the first case selected will be 10. We then include in our sample cases 10, 30 (10 + k), 50 (10 + 2k), 70 (10 + 3k), and so forth, all the way up to case 9,990 (10 + 499k). This upper limit of the sample may be stated generally as $j + (n - 1)k$, where j is the randomly drawn first selection and n is the desired sample size. In this way, we can use the random number table in combination with a centralized list to select a sample of 500 documents for analysis.

The technique of systematic random sampling has one major advantage over simple random sampling—ease of application to large populations that meet the criterion of central listing—and it has many potential uses. Still, we must keep in mind that systematic random sampling is less random than is a straight lottery selection, and it may therefore yield a less representative subgroup. We can see this at both the definitional and operational levels.

To begin with, recall that a random sample is one that permits every individual case *and* every possible combination of n cases an equal opportunity of selection. Systematic random sampling meets only one of these criteria. Because we begin to draw such a sample by using a random number table to select the first case, any case in the population has an equal chance of ultimately being included in the sample (though not necessarily on the first draw, because this is limited to the range 1 to k). However, because we then select only additional cases that are k numbers apart from one another, not every possible combination is allowed.

Thus, in the example where $k = 20$, we may select any case from 1 to 20 to begin with, but once we select case 10, it becomes impossible for us to include, say, cases 9, 14, 237, and 5,724, simply because those cases do not differ from 10 by a multiple of k. A systematic random sample is at best, then, only an approximation of a truly random sample.

Systematic Bias   This observation becomes especially important when the list from which we are sampling contains a **systematic bias**. In alphabetical or chronological lists, this is generally not a problem, but in other kinds of lists it may be a significant one. Let us say, for example, that as part of a study of political socialization, we wish to measure the intelligence level of a sample of students at a particular school where every class consists of 20 children. The school contains 100 classes, or 2,000 students in all. In response to our request, the principal of the school provides us with a roster of all students in the school, from which we hope to draw a systematic random sample of 100. However, rather than an alphabetical listing, the roster consists of a compilation of individual class rolls listed one after another. Moreover, each class roll is arranged not alphabetically but in order of the students' class standing, with the best students listed first and the lists continuing in order of decreasing accomplishment. In such a circumstance, if we take every 20th (2,000 ÷ 100) case beginning from a randomly drawn case 1, we will have a sample of only the 100 best (and, possibly, most intelligent) students in the school. If we randomly select case 10, we will sample only the middle range of students. And if we begin from case 20, we will sample only the worst students in the school.

In other words, an underlying bias in the list upon which our sample is based will lead to the selection of an unrepresentative sample. Ultimately, this will either preclude our generalizing to the larger population or, if the problem escapes our notice, will result in our drawing potentially incorrect conclusions. Although this particular example is an extreme one developed for the purpose of illustration, similarly biased lists do exist, and the researcher who employs systematic random sampling procedures must be aware of the potential danger.

Random samples, then, are an ideal to which we aspire, and systematic random samples are approximations of that ideal that are often quite useful. Very often, however, a research situation does not readily lend itself to either technique. This is particularly true in the case of survey research. For one thing, centralized lists of the population to be studied are frequently nonexistent (for example, there exists no list of all U.S. voters or of all residents of a particular city), and even the number—not to mention the identity—of all the cases may not be known in advance. Thus, one of the major preconditions for simple or systematic random sampling—the existence of individual cases that can be identified in advance—may not be met. Moreover, even when this problem can be overcome, logistical difficulties and limited resources may render either of these sampling techniques impractical. This is true because random selection of individual cases requires that *specific individuals,* who may live great distances from one another or who may be very difficult to contact, *must be included in the sample.* In a strictly random process, no substitutions are permissible. These considerations can lead to massive diseconomies of time and money that might even be so great as to preclude conducting the study at all.

Cluster or Multistage Random Area Samples   Fortunately, an alternative technique has been developed that preserves the quality of randomness we desire but overcomes most of the objections we have just noted. This technique, termed either **cluster sampling** or **multistage random area sampling,** has found wide application in survey research and may, by analogy, be applied elsewhere as well. The idea behind multistage random area sampling is that rather than identifying members of a sample as individuals, we identify them as residents of particular housing units. The reasoning here is that people move from place to place, whereas housing units remain fixed. In addition, the location of virtually every housing unit in the country is known and has been mapped, and each is part of a variety of geographically distinct areas including, among others, blocks, census tracts, precincts, legislative districts, cities, townships, counties, congressional districts, and states.

We shall see that certain of these area types have characteristics that aid greatly in drawing a representative sample. For the moment, however, the point is that by focusing on the resident of a housing unit, a unit that is always in the same place, rather than on a particular individual, who may be more mobile, we are able to stabilize and localize our sampling procedure. In effect, we are simply redefining our population. Rather than speaking of all persons living in the United States, we speak of all residents of housing units in the United States. Because both groups are, for all practical purposes, the same, however, we may sample the latter and generalize to the former. We avail ourselves of the much simpler and, for reasons to be discussed later, much less expensive technique of sampling locations, yet we are able to generalize not to places, but to the people who inhabit them. This is the principal value of multistage random area sampling.

The procedure itself is illustrated in Figure 7.3. For the purpose of illustration, let us assume that we wish to conduct a nationwide sample survey. The same procedures that we set forth here may, of course, be modified for use on smaller-scale projects.

The Multistage Process   We begin with a map of the United States, which we divide into a large number of equally populated areas (also called primary sampling units, or PSUs). It is less work than it sounds like, because the government has already made this division (or at least approximated it) in the form of 435 congressional districts, each populated with somewhat more than half a million people. We assign a number between 1 and 435 to each such district and, using a random number table, select several congressional districts for analysis. The exact number to be selected is a function of both the ultimate size of the sample to be drawn and the available resources, but in general, the more districts we select, the better the sample.

At this point, the principal cost saving of the multistage random area technique becomes apparent, for rather than having to track down respondents all over the country, we may focus our attention (and money) on a relative few areas most of which are of manageable size.

Once the subject congressional districts have been identified, each is further divided into still smaller but equally populated areas. In many instances, these may correspond to political boundaries, such as precincts or electoral districts, while in others we may find it necessary to create our own divisions. In any event, once these areas have been identified, one or more (depending again on sample size) are randomly selected within each congressional district by the random selection procedures we have outlined. These precincts or other areas are then further divided, first into census tracts, then into blocks, and finally into dwelling units (houses and individual apartments), with the random selection process employed at each stage of selection. In the end, we shall have identified a number of individual dwelling units that should correspond roughly to our desired sample size. The residents of these dwelling units will become the subjects of the research.

There is, however, one additional complication. Although we generally wish for a number of reasons to interview only one person at a given address, more than one person is likely to reside in any particular dwelling unit. Which one do we interview? Most researchers who use sampling procedures of this type provide their interviewers with a series of decision rules to apply at this point, the net effect of which is to create a set of quotas based on the age, sex, and/or family standing of the respondent. In one home, the interviewer might be instructed to seek out the youngest adult male, in another the oldest adult female, and so forth.

We can see, then, that the term *multistage random area sampling* is truly descriptive. At each of several stages, equally populated areas are selected at random until, ultimately, individual dwelling units have been identified. In each instance, the geographic location is the subject of the sampling procedure, and at each stage, several clusters of locations are identified (hence the alternative term, *cluster sampling*). Only in the final stage—identifying specific respondents—does the procedure diverge from the principle of randomness, but at so local a level, and with the use of such carefully constructed quotas, that the effects on the representativeness of the sample are probably minimal. In many instances, multistage random area sampling offers a reasonable approximation of a truly random sample at a lower cost in time and resources.

Figure 7.3
Steps in multistage random area sampling

Source: *Interviewer's Manual: Survey Research Center.* Ann Arbor, MI: Institute for Social Research, University of Michigan, 1969, p. 8–2. Reprinted by permission.

Stratified Samples   We should mention one other technique, though it is less a selection procedure than a strategy. This technique is known as **stratified sampling** and is used primarily when we wish to study in detail a population subgroup that is so small that a random sample will include too few members of that subgroup to permit detailed analysis.

Suppose, for example, we wish to study the hypothesis that presidents are more open with the news media during the first two months of their administration (often termed a "honeymoon" period) than at all later times and that we wish to test the hypothesis by analyzing the content of the transcripts of presidential news conferences. Suppose further that we are able to identify 500 such transcripts for a given period, of which only 25 (or 1 in 20) are news conferences from the honeymoon period, and that we wish to sample 100 of these conferences. If we use either a simple or a systematic random sample in this instance, we might expect that sample to include approximately 5 honeymoon-period transcripts and approximately 95 post-honeymoon transcripts. The very small number of the former makes a meaningful comparison very difficult, because it may provide too few examples to reflect accurately the range of presidential responses to reporters' questions.

Under such circumstances, when we wish to enhance the importance of a particular subgroup, we may choose to *stratify* our sample. In doing so, we choose not one but *two separate samples*. The first is a simple or systematic random sample of the smaller subgroup (transcripts from the honeymoon period) and is *larger* than the expected frequency of occurrence of the subgroup in the original sample (here, perhaps 15 rather than 5 cases). The second is a simple or systematic random sample of the larger subgroup (transcripts from all subsequent periods) and is *smaller* than its expected frequency of occurrence in the original sample (here, perhaps 85 rather than 95 cases). In the example, our sample can be described as stratified according to the date of the news conference. The effect is to provide us with relatively more cases of honeymoon-period transcripts for analysis and comparison with those from later periods than we would otherwise select.

Three observations should be made at this point. First, stratification is not a substitute for simple random sampling or some other form of sampling, but an additional step to be used under particular circumstances. In effect, it is a second-order sampling procedure. In this context, stratification is frequently used, particularly by public opinion pollsters, at the late stages of a sample in order to ensure an appropriate balance of, for example, men and women. It is thus similar in purpose to the quotas that are applied in the final stage of a multistage random area sample.

Second, because it requires the drawing of separate samples, stratification may be used only when we are able to identify the relevant subpopulations *in advance*. In our example, this is not a source of difficulty, because before sampling, we can easily distinguish the honeymoon-period transcripts from those of later periods. In much survey research, however, when we may wish to stratify along less evident variables, we can encounter serious problems.

Third, because stratified sampling uses separate samples and because one can generalize from a sample only to the particular population (or subpopulation) from which it is drawn, we must exercise great care in stating our conclusions from a study based on such a sample. The reason for this is quite clear. In stratifying to increase the number of cases of a particular type in our study, we are in effect biasing our total sample in the direction of those cases. To overcome that bias, we must state our conclusions in one of only two ways. First, we may compare with one another our findings for the groups by which we have stratified (for example, we can compare our findings for honeymoon-period conferences with those for conferences from later periods). Here we are simply comparing the results of separate samples without drawing any conclusions about news conferences as a whole. Second, we may differentially weight the groups by which we have stratified in proportion to their overall share of the population and then draw general conclusions about the population. In this case, we are taking advantage of our detailed knowledge about the smaller subgroup (honeymoon-period conferences) but are reducing its importance vis-à-vis the population of all news conferences. Under the latter procedure, a stratified sample may be used to approximate a simple random sample while providing more complete information.

Quota and Judgmental Samples   On occasion, we may find it helpful to select other kinds of samples. One such is the **quota sample,** in which the members of a population are classified according to several relevant characteristics (such as sex, age, or party identification) and individuals displaying these traits are selected in proportion to their share of the population. Another is the **judgmental sample,** in which the observer simply picks out those individual cases believed for some reason to be *typical* or representative of the population from which they are drawn. This is most common in studies of small populations and when only a very small sample can be drawn from a large population. It must be remembered, however, that such samples are in general less likely to be truly representative of their corresponding populations and are therefore usually less desirable.

Determining Appropriate Sample Size

Having defined our terms and considered our selection procedures, we are now left with the question of how many cases to sample. In many ways, an answer to that question draws upon some sophisticated statistical concepts that lie beyond the scope of this text. However, much of the rationale underlying the determination of an appropriate sample size is more readily understood and is worth some attention before we proceed.

Homogeneity   Several factors help us to determine an appropriate sample size. One of the most important of these is **homogeneity,** the degree to which the members of a given population are like one another with regard to the characteristics we are interested in studying. If every individual in a population is *exactly like* every other individual, then by sampling only one individual we can obtain a truly representative sample. If, on the other hand, every individual in the population is *completely unlike* every other individual, we will be required to conduct a census of the entire population before we can claim to have a representative group. In the first instance, the population is described as completely *homogeneous;* in the second, as completely *heterogeneous.* In reality, of course, most populations lie between the two extremes.

The closer a particular population is to homogeneity—that is, the fewer the differences among its members—the smaller the sample required to represent it.

Conversely, the closer a particular population is to heterogeneity—that is, the more diverse its members are—the larger the sample required to represent it. This has implications in particular for stratified sampling, because by the very act of stratification, we create subgroups that are more homogeneous than the overall population. We can thus use smaller samples within strata than we could for the overall population without a loss of representativeness.

Number of Categories   Similarly, the more categories (variables and response options) we wish to study, the larger the sample must be. This is true because increasing the variety and sensitivity of our measures will tend to accentuate the heterogeneity of the population we are studying. In other words, the more questions we ask or the more types of answers we allow, the more likely we will be to find differences among our subjects. The more differences we examine among our subjects, the more subjects we must examine to claim a representative sample.

Sampling Error   Another important consideration is the degree of accuracy we require. We use a sample to *estimate* the characteristics of a larger population, but any estimate is likely to include some margin of error. How much of this **sampling error** are we willing to tolerate? The answer is often determined by how we intend to use our results. If we are public opinion pollsters being paid to predict the outcome of a close election, we might be unwilling to accept more than the slightest margin of error. If we are political researchers attempting to spot general trends in attitudes or behaviors, we might tolerate considerably more. In general, the more accuracy we want, the larger our sample must be.

Related to this is a second question, that of just how confident we are that our estimates of the margin of error are correct. Most samples of a given size taken from the same population are very similar to one another and to the population itself, but once in a while a sample is drawn that happens, by chance, to be different. A sample of college graduates, for example, might be far out of proportion to that group's true share of the original population. Thus, while each sample provides us with an estimate of the characteristics of a population, such estimates differ somewhat from one another and from the population as a whole because no two samples are *exactly* alike.

The problem is that in the real world, we do not always know the underlying population parameters our sample is intended to estimate, and we do not draw a great many samples. We draw only one. And though we may be able to check the face validity of our sample by comparing it with those used in other studies of the same or a similar population, *we cannot know for sure* that the sample we have drawn is not the odd one out—an unlikely yet possible unrepresentative sample. We know from a study of statistics, however, that we may reduce the likelihood that ours is the bad apple in the barrel by increasing the size of our sample. The more cases we include, the more likely we are to have a truly representative sample—one that does in fact fall within the error range we have specified.

Confidence Interval   We can make this discussion less abstract by considering the summary of sample sizes presented in Table 7.1 (based on Table A.2 and A.3 in Appendix A). The table lists appropriate *minimum* sample sizes for several levels of

Table 7.1
Summary of sample sizes

Percentage Sampling Error Tolerated	Level of Confidence .95	Level of Confidence .99[*]
1	10,000	22,500
2	2,500	5,625
3	1,111	2,500
4	625	1,406
5	400	900
10	100	—

[*] Rounded down from .997 in the source table for purposes of explanation.

sampling error and confidence for a *random sample* of a relatively heterogeneous population of more than 100,000 cases.

The table may be used in either of two ways. First, we may wish to specify the particular level of sampling error we are willing to tolerate and the confidence level at which we shall operate. Suppose that these figures are 64 percent and .99, respectively.

The first tells us that any measurement of our sample we might make is within 4 percentage points above or below the true distribution of the same attribute in the larger population. This range is referred to as a **confidence interval**. If, for example, we find that 43 percent of our respondents in a survey report identifying with the Democratic party, we will assume that a full census of the population would show the true percentage of Democratic identifiers to be 43 percent ±4 percent, or somewhere in the range from 39 percent to 47 percent. The table tells us (if we read across at 64 percent and down at .99) that to achieve that degree of accuracy with 99 percent confidence, we must select a sample of at least 1,406 cases. If we wish to narrow the margin of error (increase our accuracy) to, say, 62 percent (that is, to refine our estimate to the range from 41 percent to 45 percent Democrats), we have to increase our sample size to at least 5,625 cases. At both levels of confidence, the table clearly demonstrates that increased accuracy requires an enlarged sample.

Confidence Level   The second number that we began with refers to the likelihood that our sample is in fact representative of the larger population within the degree of accuracy we have specified and is called the **confidence level**. In this context, .95 (95 percent confidence) means that out of 100 samples of a given size that are drawn from the same population, 95 will meet this test for accuracy, and .99 (99 percent confidence) means that 99 out of 100 samples of a given size drawn from the same population will be as accurate as claimed. The chances that any particular sample will achieve the desired accuracy, then, are 95 to 5 and 99 to 1, respectively.

As one might expect, for each level of sampling error the sample size required to attain 99 percent confidence is substantially larger than that for 95 percent confidence. Looking again at our Democrats with a margin of error of 64 percent, for instance, we find that a sample of 625 cases allows us to say with 95 percent confidence that somewhere between 39 percent and 47 percent of the whole population are Democrats, whereas a sample of at least 1,406 cases is required before we can make the same statement with 99 percent confidence. In general, the lower the percentage of sampling error and the greater the level of confidence, the better a piece of research will be. By convention, a level of confidence of either .95 or .99 is judged to be acceptable in political science research.

We may also use this type of table in a reverse manner. If, for example, we encounter a study that employs a sample of 2,500 cases, we may consult the table to ascertain the corresponding sampling error and level of confidence. A glance at Table 7.1 shows that multiple interpretations are possible. We may interpret 2,500 cases to yield a sampling error of 63 percent at the .99 level of confidence, or alternatively, to yield a sampling error of 62 percent at the .95 level of confidence. Either interpretation is equally appropriate, and the two together help to make clear the tradeoff between accuracy and confidence. With the same number of cases we may be extremely confident of a relatively less precise result or somewhat less confident of a higher order of precision.

Ideally, of course, we always prefer to operate with minimum error and maximum confidence. Unfortunately, practical considerations frequently intervene. A single personal interview in a survey project, for example, may cost as much as $50 or more in labor, transportation, and other expenses. This means that at the .99 level of confidence, the cost of reducing our margin of error from 63 percent to 62 percent may be more than $130,000. In many instances, the difference in the quality of the results is not worth the added expense, and in far more instances, the money is simply not available. Limits on resources thus play an important role in limiting the size of samples. Most national public opinion polls, as well as major political science survey research projects, use samples of approximately 1,200 to 1,600 respondents. Such studies yield results to within 3 to 5 percent accuracy at the .99 level of confidence and are regarded as both affordable and sufficiently precise.

One other point should be noted before we conclude our discussion of sample size, though it is, no doubt, less obvious and less intuitively appealing than others we have raised. As an examination of Tables A.2 and A.3 in Appendix A makes clear, once it reaches a certain limiting point, the size of a population *does not* affect the size of the sample chosen to represent it. And though the proof of this assertion is beyond the scope of this book, its implications are not. In effect this upper limit on sample sizes means that very nearly the same size sample may be equally representative of the population of Roanoke, Virginia; of New York City; of the United States; or of the entire Western Hemisphere, so long as that sample is properly drawn. Only for relatively smaller populations is population size a significant factor in determining sample size.

Conclusion

An important point that is often overlooked by the novice political researcher is that *any* time you gather data by *any* method from *any* source, if you wish to generalize at all beyond the particular cases examined in the research, then the data set constitutes a *sample* and its constituent cases should be selected with an eye toward the considerations raised in this chapter. Whether the subject of the research is elections, political advertisements, news accounts, political jurisdictions, organizations, or anything else, you must be aware of the importance of the selection process and its implications for the meaning and usefulness of your research.

Summary Points

• A sample is any subgroup of a population of cases that is identified for analysis.
• A representative sample is one in which every major attribute of the larger population from which the sample is drawn is present in roughly the proportion or frequency with which those attributes occur in that larger population.
• Representative samples are based on random sampling procedures, which ensure that (1) each individual or case in the population has an equal chance to be selected, and (2) each possible combination of individuals or cases has an equal chance to be selected.
• Sample size depends on the homogeneity of the sample, the number of categories to be analyzed, and the desired sampling error and level of confidence.

Suggested Readings and References

The statistical procedures underlying the determination of an appropriate sample size are discussed in a number of sources, which include Hubert M. Blalock, Jr., *Social Statistics,* 2nd ed. (New York: McGraw-Hill, 1979); Dennis J. Palumbo, *Statistics in Political and Behavioral Science,* 2nd ed. (New York: Columbia University Press, 1977); Sharon L. Lohr, *Sampling: Design and Analysis* (Pacific Grove, CA: Duxbury Press, 1998); Steven K. Thompson, *Sampling,* 2nd ed. (New York: Wiley-Interscience, 2002); and Paul S. Levy and Stanley Lemeshow, *Sampling of Populations: Methods and Applications,* 3rd ed. (New York: Wiley-Interscience, 1999).

   Discussions and examples of sampling procedures appear regularly in the pages of *Public Opinion Quarterly.* Several variations on sampling techniques are described, and their respective strengths and weaknesses summarized, in Delbert C. Miller and Neil J. Salkind, *Handbook of Research Design and Social Measurement,* 6th ed. (Newbury Park, CA: Sage, 2002).

Research Exercises

1. Using Tables A.2 and A.3 in Appendix A, determine the sample size needed to meet each of the following sets of criteria:

   a. 3 percent sampling error, .95 level of confidence, population of 10,000

   b. 2 percent sampling error, .95 level of confidence, population of 50,000

   c. 1 percent sampling error, .99 level of confidence, population of 2,299,999

2. Locate or construct a map of your congressional district showing all principal geographic or political subdivisions, and devise a strategy for a multistage random area sample of 1,000 persons from your congressional district. What level of confidence and sampling error will such a sample yield?

3. You are planning a study of student politics. Develop practical alternative strategies for sampling the students at your college or university, using each of the following: simple random sampling, systematic random sampling, stratified sampling (By what characteristic will you stratify? Why?); multistage area sampling; and judgmental sampling (What

criteria would you apply? Why?). Summarize the advantages and disadvantages of each approach. Which would you recommend using? Why?

Key Terms

generalizibility

population

sample

representative sample

parameter

random sample

systematic random sample

systematic bias

cluster sample

multistage random area sample

stratified sampling

quota sample

judgmental sample

homogeneity

sampling error

confidence interval

confidence level

CHAPTER 8

Survey Research

- How is a survey planned?
- How are survey questionnaires designed?
- How do we choose the appropriate survey methodology?
- How is a survey conducted?

Often the best (and sometimes the only) way to learn what people think or how they act is to ask them. Acceptance of this fact has made survey research one of the most fully developed and extensively used of social science methods. An understanding of survey research is essential to understanding a great deal of political science since 1930. This chapter provides an overview of what this method involves, when it is appropriate, and what its principal strengths and weaknesses are.

Survey research is *a method of data collection in which information is obtained directly from individual persons who are selected so as to provide a basis for making inferences about some larger population.* It is important to note that this definition excludes "surveys" not based on scientific sampling procedures. Public opinion polls and "person-in-the-street" interviews, which are based on chance samples, provide no information other than the fact that the particular individuals interviewed gave certain answers; there is no reason to believe that others would respond in similar ways.

The information collected in surveys may be obtained by direct questioning through *face-to-face* or *telephone interviews* or by having the subjects complete *mailed* or *self-administered questionnaires.* Those who answer survey questions are generally referred to as **respondents.**

Surveys provide five types of information about respondents: facts, perceptions, opinions, attitudes, and behavioral reports. *Facts* include those background characteristics (age, occupation) and personal history (place of birth, first political involvement) that may be relevant to the interpretation of the other data collected. *Perceptions* are statements of what individuals know (or think they know) about the world, such as the names of public officials or the federal government's current policy toward trade with China. *Opinions* are statements of people's preferences or judgments about events and objects. Such questions as *Do you favor legalization of marijuana?* and *Whom do you want to win the upcoming local election?* tap opinions. *Attitudes* are relatively stable evaluations of and orientations toward events, objects, and ideas. When we want to know about people's support for civil liberties or government regulation of the economy, for example, we are asking about the attitudes on which specific opinions are often based. *Behavioral reports* are simply statements of how people act (for example, how often they vote or read newspaper editorials).

In survey research, concepts are operationalized through questions, and observation consists of recording respondents' answers to these questions. The method, therefore, is especially suited for studies in which individual persons are the units of analysis and the principal concepts employed pertain to individuals. If our research involves concepts such as the average daily importation of foreign oil by the United States or the number of crimes committed with handguns each year, survey research is inappropriate, because average citizens are not likely to have the information we seek. If research focuses on the opinions, attitudes, or perceptions of individuals, a survey may well be the best method of data collection. It is, however, a very expensive and time-consuming method. Therefore, researchers should be certain that there is not some other, less expensive way of gathering the necessary data before proceeding with a survey.

Stages of the Survey Process

Having decided to use a survey as a data collection method, we must now decide what steps to go through. Survey research can be divided into fourteen basic activities. In practice more than one of these may be going on at any one time, and the researcher may, on occasion, move back and forth between activities as the survey develops. Conceptually, however, the stages of survey research can be described as follows:

1. *Conceptualizing:* Specifying the purpose of the research, developing hypotheses, clarifying concepts, and operationalizing the concepts through survey items.

2. *Survey design:* Establishing the procedures to be used and deciding on the general nature of the sample to be drawn.

3. *Instrumentation:* Drafting the questions and other items that will appear on the survey instrument (the questionnaire or interview schedule) and planning the format of that instrument, as well as designing any visual aids or other devices that will be used.

4. *Planning:* Developing methods of managing the survey and anticipating the materials and personnel that will be needed.

5. *Sampling:* Selecting the persons to be interviewed according to the method that best fits the purposes and resources of a given study.

6. *Training or briefing:* Preparing interviewers, coders, or other personnel to properly contact respondents and administer the instrument to them.

7. *Pretesting:* Administering the instrument to a small sample similar to the larger sample to be contacted so as to ensure that instructions can be correctly interpreted and that items produce the desired type of response.

8. *Surveying:* Administering the instrument (by mail, phone, or personal interview) to members of the sample.

9. *Monitoring:* Ensuring that the proper persons are being contacted as respondents both by requiring records of contacts and refusals, and by checking on the administration of instruments.

10. *Verifying:* Using follow-up contacts to make sure that interviews have actually been performed, that mailings have reached potential respondents, and that questionnaires have been returned.

11. *Coding:* Reducing to numerical terms the data collected.

12. *Processing:* Organizing the data for analysis.

13. *Analyzing:* Working the data with statistical and other tools in order to reach conclusions about their content.

14. *Reporting:* Summarizing findings into research reports.

The remainder of this chapter highlights some of the primary points the survey researcher should take into consideration when engaged in each of these activities.

Conceptualizing

In this stage, a general research question is reduced to a far more specific set of questions that can be addressed through empirical investigation. Decisions made in the conceptualizing stage have important implications for the choices that are available in sampling and survey design. For instance, in deciding to whom our theory applies, we determine what our sampling frame should be. In selecting an operationalization that requires personal interviewing, we are dictating the level of research support needed. Even when first thinking through the theoretical aspects of the project, then, we have to be sensitive to the issues of resources and accessibility of respondents.

Survey Design

Surveys are generally either exploratory, descriptive, or explanatory in purpose. *Exploratory* surveys help us acquire information that can be helpful in formulating research questions and hypotheses more precisely when we know little about a phenomenon we want to study. *Descriptive* surveys provide precise measurement of variables that may be important in theorizing but provide no basis for making causal inferences. *Explanatory* surveys test causal hypotheses and help us understand observed patterns in terms of a theory. They must be designed so as to allow us to rule out alternative rival hypotheses. Data for each type of survey can be collected through *personal interviews, mail questionnaires, telephone interviews,* or *self-administered questionnaires.* Deciding on the objective of the survey and choosing the appropriate data-collecting method are the first steps in survey design. The purpose will be dictated largely by our level of theoretical and empirical knowledge of the subject. Which data collection technique is appropriate will be determined by the operationalizations we have chosen and by the resources that are available.

Cross-Sectional Surveys   We must next select a way to organize the survey. The basic choice is between *cross-sectional* and *longitudinal* designs. In **cross-sectional surveys,** data are collected from respondents only once. If we have a representative sample, this design allows us to describe populations and relationships between variables in those populations at a given time, but it does not allow us to say how the characteristics or relationships have developed or will develop over time. Cross-sectional surveys offer a snapshot of a moving target. They are best suited to exploratory and descriptive studies, but together with a strong theory and proper data analysis, cross-sectional surveys can provide some basis for explanation. For example, in a study of the relationship between personality and political behavior, we may be willing to assume that a person's level of self-esteem is a relatively stable personality trait that precedes one's level of political involvement. If we find, then, that those with a high level of self-esteem tend to be more politically involved than those with low self-esteem, we might feel safe in arguing that high esteem leads to or causes high political involvement, even though we have data from only one time.

Longitudinal Surveys   Longitudinal surveys are those in which data are collected from respondents on more than one occasion. The main types of **longitudinal surveys** are *trend, cohort,* and *panel* studies.

In **trend studies** samples are drawn from the same population at different times and surveyed. *Different persons* may be included in each survey, but the results will be representative of trends in the *same population,* because, as was explained in Chapter 7, each properly selected sample will be equivalent to every other sample from that population. Thus, if we find different degrees of partisan identification in two samples of the same population surveyed at different times, we may infer that there has been a change in the level of partisan identification *in the population* during the time that separates the surveys. We might also explore changes in the relationship between variables through trend studies. If we find, for instance, that the relationship between gender and political activity is weaker in the second of two surveys of samples from the same population, we might conclude that there is a trend toward the breaking down of sex roles in the political life of that population.

Whereas trend studies are representative of a *general* population at different times, **cohort studies** focus on the same *specific* population over time. Members of the population sampled in trend studies will change with time, but cohort studies draw samples from the *same* population each time even though different members might be included in the samples. For example, we might want to draw a sample from among all of the Mexican citizens who legally immigrated to the United States in 2005 and sample that same group again three years later to study their adaptation to life in the United States. Though there may be some loss from this population as members die or move out of the United States, no new members will be added.

Both trend and cohort studies allow us to document change in a population over time, but because different samples are drawn for each survey, we cannot identify *which* members of the population are changing. This makes it more difficult to discover causal patterns. **Panel studies,** by contrast, use the *same sample at different times.* This allows us to see which members of a population are changing and to identify the characteristics or experiences that are associated with changes. For example, we might interview the same sample of registered voters before, during, and after an election campaign in an effort to determine what aspects of a campaign are most likely to lead people to change their choice of candidates.

This important advantage of panel studies must be weighed against some disadvantages. First, panel studies are very costly, because the expense of keeping track of sample members over time must be added to the costs of conducting several interviews. Second, there can be problems of reactivity of the type discussed in Chapter 6. The very fact that people are being interviewed, perhaps repeatedly, about a subject may cause them to alter their behavior or attitudes with regard to that subject in ways they would not were they not being interviewed. This creates a kind of test effect that can distort results. At the very least it means there is a risk that the sample will become *unrepresentative of the larger population* by virtue of being included in the study. Third, *attrition* from the sample can compromise the validity of panel studies. Attrition occurs when respondents in the first wave of surveying do not respond in subsequent waves. If those who drop out of the panel share characteristics that are relevant to the study but not shared by those who do not drop out, their withdrawal may create a highly biased sample that both distorts results and prevents generalizing to the larger population.

Despite these drawbacks, panel studies are still the strongest design for most explanatory purposes, and they often justify their expense by the additional information they yield.

Instrumentation

Whatever study design is employed, the survey researcher will have to develop a set of questions to use as tools in obtaining measures. This is an extension of the operationalization process begun in the conceptualization stage and produces a *survey instrument,* which may be either a **questionnaire,** to be filled in by the respondent, or an **interview schedule,** which guides an interviewer in a personal or telephone interview. When developing these instruments, the researcher must consider (1) the content, (2) the form, (3) the format, (4) the wording, and (5) the order of questions.

The *content* of questions determines what information can be obtained from responses to them. It is dictated by the hypothesis being tested or the question being studied. What must we know to resolve the research question, and what must we ask to obtain that information? These are the questions that should guide the choice of what to ask. It is essential to be very clear both about what information is expected from responses to each item on a survey instrument and about how that information will be used in data analysis. What will it contribute to our ability to answer the research question?

There are an infinite number of questions to be asked about almost any important subject, but survey instruments must be kept relatively short if respondents are to complete them. Personal interviews should last no longer than 45 minutes under most circumstances, and telephone interviews no longer than 20 minutes. Mail questionnaires should generally be no more than four pages long. The need for brevity, however, must be weighed against the need to obtain all the information necessary to rule out the various rival hypotheses encountered in data analysis or the need to seek explanations for unanticipated results. One way to approach this problem is to follow two general rules. First, keep the number of hypotheses being tested or research questions being addressed in a survey very limited. This will restrict the number of variables on which information is needed. Second, when selecting items for inclusion, exclude any for which there is no clear and immediate role in the anticipated data analysis.

Surveys usually contain both questions that are specific to the study and general background questions that measure characteristics that past research has shown to be strongly associated with differences in the political behavior under study. The latter items are included to allow us to rule out rival hypotheses pertaining to background characteristics and to refine our understanding of relationships by seeing how they differ in different **demographic groups.** Questions that seek information on the following characteristics are often at least *considered* for inclusion in any survey instrument:

Sex	Marital status
Age	Home ownership
Race	Household composition
Income	Party identification
Religion	National origin
Education	Length of residence
Occupation	Organizational memberships

Types of Questions   Survey questions can be either *open-ended* or *closed-ended.* **Open-ended questions** allow respondents to answer in their own words; no options are imposed on them. For example, *What do you consider to be the most important single issue in this year's local election?* is an open-ended question. Such questions have the advantage of allowing the researcher to discover unanticipated patterns in people's answers. They also prevent the researcher's selection of response options from biasing answers or concealing information. Open-ended questions have some disadvantages, however: They make comparison of respondents' answers extremely difficult, because each person may not use the same frame of reference in answering. In addition, they could encourage long or irrelevant answers, which are often difficult to analyze.

Closed-ended questions force the respondent to choose an answer from a limited number of options and have the advantages of making comparison of responses simple, allowing quick processing, and ensuring the relevance of responses. For example, *Do you consider yourself to be a conservative, a moderate, or a liberal?* is a closed-ended question. The options offered in closed-ended questions should be *exhaustive* (they should include all possible responses that might be expected) and *mutually exclusive* (they should not allow more than one choice as a response to any single question). The options should also allow respondents to express differences in the *intensity* of their response when this might be relevant. A question like *Some people feel that the federal government should sponsor free abortion clinics for low-income women. Do you agree or disagree with this position?* calls for a more complex set of choices than just agree and disagree. *Strongly agree, agree, neutral, disagree, strongly disagree,* and *no opinion* would better reflect the range of opinions people are likely to hold.

Even when they are well constructed, closed-ended questions run the risk that the researcher's choice of options may influence responses. A question like *Which of the following would you say is the most important issue facing the United States today?* assumes that the researcher can list all the issues people will consider the most important. Use of this closed-ended form may prevent our discovering something we have not anticipated about public opinion. The choice between open- and closed-ended questions must be made on the basis of both the resources that will be

100° Very warm or favorable feeling

85° Quite warm or favorable feeling

70° Fairly warm or favorable feeling

60° Slightly warm or favorable feeling

50° No feeling at all

40° Slightly cold or unfavorable feeling

30° Fairly cold or unfavorable feeling

15° Quite cold or unfavorable feeling

0° Very cold or unfavorable feeling

Figure 8.1
The feeling thermometer as a visual aid in survey research

available for data processing (open-ended requiring more) and the theoretical and empirical knowledge we have of our subject (closed-ended requiring more).

It is also important to think about how a question is presented and answered. Though the straightforward oral or written question-and-answer format is most common, a variety of other techniques is available to help respondents conceptualize choices and understand what is being asked. Many of these involve visual aids, such as charts, photographs, or cards that can be sorted into boxes. One example is the "feeling thermometer" developed at the Survey Research Center of the University of Michigan. Respondents are shown a card with a drawing like that in Figure 8.1 and asked to report how warm or cold they feel toward an object or a person by choosing a temperature reading from the thermometer. This instrument facilitates the ranking of more cases (potential presidential candidates, for example) than respondents could reasonably be expected to rank in an abstract mental exercise. The researcher simply asks about each case individually and compares thermometer readings. The more complex the mental task respondents are being asked to perform, the more useful visual aids and other variations on the question-and-answer format can be.

Question Wording Question wording is crucial to the success of a survey. Researchers can make it easier for an interviewer to do a good job by providing clear instructions and by carefully wording questions. Properly phrased questions can often prevent problems in the field. For example, it is easier for the interviewer to establish a good relationship with the respondent and to avoid the appearance of "grilling" if questions are phrased so that respondents do not have to admit that they do not know some fact or have given no thought to the subject. A phrase such as . . . *or haven't you had a chance to read about that?* at the end of a question can considerably ease potentially tense situations.

No one can provide precise guidelines for correct wording, because the questions that have to be asked are determined by the subject under study. We can, however, describe some common errors in question wording that should be avoided. Here are some features questions should *not* have:

1. *Excessive length.* If there is a general rule about question wording, it is to use the shortest form of the question that communicates effectively. Longer questions not only consume more time but are also more likely to lose or confuse respondents. Avoid conditioning phrases and unnecessary adjectives. For example, the question *If the presidential election were to be held at this point in time, rather than in November, which of the following several candidates do you think you would vote for?* can profitably be shortened to *If the presidential election were held today, whom would you vote for?* followed by a list of candidates.

2. *Ambiguity.* The quest for brevity should not lead to incomplete or imprecise wording. To be certain that questions contain all the information necessary to elicit an informed response, ask yourself whether the respondent might have to answer the question with a question. For instance, when asked, *Do you ever complain about public services?* a respondent might answer, *Complain to whom? Public officials? Neighbors?* Questions are often ambiguous if they are too general *(Do you feel that people think too much about politics?)* or indefinite about time, location, or point of comparison *(Did you vote in the last election? Do many Asians live here? Do you think Smith is the best candidate?).*

3. *Double-barreled questions.* These questions are often impossible to answer with a single response because they contain two distinct questions. For example, *Do you feel that we are spending too much on the military, or do you feel it is important to maintain a strong national defense?* cannot be answered with "yes" or "no" if the respondent feels that it is important to have a strong defense but also thinks that current expenditures are higher than necessary for that purpose. To avoid double-barreled questions, examine any question containing *and* or *or* to be certain it does not combine two questions that should be asked separately.

4. *Bias.* Questions can be worded so as to encourage one response rather than another. Such questions are often referred to as *loaded questions.* When asked, *You are opposed to busing innocent schoolchildren all the way across town just to achieve racial balance in the schools, aren't you?* respondents will be far more inclined to agree than if asked, *Do you favor or oppose the use of busing to achieve racial balance in the public schools?* Phrases that evoke social norms (such as, *How often do you fulfill your civic duty by voting?*) clearly bias responses. Phrases that associate a position with authority figures or socially disapproved persons or groups can also distort results. For example, questions that begin with, *Do you agree with the Supreme Court that . . .* or *Do you share the neo-Nazi view that . . .* will probably produce biased results.

If there are opposing positions on an issue, it is important that questions be worded so as to make each seem legitimate. A useful approach here is to word items as follows: *Some people feel that the federal government should take control of the nation's oil companies and operate them as public utilities. Others think that would be a serious mistake. How do you feel about it? Do you think the federal government should take control of U.S. oil companies?*

5. *Response set bias.* People have a tendency to agree with statements, regardless of their own positions. Question items that fail to take this into account are said to exhibit a *response set bias.* We can see the effects of this if we measure political conservatism first by using six statements with which we expect conservatives to agree, and then again by using six statements with which we expect them to disagree. The first measure will almost always "show" that there are significantly more conservatives than will the second regardless of the actual number of conservatives in the sample. Items should be mixed so that we sometimes expect agreement to reflect a given attitude or position and sometimes expect disagreement to reflect that attitude or position.

6. *Argumentativeness.* Though it is sometimes necessary to provide background for questions, it is a mistake to argue a position. For instance, it is not wise to ask, *Since there are so many dangers associated with the operation of nuclear power plants, some people argue that it is foolish to invest so much in developing nuclear power when we could be devoting resources to the development of safe and inexhaustible energy sources such as solar or wind power. Do you agree that our nation should sharply curtail its investment in nuclear energy?* In addition to being far too long, this question will probably bias responses because it omits alternatives to the position stated.

7. *Encouragement of conditioned responses.* Special problems of wording are posed when we have to ask questions that touch on sensitive subjects. Most people are reluctant to talk to strangers about such matters as their income, family life, sexual behavior, or even political preferences in some cases. For example, consider the case of questions for which society largely prescribes certain responses. Unless questions are carefully phrased, respondents will tend to give the socially acceptable answer regardless of their own opinions. Racial prejudice is a case in point. Since bigotry is generally condemned in American society, people may be reluctant to express prejudiced views.

   We can suggest three tactics to use in getting genuine responses rather than conditioned or socially approved answers. The first is to indicate that socially unacceptable views are widely held or can be viewed as legitimate. For instance, ask, *Many people feel that having African Americans in a neighborhood causes it to go downhill. Others don't think African Americans make that much difference in a neighborhood. Do you agree or disagree with the idea that African American residents generally cause neighborhoods to decline?* A second approach is to word questions so as to appear to assume that respondents engage in socially proscribed behavior or hold unpopular views so that they are forced to deny it if they do not. This makes it easier for them to "confess" to socially unapproved opinions. For instance, the question *How much harm do you think it would do to this neighborhood if African Americans began to move in?* makes it easier to express prejudice than a more neutral wording such as, *Do you think it would be harmful to this neighborhood to have African Americans move in?*

8. *Forcing a response.* Many people feel that it is socially undesirable not to have an opinion on political issues and may express opinions on matters to which they have given no thought. This can distort survey results. To avoid such responses, it is generally wise to provide a no-opinion category in response options or to word questions so as to make having no opinion seem acceptable. For instance, try opening a question with wording such as, *Some people consider the national debt to be an important political issue while others are not too concerned with it. Do you think . . . ?*

Questionnaire Structure   In addition to constructing individual items, survey researchers must be concerned with the overall format and organization of the survey instrument. Sound questionnaires or interview schedules generally consist of four main parts: the explanation, some warm-up questions, the substantive questions, and the demographic questions.

The *explanation* informs respondents of the purpose of the study, and it should convince them that the survey is important enough to warrant their time and attention. This can often be done by associating the study with a respected authority or with a worthwhile goal. If the survey has a prestigious sponsor, a line such as, *We are conducting a study for the Center for Survey Research . . .* can have the desired effect. In stating the purpose of a study, the researcher should not use terms beyond the everyday language of respondents. It would be unwise, for example, to say, *We are conducting a study of mass-elite linkages to determine the extent to which formal mechanisms of representation are a facade for social control by political elites,* even if this were the purpose of the study. A more effective statement would be, *We want to know what kind of contact people like you have with their elected representatives, and we hope that the results of this study will help improve the operation of our government.* Though it is never advisable to lie to respondents, the explanation should not reveal study information that would bias responses. If respondents are told that a study focuses on racial prejudice, they may give different answers from those they would give if told only that the study deals with citizens' attitudes or some other neutral term. The explanation can help interviewers establish a good rapport with respondents or encourage respondents to complete a questionnaire by assuring them that the researchers are open about what they are doing and by eliminating any fear that the study might be a front for a sales pitch.

Warm-up questions, too, can help establish a good relationship with respondents. These are impersonal, non-threatening items used to initiate an interview or questionnaire. Asking respondents about their length of residence in their present location or what they think are the most important problems in their community or in the nation can be useful warm-ups. Any questions that are selected for this purpose, however, should be relevant to the study and have a definite role in the analysis. Otherwise, they are wasted. Warm-up questions should not be created especially for that purpose but should be selected from questions that are to be asked anyway.

Substantive questions constitute the bulk of the items on most instruments. The ordering of items within this group is determined principally by the need to achieve a logical flow in the questioning. Question ordering is not always neutral, however. For instance, researchers often want to ask the same question in different ways. When this is done, the different forms of the question should be separated so that respondents do not find the interview repetitive. Similarly, if both general and specific questions about a phenomenon are to be asked, it is usually best to ask the general questions first in order to get a response that has not been conditioned by a series of specific inquiries. It usually makes sense to place open-ended questions about a subject before closed-ended questions on that same subject in order to prevent the options offered in the closed-ended items from biasing responses to the open-ended items.

Demographic items seek factual information about respondents that is often regarded as personal or sensitive. They are usually placed at the end of an instrument to prevent having other parts of the interview or questionnaire affected by respondents' being ill at ease or feeling as if the researchers are snooping. Though people are generally willing to provide information on such personal matters as their income or marital status, getting adequate answers to demographic questions requires careful wording.

Placing demographic questions at the end of an instrument has the added advantage of postponing, until more interesting questions have been asked, what some people consider dull questions of the sort they frequently have to answer in filling out official forms. This can be especially important with self-administered questionnaires, because a set of routine questions at the outset can make completing the form seem like work and lead respondents to abandon the questionnaire.

Questionnaire Format   Once the principal sections of the instrument have been designed, decisions about how they will be placed on paper must be made. These decisions determine the *format* of the instrument. Earl Babbie (1990, p. 135) argues:

> The format of a questionnaire can be just as important as the nature and wording of the questions asked. An improperly laid out questionnaire can lead respondents to miss questions, confuse them as to the nature of the data desired, and, in the extreme, result in respondents throwing the questionnaire away.

The format of an interview schedule can be just as important. A poorly laid out schedule can confuse interviewers in ways that lead them to skip items, incorrectly record responses, and alienate respondents by appearing clumsy. We can offer some guidelines for setting up both questionnaires and interview schedules.

The first rule for both types of instruments is *Do not crowd items*. It is difficult to overstress the harm that can be caused to a survey by crowding print on a page. To prevent errors, leave plenty of white space on each page of the instrument. Especially in self-administered questionnaires, this helps respondents avoid misreading or mismarking and can give them the sense that the questionnaire is easy to complete. It is better to have a few questions on each of a large number of sheets in a questionnaire than to have many questions on each of a few sheets. The total number of pages matters less than the clarity of each page, but a rule of thumb is that it will take approximately 30 minutes to administer an instrument of 10 well-spaced pages, and 30 minutes is about as long as researchers can count on to hold their respondents' attention under most circumstances.

Precoding   In setting up an interview schedule, researchers must balance the needs of interviewers with the needs of those who will code information from the completed form and those who will prepare that information for data entry. One of the basic questions here is whether or not to use a **precoded instrument.** Coding is basically a process of assigning numbers to represent verbal responses. A precoded instrument has these numbers already associated with the responses; one that is not precoded does not. Figure 8.2 presents an example of a portion of a precoded interview schedule. The numbers in parentheses beside the coded responses indicate the column of a computer line or entry in which the code is to be entered. Major divisions are made in the interview schedule to signal the data entry operator to move to a new line or entry.

Precoding has two advantages. First, it can speed the interview process by making it easier for interviewers to record responses. In most cases, it takes less time for the interviewer to circle or write down a number to represent a response than to write out the response. This can also reduce the number of mistakes made in interpreting the completed interview schedule. Second, precoding allows data entry directly from the completed survey instruments rather than requiring an additional step in transferring information from survey instruments to a form that can be used in data entry.

Although there are many specific techniques for setting up precoded instruments, it is important to keep all responses on the same side of the paper whenever possible. This means that neither interviewers nor those who process the data will have to move their eyes continually across the page when recording or entering data. In self-administered questionnaires, however, the numerous parenthetical numbers can confuse respondents, and researchers should carefully pretest the effect of precoding before using it in a questionnaire.

One of the most important items to be built into a precoding system is a means of *identifying individual respondents* and keeping together all computer entries that contain their responses. This is done by assigning each respondent a unique number. The number must appear on each page of the interview schedule or questionnaire so that recorded data can be checked against the raw data.

Providing instructions that ensure that respondents answer all appropriate questions in the proper order is one of the most difficult parts of designing survey instruments. Interviewers can be trained and given an opportunity to virtually memorize an interview schedule, but clear instructions are still needed when complex choices are involved. This need is even greater when self-administered questionnaires are used, since the respondent sees the instrument only once. Figure 8.3 illustrates some means of helping respondents follow question sequences on questionnaires. Note that a number is associated with each response. Respondents would be instructed to circle the number corresponding to their answer, and arrows direct respondents through the proper sequence of questions.

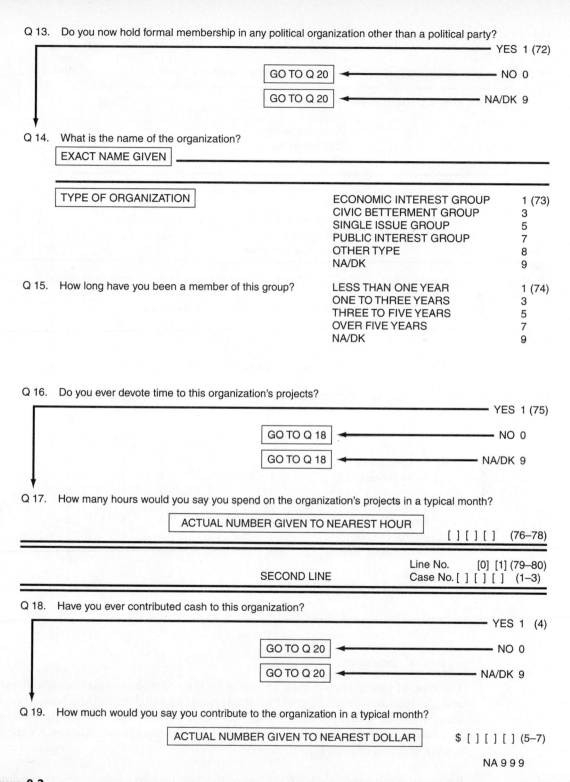

Q 13. Do you now hold formal membership in any political organization other than a political party?

YES 1 (72)

GO TO Q 20 ←———————— NO 0

GO TO Q 20 ←———————— NA/DK 9

Q 14. What is the name of the organization?

EXACT NAME GIVEN _____

TYPE OF ORGANIZATION	
ECONOMIC INTEREST GROUP	1 (73)
CIVIC BETTERMENT GROUP	3
SINGLE ISSUE GROUP	5
PUBLIC INTEREST GROUP	7
OTHER TYPE	8
NA/DK	9

Q 15. How long have you been a member of this group?

LESS THAN ONE YEAR	1 (74)
ONE TO THREE YEARS	3
THREE TO FIVE YEARS	5
OVER FIVE YEARS	7
NA/DK	9

Q 16. Do you ever devote time to this organization's projects?

YES 1 (75)

GO TO Q 18 ←———————— NO 0

GO TO Q 18 ←———————— NA/DK 9

Q 17. How many hours would you say you spend on the organization's projects in a typical month?

ACTUAL NUMBER GIVEN TO NEAREST HOUR

[ ] [ ] [ ] [ ] (76–78)

SECOND LINE

Line No.   [0] [1] (79–80)
Case No. [ ] [ ] [ ] [ ]   (1–3)

Q 18. Have you ever contributed cash to this organization?

YES 1 (4)

GO TO Q 20 ←———————— NO 0

GO TO Q 20 ←———————— NA/DK 9

Q 19. How much would you say you contribute to the organization in a typical month?

ACTUAL NUMBER GIVEN TO NEAREST DOLLAR

$ [ ] [ ] [ ] (5–7)

NA 9 9 9

Figure 8.2
Excerpt from a hypothetical precoded interview schedule*
* To simplify the example, some questions have been modified from the form in which they would actually appear.

9. Have you ever complained to local officials about public services?   Yes 1   No 2

9a. To which type of official have you complained most often?

Mayor 1

Council member 2

City agency head 3

Other official 4

9b. How many times have you complained to local officials about poor public services in the past year?

Once or twice 1

Three or four times 2

Five to ten times 3

More than ten times 4

10. How would you say the public services in your neighborhood compare with the services found in other neighborhoods of this city?

Much better than in other neighborhoods 1

Somewhat better than in other neighborhoods 2

The same as in other neighborhoods 3

Somewhat worse than in other neighborhoods 4

Much worse than in other neighborhoods 5

11. How would you rate the quality of each of the following public services as they are delivered *in your neighborhood* today?

	Excellent	Good	Fair	Poor	Very bad
Fire protection	1	2	3	4	5
Police protection	1	2	3	4	5
Streets and sidewalks	1	2	3	4	5
Trash collection	1	2	3	4	5
Street lighting	1	2	3	4	5
Animal control	1	2	3	4	5
Recreational facilities	1	2	3	4	5

Figure 8.3
Excerpt from a hypothetical mail questionnaire

Types of Surveys

The type of survey required is determined by the research question being addressed, and the type *possible* is dictated by the resources available. But the basic choice is always among four options: *personal interviews, mail surveys, telephone surveys, and Internet surveys.* In making that choice, the researcher should consider the following features of each type of survey.

Personal Interviews   One of the most flexible of survey methods are **personal interviews** because they allow the use of a variety of questioning techniques (visual aids, for example) and give interviewers a chance to pursue questions in order to ensure appropriate responses and prevent respondents from misunderstanding questions or instructions. Personal interviews also provide the largest amount of data per interview, because an interviewer can normally hold a respondent's attention longer in face-to-face interaction than over the phone or through a questionnaire. The response rate is also generally higher for personal interviews.

These interviews are not without disadvantages, however. In the first place, they are very expensive, and only the most important of projects can generally command the funds necessary to employ the technique. Second, personal interviews can produce biased data because of the features of the interview process itself. Recorded responses may reflect real-world facts or attitudes less than they reflect the effects of the setting in which the interview occurs, the reactions of respondents to a given interviewer, the biases of the interviewer, the liberties the interviewer takes in asking questions, or the interview style employed. In addition, personal interviews are difficult to monitor to ensure quality control. The researcher is unable to observe the interviewers in the field and must rely on a variety of post-interview techniques to ensure that interviews were properly conducted. Though such techniques as contacting respondents to see if they were actually interviewed and comparing the responses reported by different interviewers can be effective, they are not foolproof and are costly and time-consuming.

Mail Surveys In cases where personal interviews are impractical, **mail surveys** are a good alternative and offer several advantages:

1. Because mail surveys cost much less to conduct, larger samples can be drawn and a wider distribution of the instrument can be achieved.
2. Many of the biases in distribution of the instrument can be avoided. Among these are biases relating to the reluctance of interviewers to work in certain types of neighborhoods and their inability to obtain interviews with certain types of individuals.
3. Response biases associated with the interviewer are avoided.
4. There is a greater chance of obtaining truthful responses both because a greater anonymity is implied by a mailed instrument and because the biasing effects of respondent-interviewer interaction are removed.
5. Respondents have more time to give thoughtful replies that may reflect their true feelings more accurately than do the hurried responses given in an interview.
6. Fewer personnel need be involved in the survey. This saves money and time.

Unfortunately, mail surveys have their limitations as well. In the first place, they require a mailing list that can be used as a sample frame and provide a representative sample. No such list exists for many of the populations to which researchers may want to generalize. Second, questionnaires have to be kept short if an adequate response rate is to be obtained. This means that less information can be secured from each contact. Third, the researcher has little control over who responds to the questionnaire. This can pose problems both because someone other than the person to whom it is addressed can complete a questionnaire and because it is difficult to obtain an adequate response rate with a mailed instrument.

The most significant problems associated with mail surveys are low response rates, biased response patterns, and improperly completed questionnaires. In general, a response rate of 40 percent is considered acceptable for mail surveys, and a rate of 60 percent or more is considered very good. A demonstrated lack of bias in responses is more important than a high response rate, however, because low response rates challenge the value of results chiefly by rendering the sample unrepresentative. The following techniques are available for encouraging better response rates:

The usual procedure for mail surveys is to send a questionnaire, a letter explaining the purpose of the survey, and a return envelope all in one envelope. Research has shown that using *self-mailing questionnaires* increases response rates. Self-mailing questionnaires can be folded, sealed, and mailed without an additional envelope. That seems to make it easier for respondents to return the instrument and averts the problem of respondents losing the return envelope.

Follow-up mailings can substantially increase return rates both by reminding respondents of the survey and by locating people who, for some reason, have not received the initial letter. Generally, three mailings (an original and two follow-ups) are best. If individual respondents can be identified from returned questionnaires, then mailing follow-ups only to non-respondents can save money. If respondents cannot be identified, it is a good idea to do a blanket mailing to all members of the sample, thanking those who have responded and encouraging those who have not to do so. The follow-up mailing should contain both a letter reminding people to send in their completed questionnaire and a second questionnaire in case the first was lost or never arrived.

It is often wise to include in all mailings a phone number that respondents can call to get answers to questions about the survey. This can both increase the response rate and reduce the number of returned questionnaires that were improperly completed. Response rates can also be enhanced by carefully avoiding any marks on the questionnaires (sequence numbers, for instance) that respondents could interpret as a device for identifying their questionnaire. People are generally more likely to cooperate if they feel their responses will be anonymous.

Telephone Surveys   Telephone surveys fall between personal and mail surveys in many ways. The number of questions that can be asked is generally larger than for mail instruments but shorter than for personal interviews. Response rates are usually lower than for personal interviews but higher than for mail surveys. Though interviewer-related sources of bias are not totally removed, a voice over the telephone is normally less likely to create biasing effects than is a person in the respondent's living room. Finally, the personnel requirements of telephone surveys are between those of mail and personal surveys.

The advantages of telephone surveys include the speed with which they can be completed, the control they provide over who responds, and the flexibility they offer in allowing an interviewer to ensure appropriate responses. Their chief limitation arises from the possibility that an unbiased sample cannot be obtained. Those who do not have a telephone or who have an unlisted number may also be distinctive in ways that are relevant to the study. If so, leaving them out of a sample may provide misleading results. For example, many service professionals (doctors and lawyers, for example) have an unlisted home telephone number in some communities, and very poor people often do not have a telephone. This can be crucial to a study of the relationship between income and political attitudes.

A sampling technique known as **random-digit dialing** (RDD) has enabled survey researchers to overcome the bias associated with unlisted numbers and inaccurate listings, and has significantly increased the speed with which telephone surveys can be conducted. Surveys conducted with the RDD method rely on random samples of computer-generated telephone numbers. This is usually done by combining the three-digit telephone exchanges (or prefixes) of the geographic area where the survey is to be conducted with randomly generated four-digit root numbers. The advantage of such RDD samples is that they not only guarantee a completely random selection of households to be contacted, but also contain numbers of unlisted households which would be otherwise unreachable.

Internet Surveys The growing popularity of the Internet and the continuing decline of telephone poll response rates have led to the development of surveys that can be distributed through the Internet. In recent years, **Internet surveys**, which usually are administered through e-mail, Web pages, or a combination of both, have become a standard research tool in government, business, academia, and the mass media.

The proliferation of Internet surveys is driven by a number of important advantages this type of survey has over more traditional interviewing methods. First, Internet surveys allow cost-efficient access to potentially millions of national or international respondents. Since Internet surveys are self-administered and distributed online, they eliminate the need for interviewers, long-distance phone charges, or printing and mailing costs. Thus, it is fairly cheap to administer Internet surveys to a large number of respondents regardless of where they live or work. In addition, because in most Internet surveys data are entered directly by the respondents (by clicking on answer choices provided on a survey Web page, for example) and instantly downloaded and saved by a central computer, there is no need for additional data entry, again saving money.

Second, Internet surveys allow a variety of instrument designs that can be tailored to the specific needs of the research project or the targeted respondents. Questionnaires administered through the Internet can, for example, incorporate images or short video clips—something that is impossible in telephone surveys. This enables researchers to expose respondents to visual cues (for example videos about cars or images about different product designs) and ask about what has been seen. In addition, to accommodate the needs or preferences of specific respondents, the format of Internet questionnaires can be easily adapted to feature, for example, different colors and designs (appealing to men rather than women, for instance), various languages (for non-English speakers), or larger type-fonts (for people who cannot read small print).

Third, Internet surveys permit respondents to complete the questionnaire whenever it is convenient for them—and not when an interviewer calls them or knocks on their door. Since many people are annoyed with the often intrusive and repeated calls by marketing and surveying organizations, surveys delivered through e-mail or the Internet might offer a solution to the declining response rates that have been observed in more traditional telephone surveys.

While Internet surveys are attractive because of their low cost and simple administration, this survey method has significant drawbacks which severely limit the type of data that can be gathered.

The biggest disadvantage of Internet surveys is related to the fact that not everybody has access to the Internet. While Internet usage has increased in the past few years, many people still do not have access to the Internet. In the United States, for example, only about 69 percent of all Americans used the Internet in 2004 (Nielsen//NetRatings, 2004). Moreover, those who are online tend to be younger, more educated, and wealthier than those who do not have Internet access (Pew Internet & American Life Project; see www.pewinternet.org). Both of these factors make it extremely difficult to obtain a nationally representative sample of survey respondents. After all, even if we were able to obtain a complete list of Internet users in the United States (or anywhere else, for that matter), randomly selecting respondents from such a list would result in strongly biased samples that are not representative of the overall population. Obviously, such a sample would not only exclude all those who do not use the Internet, but also would contain more younger, educated, and wealthier people than can be found in the general population.

Because of the difficulties associated with drawing representative samples for Internet surveys, it is advisable to verify whether existing Internet surveys rely on self-selected respondents (as many do), or whether they are based on truly representative samples. Many of the online "polls" that are published by media organizations such as *CNN.com*, for example, are based on responses from people who happen to visit a particular Web page at a certain time—and who actually decided to answer the poll questions. It is no surprise then, that Internet surveys that are based on such self-selected respondents provide virtually no information about the opinions or attitudes of any group or population. On the other hand, Internet polls conducted among a self-contained group of people (for example, all employees of *Microsoft*) can be representative if the sample has been drawn from a complete list of possible respondents who all have access to the Internet.

It should be noted here that some survey companies have successfully provided access to representative samples of respondents through the Internet. *Knowledge Networks* (www.knowledgenetworks.com), for example, relies on samples of respondents who are first chosen through traditional random-digit dialing procedures (as in telephone surveys) and are then provided with Internet access in return for their cooperation with surveys sent to them via the Internet. Such a methodology is obviously very expensive and requires the periodic replacement of those people in the sample who have become "professional" survey respondents.

Another big disadvantage of Internet surveys is the lack of control over the administration of the instrument. Since most online polls are self-administered, there is no possibility for interviewers to answer potential questions respondents might have about the survey, or probe any of the respondents' "don't know" or "refusal" answers. In addition, the survey administrator has to make sure that the questionnaire is completed by the targeted respondent and not somebody who happens to stumble across the questionnaire while surfing the Internet (this is usually accomplished by using password-protected survey Web sites).

Finally, researchers interested in using Internet surveys should be aware of the fact that the technology used to access the Internet can differ significantly from one user to the next. For example, while a significant number of people have fast broadband Internet access either at work or at home, some still use the much slower telephone modems to go online. Thus, it might be difficult for respondents with slower Internet connections to receive and answer questionnaires that contain, for example, large video clips or images that cannot be downloaded within a reasonable time. In addition, there are potential technological problems with different browsers or hardware configurations, which can significantly affect the way survey questionnaires are displayed on respondents' computer screens.

Overall then, Internet surveys are most suited to collect data from respondents who belong to finite groups with complete access to the Internet. Research projects that require representative samples of the general population, however, are better served with more traditional forms of surveys, such as personal interviews or telephone surveys based on random-digit dialing procedures.

Training and Briefing Personnel

The personal interview is simultaneously one of the worst and one of the best data collection tools available to political scientists. The most significant disadvantages of the interview stem from the fact that the interview situation is rich with opportunities for *reactivity* to affect measurement. Respondents' reactions to the appearance or behavior of the interviewer, to the wording of questions, or to the interview setting can create artificial data that contain less information about the real world than about the interview process itself.

Because respondents react not only to questions but also to the person asking the questions and the manner in which they are asked, characteristics of interviewers that should be totally unrelated to the interview can, in fact, be crucial to its success. In order to minimize error in survey research, the interviews must be standardized. This means that each question should mean the same thing to each respondent, and that each response must mean the same thing when given by different respondents. The presence of an interviewer, ideally, should not affect the respondent's perception of a question, nor the kind of answer that is given. In order to increase response rates and accuracy, interviewers should do what they can to persuade respondents to complete the interview. It is important to interview busy and less cooperative people as well as people who willingly complete the survey.

Interviewer Guidelines   The following guidelines should help to reduce interviewer error considerably:

1. Use an informal, conversational style when asking the questions in the survey. You should be matter-of-fact and casual in your approach to questioning, as if there were absolutely no reason to expect people to refuse to answer.
2. You should be sufficiently familiar with the questions so that you sound as if you are not reading them. Do not conduct the interview in a monotonous voice, since this might make you sound disinterested in the respondents' answers. Try to make the respondents feel that you are listening to what they say by using affirmations such as *I see* or *okay*.

3. Do not express your own opinions during an interview by expressing agreement or disagreement with the respondent. Remain neutral and never suggest answers to the respondent even if you think you "know" what the respondent thinks. Also, do not allow yourself to be drawn into conversations with the respondent about the subject of the survey, because your remarks may bias responses.

4. Let the respondents determine the speed at which you read the survey. It is, however, important to move the interview along as quickly as possible in order to avoid opportunities for the respondent to terminate the interview.

5. Do not intentionally alter the wording or the order of items. All questions should be read exactly as they are written and in the order in which they are presented. Just as survey results can be distorted when questions are reworded, they can also be distorted when questions are asked out of sequence.

6. Do not attempt to interview from memory. Always have the questionnaire before you, and refer to it for question wording and order even if you are so familiar with the instrument that it takes only a glance to remind you of the items.

7. If you are to record respondents' comments, record them in exactly the words the respondents use rather than summarizing them.

8. If respondents give indefinite answers, probe for more specific responses. Your probes should be neutral and should not suggest answers. The most effective neutral probe is repeating the original question or response categories. In well-constructed surveys, appropriate probes are indicated on the questionnaire for any question that is likely to require them.

9. Do not accept *I don't know* or *no opinion* as a response without at least one probe. Repeat the question and perhaps offer a little encouragement such as *I know some of the questions might be difficult to answer, but what is your best guess?*

10. If respondents object to question wording or the alternative answers offered, do not defend the survey instrument but merely explain that you must ask the questions as written and that you are not responsible for them.

11. Never tell respondents what others have answered in response to a given question even though respondents may ask.

12. Be prepared to answer any questions the respondent asks you about who is doing the survey and why. Each study should have a sheet prepared by the project manager that provides brief answers to these questions.

Pretesting

Pretesting a survey instrument and all the accompanying procedures of data management is as important to successful survey research as a test drive is to buying a good used car. Also called a **pilot study,** this trial run helps identify problems that will show up only under actual field conditions.

Pretests are conducted by administering the survey to a small sample of respondents similar to those who will be in the larger sample. The pretest sample need not be representative of the larger population. It is more important to draw the pretest sample in such a way as to ensure that members of all groups of respondents that may react differently to the instrument be included in the pretest than it is to draw a representative sample for the pretest. If, for example, less educated people are likely to have difficulties with the instrument, the researcher should take special pains to include respondents with little education in the pretest, even if they represent only a small portion of the population of interest.

Pretests can serve both to verify the utility of an instrument in which the researcher has a good deal of confidence and to help in the development of an instrument when the researcher knows less about the phenomena under study. In the former case, the instrument should be administered in the pretest in what is expected to be its final form. In the latter case, however, the researcher might want to experiment with different forms in order to learn what works best. A pretest of that type can involve:

1. Different versions of the instrument that test different question wordings or instrument formats.
2. Administering a final questionnaire through actual interviews in order to identify problems in communication.
3. Open-ended questions that help develop response categories for closed-ended questions to be used in the final version.

When these types of devices are used to refine an instrument, the researcher should pretest the instrument that is finally developed, so as to identify any remaining or newly created flaws.

When pretesting an instrument that calls for interviews, researchers often find it useful to conduct a number of the interviews themselves in order to get a feel for the dynamics set up by their instrument and a sense of whether or not it communicates effectively with typical respondents. At the very least, the researcher should meet with the interviewers as soon as they return from the field and go over the instrument and accompanying procedures in detail in order to identify any points at which instructions are unclear, specified procedures are awkward, or respondents seem confused by questions.

Often a pretest is as much a test of the sampling technique as it is of the survey instrument. If interviewers using the specified sampling procedure turn up an unusually small number of qualified respondents or an obviously unrepresentative sample in the pretest, the applicability of the sampling technique to that research situation should be reexamined. If personnel find it difficult to record data using the procedures selected for the pretest, then other procedures should be developed for the full-scale survey.

Pretesting is costly and time-consuming, but it is an absolutely essential investment, because without it the researcher risks producing useless or misleading data. Think of it as buying insurance against finding yourself with a mountain of very expensive data that are useless because of flaws in the survey that you could have corrected if only you had been aware of them.

Surveying

After all these preparations, we are ready to conduct the actual survey. This is the heart of the study because it is where the data are actually collected. What is done in this stage depends on what type of survey is being conducted.

Most surveys are based either on personal interviews or on telephone interviews. Researchers generally prefer to use face-to face interviews for longer surveys or questionnaires that contain sensitive topics that respondents might be reluctant to talk about on the telephone. Of course, face-to-face interviews are relatively expensive because interviews have to be conducted at the respondent's home or at a central interviewing facility to which each respondent has to be invited. In addition, surveys that rely on face-to-face interviews can be difficult to conduct in certain areas of the United States (for example in high-crime neighborhoods or extremely rural areas) and usually take much longer to complete than telephone surveys. Based on the assumption that almost all Americans can be contacted by telephone, a large number of surveys carried out in the United States are conducted by telephone.

Computer-Assisted Telephone Interviewing (CATI)   The proliferation of computers in the past twenty years has led most survey organizations today to use computers in order to manage and conduct telephone interviews. **Computer-assisted telephone interviewing** has mostly replaced the traditional "paper-and-pencil" method, which forced interviewers to read printed questionnaires to respondents and then manually record their answers.

A typical CATI system consists of twenty or more networked computers that are controlled by a server (or main computer) that functions as a central storage location for the sample and the data. The server controls and displays the interview schedule on each interviewer's computer screen, selects telephone numbers, and dials them automatically for the interviewer. As soon as somebody answers the telephone, CATI prompts the interviewer to take the call and then read an introduction to the study (*Hello, my name is . . .*). The introduction typically identifies the survey organization and the study sponsor, in addition to briefly explaining the purpose of the survey. If respondents agree to participate in the survey, interviewers start to read each question directly from the computer screen and enter responses with their keyboards.

While most questions require the interviewer to enter only numerical codes for each answer (for example 1 for *agree* and 2 for *disagree*), interviewers can also record longer responses by typing them into blank boxes displayed on their screens. As soon as the interviewer has entered a response, the CATI system automatically displays the next question until the end of the survey has been reached. After completion of the interview, respondents' data are saved on the server and are available for immediate analysis.

The CATI system offers several advantages over the "paper-and-pencil" method of conducting telephone interviews. First, it increases the efficiency and accuracy of surveys by displaying questions and answer categories on the interviewer's computer screen. Since the CATI program automatically guides the interviewer through the questions and records responses as they are entered, the possibility of interviewer error is greatly reduced.

Second, CATI systems allow survey organizations to administer very complex and individualized interview schedules. Based on responses to previous questions, for example, CATI can adjust the interview schedule and skip over questions not intended for certain respondents. This so-called **question branching** would be difficult to implement if an interviewer had to flip through pages of a printed interview schedule in order to get to the next appropriate question. CATI also has the ability to take responses and automatically insert them in subsequent questions, thus allowing the interviewer to ask highly individualized questions that are appropriate to each respondent. In addition, most CATI systems allow multilingual interviews (important for surveys targeting non-English speakers), voice capturing of open-ended question responses (eliminating the need to type them), and the playback of short audio clips (to test commercial jingles, for example).

Third, CATI systems are able to monitor and control interviewers unobtrusively during the interviews. Researchers can listen in on any interview at any time to catch and correct interviewers' mistakes. Interviewers who, for example, mispronounce names or forget to probe *don't know* answers can then be retrained or pulled entirely from the study.

Finally, because respondents' answers are directly entered into the computer during the interview, researchers can request distributions or tabulations of responses at any point during a survey project. Most CATI systems feature integrated statistical software packages that allow instant analysis of the survey data, thus eliminating the need to reformat and then export data into other statistical programs.

While the introduction of CATI systems has improved and automated the way telephone interviews are conducted, computers have also simplified the administrative functions associated with interviewing, such as scheduling of callbacks, interviewer productivity reporting, and sample management. Moreover, integrated text editors enable researchers to write, test, and revise questionnaires easily and quickly within CATI, thus reducing the time needed between the development and implementation of new survey schedules.

Monitoring

Surveys are monitored to ensure the validity and generalizability of results. Low or unbalanced response rates can be identified and, perhaps, corrected through careful monitoring. For all types of surveys this involves keeping careful records of completed instruments as they come in.

With mail surveys, returned questionnaires should be opened, checked for proper completion, and filed. Each questionnaire should be assigned a serial identification number so that the time of its return can be determined later. The number of questionnaires that is received each day should be logged so that the researcher can keep track of the response rate. If respondents can be identified from the returned questionnaires, the researcher should record incoming questionnaires in a manner that will reveal imbalances in the return as they develop. If a certain geographic or demographic group is making an extremely low response, some extra follow-up mail effort may be called for to keep the sample from becoming unrepresentative. In addition, examination of the incoming questionnaires may reveal mistakes made by respondents, such as overlooking the last page of the instrument or misreading directions about how to mark items. If respondents are identified, a phone call or second mailing can sometimes save questionnaires that otherwise have to be discarded.

With personal surveys, monitoring is done principally through a debriefing session as interviewers return from the field. The researcher or a trusted assistant should check the completed interview schedules to determine whether (1) the correct people in the correct households have been interviewed, (2) all completed interview schedules have been returned, (3) each instrument fully identifies the respondent and provides information on the time and date of the interview, (4) each instrument contains an identification number for the respondent and for the interviewer, and (5) all refusals are explained and any outstanding callbacks have been made. All this helps ensure proper sampling and assists in verification.

Monitoring telephone surveys usually involves the researcher or field director listening in on interviews randomly without being detected. This provides both an incentive for interviewers to be responsible and a means of detecting and subsequently correcting flaws in interviewers' administration of the instrument.

Internet surveys are routinely monitored by checking the received data for possible problems with the sample or the questions themselves. Since most Internet surveys allow "peeks" at the data even while the survey is in progress, it is relatively simple to get information about who is responding and how questions are answered. Potential problems such as non-response, for example, can then be easily addressed by contacting respondents with reminders or sending the survey questionnaires again.

Verifying

Verification is especially important with personal surveys, when unethical interviewers have both an opportunity and an incentive to falsify interviews and when even well-meaning ones can interview the wrong people. Verification procedures allow researchers to catch this type of error and to be sure that the sampling procedure is being followed correctly.

Verification of personal interviews usually involves contacting the intended respondent to determine (1) whether the interview has occurred and (2) whether the interviewer has asked and correctly recorded answers to all questions. To do this, ask when the interview occurred and approximately how long it took. If respondents report that the interview has been conducted, ask them to re-answer two simple questions—one from the middle and one from near the end of the questionnaire—under the pretext that the answers were not clearly recorded in the field. Then check their answers against those that were recorded.

In large surveys, verification is done on a spot-check basis because contacting all respondents would be too costly. If spot checks reveal falsifications or significant errors in any of an interviewer's forms, all of his or her interviews should be verified.

Secondary Analysis of Survey Data

It is important to recognize that most political scientists, perhaps even most political scientists who publish books and articles based on survey data, *never conduct a survey*. They do not conduct surveys both because it is difficult to obtain the necessary funding and because it is often possible to answer the research question they want to explore by using survey data others have collected. Studying data collected by someone else is called **secondary analysis**. Such analysis is very common with survey data because they are so expensive to collect.

Secondary analysis is highly desirable for several reasons. In the first place, the results of almost any survey contain data that are never used by the original researchers because they turn out to be only marginally relevant to the particular research question under study. Another researcher may find these data perfectly suited to answering some other research question. Secondary analysis allows fuller use of data and conserves resources by saving the cost of new surveys when sufficient data already exist. Second, surveys run the risk of *contaminating the population.* This means that repeated studies of some subject among a population may actually cause changes in the phenomena in question or make people reluctant to cooperate with future research. By allowing research to be conducted without yet another survey, secondary analysis minimizes the risk of contamination. Third, although there are a great many data analysis techniques available to political scientists, any one researcher is likely to use only a few in a single study. Secondary analysis allows other researchers to apply different techniques that may expand our understanding of the subject or may even produce different answers to the original research question.

The most fruitful approach to secondary analysis is to select a research question, devise hypotheses to be tested, and then seek completed studies that contain the data necessary to test those hypotheses. Working in reverse (locating a sound data set and examining it in hopes of coming up with valuable research questions it can help answer) can sometimes pay off, but it significantly constrains the range of questions that can be investigated.

The first requirement of a useful data set is that it be based on a sample of the *appropriate population.* If we want to generalize to women in the United States, a study sampling voters in Kansas will be of no use. The second requirement is that the survey instrument contain *appropriate operationalizations* of the key variables in the hypotheses to be tested. If, for example, differences between African Americans and whites are central to an investigation but the data set has recorded race only as "white" and "nonwhite," it will be of little use, as racial groups other than African Americans (for example, Asians and Native Americans) are included in the nonwhite category.

How do we find out if a study is usable? Good reports of research state what sample has been used and describe the operationalizations of key variables that have been employed. Consequently, books and journal articles sometimes provide enough information about a data set for us to judge its suitability, and a literature search can turn up a source of data for secondary analysis. Individual political scientists are often willing to share data sets with others when asked, so it is sometimes possible to obtain a data set through a letter to an author.

Data Archives Fortunately, there is a more systematic and reliable way to locate and gain access to data for secondary analysis. There are a number of institutions that collect data sets in the same way that libraries collect books. These institutions are generally referred to as **data archives.** They classify data sets for easy location and put them in a form that facilitates the sets' use by people who were not involved in the original project in which the data were collected. Some of the more important social science data archives are listed here, along with brief descriptions of their holdings.

- *Roper Center for Public Opinion Research,* University of Connecticut, Storrs. One of the nation's largest archives containing data from surveys conducted in many nations and covering a wide variety of subjects (www.ropercenter .uconn.edu).

- *Inter-University Consortium for Political and Social Research (ICPSR)*, University of Michigan, Ann Arbor. A very large, general collection of surveys in the United States and abroad, stressing political variables and including cross-national data sets and extensive data on political behavior in the United States (www.icpsr.umich.edu).

- *National Election Studies (NES)* produce data on voting, public opinion, and political participation that serve the research needs of social scientists, teachers, students, policy makers, and journalists concerned with the theoretical and empirical foundations of mass politics in a democratic society (www.umich.edu/~nes).

- *National Opinion Research Center (NORC)* at the University of Chicago (www.norc.uchicago.edu) conducts the General Social Survey (GSS), an almost annual survey of U.S. households. The first survey took place in 1972 and since then more than 35,000 respondents have answered more than 2,500 different questions (webapp.icpsr.umich.edu/GSS).

- *Louis Harris Data Center* at the University of North Carolina, Chapel Hill maintains a collection of surveys of the U.S. population conducted by the Louis Harris public opinion polling organization (www.irss.unc.edu).

- *International Social Survey Programme (ISSP)* is an annual program of cross-national collaboration on surveys covering topics important for social science research. It brings together preexisting social science projects and coordinates research goals, thereby adding a cross-national, cross-cultural perspective to the individual national studies (www.issp.org).

- *European Union (EU)* provides access to European public opinion including *Eurobarometer, Europinion,* and links to other social sciences data archives (europa.eu.int/comm/public_opinion).

- *Data and Program Library Service (DPLS)* is the central repository of data collections used by the social science research community at the University of Wisconsin–Madison (dpls.dacc.wisc.edu).

- *Pew Research Center for the People and the Press* in Washington, D.C. is an independent opinion research group, sponsored by the Pew Charitable Trusts. The center studies public attitudes toward the press, politics, and public policy issues (www.people-press.org).

Each of these institutions publishes a list of the data sets it has and provides a general description of the data. Once a promising-sounding study has been located in a listing of archive holdings, we can determine the actual utility of the study by obtaining the **codebook** for the survey. This lists all questions asked and tells how the responses have been coded, and it will allow us to judge the fit between the study's operationalizations and the hypotheses to be tested.

Conclusion

Without question, surveys are the most efficient way to collect information about how people think. Technological developments such as computer-assisted telephone interviewing and online polling has increased the number of surveys conducted each year. In fact, there are now so many surveys that many people have become annoyed by the seemingly constant intrusion into our private life. Successful survey studies therefore require a carefully planned design, well-written questions, and a representative sample of respondents who are contacted with the most appropriate type of survey (face-to-face, telephone, online, etc.).

Summary Points

• Surveys have to be planned carefully to ensure that the data collected will provide enough information to answer research questions or to test hypotheses. In the planning phase of a survey, researchers have to consider the conceptualization of hypotheses and concepts, the type of survey required, the design of the survey instruments, the required sample and sampling procedures, the interviewer training, and the pre-testing of the instrument.

• Survey design focuses on the development of a questionnaire and an interview schedule. Survey questions can be either open-ended or closed-ended and should be worded carefully in order to avoid bias and other related problems. The structure of the questionnaire should encourage respondents' participation.

• The required survey type (personal interviews, mail, telephone, or Internet survey) is determined by the research question and by the resources available. Each survey type has distinct advantages and disadvantages that have to be considered before the start of any research project.

• Surveys are conducted either by personal interviews, mail, telephone, or through the Internet. The surveying process requires monitoring and verification of the conducted interviews, data coding, processing, and analysis.

Suggested Readings and References

The literature on survey research is one of the largest in the social sciences. Most of it reflects the fact that the method is widely used in sociology and psychology as well as in political science and other fields. A relatively comprehensive overview of the method is provided in Floyd J. Fowler, Jr., *Survey Research Methods*, 3rd ed. (Newbury Park, CA: Sage, 2001). Other excellent introductions are found in Earl Babbie, *Survey Research Methods*, 2nd ed. (Belmont, CA: Wadsworth, 1990); Herbert F. Weisberg, Jon A. Krosnick, and Bruce D. Bowen, *An Introduction to Survey Research, Polling, and Data Analysis*, 3rd ed. (Thousand Oaks, CA: Sage, 1996); Louis M. Rea and Richard A. Parker, *Designing and Conducting Survey Research: A Comprehensive Guide*, 2nd ed. (San Francisco, CA: Jossey-Bass, 1997); Arlene Fink and Jacqueline Kosecoff, *How to Conduct Surveys: A Step by Step Guide*, 2nd ed. (Thousand Oaks, CA: Sage, 1998). See also *The Survey Kit*, by Arlene Fink, 2nd ed. (Thousand Oaks, CA: Sage, 2002).

The subjects of question wording and questionnaire design in general are addressed in Abraham N. Oppenheim, *Questionnaire Design and Attitude Measurement* (New York: Continuum International Publishing Group, 1999); William H. Foddy, *Constructing Questions for Interviews and Questionnaires: Theory and Practice in Social Research* (New York: Cambridge University Press, 1994); Floyd J. Fowler, *Improving Survey Questions: Design and Evaluation* (Thousand Oaks, CA: Sage, 1995); Douglas R. Berdie, John F. Anderson, and Marsha A. Niebuhr, *Questionnaires: Design and Use*, 2nd ed. (Lanham, MD: Rowman & Littlefield, 1992). Interviewer skills are covered in Floyd J. Fowler, Jr. and Thomas W. Mangione, *Standardized Survey Interviewing: Minimizing Interviewer-Related Error* (Newbury Park, CA: Sage, 1989).

A very detailed discussion of how to conduct surveys by mail rather than through personal interviews is found in Thomas W. Mangione, *Mail Surveys: Improving the Quality* (Thousand Oaks, CA: Sage, 1995). Telephone survey methods are covered in James H. Frey and Sabine Mertens Oishi, *How to Conduct Interviews by Telephone and in Person*, (Newbury Park, CA: Sage, 1995) and in Paul J. Lavrakas, *Telephone Survey Methods: Sampling, Selection, and Supervision*, 2nd ed. (Newbury Park, CA: Sage, 1993). One of the most widely referenced books on these techniques is Don A. Dillman, *Mail and Internet Surveys*, 2nd ed. (New York: Wiley, 1999).

A good introduction to the practical applications of Internet surveys is provided by Samuel J. Best and Brian S. Krueger, *Internet Data Collection* (Thousand Oaks, CA: Sage, 2004) and by Matthias Schonlau, Ronald D. Fricker, Jr., Marc N. Elliot, *Conducting Research Surveys Via E-Mail and the Web* (Thousand Oaks, CA: Sage, 2002). Both books also contain a good selection of references for methodological issues in Internet research.

Political scientists who are not conducting their own surveys but are planning to use data collected by others might want to turn to Herbert H. Hyman, *Secondary Analysis of Sample Surveys* (Middletown, CT: Wesleyan University Press, 1987) or to K. Jill Kiecolt and Laura E. Nathan, *Secondary Analysis of Survey Data* (Thousand Oaks, CA: Sage, 1985).

Research Exercises

1. Write a series of three to five statements with which you might ask respondents to agree or disagree in order to get a measure of each of the following concepts:

   support for the Democratic party
   opposition to gun control legislation
   political efficacy
   political activism (participation)
   political liberalism

2. Select a politically relevant topic of interest to you and identify a dependent variable and three independent variables you might want to use in a study of the subject. Devise an interview schedule designed to provide measures of these four variables, and write it out in a form that can be used in interviewing. Include a system of precoding for answers.

3. Devise a simple theory (one involving only a few independent variables) to explain why people differ on *one* of the following variables:

   party identification
   political alienation
   regularity of voting
   membership in voluntary associations

4. Write out the theory as a set of testable hypotheses, carefully identifying the variables involved. Now locate an existing survey research data set on the Internet that you can use in a secondary analysis to test these hypotheses. Find some promising-sounding studies, get a copy of the code book for each so that you can see exactly what questions were asked, and make your selection on that basis.

Key Terms

survey research	precoded instrument
respondents	personal interviews
cross-sectional surveys	mail surveys
longitudinal surveys	telephone surveys
trend studies	random-digit dialing (RDD)

cohort studies
panel studies
questionnaire
interview schedule
demographic groups
open-ended questions
closed-ended questions
question wording

Internet surveys
pretests
computer-assisted telephone
  interviewing (CATI)
question branching
secondary analysis
data archives
codebook

CHAPTER 9

Scaling Techniques

- What is scaling?
- When are scales used?
- What types of scales are available?

One of the most common problems we encounter in designing survey or other instruments arises when we must find a way to assign a single representative value or score to a complex attitude or behavior. As an example, consider how one might go about measuring the degree of people's prejudice toward college students. Such prejudice can take a number of forms, depending on which attributes of college students a particular individual might focus upon. That is, some people might judge college students by students' dress, others by their mannerisms, and still others by their behavior, their social or economic status, or even their personal hygiene. Some people might hold stereotypic views based on one or two encounters, either pleasant or unpleasant, with specific students, and others may barely differentiate between college students and other members of the community. These elements of judgment may vary quite widely in substance, direction, and degree, but each is, at least potentially, a component of the larger concept *prejudice*.

As researchers hoping to tap these factors, we must design an instrument that is at once sufficiently broad to detect and measure as many of these component elements as possible and sufficiently concise to allow us to summarize in some meaningful way the extent to which the more general concept in question is present. Put another way, we need a device that captures or represents a notion such as prejudice in all its complexity *and* tells us how much of it each respondent (or case) has. One important means by which we can accomplish this is through *scaling*.

Scaling is a procedure in which we combine a number of relatively narrow indicators (in the example, survey questions about specific perceived traits of college students) into a single, summary measure that we take to represent the broader, underlying concept of which each is a part (prejudice). Thus, we might measure a respondent's attitudes about various behaviors of college students (that they drink too much or have too many loud parties, for example) or about their mannerisms (that they are snobbish or self-important or inconsiderate), but we would not take any one of these items *alone* to stand for so broad a concept as prejudice. Rather, we must pull together *several* of these narrow measures in some way that allows us to draw conclusions about the more general point of view to which each may contribute or that each may reflect. And more than that, we must accomplish the task in such a way that we can compare the amount of prejudice (or whatever it is we are measuring) that characterizes one respondent with the amount that characterizes another, in effect making a judgment (in the example) about which is *more* prejudiced. The unifying measure that represents a given underlying concept is called a

scale. The individualized assessment of the degree to which any given case manifests that underlying concept is called a **scale score.** Scaling, or scale construction, is simply the procedure by which we build scales and assign individual scale scores.

Scale Construction: Two Basic Concerns

Scaling, then, seems to be a fairly straightforward process. The task of the researcher is simply to identify several components of the underlying concept, to develop indicators to measure each, to combine those indicators into a summary score by reciting a few magic words or statistical incantations, and—presto—it's done. Unfortunately, this apparent simplicity is deceptive, for there are some potential dangers to which we must be especially sensitive when selecting and interpreting scale components. Most important among these are two with which we are already familiar: the concerns posed by the notions of validity and reliability.

Validity In the present context, validity questions whether there is reason to believe that each of the individual components (specific questions) in a given scale is actually related directly to the underlying concept and whether, collectively, those components capture the full essence of it. Putting that another way, we must ask ourselves whether it really makes sense to combine a particular set of indicators *and,* once we have done so, whether it really makes sense to attach to this set of indicators the particular label we have chosen. Thus, in our example, we must ask ourselves first whether persons' attitudes toward student behavior really have anything in common with their attitudes toward student mannerisms or styles of dress, and second whether all these attitudes together can really be considered to reflect the degree of those persons' prejudice toward students.

Reliability In scaling, reliability becomes a concern with whether the various component indicators of a scale are in fact related to one another in a consistent and meaningful manner. In effect, we are asking not whether a particular set of questions or indicators differentiates between apples and oranges, but rather whether, once the apples have been identified, it provides us with consistent standards for sorting them by size, color, and variety. If so, then combining the measures will tell us more about apples than will any single measure. But if our standards are inconsistent or ambiguous, then our observations based upon them may prove misleading.

An Example Consider a scale in which each respondent is instructed to express either agreement or disagreement with each of the following statements:

1. The Cubans are evil and cannot be trusted.
2. The French are evil and cannot be trusted.
3. The Japanese are evil and cannot be trusted.
4. The Chinese are evil and cannot be trusted.

Let us suppose that this scale is intended to measure *xenophobia*—the fear and distrust of foreigners. Presumably, the more statements with which particular respondents agree, the more xenophobic we may take them to be. But is that really the case? A person who believes only the Cubans and the Chinese are evil and not to be trusted may, in effect, be expressing anticommunism rather than xenophobia. A person who believes only the Japanese and the Chinese are evil and not to be trusted may, in effect, be expressing racism rather than xenophobia. Even a respondent who regards all four groups as evil and untrustworthy may, upon closer inspection, be expressing not xenophobia but a feeling that *all* people or *all* governments, even the respondent's own, are evil and not to be trusted. Because we cannot say with any assuredness that this scale measures xenophobia per se, the scale lacks validity. And what of reliability? Even if the scale were measuring xenophobia, could we claim that its components measured consistently? Fear and distrust of the Chinese, for example, may be an indicator of at least two very different characteristics—one ideological and the other racial—and two respondents might give the same answer for very different reasons. Is our anticommunist respondent in some meaningful sense *equally* as xenophobic as is our racist one? Probably not. To combine these particular items into a single measure by simply adding them together, then, is at best an exercise in futility and at worst a source of erroneous conclusions.

Problems of this type cannot always be overcome easily, and as a result, scaling must be used with great care in some instances and must be forgone in others. Yet the overriding advantages inherent in the ability to develop a single number or score to represent a complex attitude or behavior provide a substantial incentive to employ scaling techniques in a great many instances. In the remainder of this chapter we discuss four different approaches to the development of meaningful scales. Each of these should be viewed not only in terms of its procedures but also in terms of its strengths and weaknesses in overcoming the problems of validity and reliability.

Likert Scaling

The first such technique, and probably the least satisfactory in these terms, is **Likert scaling**—a simple technique by which each respondent is presented with a series of statements requiring a value judgment. Figure 9.1 illustrates a typical series of such items, which might constitute a measure of prejudice toward college students. In each instance, respondents are asked whether they agree strongly, agree, disagree, or disagree strongly with the statement. Each such respondent is assigned a numerical score, with 5 representing the strongest agreement and 1 representing the strongest disagreement. A middle or neutral response is assigned the value 3. To obtain the summary measure of prejudice for a particular individual, one adds all the individual scores and divides by the number of statements. Thus, a respondent who has answered questions 1 through 6 as follows:

Item 1: Agree (4).

Item 2: Strongly agree (5).

Item 3: Neutral (3).

Item 4: Agree (4).

Item 5: Disagree (2).

Item 6: Agree (4).

Please indicate whether you *agree strongly, agree, disagree,* or *disagree strongly* with each of the following statements:

1. There may be a few exceptions, but in general college students are pretty much alike.
2. The trouble with letting college students into a nice neighborhood is that they gradually give it a typical student atmosphere.
3. To end prejudice against college students, the first step is for the students to try sincerely to get rid of their harmful and irritating faults.
4. There is something different and strange about college students; it is hard to tell what they are thinking and planning, and what makes them tick.
5. Most college students would become overbearing and disagreeable if not kept in their place.
6. College students prove that when people of their type have too much money and freedom, they just take advantage and cause trouble.

Figure 9.1

Typical Likert scale items

SOURCE: Adapted from the E (Ethnocentrism) Scale used by Theodore Adorno et al. in *The Authoritarian Personality* (New York: Harper & Row, 1950).

NOTE: In this figure statements have been worded in only one direction (that is, all agreements with the items reflect the presence of prejudice) for purposes of illustration. In practice, some items would be reworded so that the negative responses evidence prejudice, and the score values would be reversed accordingly. The goal of such a procedure is to minimize *response set bias*—the tendency of some respondents to give the same answer to every question.

is assigned the summary score 3.67 ([4 + 5 + 3 + 4 + 2 + 4]/6), which might be rounded to 4.

In general, the higher a person's scale score, the more of the measured characteristic (in this case, prejudice toward college students) he or she is presumed to have.

The problems here are precisely those already noted in our xenophobia scale, which was, in fact, an oversimplified Likert-type scale. For one thing, we know nothing about the relationships among the component items. Each may in fact measure different aspects of the same underlying trait, and on its face each appears to do so, but we cannot be sure.

The items that compose a good (or reliable) scale should have high internal consistency—that is, they should be highly correlated with each other. Different statistical models exist for measuring internal consistency. Probably the most commonly used reliability coefficient for items that have three or more answer categories is *alpha* (also called *Cronbach's alpha*), which is based on the average inter-item correlation. For items with two answer categories (true/false or agree/disagree, for example), the related *Kuder-Richardson 20 (KR20)* coefficient usually is used.

One point that should be clear even now, however, has to do with the way in which the summary (average) score is determined: one simply adds the individual item scores and divides by the number of items. But if we look more closely at the response categories (that is, *strongly agree, agree,* etc.), we find that they represent measurement at the ordinal level. That is, they distinguish between mutually exclusive categories and rank each relative to the others. They do not, however, establish known and equal intervals (the difference between *strongly agree* and *agree* is not always the same, either from item to item or from one respondent to the next). Accordingly, it is meaningless and misleading to add these numbers together, let alone to average them. A more appropriate procedure, but not a commonly used one, is to calculate a different kind of average, called a *median,* for each respondent's answers and to assign this as the scale score. Determination of the median is discussed in Chapter 16.

Guttman Scaling

Many of the problems associated with Likert scaling can be overcome in certain circumstances by using a more sophisticated technique known as *Guttman scaling.* **Guttman scaling** begins from the assumption that certain attitudes (and behaviors) are related to one another in such a way that holding (or engaging in) one is more difficult or requires more effort than holding (or engaging in) another. Perhaps the best analogy here is to a person standing on a ladder. A person standing on the fifth rung quite likely has climbed there by stepping on the first, second, third, fourth, and fifth rungs. It is possible but less likely that the person skipped one or more of the lower rungs on the way up. It is most unlikely that someone would step directly from the ground to the fifth rung of the ladder, at least without enduring some pain. In effect, then, our climber has reached the fifth rung by engaging in a series of progressively higher-order behaviors and can reasonably be *assumed* to have traversed the lower positions to reach the highest one.

Similarly, even if we know that a particular person has voted in a presidential election—an act we know from many studies to be one of the most common and least demanding in politics—we cannot assume with any degree of assurance that the same person has also participated actively in some political organization—a far more demanding and much less common action—or has run for public office—one of the most demanding and least common political acts of all. Yet if, on the other hand, we know that an individual has been active in a political organization, we *may* assume with some degree of confidence that that person has also engaged in such lesser political acts as voting, though not that the person has taken the further step of running for office. And by extension, if an individual has been a candidate for office, we have reason to assume that the person has also voted and engaged in organizational activity. These assumptions will not always prove correct, but they will be supported far more often than not.

Certain attitudes may be seen to relate to one another in much the same way. We can see this illustrated in Figure 9.2, which represents an alternative approach to measuring a person's degree of prejudice against students. In a procedure similar to that for Likert scaling, respondents are asked whether they agree or disagree with each item in a series of statements. The response that most reflects the trait being measured (for example, prejudice) is scored with a plus (+), and alternative responses are scored with a minus (−). Thus, agreement with item 1 would be scored plus (+) as reflecting prejudice, and agreement with item 2 would be assigned a minus (−), reflecting its absence. The statements themselves may be seen to bear a relationship with one another such that the various responses reflect the degree of one's prejudice or freedom from it. In effect, the closer a perceived threat comes to one's own family or self, the more difficult it presumably is for one to

Please indicate whether you *agree* or *disagree* with each of the following statements:

1. Given a choice, I would like to see college students kept out of my community.
2. It is okay for college students to visit my community.
3. If a college student wanted to live in my community, that would be okay with me.
4. I would not want to see a college student living in my neighborhood.
5. I would have no objection to someone in my family bringing home a college student as a guest for dinner.
6. I would be displeased if someone in my family were to marry a college student.

Figure 9.2
Typical Guttman scale items
SOURCE: Adapted from the Social Distance Scale developed by E. Bogardus in *Social Distance* (Yellow Springs, OH: Antioch Press, 1959).

NOTE: In this figure, the statements have been arranged in order of their degree of difficulty for purposes of illustration. In practice, their order should be mixed to obscure any implicit ranking.

remain free of prejudice. What this means is that there is, at least potentially, a logical, ordinal relationship among the items in the scale—a factor that is missing under the Likert procedure.

Moreover, Guttman scaling provides appropriate procedures not only for summarizing the degree of a characteristic possessed by a given respondent but also for assessing the degree to which a particular set of components meets the assumption of ordinality in the first place. These procedures are illustrated in Table 9.1, which reports the responses of 170 hypothetical persons to the statements presented in Figure 9.2.

Several points in the table are worthy of note. To begin with, the items are ordered on the left-hand side of the table in ascending order according to their number of supportive responses (+). This number is ascertained by summing the number of cases (*n*) for which a plus (+) has been recorded for a particular item. The assumption here is that the number of agreeing responses will decrease as the difficulty of holding a particular attitude increases. In the example, this ranking happens to correspond with our expectations in that the observed ranking is in the same order as our initial ranking, but this is not always the case.

Each line in the table represents a group of individuals who have given a particular combination of responses to the six items. Thus, the first line represents those ten people (*n* = 10) who have responded to each of the six questions in a manner reflecting prejudice toward students. The second line represents those 20 respondents whose answers indicate prejudice on items 2 through 6, but not on the more extreme item 1, and so forth. The first seven lines in the table represent those combinations of responses that are wholly consistent with the assumption that the six items are ordinally related with one another. Persons displaying any one of these combinations of responses are termed *perfect scale types*.

In Guttman scaling, there will always be one more perfect scale type than there are items in the scale, because the total absence of the characteristic being measured (*no* prejudice, as in line 7) is regarded as a perfect score. Each perfect score is assigned a number from 1 to *i* + 1, where *i* is the number of items, with 1 identifying those respondents possessing the lowest level of the trait in question and *i* + 1

Table 9.1
Hypothetical distribution of Guttman scale responses*

Item 1	Item 2	Item 3	Item 4	Item 5	Item 6	n	Error (e)	n(e)	Scale Score
+	+	+	+	+	+	10			7
−	+	+	+	+	+	20			6
−	−	+	+	+	+	30			5
−	−	−	+	+	+	30			4
−	−	−	−	+	+	10			3
−	−	−	−	−	+	10			2
−	−	−	−	−	−	5			1
+	−	+	+	+	+	30	1	30	(7) or (5)
+	+	+	+	−	−	5	2	10	(7)
−	+	−	+	+	+	20	1	20	(6) or (4)
45	55	95	145	150	160	170		60	

Marginals
(used for ordering items)

Totals

* + Indicates a response reflecting prejudice.

those possessing the highest. The appropriate score is then recorded for each respondent. Thus, in the example, each of the 10 persons in line 1, whose responses reflect the highest degree of prejudice, are assigned the score 7 ($i + 1 = 6 + 1 = 7$), each person in line 2 the score 6, each in line 3 the score 5, and so on, until the five respondents in line 7 are each scored 1. These scores rank each respondent vis-à-vis every other respondent according to his or her degree of prejudice.

We have yet to account, however, for the 55 respondents represented by lines 8, 9, and 10 in the table. One or more of the responses of these individuals do not fit the pattern predicted by our ordering of the items. These are, in effect, people who skipped one or more steps while climbing the ladder. Accordingly, these sets of responses are said to contain one or more *errors*. The term *error* here refers not to a mistake by the respondent but to a failure of the assumptions of Guttman scaling to apply to these cases. When such errors occur, and they are quite common, we proceed on a line-by-line basis as follows. First, we count the *minimum* number of changes in the line that, if made, would result in a perfect scale score. In line 8, for instance, we can change the plus (+) in column 1 to a minus (−) to obtain a response of 5, or alternatively, we can change the minus (−) in column 2 to a plus (+) to obtain a response of 7. In either event, we are changing only one item, and so we say line 8 contains one error. This is indicated in the column labeled "error (*e*)." We then multiply the number of errors (1) by the number of cases in which the error occurs (30) and enter our result in the next column. Finally, we assign to each case the scale score it would receive if the error did not occur. Though we have only one error in line 8, we have a choice of two possible corrections, one of which yields a score of 5 and the other a score of 7. Unless there is some compelling reason to choose one of these scores over the other, the standard practice is to assign each of the 30 cases randomly to one or the other scale category.

We move next to line 9 and repeat the procedure. Here we are required to make a minimum of two changes, for we must convert both minus (−) scores to plus (+). Again, we note the number of errors, multiply by the number of cases, and assign a scale score. Here, however, only one score is possible, since we have no options when making our corrections. The procedure is then repeated for line 10, as it is for any additional nonscalar combinations.

In proceeding through lines 8, 9, and 10, we have, of course, assigned scores to each case as if it fitted our scale perfectly, though we know for a fact that it does not. This means that to the extent that we rely upon our scale scores to describe those 55 cases, we risk reaching an improper conclusion. The question thus arises of just how serious a risk this is. Fortunately, Guttman scaling procedures suggest an answer.

Recall that we have kept track of the total number of errors in the scale. In effect, an assessment of risk requires us to ask whether this total error is relatively small and therefore unimportant or whether it is so large as to invalidate the scale itself. We may answer this question by calculating a statistic called the *Guttman coefficient of reproducibility* (C_R), the formula for which is as follows:

$$C_R = 1 - \frac{\sum n(e)}{i(N)}$$

where n = the number of cases in lines in which errors occur

e = the number of errors in each line

i = the number of response items

N = the total number of cases

For the example, the coefficient of reproducibility is determined by substituting the appropriate values:

$$C_R = 1 - \frac{30 + 10 + 20}{6(170)} = 1 - \frac{60}{1,020}$$

$$= 1 - 0.06 = .94$$

In this formula, the quantity $\sum n(e)$ represents the total number of "mistakes" in the scale, and the quantity $i(N)$ represents the total number of possible mistakes if *no* items or respondents fit the scale. The fraction

$$\frac{\sum n(e)}{i(N)}$$

thus tells us what proportion of all possible mistakes have in fact been made. By subtracting this proportion of error from one, we ascertain the proportion of scale entries that are error free. As a matter of convention, any Guttman scale with a C_R of .90 or higher is accepted as sound, and any scale with a lower C_R is considered suspect and is generally not used for purposes of analysis.

We can see, then, that for items that meet the criterion of inherent ordering by degree of difficulty, Guttman scaling is a potent technique by which we may bring together a number of indicators into a single summary value that meaningfully represents a more general characteristic of a respondent.

Thurstone Scaling

Yet another technique for creating summary measures, though one intended to solve a rather different problem, is the *Thurstone equal-appearing interval scale.* You will recall from our earlier discussion that in phrasing questions to measure such variables as social class, the researcher may choose to measure respondents' characteristics according to some externally imposed criterion, such as income or occupational prestige, or may alternatively permit respondents to apply their own standards of judgment, as by asking them what social class they *identify* with. The first approach enhances the comparability of data from case to case; the second may yield less comparable but more meaningful data. **Thurstone scaling** is a procedure for pursuing the second strategy (but with improved comparability) by letting a few members of the population to be studied actually participate in designing the scales that will be used to measure the characteristics of the population itself. By providing for the internal definition of the meanings of indicators, the Thurstone technique enhances the validity of a scale. By eliminating from consideration all but the most widely agreed upon scale items, we enhance the reliability of the scale as well. The technique is rather complicated, but once we have these goals clearly in mind, it is not difficult to understand.

In constructing a Thurstone scale, the researcher first gathers a large number of statements, perhaps as many as 100, that reflect a variety of attitudes about some object. A number of "judges" is then selected at random from the population to be studied. These are simply individuals on whom the list of statements will be tried out. The judges usually number at least fifty, and they may include as many as several hundred persons when resources permit. Each judge is presented with an 11-point scale—ranging from *favorable* (11) to *neutral* (6) to *unfavorable* (1)—and with a stack of cards on each of which is printed one of the statements. The judge is asked to examine each statement as it relates to the object in question and to place each card in one of 11 piles corresponding to his or her evaluation. Thus, those statements a judge regards as most favorable toward some object, such as college students, may be placed in pile 11, those slightly less favorable in pile 10, and so forth. In this manner, the researcher obtains every judge's understanding of the evaluative meaning of each statement.

At this point, each statement is assigned a scale score indicating its relative position on the favorable-unfavorable continuum, with higher scores going to those statements that are seen as more favorable. Many researchers assign these scores by calculating a mean, that is, by summing all of the individual scores for each item and dividing by the number of judges. A more appropriate procedure is to find the median value assigned to each statement (see Chapter 16) and to treat this as the scale score. Those items that are assigned widely divergent scores by different judges (for example, those that are spread over five or six categories) are eliminated at this point. From the remaining list, some fifteen to twenty final items are selected for inclusion in the questionnaire. The items should be those on which the judges most closely agree, and they should collectively cover the full spectrum of evaluations. Figure 9.3 illustrates a few typical statements that might be included in a Thurstone scale of attitudes toward college students.

Please consider each of the following statements and indicate which ones you *agree* with:

1. It may not be widely known, but far more college students have volunteered for the military services than one would expect on the basis of their percentage in the population as a whole.
2. Some college students are definitely much superior in intelligence to other people in this community.
3. Whatever their faults, college students contribute a great deal to the quality of life in this community.
4. There is little truth in the image of college students in this community as being less ambitious or hard-working on the average than many other groups.
5. Some college students are clean and some are dirty, but the average college student does not differ in any way in his personal habits from the average person.
6. When you come right down to it, college students are just like anybody else in this community; they have their good points and they have their bad points.
7. While there are no doubt a few exceptions, in general college students tend to be especially clannish and to stick together.
8. While every group has a right to get ahead, college students are a little apt to disregard the rights and possessions of other people.
9. College students sometimes try to enter stores, hotels, and restaurants where they are just not welcome.
10. Many people in this community would accept college students more easily if there were less drunkenness, self-righteousness, and public demonstrations of sexual looseness and immorality among them.
11. It is a fairly well-established fact that college students have a less pleasant body odor than other people in this community.

Figure 9.3
Typical Thurstone scale items

SOURCE: Adapted from a scale reported by H. Schuman and J. Harding in "Prejudice and the Norm of Rationality," *Sociometry*, 27 (1964), pp. 353–71.

NOTE: These statements have been ordered from most favorable through neutral to most unfavorable for purposes of illustration. In practice, their order should be assigned randomly to obscure any systematic relationships. Scale values should not be shown on the questionnaire.

When these final items reach the interview stage, respondents in the study sample are asked either which of the statements they agree with or, alternatively, which two or three statements are closest to their own view of the object in question, in this case, college students. The median value of the items so designated by each individual is then determined and is assigned as that respondent's scale score, the summary of his or her views toward the object. When the responses of a given individual are scattered widely over several noncontiguous items, the researcher generally concludes either that the individual has no attitude toward the object in question or that his or her attitude is organized differently from the structure assumed by the scale. In such cases, no scale score is assigned. But when, as is much more often the case, the responses do cluster tightly in one portion of the continuum, the researcher can have reasonable confidence in the validity and reliability of the measure. This is due in no small part to the role of the judges in designing the research instrument.

Listed below are several pairs of words that could be used to describe college students. Between the words in each pair are several blanks. Please put an *X* on the blank for each pair that best describes how you feel about college students.

In general, college students are:

1.	Boring	— — — — — — —	Interesting
2.	Clean	— — — — — — —	Dirty
3.	Emotional	— — — — — — —	Rational
4.	Gentle	— — — — — — —	Violent
5.	Good	— — — — — — —	Bad
6.	Dishonest	— — — — — — —	Honest
7.	Serious	— — — — — — —	Humorous
8.	Idealistic	— — — — — — —	Realistic
9.	Noisy	— — — — — — —	Quiet
10.	Pleasant	— — — — — — —	Unpleasant
11.	Rich	— — — — — — —	Poor
12.	Pleasing	— — — — — — —	Annoying
13.	Sincere	— — — — — — —	Insincere
14.	Superficial	— — — — — — —	Profound
15.	Valuable	— — — — — — —	Worthless

Figure 9.4
Typical semantic differential items

The Semantic Differential

The fourth and final scaling procedure we shall discuss is termed the **semantic differential.** This procedure, which is quite different in structure and purpose from those already discussed, relies on a series of adjective pairs to bring out the meaning a given individual attaches to a particular concept. A typical series of these adjective pairs is illustrated in Figure 9.4. Respondents are presented with such a list, usually on a separate card, and are asked to rate a particular object, again in the illustration using college students, on a 7-point scale from one adjective to the other. Measurement of this type allows for variation in both the intensity and the direction of the attitude being measured, with neutrality being represented by the midpoint on the scale. The ordering of adjectives in each pair is determined randomly to prevent response set bias.

Although some researchers do break such scales into various underlying dimensions and sum the responses within each, most agree that semantic differential scales do not readily yield scale scores in the same way as the other techniques we have discussed. Rather, semantic differential scales are useful primarily either for purposes of comparison from object to object (Are ostensibly similar objects viewed by respondents in similar terms?) or for the development of scales measuring more general concepts (for example, what types of actions or views are regarded as either liberal or conservative?). In effect, then, the semantic differential serves a somewhat different and more fundamental purpose in the research process—that of helping to construct and evaluate definitions—than do the Likert, Guttman, and Thurstone techniques.

Conclusion

Researchers often use scales to assess "unmeasurable" constructs such as political participation or social power. Since most complex constructs cannot be measured with a single indicator, one simple solution is to combine a number of related indicators into a single measure that is assumed to represent a broader construct. The most common scales used in political science research are Likert, Guttman, Thurstone, and semantic differential scales.

There are, we should note, several other scaling techniques that one might employ in survey research. Those we have discussed are the most common, and within the limits noted, among the most useful. Together they should suggest the types of options available, and the criteria one must consider, when it becomes necessary to develop multiple, but narrow, measures of broad, underlying concepts.

Summary Points

• Scaling is a procedure which combines a number of relatively narrow indicators into a single, summary measure that represents the broader, underlying concept of which each is a part.
• Scales allow the creation of a single indicator for potentially complex concepts that are based on a large number of individual, but related, measures.
• The most frequently found scales are Likert scales and Semantic Differential scales. Other, but less frequently employed, scaling techniques are Guttman and Thurstone scales.

Suggested Readings and References

For a comprehensive survey and discussion of many specific scales found in the literature of social science, see John P. Robinson et al., *Measures of Political Attitudes* (San Diego, CA: Academic Press, 1998), and John P. Robinson, Phillip R. Shaver, Lawrence S. Wrightsman, eds., *Measures of Personality and Social Psychological Attitudes* (San Diego, CA: Academic Press, 1991).

Application-oriented introductions to scaling are provided by Robert F. DeVellis, *Scale Development: Theory and Applications*, 2nd ed. (Thousand Oaks, CA: Sage, 2003) and by Richard G. Netemeyer, William O. Bearden, and Subhash Shama, *Scaling Procedures: Issues and Applications* (Thousand Oaks, CA: Sage, 2003). Gary M. Maranell has brought together many of the seminal works in the literature on scaling in *Scaling: A Sourcebook for Behavioral Scientists* (Chicago: Aldine, 1974). Lee F. Anderson et al., in Chapter 6 of *Legislative Roll-Call Analysis* (Evanston, IL: Northwestern University Press, 1966), provide an especially useful summary of Guttman scaling techniques. John P. McIver and Edward G. Carmines provide succinct overviews of Likert, Guttman, and Thurstone scaling at a slightly more sophisticated level than that presented here in "Undimensional Scaling" in *Quantitative Applications in the Social Sciences* (Beverly Hills, CA: Sage, 1981).

For an example of scale construction, see Ada Finifter, "Dimensions of Political Alienation," *American Political Science Review,* 64 (1970), pp. 389–410.

Research Exercises

1. Select a multifaceted concept (for example, *political alienation*) and identify twenty survey items that might be considered indicators of the concept. Construct both a Thurstone scale and a Likert scale from these items. Administer the survey items to ten friends or classmates and assign each a score on both the Thurstone and the Likert scales. Compare the results.

2. When carrying out Exercise 1, also ask respondents for information on their actual behavior that can be used to check the validity of the scale scores you obtain as indicators of the concept. (For example, do people who score high on political alienation act as we would expect alienated people to behave, whereas those who score low on alienation report what we would regard as non-alienated behavior?) Now compare the scale scores with the behavioral reports and write up your findings by comparing the Thurstone and Likert scales for validity.

3. Select a series of adjective pairs to construct a semantic differential scale measuring perceptions of the heads of state of five countries. Prepare an instrument like that in Figure 9.4 and administer it to a sample of your classmates. Compute a summary score for each descriptor pair and each head of state. What have you learned about your classmates? What have you learned about their perceptions of each head of state and of heads of state generally? Which adjective pairs were most useful in drawing meaningful distinctions and conclusions? Why were these most useful?

Key Terms

scaling
scale
scale score
Likert scaling

Guttman scaling
Thurstone scaling
Semantic Differential

CHAPTER 10

Content Analysis

- What is content analysis?
- What is the research process for content analysis?

Political scientists may learn a great deal about individuals, groups, institutions, or even nations through a careful examination of their communications. Do campaign advertising and election year news reports provide much information about candidates' preferences and abilities? Do the internal memoranda of a large corporation reveal a systematic plan on the part of management to bribe representatives of foreign governments they wish to deal with? What does the *Congressional Record* tell us about the relative influence or importance of each U.S. senator? Do diplomatic communiqués between the United States and Russia reflect the public perception of a reduction in the level of conflict between these two nations?

These questions and others like them may best be answered by a direct examination of various items of communication. In general, these items fall into one of three classes, depending upon the material's source and its intended audience: (1) those that are internally generated by the individual, organization, or government we are studying and internally directed (such communications as corporate memoranda, which represent or reflect the decision-making process itself); (2) those that are internally generated and externally directed (such publications as the *Congressional Record,* which are purposefully molded to create a particular image for the source among outsiders and which may reflect or obscure the process and outcome of decision-making); and (3) those that are externally generated and externally directed (such as campaign news stories that are read by potential voters). Each class of communication may be different in purpose or effect, as well as in accessibility and usefulness for research, but each provides potential opportunities to further our understanding of political behavior.

Defining Content Analysis   In each instance, the most appropriate technique for pursuing these opportunities is **content analysis**—the systematic counting, assessing, and interpreting of the form and substance of communication. Content analysis provides us with a method—really a set of methods—by which we may summarize fairly rigorously certain direct physical evidence of the behaviors of, and the relationships between, various types of political actors.

In this chapter we shall discuss when it is appropriate to use content analysis, how the technique is applied, and how the results of content analysis should be interpreted, as well as certain limits of content analytic procedures.

Preparing to Use Content Analysis

Content analysis may be used to answer research questions whenever there is a physical record of communications by, to, within, or among the political actors we are interested in, as long as the researcher has access to that record. Examples of such a record include books, pamphlets, magazines, newspapers, phonograph records or CDs, audiotape and videotape recordings, photographs, Web pages, transcripts of meetings or proceedings, government documents, memoranda, films, diplomatic communiqués and instructions, political posters and cartoons, political advertising, speeches, and even letters and diaries. Some of these records may be extremely detailed and precise (as is a verbatim transcript of a congressional hearing), while others are much less so (for example, the agenda for the same hearing). Many will have been created independently of the research process (as are newspaper articles by or about the person or group we wish to study), while others must be created by the researchers themselves (for example, videotapes of television news programs). But all sources of data for content analysis will have in common one principal characteristic: the existence of a physical record of communication. Whenever such a record exists or can be created, content analysis may serve as an appropriate research method.

Choosing a Population   The first step in preparing to undertake a content analysis is to define the population of communications we want to study. Here we have a number of options. Which is the best will be determined by our particular research question. For example, if we are interested in studying the development of political themes in twentieth-century American novels, we might define our population as all novels (the type of communication) written by Americans (the type of communicator) and published in the United States (the location of communication) between January 1, 1954, and December 31, 2004 (the time period of communication). If we wish to study newspaper coverage of a political campaign, we might define our population as all campaign-related newspaper articles (the type of communication) of 2 column inches or more in length (the size of the communication) published in daily newspapers (the frequency of communication) that are home delivered (the distribution of the communication) in the Sixth, Seventh, and Eighth Congressional Districts of Ohio (the location of the communication) during the period September 1 to November 5 of the election year (the time period of communication). Or, similarly, if we want to study the level of tension between the leaders of the United States and those of Serbia, we might define our population as all diplomatic messages (the type of communication) passed between the governments of the United States and Serbia (the parties to the communication) during a given time period.

In each instance, we define the population of messages to be studied by establishing sets of criteria to be met by each item. In the examples, these criteria include the type of communication (novels, newspaper articles, or diplomatic notes), the type of communicator, the parties to the communication (the sender or the receiver or both), and the location, frequency, minimum size or length, distribution, and time period of the communication. Although other criteria may be used on occasion, some or all of those listed here will be found in most studies that employ content analysis. The first task in preparing for a content analysis is to choose those criteria that relate most directly to the research question at hand.

Once we have defined our population, we are faced with the problem of deciding which particular cases we shall examine in detail. Because the cases to be analyzed are often limited in number and relatively accessible and because content analysis is generally less expensive per case than other methods (most notably survey research), we are sometimes able to examine every case in a given population—to conduct, in effect, a census. Indeed, the opportunities it offers for the examination of large numbers of cases is one of the major attractions of content analysis as a research technique. More often than not, however, even content analysis must be based on a more limited sample drawn from the larger population. Since documents, newspaper articles, and the like are frequently indexed or otherwise listed in some central location and since such indexes or lists may easily be created by the researcher, the most common sampling procedures used in content analytic studies are the simple random and systematic random techniques. Even when sampling is required, however, the accessibility and relatively low cost of researching messages of various types come into play, and the sample sizes drawn for content analysis may be substantially larger than those employed in other types of research. The result, of course, is a reduction in sampling error and an increased level of confidence in generalizing from our results.

Choosing a Unit of Analysis   Finally, in preparing to undertake a content analysis, we must decide on our unit of measure, or, as it is more commonly termed, our *unit of analysis*. The **unit of analysis** for content analysis is simply the particular element or characteristic of a given communication that we shall examine, count, or assess. The most basic element of a communication, for example, is the *word,* and it may be employed in a fairly straightforward manner. As reflected in each one's public statements, was George W. Bush, Bill Clinton, George H. W. Bush, Ronald Reagan, Jimmy Carter, Gerald Ford, or Richard Nixon most directly concerned with world peace? We might simply sample the statements of each and count the number of times the word *peace* (and, perhaps, some other related words as well) occurs in the text. In speeches before the United Nations during the period 1975 to 2005, which country was most conciliatory on questions of eliminating conflict in the Middle East: Israel, Egypt, Syria, or Saudi Arabia? Again, we might examine the record of all such speeches and count references to such words as *peace, brotherhood,* and *compromise.* In each instance, we identify certain important words and count the frequency with which they appear.

Even in so simple a procedure, however, we must take care to avoid at least two pitfalls. First, we must remember that nonstandardized measures can lead to biased results. If over the years in question, the Israelis have uttered a total of 100,000 words, including fifty salient references (to the words we wish to count), and the Egyptians have uttered some 200,000 words, including 100 salient references, we might reach either of two conclusions from a study of these speeches depending on whether or not we have chosen to standardize our indicator. If we simply count salient references, we will conclude that the Egyptians have been twice as concerned as the Israelis with procuring a settlement. If, however, we standardize our measure to obtain the *proportion of* all words that are in fact salient (for example, salient references *per 1,000 words*), we will conclude that both sides have shared an equal concern about settling their differences. Which approach is better? This is a fundamental problem in operationalizing variables, and the answer is best determined by looking closely at how we have conceptualized the research question initially. The point here is that the use of even such a seemingly concrete indicator as *number of salient words spoken* can entail some ambiguity. The researcher must recognize and deal with that ambiguity, because the decisions made (or overlooked) can have a substantial impact upon the conclusions one draws.

A second potential pitfall in the reliance upon raw word counts arises because the same word may be used in many different ways: "We seek peace, *but* . . ."; "The Arab brotherhood *can never allow* . . ."; "There will be *no* compromise." In the absence of any sort of control, references such as these to peace, brotherhood, and compromise will be included as positive references and will, at the very least, inflate our assessment of the interest on the part of one or both sides in reaching an accommodation. If such usages are sufficiently common, they may well mislead us altogether. For this reason, if we choose to count words, we should in most instances choose to count them in context.

At least two alternatives exist for doing so. First, we may use *judges* or **coders**—people who are part of the research team or are employed by it—to read each salient reference *in context* and to judge that context as positive, neutral, or negative. Usually more than one coder should read each reference, and a relatively high level of agreement among coders should be required before a final determination is reached. (We say more on this point later in this chapter.) This contextual judgment can then be used to enrich our data by allowing us to count and interrelate not only all references to the words we are focusing on but also the proportions of positive and negative references.

Another possible response to the problem of interpreting individual words in context, though it is at best only a partial solution, is to move to, or add, a second unit of analysis—the *theme*. A theme is a particular combination of words or ideas, such as a phrase, a sentence, or even a paragraph. In effect, when we count themes, we search for recurring subjects in a text, as, for example, the expressions *cold war, refugee problem, national health insurance,* or *faith-based politics*. The procedure is similar to that for counting words and represents an improvement to the extent that themes incorporate the modifiers (adverbs, adjectives) and explanatory text that both accompany usage of a particular word and help to establish its meaning.

The problem with analysis at the thematic level is that, although it does make clear the context in which individual words are used, it does so at the cost of much added complexity. This is true in that the same theme may be referenced in very different ways and by very different sets of words. Sometimes these references may be very subtle, displaying few or none of the overt characteristics we are looking for. References to immigration issues, for example, may be veiled in conciliatory words about political asylum, whereas those applied to religion in politics may be cloaked in nationalistic rhetoric. Do such words and rhetoric constitute salient references? Is the theme present, or is it not? These questions do not have simple answers. To the contrary, they generally require us to arrive at some clearly stated but potentially limiting definitions and to develop a series of highly formalized decision-making rules (for example, allowing only overt references that contain one or more words or phrases from a given list to be counted), which may make our findings more reliable but at the same time less meaningful.

A third unit of analysis commonly used in content analysis research is the *item*—the communication itself taken as a whole. What proportion of *books* published in the United States in 1935 advocated socialism? Which presidential candidate in 2004 was the subject of the greatest number of favorable newspaper *editorials*? How did *letters* written by Richard Nixon after his resignation from office differ from those written earlier? In each instance, we treat the item of communication as a unit and we examine its *overall* characteristics. Does it or does it not deal with a particular issue? Does it or does it not reflect a certain set of values or preferences? Such questions lose some of the subtlety of judgment required by lesser units of analysis and they necessitate the making of summary evaluations. For precisely these reasons, however, their analysis is generally more manageable than is that of words or themes, in a sense making fewer demands of the researcher. This is true because variables may be operationalized at a less specific level, one on which events (that is, occurrences of a salient reference) are often more apparent and on which measurement is often more reliable.

An Example   Item-based studies of the use of words and themes have become in recent years much easier to perform due to the availability of online, searchable databases such as *LexisNexis,* which was discussed in Chapter 3. Suppose, for example, we wanted to know how often George W. Bush referred to Saddam Hussein as "evil" during the months leading up to the Second Gulf War, with troops entering Iraq in March, 2003. Using *LexisNexis,* we could request both a full-text search to count all of the articles in *The New York Times* (or any of a large number of other newspapers, magazines, or broadcast transcripts) in which the words "George Bush," "Saddam Hussein" and "evil" appeared for each given month of the period under review. Once in the relevant file, and depending on the software one used for access, the instruction might look something like this:

((George Bush) OR (President Bush)) AND ((Saddam Hussein) w/10 evil) AND
(Date = February 2003)

This string of terms would identify any article published during February 2003 in which Mr. Bush's named appeared *and* in which Mr. Hussein's name also appeared *within 10 words in either direction* from the word "evil." Similar searches also could be conducted to test (1) whether Mr. Bush was referred to more often by title rather than by first name as the crisis moved more clearly toward military conflict (as might be the case, for instance, if the media were subtly enhancing his stature as the nation approached war); (2) whether Mr. Bush led or lagged behind other political leaders (and *which* leaders used this more) in his use of the "evil" terminology; or (3) numerous other hypotheses related to the framing of public perceptions of the conflict.

The results of item analysis may be at least as meaningful as those of component analysis in many instances. Is it more important that the Egyptians have made, say, seven conciliatory references in a given speech at the United Nations, or simply that they have made a conciliatory speech? Is it more important that the United States has sent a note to Iraq with four overt references to military intervention, three veiled references to the failure to disarm, and two sharply critical references to the possible presence of weapons of mass destruction, or that the United States has issued a note that can be characterized as contentious in tone? In content analysis we always risk losing sight of the forest for the trees or, more precisely, of the overall significance of a communication for its component parts. For this reason, we must be very careful to select a unit of analysis that will allow us the particular perspective on our research question that will prove most advantageous.

Computer-based Content Analysis   While *LexisNexis* provides basic word counts for text within its own database, those who are interested in analyzing text from other sources (for example, transcripts of speeches, e-mail messages, or Web pages) have to use more specific software packages written for content analysis of digital documents. Among some of the better-known programs for sale are, for example, *Concordance* (www.rjcw.freeserve.co.uk), *Diction 5.0* (www.scolari.co.uk), and *WordStat* (www.simstat.com/wordstat.htm). Other programs are free for academic use; these include the popular *VBPro* (mmmiller.com/vbpro/vbpro.html) and *General Inquirer* (www.wjh.harvard.edu/~inquirer).

All of these content analysis programs provide basic text analysis functions such as *word frequency counts* and *category frequency counts*. **Word frequency counts** provide a list of all the words that occur in a text and the number of times they occur. In most of these programs, text can be split into subparts and then compared either visually or statistically to see if there are significantly more mentions of particular words in one part or the other. Another advantage of these software packages is that they often make use of synonym lists in order to merge word counts. Thus, instead of counting all words in a given document, the program first removes the grammatical structure and then counts as identical those words that share the same stem. In such a frequency count, for example, 'politics' and 'political' would be counted as the same word. In **category frequency counts,** on the other hand, a set of words or phrases are first grouped into categories, then the program shows how many times each category occurs in the document. For example, the category "election" might consist of the words voting, vote, voter, election, electorate, choice, participation, ballot, poll, and survey that would then be counted as part of one category only. Thus, category counts allow a slightly more sophisticated text analysis, because users can define more specific or complex models of content.

Some of the programs also allow the user to generate so-called concordances (or KWIC as in "key words in context"), which basically analyzes the context in which certain key words appear in the text. For example, a concordance analysis of the key word "liberal" might provide some important insights about how often this term has been used to describe either a politician or a policy. Concordances also are useful for finding lists of words that co-occur reliably in a particular text that then can be combined and used in the category frequency counts described above.

The main advantage of such computer-based content analyses is the fact that as long as the unit of content is short, simple, and well-defined (such as words or small group of words), it is relatively easy to analyze a lot of information. Thus, as long as the text is available in digital form, even documents spanning many thousands of textpages can be analyzed in only seconds. In addition, since the drudgery of content analysis is done by the computer, there is no need to train and employ human coders.

A disadvantage of software-aided content analysis is that computers cannot easily code and analyze latent content, such as meaning or bias. An analysis of whether

President George W. Bush has been portrayed by *The Washington Post* in a more positive or negative light, for example, still requires the input of the researchers (defining the codes for "positive" and "negative") and human coders (evaluating the text as positive or negative).

Undertaking a Substantive Content Analysis

Once we have settled upon a population, a suitable sample, and an appropriate unit of analysis, we are ready to get under way. **Substantive content analysis** is based on a study of words, themes, and items that focuses on the *substantive content* of a given communication. Thus, in preparing to analyze these elements, we must anticipate their substance and we must define each possible observation in accordance with our expectations.

Creating a Dictionary   What this means, in effect, is that as the first step in undertaking a content analysis of this type, we must create a sort of dictionary in which we define each and every observation we might make according to the particular category it fits. Suppose, for example, we are interested in studying all of the sixth-grade schoolbooks used in Havana, Cuba, last year and in identifying in them all references to Americans and the United States? Before we can proceed with such an analysis, we must define just what constitutes a salient reference. Do we look only for the words *American* and the *United States*? If we do so, we may miss a great many salient references using such derogatory terms as *Yankee aggressors, northern imperialists, gringos, invading forces at Guantanamo,* and *the outlaw regime in Washington.*

A parallel but more difficult problem arises when the *absence* of a word or phrase has substantive meaning and must be captured. For example, maps in a sixth-grade civics text published in 2000 for use in Palestinian schools pictured a long green shape separating the West Bank from the Gaza Strip, but it did not label that strip, which, of course, was Israel. Nor did the Israeli capital of Tel Aviv appear on these maps. These omissions are meaningful and significant, and a content analysis scheme for studying such books must capture them. Incidentally, as with our hypothetical Cuban texts, these real books characterized Israel in such oblique terms as "the occupier" (Hockstader 2000).

The point is that we must anticipate not only the references we are likely to encounter but also the contextual elements of their use, and we must devise a thorough and systematic set of decision rules for judging each usage as it occurs. This problem is usually resolved by a combination of pretesting the population of communications to be analyzed (that is, reading through a selection of items to identify the types of salient references most likely to be encountered in a subsequent and more thorough analysis) and developing informed judgments about the contexts and uses of terms. Here, as in the later formal analysis, the observations of several researchers are preferred over those of one.

A more difficult problem arises when we must assign *evaluations* to salient references—when we must decide whether a particular reference is good or bad, favorable or unfavorable, pro or anti, and so forth—and when a series of such references must be ranked according to their intensity (which is most favorable, which

Best of a bad lot	Best available
Better than the opponent	Our first choice
Urge you to vote for	Finest candidate in a crowded field
Everything the people of this state could ask for	Woman (Man) of the hour
An outstanding leader	Promising
One of the nation's best	Lesser of two evils
Best the selection process could produce	Our perennial favorite
Acceptable	Most acceptable
Recommend with reservations	Recommend without reservations
Wholeheartedly endorse	Warmly recommend
Offer our support	Enthusiastically commend to your attention

Figure 10.1
Sample phrases in newspaper editorials endorsing a candidate (random order)

is next most favorable, and so forth). Here we are concerned with developing and applying indicators that are sufficiently refined to tell us not only how the political actor feels but also how strongly the actor feels that way. A situation of this type is illustrated in Figure 10.1. The figure summarizes a number of ways in which a newspaper might endorse a candidate. If our goal is to determine which of several newspapers most strongly supports that candidate, then our immediate task is to decide how to rank these statements according to the intensity of support that each reflects.

Pair-comparing   Several techniques are available to assist us in making these decisions. One of the most prominent of these ranking techniques is **pair-comparison scaling.** Like the Thurstone scaling technique described in Chapter 9, it relies upon the decision of a group of judges about the meaning or intensity of a term, though here the judges may be drawn from the issuers of the communication, the receivers of the communication, a group of scholars familiar with the general subject area under study, the general population, or the researchers themselves.

The goal of pair-comparison scaling is the same as Thurstone scaling, but the procedure itself is rather different. Each item to be evaluated by the judges is paired with *every* other item, in a series of comparisons, and each judge is asked to decide which word or phrase in each pair is the stronger or more intense. Thus, if we have five statements for comparison, each judge compares item 1 against items 2, 3, 4, and 5; item 2 against items 3, 4, and 5; and so forth—in each instance designating one or the other as more intense. By counting the number of times each statement is so designated by each judge, by totaling these numbers for each item for all judges, and by dividing by the number of judges (that is, by calculating the average score the judges as a group have assigned to a particular statement), we are able to arrive at a quantitative ranking of the intensity of each item. The higher its mean score, the stronger the judges consider a statement.

One of the problems associated with the pair-comparison procedure is the fact that it relies entirely on the decisions of judges whose criteria for judgment may or may not be appropriate or consistent. The standards for expertise in such undertakings are not always clear, or at least are not always clearly stated, and as a consequence, the judgments themselves are open to question. Indeed, it is not uncommon for a single judge to assign different scores to the same statement in a series of identical tests. Because we are sampling content and not humans here, there is neither a clear reference population, as there is in Thurstone scaling, nor a set of underlying parameters to be approximated. The selections made by judges are necessarily arbitrary. Consequently, the reliability of results derived by depending upon such judges may be minimal.

Undertaking a Structural Content Analysis

In addition to, or in lieu of, words, themes, or other elements that denote the substantive content of a communication, several units of analysis are available that allow **structural content analysis.** Here we are less concerned with *what* is said than with *how* it is said, and while we must retain a concern with the subject matter, we measure something else.

We may be concerned, for example, with the amount of space or time devoted to a given subject in a particular source. How many words or column inches of newspaper coverage have been accorded each candidate in a particular election campaign? How many articles or pages in political science journals published in the United States are devoted each year to an analysis of governments and politics in Africa? Has the number changed, or has it remained constant over the past three decades?

Alternatively, we might be concerned with other, and perhaps more subtle, aspects of the communication format. Is a particular news item accompanied by a photograph or illustration of some sort? Those that are have been found to attract more attention from readers than those that are not. How large a headline accompanies a news item? Does coverage of a particular subject receive front-page prominence, or is it buried among the truss ads? In answering questions like these, we are less concerned with subtleties of meaning than with styles of presentation. We watch for the presence or absence, the prominence, and the extent of treatment of general themes rather than for substantive nuance. The result in many cases is an analysis whose measurements are much more reliable than those employed in a more substance-oriented study (since there is less ambiguity built into the indicators), but one whose lessons may, as a direct consequence, be less rich.

Figure 10.2 illustrates a typical coding sheet for recording data from a structural analysis of content. Drawn from a study of newspaper coverage of congressional elections (Manheim 1974), the unit of analysis for this particular study was the *candidate insertion,* which was defined as any newspaper item that mentioned by name or implication any candidate for Congress in the district in which the newspaper was distributed. Thus, each row on the coding sheet summarizes the characteristics of a single candidate insertion. After each item was assigned a unique identification number, it was classified according to type (news story, feature article, editorial, letter to the editor), the date of publication, the candidate it referred to, the newspaper in which it appeared, the general preferences expressed in the item (if any), its prominence of

ID Number	Article type	Publication Date	Candidate	Newspaper	Preference	Prominence	Graphics	Headline	Content	Total	Column	Inches	Candidate	Column	Inches

Figure 10.2
Typical coding sheet for structural content analysis

placement (front page, inside page), the presence or absence of accompanying photographs or drawings, reference to the candidate in the headline of the item, the primary content of the item (news of a campaign event, content of a speech, endorsement), the overall size of the insertion, and the proportion of the insertion actually relating to the candidate in question.

Structural Versus Substantive Content Analysis   Identifying the frequency of occurrence of a name or other item requires only a general concern with the actual substance of each insertion rather than the highly detailed and specific judgment necessary in the substantive approach discussed earlier. As a result, structural content analysis is usually easier to design and carry out, and therefore less expensive and often more reliable, than is substantive content analysis. And though its results may be less satisfying in that they provide us with what amounts to a sketch of a communication rather than a finished portrait, those results often prove entirely adequate in answering a particular research question.

Special Problems in the Use of Content Analysis

Although content analysis is a relatively inexpensive technique that draws on a relatively accessible database, and although there are few special ethical dilemmas that we are likely to encounter in undertaking it (unless we are analyzing confidential or classified communications), we must still be careful to avoid several potential difficulties when we use this method.

Biased Content   We must be aware that communications are issued, and may be specifically designed, for a purpose, whether it be description, persuasion, exhortation, direction, self-protection, or even obfuscation. In analyzing such communications, therefore, we must attempt to interpret their content in the context of their apparent purpose. For example, it is common to find in the Chinese press statements of the type, "*All of the Chinese people believe* that membership in the World Trade Organization is a major step forward in the progress toward social revolution."

Taken at face value, such statements are demonstrably false, since not every one of many millions of people would be aware of, let alone agree upon the value of, any single policy. From this perspective, we might be inclined to view these statements as the most blatant form of propaganda. We have learned from studying the Chinese press, however, that statements of this type are not printed for purposes of external propaganda at all, but rather are intended to suggest to the Chinese people themselves the beliefs that their government wishes them to hold. In other words, the purpose of such statements of consensus is not descriptive, but directive. Knowing this, we may interpret them as useful indicators of the policy interests of the Chinese leaders rather than as meaningless items of propaganda, and we may employ them to some advantage. The purpose of a communication, then, can provide an important context for understanding its content, and we must attempt, when possible, to ferret out this information.

Intended Audience   The distribution that is accorded a particular item of communication can have significant implications for its meaning. A pamphlet that circulates only among Chinese dissidents, a solicitory letter from a candidate or special interest group that reaches only those people on a particular mailing list, a document that circulates only among a small group of persons—each is an example of a communication with a limited or specialized distribution. Even a newspaper that is generally available may have a limited or specialized clientele. *The New York Times,* for example, has a readership that is generally more affluent and better educated than that of the *New York Daily News,* yet both are readily available to all of the city's newspaper readers. *The Wall Street Journal* has nationwide distribution, but its readership does not extend equally to all socioeconomic classes. Very often, if we are to assess properly the significance of a communication, we must know whom it reaches. Whether by judgment (rendered, for example, by knowledgeable experts, as might be the case in studying communication among Chinese dissidents), by inquiry (as when we ask a candidate or group which mailing lists were used), by self-evidence (which we have when a document is accompanied by a routing slip listing, and perhaps initialed by, all who have read it, or when a Web page includes a counter showing the number of visitors), or by reliance on an audience survey (such as the kind usually taken by newspapers to document their circulation claims), we must attempt to measure or to estimate how widely a message has been disseminated and to whom. Having this information enables us to judge the value or the importance of the material we analyze.

Representative Sample   We must try to gauge the degree of our own access to the items at issue. Have we been provided with free choice over the materials we shall analyze? Are those materials available in an unbiased manner (that is, do we have access to *all* of them), or has some external control been imposed by someone other than the researcher? Do we, for instance, have access only to documents that have been declassified, only to Chinese newspapers that are published for and distributed primarily to foreigners, only to records of *formal* meetings of a government commission? The issue here is one of generalizability, and the question is whether the research population itself, not to mention the sample, is truly representative. If it is not, the researcher may, if not exercising care, at the very least be misled and at the worst be manipulated.

The difficulty in overcoming these challenges to a successful content analysis is that the information we require in order to make informed judgments may simply be unavailable. We may not know, and may be unable to ascertain, the purpose of a communication, its distribution, or the degree of access to it that we have been accorded. The dangers here are manifold, and the content analyst must be sensitive to them. We must not allow appearances to cloud our judgment but must maintain a healthy skepticism regarding our data as long as these questions remain unanswered. That is not necessarily to say that we should not undertake content analysis under conditions of uncertainty, but merely that we should not lose sight of the uncertainty itself once the analysis is under way.

Intercoder Reliability   We should say a few words about *intercoder reliability*. With the exception of raw word counts and other content analysis procedures that have been thoroughly computerized (several programs embodying concept dictionaries and search or count procedures have been developed), all content analysis depends on human judgments about communication content. Messages, after all, do not analyze themselves. They are poked and prodded, counted and classified by *Homo sapiens* in the form of the researcher. Therefore individual researchers may differ from one another in their understanding of the content of a given communication. Indeed, only when some degree of consensus can be reached about that meaning can we have real confidence in our measurements. **Intercoder reliability** is the term political scientists use to describe the degree of that consensus. The higher it is, the better. In general, intercoder reliability may be promoted by taking three basic steps:

1. Operationalize all variables carefully and thoroughly. Make sure that all meanings have been clearly stated and as many ambiguities as possible have been eliminated. In effect, this will create *common standards of judgment* that can be used consistently in classifying and measuring content.

2. Use as many observers (coders) as possible. The larger the number of subscribers to the consensus, the more confidence we can have in it. This may, of course, mean more work and considerable duplication of effort (and, if proper training is not provided, it carries a risk of increased measurement error), but the payoff can be substantial. The limiting factor here is usually cost.

3. Maximize the interaction among the observers. Hold common practice sessions and argue out all differences of interpretation so that ultimately the consensus extends not only to the data but also to the real meanings of the operational definitions themselves.

Calculating Reliability   The success of this process can be measured in either of two ways, both of which draw upon statistical concepts that we develop more fully in Chapter 16. One approach, used primarily in substantive content analysis, is to have all observers who are working on a given project analyze and code independently (assign their own numerical values to) the same communication, then to calculate a statistic called a correlation coefficient (Pearson's r) among the codes recorded by each pair of observers. This coefficient (discussed in detail in Chapter 17) measures the degree of correspondence in the judgments of the researchers on whether and how often a particular word or theme is present. The coefficient ranges from -1 to

+1, and readings of +.90 or better are usually interpreted as indicating a high degree of intercoder reliability.

An alternative measure may be more useful for structural content analysis, in which we are less concerned with the treatment of themes than with their presence or absence and in which duplicated measurement is less necessary. Here we treat the differences between observers as a variable in their own right, and we ask whether that variable is associated with systematic differences in any other variable we have measured. In other words, we are concerned with the possibility that one or more observers have recorded results consistently differently from the others. If it can be assumed that all cases have been distributed to the observers in an unbiased manner (some effort is generally made to distribute them *randomly*), any systematic differences we observe are more likely to be the result of differences between coders than of underlying differences in the cases that happen to have been assigned to the aberrant observer. The coefficient of intercoder reliability here takes the form $(1 - \eta^2)$, where η^2 is a measure of the variance in each subject variable that is accounted for by differences between coders (Freeman 1965, 120–129). By subtracting this "observer error" from 1, we obtain the proportion of error-free observations. The coefficient is calculated separately for each variable and should exceed +.90 if we are to have confidence in the reliability of our measures.

Conclusion

In sum, content analysis is a widely applicable technique with advantages in cost, sample size, and, often, access to data. Perhaps more than any other technique, however, it demands careful operationalization of all variables and constant monitoring of the process of observation. Its results may be highly informative, but they must be understood in a context that it is often beyond the scope of the content analysis technique itself to describe. For this reason, content analysis is often used to best effect in combination with other data-gathering methods (surveys, direct observation) in what are termed *multimethod designs*.

Summary Points

- Content analysis assesses written or textual information that people receive.
- Before conducting a content analysis, you need to determine the population of interest, select a sample of documents, choose a unit of analysis, and decide whether computerized or human coders are most appropriate.

Suggested Readings and References

The most thorough and accessible content analysis texts available today are written by Kimberly A. Neuendorf, *The Content Analysis Guidebook* (Thousand Oaks, CA: Sage Publications, 2002) and by Klaus Krippendorff, *Content Analysis: An Introduction to Its Methodology*, 2nd ed. (Thousand Oaks, CA: Sage, 2004). Computer-based content analyses are specifically covered in Mark D. West, ed. *Applications of Computer Content Analysis* (Westport, CT: Ablex, 2001), Mark D. West, ed., *Theory, Method, and Practice in Computer Content Analysis* (Westport, CT: Ablex, 2001), Roel Popping *Computer-assisted Text*

Analysis (Thousand Oaks, CA: Sage, 2000), and Ephraim Nissan and Klaus Schmidt, eds., *From Information to Knowledge: Conceptual and Content Analysis by Computer* (London: Intellect, 1995).

Some of the more interesting examples of content analysis at work are Bruce Bimber and Richard Davis, *Campaigning Online: The Internet in U.S. Elections* (New York: Oxford University Press, 2003), which compares the content of presidential campaign Web sites with how candidates present themselves in other media; Paul M. Kellstedt, *The Mass Media and the Dynamics of American Racial Attitudes* (Cambridge: Cambridge University Press, 2003), operationalizes a summary measure of "racial policy preferences" with a systematic analysis of news media content spanning almost fifty years; Stuart N. Soroka, *Agenda-setting Dynamics in Canada* (Vancouver: University of British Columbia Press, 2002), which tracks various groups' issue agendas, using a decade of articles from newspapers across Canada. Examples of content analysis in use, together with discussions of related methodological issues, appear regularly in the pages of *Journalism and Mass Communication Quarterly, Journal of Communication,* and *Political Communication.*

Referenced work: Lee Hockstader, "Israel Not on Map in Palestinian Textbooks," *Washington Post*, September 3, 2000, p. A1. Jarol B. Manheim, "Urbanization and Differential Press Coverage of the Congressional Campaign," *Journalism Quarterly*, 51 (1974), pp. 649–653, 669. The standard intercoder reliability formula and computational procedure, which is a measure of association between one nominal and one interval variable, may be found in Linton C. Freeman, *Elementary Applied Statistics: For Students of Behavioral Science* (New York: Wiley, 1965), pp. 120–129.

Research Exercises

1. List as many words or phrases as you can that might constitute references to human rights abuses in news stories about China, Indonesia, Mexico, and the United States. Using a pair-comparison procedure, rank these terms in order of intensity. Compare the countries' rankings.

2. Design a study using *structural* content analysis to answer this question: Is *The New York Times* biased in its coverage of the Middle East? What are the principal variables to be measured in such a study? Next, design a *substantive* content analysis to answer the same question. Will the principal variables in this second study differ from those in the first? In what ways? If you had to choose, which method would you pick as most appropriate to answer the research question? Why?

3. The journal *Political Communication* publishes many research articles that employ content analysis. Locate and read one such article, then summarize and evaluate the content analysis procedures employed by the author(s).

Key Terms

content analysis
unit of analysis
coders
word frequency counts
category frequency counts

substantive content analysis
pair-comparison scaling
structural content analysis
intercoder reliability

CHAPTER 11

Sources and Applications of Aggregate Data

- What is the distinguishing characteristic of aggregate data?
- What is the most common pitfall to avoid when analyzing aggregate data?

Scientists are interested in individual cases only to the degree that these examples help them to test more general hypotheses. Similarly, political scientists typically observe individuals solely in an effort to learn more about that type of individual. For example, we may study the behavior of a particular governor not because we want to know about Governor John Doe, but because we think we can better understand or predict the behavior of governors in the United States from what we observe about Governor Doe. Political scientists are usually interested in the study of groups or collections of persons or institutions, such as American voters, Indian peasants, Russian bureaucrats, or European parliaments.

Defining Aggregate Data   Sometimes, in order to study these groups we have to gather information on the individual members of the groups (or a representative sample of them) and combine or *aggregate* that information to secure information about the group *as a group*. Often, however, there already exists aggregated information about the group. Data on the characteristics of an entire group or aggregate of individuals are referred to as **aggregate data.**

There are two general categories of aggregate data. The first category— **summative indicators**—includes large sets of measures of group characteristics that are created by combining the behavior of all members of the group. For example, the population of a nation is an aggregate datum derived by adding inhabitants as units. Birth, death, literacy, suicide, and crime *rates* are aggregate data created by adding up the number of particular events (births, deaths, crimes, etc.) in a group and expressing it in a standardized unit such as *per thousand persons in the population*. In each case, the aggregate datum quantifies some *group* characteristic that individual members of the group cannot possess. Individuals may be born or learn to read and write but cannot have a birth or literacy *rate* in the same sense that a nation does. These data are measures of aggregate characteristics.

A second general category of aggregate data consists of those measures that quantify group characteristics that are derived not from any combination of individual members' characteristics but from qualities of the group *when acting as a group*. They are often referred to as **syntality indicators.** For example, *form of government* is a system-level variable, and a given nation may have a democratic or a nondemocratic form of government regardless of whether its individual citizens hold democratic or nondemocratic values and attitudes.

Types of Groups   Data from each category are available on many different kinds of groups from a variety of sources. Such groups may be broadly classified into **areal groups** (those defined by residence within a geographic area, such as a nation, city, or census tract) and **demographic groups** (those defined by personal characteristics, such as age, race, or occupation).

In this chapter you will learn that proper use of aggregate data involves solving some challenging methodological problems. The advantages of using such data, however, often far outweigh the costs. Political scientists may find the use of aggregate data necessary or desirable because individual-level data are either unobtainable or too expensive to obtain.

As examples of studies for which individual data might be impossible to obtain, consider the following cases. (1) If we want to do a historical study, at least some of the groups on which we need data (for example, the population of Chicago in 1880) may be dead. (2) Members of some politically important groups such as international terrorist organizations may absolutely refuse to be identified or interviewed. (3) Often, political scientists find themselves in situations in which it is theoretically possible to collect individual level data, but such collection is prohibitively expensive. This is especially likely to be the case when we are interested in comparing nations, because the cost and logistical problems of multinational survey research are enormous.

If you are interested in research questions for which individual-level data are unavailable, you may find it worthwhile to search for aggregate data that contain the basic information needed. In this chapter we introduce you to the types of aggregate data that are available, suggest some sources of these data, discuss some of the methodological problems encountered in using aggregate data, and, finally, offer some guidelines for collecting aggregate data. You will soon recognize that the proper use of aggregate data requires the mastery of data collection, processing, and analysis techniques. As a student and as a professional political scientist, however, you are probably more likely to work with aggregate data than with data collected through any of the methods described in preceding chapters, because aggregate data are so readily available.

Types of Aggregate Data

Most of the aggregate data available to political scientists are gathered by non-social scientists for reasons other than research. Therefore, they often seem to bear only a tangential relationship to our research. In fact, one of the most challenging aspects of aggregate data analysis is often that of finding some way to use existing data as indicators of concepts of immediate theoretical interest to the researcher. For example, at first glance there is little reason to believe that a political scientist will be concerned with the number of radios or newspaper subscriptions purchased in some nation. We are not, after all, marketing agents for the press. But these figures may be useful as partial indicators of the amount of political communication that goes on within a nation or of its level of economic development, and these clearly are appropriate concerns for political scientists. Similarly, the number of hospital beds per thousand persons in the population takes on political significance when it is viewed as an indicator of, say, the distribution of health care facilities among groups within a city or state.

The point is that aggregate data are often of no intrinsic interest and have to be transformed in some way to be of use. Do not look only for ready-made indicators of concepts, but be alert to the possibility of combining seemingly unrelated measures into useful indicators.

We can identify six types of aggregate data (Merritt 1970). They are explained here in roughly *descending* order of the extent to which they are likely to be valid and reliable.

1. *Census data.* Many of the world's nations attempt to survey their entire population (or at least all households) periodically in order to gather information to be used for such purposes as levying taxes and planning public policy. The data commonly collected includes such information as number of people in the family, sex of the head of the household, length of residence, educational levels, family income, and condition of housing. Though census data are collected from individuals, by the time they become available to researchers as part of the public record, they usually appear as summary figures (the total number of persons who own a car in a given geographic area, for instance).

   Census data have several desirable characteristics that make them extremely valuable in aggregate data analysis. First, although errors can occur, census data are generally quite reliable. Second, because the variables measured are normally straightforward, census data are usually regarded as highly valid. Third, some nations have been collecting relatively standardized data for many years. Thus, census data provide an opportunity to trace historical trends or to test hypotheses about change over time. Fourth, because census data are generally standardized (that is, they contain responses to the same questions and classify responses in the same categories) within nations and are often comparable between nations, they are useful in comparing different cities, regions, or nations. In addition, census data are easily available. Many nations publish reports of both major census projects (generally undertaken once every ten years) and any of a wide variety of specialized surveys undertaken in between. The United Nations (www.un.org) publishes the annual *Demographic Yearbook,* describing the census data available from various countries. In the United States, the Bureau of the Census (www.census.gov) maintains a large User Services Division that can assist social scientists in gaining access to and working with the wide variety of data available from the bureau.

2. *Organizational statistics.* In every nation, the various levels of government, businesses, and organized groups such as labor unions and professional associations gather data related to their own operations. If these statistics happen to fit the requirements of a particular social scientist's research project, they can be of great value.

   Some organizations collect their own data, as does a multinational corporation keeping a record of its capital investments, a hospital recording information on patients, or a city government recording property assessments for tax purposes. Others use data generated by other agencies, such as the United States Department of Commerce (www.doc.gov), to create data in the form of various indices of, for example, economic performance or population shifts.

With either type of official statistics, there can be problems. The first, and perhaps greatest, problem is that of gaining access to the data. Data compiled by government agencies are generally part of the public record and readily available, but data collected by nongovernmental organizations are private property. Some organizations, especially businesses, consider their data sensitive and are most reluctant to share them. Often the problem is less one of gaining access to the data than one of simply learning of their existence. There are no central listings of the statistics collected by the thousands of public and private organizations engaged in such record keeping. Researchers may, therefore, miss major opportunities because of a lack of information about the existence or content of particular statistics.

A second problem is that the content and quality of the data may vary greatly, making comparisons and generalizations difficult. If teachers' unions in Indiana and Ohio do not collect comparable data on their members, we cannot use their statistics to make meaningful comparisons between them. In addition, if we do not know how data have been collected, we may not know how much confidence to place in the figures.

Finally, data may not be in a usable form. A local government's vital statistics (records of births, deaths, marriages, deeds) may be available only in unaggregated form and only in a central location, so that a researcher has to sit for countless hours in a government office tediously hand-recording the data so that they can be converted to a machine-readable (i.e., computerized) form and totaled. This can require an unjustifiable investment of time and money.

These problems are not found in all official statistics, and even when they are encountered, the potential payoff in economical research is generally worth the effort required to solve them.

3. *Sample surveys.* Survey research is designed to gather individual-level data. When surveys are based on samples that are representative of a population in which we are interested, it is often possible to use their results as aggregate data. Suppose, for example, we want to compare the political information level of two nations' citizenry. If each nation has a public opinion polling organization that regularly surveys a national sample (as Gallup and Roper do in the United States) and that asks questions about such behavioral matters as frequency of watching TV news reports or subscriptions to news magazines, we might use the results to construct aggregate measures of our variable. Similar use can sometimes be made of individual surveys conducted for academic purposes. Survey data, if properly collected, have the advantage of being quite reliable, and they can be as valid as the researcher is wise in constructing indicators. They are also generally available (at least for a price) from the agencies or scholars who have collected them, and they are often in a readily usable form.

4. *Publications' content.* In a construction of aggregate data, content analysis can be applied to publications sponsored by or distributed among particular groups. For example, if we are examining political socialization processes in Great Britain, we might content analyze the textbooks used in civics courses to determine the extent to which they stress democratic values, and we might then use the combined results as one indicator of the nation's democratic orientation.

Similarly, we might rely on content analysis of the major newspapers of developing nations to derive an indicator of those nations' relative attention to international and domestic events or of their support for the United Nations. In each case, the product of the content analysis is an indicator of a group characteristic.

This type of aggregate data is generated by the researcher specifically for the purpose of a given research project instead of being collected from a primary source, such as a census report. As a result, access to such data depends on the availability of the publications or databases (such as *LexisNexis*) needed for a content analysis and on the researcher's having the resources necessary to perform the content analysis. The reliability and validity of the data depend, in turn, on the skill with which the researcher applies the rules discussed in Chapter 9. Aggregate data collected through content analysis of publications have the advantage of being adaptable to an individual study but generally provide only highly imperfect indicators of underlying concepts. Ask yourself, for instance, how confident you would feel in making statements about the kind of political values British schoolchildren learn from an analysis of their civics texts.

5. *Event data.* Often, political scientists are interested in the occurrence of discrete events that are not recorded in census reports or organizational data because they are too infrequent or fall outside the responsibility of any one agency. Riots, revolutions, assassinations, the breaking of diplomatic ties, protest demonstrations, indictments of public officials for crimes in office, *coups d'etat,* and the creation of new political parties are all examples. Information on these events can be useful in the construction of indicators of group properties. For instance, we might want to measure a nation's political stability by counting the number of acts of political violence occurring there in a given time period or want to compare the level of political corruption in several cities by counting the number of indictments of public officials for bribery.

Event data are gathered by a process very similar to content analysis. After deciding what events are important to our study and carefully operationalizing them (for example, deciding what actions constitute a riot), we systematically survey sources such as newspapers, yearbooks, and radio broadcast transcripts that are likely to contain reports of them, and we take a tally (being careful to avoid double-counting the same event when it is reported in more than one source). In addition, we can use content analysis techniques to produce more detailed data about these events. We can, for example, classify riots according to their duration, their level of violence, or the number of people involved in order to produce a measure of severity.

Event data can be made relatively reliable by careful training and supervision of those who read the source materials. However, it is extremely difficult to make event data *valid.* The major problem is comprehensiveness in reporting. Even when all known sources or reports of some type of event have been reviewed, the researcher cannot be sure that some such events have occurred but have not been reported. In some nations the government carefully controls reports of political events in order to present the preferred image to the world, so that many important happenings (such as the use of troops to break a strike) may not be reported and no valid measure of the events can be constructed. A second and related problem grows from the potential inaccuracy of reports. Even when events are recorded, the details of their occurrence can be distorted intentionally or unintentionally. Such problems are not insurmountable, but researchers must be aware of them in designing their studies around event data, and they must realistically assess their chances of acquiring valid measures by this means.

6. *Judgmental data.* Occasionally there simply are no data available to use for construction of measures of particular aggregate properties. In these cases, researchers can sometimes use as data the opinions of experts or persons with special knowledge.

Consider the example of a study of the lobbying efforts by several interest groups for and against environmental protection legislation. There may be no public record on the subject, but researchers can ask key legislators about their judgment of whether and how strongly each group supports or opposes such legislation in its lobbying efforts. Similarly, if researchers are unable to gather data on the force governments employ to stay in power in various nations, they can ask other scholars who have studied those nations' political systems for their judgment about the coerciveness of the governments.

Obviously, judgmental data suffer from some limitations. In the first place, their accuracy is subject to the biases and limited experiences of the judges. Using many judges and checking their estimates against one another represent one way to avoid relying on false or partial judgments. It is often difficult, however, to find several qualified judges who differ in their background and their experience with the subject matter, so that even using multiple judges is no guarantee against inaccurate data. Second, even when judges provide perfectly accurate information, judgmental data are generally imprecise. We are, after all, asking for opinions and impressions of complex phenomena, not counts of discrete events. These limitations need not be debilitating, however. It is important only that researchers recognize them in designing studies and in analyzing judgmental data. It would be an error to treat judgmental data as more reliable and precise than such data are.

Limitations in the Use of Aggregate Data

From the foregoing discussion you can see that the specific types of problems encountered in aggregate data analysis vary with the types and sources of data being used. There are, however, some general problems that may be confronted in any use of aggregate data analysis. We discuss two. Our purpose is not to provide solutions but to alert you to the need to be on the lookout for these problems in your research and the research of others.

Ecological Fallacy   It is important to consider first the general problem referred to as the **ecological fallacy,** because knowledge of it should guide the design of research and the specification and operationalization of variables, as well as the very decision to use aggregate data to address a specific research question.

Researchers run the risk of committing one of several types of ecological fallacy anytime they attempt to generalize to one level of analysis from data collected at another. For example, if we collect data on the racial characteristics of individual welfare recipients in each *state* in the United States and find a strong positive relationship between being nonwhite and receiving public assistance, we may be tempted to generalize "up" to the national level, claiming that this relationship holds for the nation as a whole, or to generalize "down" by assuming that the relationship found in any given state will also be found in each of its counties. If, however, we actually do aggregate our data at the national or county level, we may find that the relationship is significantly different from that found when data are aggregated at the state level. Empirical studies of the ecological problem have shown that relationships may not only be weaker or stronger at different levels but may even change directions. When researchers generalize from one level of analysis to another, they run the risk of seriously misinterpreting their data and reaching conclusions that are simply wrong.

Does this mean that we must use only data that are aggregated at the level of whatever units of analysis we choose for our studies and can never generalize up or down in research? No. There are techniques of data analysis that, under some conditions, can at least minimize the risks involved in making inferences between levels of analysis. If researchers find that they must use data aggregated at a level other than that with which they are concerned, they should plan to employ one or more of these data analysis techniques outlined by King (1997) or Achen and Shively (1995), and should take care that their data meet the requirements of this type of analysis before investing time and resources in gathering them.

Awareness of the risks of ecological inference should make researchers extremely cautious when planning a study and operationalizing concepts. Whenever possible, they should avoid selecting indicators that require inferences between levels of analysis. For example, suppose we are studying the relationship between union membership and support for the Democratic party in the United States, and we discover aggregate data for congressional districts that give the percentage of each district's labor force holding union memberships and the percentage of each district's voters that have voted Democratic in recent elections. We will be able to use these data if congressional districts are our unit of analysis and our goal is to be able to make statements such as, *Those districts with proportionately more union members tend to elect Democratic candidates.* However, if individual voters are our units of analysis, we will want to be able to make statements such as, *Labor union members tend to support Democratic candidates.* In this case we *cannot* use with any confidence the aggregate data from congressional districts, and we will be wise to seek data on *individuals'* union membership and voting behavior.

Variable Precision   A second, and related, set of problems often encountered in aggregate data analysis relates to the difficulties of creating valid indicators from aggregate data. It is rare to find aggregate figures that can be used directly as a measure of some concept of interest to political scientists. Most frequently, we find numbers representing variables that can be viewed as part of the larger phenomena to which our concepts refer. In studying the political impact of modernization, for instance, researchers may not be able to find aggregate data that directly report the level of modernization of various nations. They might, however, be able to find information on the proportion of each nation's population that lives in communities of more than 25,000, is engaged in nonagricultural employment, or is literate, all of which can be considered components of modernization. Such figures are often referred to as **raw data;** they are of no intrinsic interest in themselves but can be used to create indicators of concepts that are of interest.

Developing Useful Measures   The challenge that aggregate data analysts face is one of finding theoretically and methodologically justifiable ways of converting raw data into useful measures. Two basic approaches to this are the creation of indices and the transformation of data.

Index construction is a means of reducing complex data to a single indicator that more fully captures the meaning of a concept than does any of its components. Three commonly used types of index are additive, multiplicative, and weighted. An **additive index** is appropriate when available data represent different measures of the *same* underlying variable. For example, we might want simply to add together reported numbers of exported bushels of wheat, corn, and soybeans in order to obtain an indicator of the concept *agricultural exports*.

Often, however, aggregate data represent measures of *different* aspects of a phenomenon and cannot be added. There is, for instance, no mathematical logic by which we can add the number of people involved in a riot to the number of hours it lasts in order to create an index of riot severity. Number of participants and length of duration are nonadditive elements of the phenomenon we call *riots*. We can, however, argue that those two elements interact with one another to determine how severe a riot is. By this logic we might *multiply* the number of participants by the number of hours of duration to create an indicator of the severity of the riot by measuring the "demonstrator hours" devoted to it. Such an indicator is called a **multiplicative index.** Indices of this type are called for anytime we have measures of different aspects of a concept.

In some circumstances raw data have to be weighted by some standard to become a useful indicator of concepts. For example, the *number* of persons attending antigovernment rallies is a useful indicator of the legitimacy accorded a government only when it is expressed as a percentage of the population. When we do this we are weighting one variable (the number attending antigovernment rallies) by a second (the population) to create a **weighted index.** Similarly, we might want to weight the number of antigovernment demonstrations by the variable *time* to create an index of demonstrations per year on the assumption that ten demonstrations in one year indicate more political unrest than ten demonstrations spread over ten years. This particular type of weighting is known as *standardization*.

Weighting is technically simple to do, but it is often conceptually difficult to determine whether a measure should be weighted and by what it should be weighted. For instance, it is not clear whether arms races are triggered by the absolute level of armaments held by nations or by the ratio of one nation's armaments to another's. Should a nation's armament level be weighted by its opponents' armament level before the figure can be used as an indicator in a study of arms races? Answers to such questions are often to be found in an empirical examination of how the use of weighted and unweighted indicators affects the results of statistical analysis.

Figure 11.1
Effects of logarithmic transformation on hypothetical data from abortion rights demonstrations in 57 U.S. cities

Often, in the use of aggregate data, measures are encountered that cannot be made useful simply by combining them with others, but that must be individually modified. Sometimes even indices can be made more useful if they are modified. Such modifications are referred to as **data transformations.** Data are transformed principally in order to meet the requirements of certain statistical procedures that researchers want to employ in data analysis. In general, the justification for transforming data is to avoid having the results of statistical analyses distorted by features of the distribution of the raw data.

There are many techniques of data transformation, and each is designed to correct different flaws in raw data. However, the *logarithmic transformation* can serve as an example of how transformations work. Some of the most useful statistical procedures can legitimately be applied only to data that are normally distributed. (We discuss normal distributions in Chapter 16.) Application of these procedures to data that are not normally distributed can result in serious underestimates of the strength of relationships between variables, as well as other misleading results. Yet raw aggregate data are often not normally distributed. Logarithmic transformations are designed to make data more nearly approximate a normal distribution. The basic procedure is to add a constant to the score for each case on the raw data and then substitute the appropriate logarithm for the original score by using a log table. The effects of such a transformation on data are suggested in Figure 11.1, which shows the results of transforming hypothetical data on the number of people taking part in abortion rights demonstrations in fifty-seven U.S. cities. The distribution of the transformed data in Figure 11.1(b) does not form a normal, or bell-shaped, curve, but it is much more nearly normal than the distribution of the raw data in Figure 11.1(a).

You should not interpret anything we have just said as meaning that having multiple measures of some concept is a problem that must be solved. On the contrary, it is highly desirable to have *multiple indicators* of concepts, and though it is often useful to combine measures into indices, it is usually wise also to record the individual measures and examine them separately at some stage of the data analysis. The reason is that multiple indicators can be used to check the validity of our operationalization of concepts.

For example, suppose we want to measure the concept *gender discrimination in employment* among the American states. We might be able to find aggregate data on the following variables:

The ratio of the average salary paid to women to the average salary paid to men

The proportion of all professionals in the state who are female

The ratio of the unemployment rate for women to the unemployment rate for men

We can use all three indicators by scoring each state on each variable and comparing the results. If those states that appear to have the most discrimination by one measure also rank high on discrimination by the other measures, we will feel more confident that each measure is a valid indicator of the underlying concept *gender discrimination in employment.* If, on the other hand, we find that those states that rank high on discrimination as measured by two of the indicators rank low on discrimination as measured by the third, we will be reluctant to use the deviant measure as an indicator of our concept.

The more independent indicators we can locate for each concept, the better, for with more indicators we can provide more convincing tests of the validity of each. For instance, in the preceding example, with only three measures, we might not be altogether sure that the deviant measure is not, in fact, the valid one and the other two invalid. It may be its very validity as an indicator of our concept that makes it stand apart from the others in the way it ranks states. If, however, we have five or ten measures that produce consistent rankings of states and one that stands apart, we can feel quite confident that it is the deviant measure that is invalid. A variety of techniques is available for using multiple measures to test and enhance the validity of our indicators (see Suggested Readings and References).

There is one additional important issue to consider when using aggregate data. This potential problem stems from the fact that aggregate data are often available in a form that does not allow valid comparisons across units. For example, if we are interested in the degree to which different states in the United States exhibit a commitment to public education, we might find data on how much each state spends on education each year. It would be inappropriate, however, to compare the total number of dollars Texas spends on education to the total number of dollars Rhode Island spends, because the two states differ so radically in size and wealth. Rhode Island may spend only a fraction of the amount Texas does and yet exhibit a stronger commitment to education because it is spending far more *per school-age child* or a far greater *portion* of its total state budget on schooling. To make a valid comparison among the states, it would be necessary to restate the amount they spend on education in some way that controls for differences in population and wealth. Unless we do this, we will not have a valid indicator of our concept, and our conclusions will be determined by the relative size and wealth of states rather than by their relative commitment to education. Additionally, of course, our research report will have to justify the apparently logical connection between the concept of "commitment to education" and the variable "per child public school spending."

Situations like this require that we *standardize* our measures in some way. A **standardized measure** is one that is stated in a way that, in order to allow valid comparisons, takes into account the differences that might exist among cases on variables other than the one it represents. It is very often necessary to standardize aggregate data prior to making comparisons among units of analysis. This may involve collecting data on variables that are of no direct relevance to the project. For example, in a study of commitment to education, we might need to collect data on the populations and total governmental expenditures of the states in order to standardize their educational expenditures by stating them as dollars per school-age child or a percentage of total state expenditures. Similarly, if we wanted to measure the concept *militarization* by observing the amount of money nations spend on the military, we would need to standardize the measure by stating it as a percentage of a nation's gross national product (the total value of all goods and services produced in the country) before making comparisons. Unless we did this, a wealthy nation might look more militaristic than a poor nation even though it devoted only a tenth as much of its total wealth to the military as a poor nation did.

Whenever you anticipate making comparisons among groups (nations, cities, organizations, etc.), you must be alert to the need to standardize your measures and must plan to collect the additional data necessary for this standardization. Standardization is generally achieved by stating measures either as a percentage or proportion of some other variable or as so many units per unit of some other variable. This often results in the computation of a *rate* such as a crime rate (crimes per 10,000 persons), literacy rate (literate persons per 1,000 population), or infant mortality rate (infant deaths per 1,000 live births). The additional work of collecting data on the variables on which your key variable must be standardized is *absolutely necessary* for valid comparisons among cases that differ significantly in theoretically relevant ways.

The point of this section has been that aggregate data analysts should not only be cautious about using raw data as indicators of concepts but should also be alert to the potential uses of multiple indicators and the possibility of improving indicators by combining, standardizing, or transforming measures.

Sources of Aggregate Data

The amount of aggregate data available in the world is so great that one is inclined to believe it possible to find indicators for almost any empirically useful concept. In fact the very abundance of the available data sometimes poses problems as researchers find themselves having to search scores of sources to find all available indicators. Yet, even with this reservoir of data, researchers are sometimes unable to locate exact indicators of the concept they want to measure, for exactly the right time period, and aggregated at exactly the right level.

We cannot begin to list *all* the sources of aggregate data here. We can, however, list those sources of general data that are most likely to be of use to political scientists. Whereas some data sources contain data on a variety of subjects and cannot be neatly characterized as a source of one particular type of data, we have classified the sources listed here by the major type of data they are likely to yield. Most college and university libraries have the publications listed here or are able to help you locate them.

The key to successful use of any of the documents or data archives described here is knowing precisely what type of measures you are seeking. The hypotheses you are testing, the theory you are working from, or a precise statement of your research question can tell you what type of data (such as a measure of nations' economic productivity or of the size of their military forces) is needed to operationalize the concepts utilized in your research. If you simply go to the library with the idea of poking around in available data sources until you run across some indicators that look useful, you will almost certainly meet with failure. If, on the other hand, you approach the task of gathering data with a clearly conceptualized research strategy in mind, you should be able to tell the reference or social science librarian what you need.

1. *Demographic and related data on the United States.* All statistics released by agencies of the federal government are indexed in the *American Statistical Index,* which can be used to locate sources for specific measures. In addition, statistics on economic and population trends, foreign trade, energy use, and other issues collected for more than 100 federal agencies can be accessed through the Internet at FedStats (www.fedstats.gov). The publications of the Bureau of the Census are indexed in the *Catalog of United States Census Publications,* which describes the data available from the censuses of housing, population, governments, and agriculture, among others. Many of these data are summarized each year in the publication *Statistical Abstract of the United States,* which presents selected statistical profiles of the United States and its subdivisions and contains an extensive guide to public and private data sources. Each of the various censuses of the United States is summarized in *Subject and U.S. Area Reports.* The *Bureau of the Census Catalog* describes all census bureau materials, published and unpublished. It is indexed by subject and state and local area and is published quarterly.

   Some frequently used sources of specialized data about the United States are the *Congressional District Data Book,* which provides demographic and economic information and voting records for United States congressional districts, and the *County and City Data Book,* which contains demographic and economic data for states, counties, cities, unincorporated places of more than 25,000 in population, and urbanized areas in the United States on an annual basis. Similar data are presented in the *State and Metropolitan Area Data Book* from the Bureau of the Census. Voting data are summarized in the *Guide to U.S. Elections,* which gives returns for presidential, Senate, House, and gubernatorial races since 1824, and in *America Votes,* which covers national elections and primaries since 1952.

2. *Demographic and related data on other nations.* Recognizing the difficulties in locating comparable measures of any given variable for different countries, a variety of sourcebooks contain data collected by different nations and international bodies. Researchers who use these must be especially sensitive to the need to ensure the comparability of reported figures before basing comparisons on them.

The United Nations Statistics Division (unstats.un.org/unsd/) publishes three especially useful documents: The *Statistical Yearbook* summarizes data on population characteristics, economic activity, education, communications, and other matters for the world's nations each year; the *Yearbook of National Accounts Statistics* reports detailed information on economic activity; and the *Demographic Yearbook* gives historical data on population characteristics and annually examines a special subject, such as population distributions, mortality rates, or ethnic compositions. In addition, the United Nations Educational, Scientific, and Cultural Organization (UNESCO) publishes the *Statistical Yearbook* (www.uis.unesco.org/), which summarizes data on education, communication, science, and technology in more than 200 countries.

The *Statesman's Yearbook* provides detailed information about nations that has been compiled from a variety of national and international sources. The European Union publishes the *Eurostat Yearbook,* which provides demographic, social, political, and economic data for EU member states and candidate countries for leading EU economic partners (europa.eu.int/comm/ eurostat/). Further summary figures on national characteristics can be found in the *World Almanac* and *Worldmark Encyclopedia of Nations* in well-indexed form. A good deal of economic data can be found in the *Yearbook of International Trade Statistics.*

3. *Data on governments in the United States.* U.S. federal, state, and local governments turn out thousands of publications reporting figures on their own operations and on the social conditions that either call forth or result from public policies. The federal government is by far the most prolific producer of data. Its many publications are listed in the *Monthly Catalog of U.S. Government Publications* (MOCAT). An Internet version of MOCAT can be accessed through the Government Printing Office (www.gpo.gov). If you know what agency or branch of the government is likely to produce the data you are seeking, you can locate its publications in the *Monthly Catalog.* Correspondingly, if you know what you are looking for, the index of the *Monthly Checklists of State Publications* can be used to direct you to specific state publications. The *County Yearbook* and the *Municipal Yearbook* provide data on political, economic, and demographic variables at local levels.

4. *Event data.* By their nature, event data are not reported in regular, summary form. They have to be discovered in running records of daily events that are not necessarily compiled with the social scientist in mind. Two of the most comprehensive reference sources for events reported in newspapers are the indexes for the *Times of London* and *The New York Times. Facts-on-File* is a weekly digest of current events classified by subject and compiled into the annual *News Dictionary,* which stresses events in and related to the United States. Perhaps the most extensive general news digest is *Keesing's Contemporary Archives: Weekly Diary of World Events,* which contains transcripts of important speeches, some election and statistical data, and news summaries, and is indexed by subject and proper name.

5. *Survey data.* All of the sources named thus far present data in printed form. Using them for large studies requires recording the data and transferring them to

machine-readable form. The most useful sources of survey data, by contrast, are actual data sets (i.e., machine-readable records of raw data). These are available from a variety of data archives, several of which were identified in Chapter 8.

In addition to these sources, it is important to recognize the rich variety of private sources of data. Which of these are appropriate to any given study will be suggested by the subject of the study. For a study of the investment patterns of West European firms, for example, useful data may be held by individual banks or by national and international associations of banks.

Collecting Aggregate Data

Once the sources of data needed for a study have been identified, unless the data are already available on computer files, researchers face the task of transferring the data from a source to their records in a machine-readable form. The basic challenge is one of systematically coding and recording data.

Though this takes only a fraction of the time required to collect the same data through field research, it can be a very time-consuming task. It is important, then, to do it as efficiently as possible. The way to begin is by carefully thinking through in advance the research design and the data analysis you intend to perform so that you can specify exactly which cases you want data on and what measures you want to record for each. Failure to do this advance preparation will often lead to your wasting time recording data for which you ultimately have no use. Moreover, if you have carefully planned the study, you can list all cases and variables in some order of importance so that if you run short of time or funds in the data collection stage, you can make a rational choice to leave out certain cases or variables in order to terminate data collection in the least harmful manner. Keeping this option open means that you must proceed sequentially, either collecting all data on each case one at a time (if you want to be able to drop cases but need all variables) or collecting data for all cases on each variable one at a time (if you need all cases but want to be able to leave out some variables).

In either event, you need two basic tools for data collection: a set of *data specifications* and a *recording form*. **Data specifications** are simply detailed descriptions of the data that are to be recorded for each case and variable, including any coding instructions. Sometimes a single phrase will serve as a data specification for census data or organizational statistics—for example, *total number of municipal employees in 1990* or *adult population in 1990*. However, apparently simple pieces of data can require extensive qualifications. For instance, if we want a figure on total state expenditures for public welfare programs in a given year, we have to identify those programs that qualify as welfare for purposes of the study; if we want a measure of the number of persons in nations' armed forces, we have to include instructions for excluding domestic police from the count for countries in which the police are formally part of the military. Being able to provide these details in data specifications requires prior study of the subject and the reporting systems of your units of analysis. Even then, unexpected difficulties can arise. You may, for example, discover that budgeted and actual welfare expenditures differ considerably or that corrections for inflation have to be added in time-series studies. The adjustments you make in

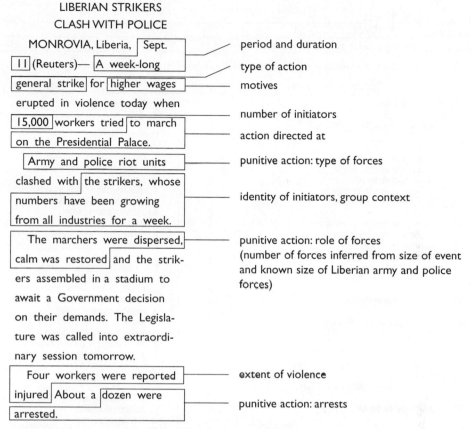

Figure 11.2
Coding of an article for aggregate data analysis
SOURCE: Ted Robert Gurr, *Politimetrics,* Englewood Cliffs, NJ: Prentice Hall, 1972, p. 93. Reprinted by permission.

response to these problems must be both technically correct and consistent with the meaning of the concept operationalized by the measure.

When collecting event data, a coding manual will help to document your data specifications, particularly noting essential distinctions in definitions. You will want, for instance, to be able to distinguish between riots and peaceful demonstrations or between pro-government and anti-government demonstrations. The most dependable way of doing this is to develop a **coding manual** (or **codebook**) that records the details of those characteristics that distinguish events in which we are interested from one another. (We say more about the use of coding in Chapter 14.)

The coding manual is then used in completing each **recording form**. It is similar to an interview schedule in survey research in that it is a means of systematizing and coding observations. If data are to be placed in electronic files, the columns to be used for each piece of information can be indicated on the recording form in order to speed data entry. Ted Robert Gurr provides an example of how recording forms for event data should be constructed. Figures 11.2 and 11.3 reproduce his illustrations. Clearly, those using the form must be carefully instructed in how to record events on it.

CIVIL STRIFE CODING SHEET (rev. 6/66) Polity __Liberia__

Coder ___Tg___ Month and Year of Coding __7/66__

Source(s) ___N.Y. Times___

Issue and Pages ___9/13/61   p.21___

Summary ___Clashes with police in general strike___

col. num.	contents of columns	col. num.	contents of columns
1–3	Polity I.D. Number _0_ _6_ _0_	(18)	8 some, undifferentiable 9 other _____
4–7	Polity Population (100,000's) _0_ _0_ _1_ _0_	19	Regime Classes ⓪ none or insignificant 1 military/police 2 public employees 3 political elite 4 military/police, employees 5 political elite, employees 6 military/police, elite 7 all three 8 some, undifferentiable 9 other _____
8	Character of Report 1 single report, current period, continuing event 2 single report, all of continuing event, to date ③ single report, concluded event 6 cumulative report, current period, continuing event 7 cumulative report, continuing event, to date 8 cumulative report, concluded event		
9–10	_6_ _1_ (Year Event Began)	20	Domestic Initiators, Summary 0 none or insignificant ① lower classes only 2 middle classes only 3 regime classes only 4 lower and middle classes 5 lower and regime classes 6 middle and regime classes 7 all domestic classes
11–16	Period Covered by Report from (_9/5/61_) to _6_ _1_ _0_ _9_ _1_ _1_ Year Month Day		
	I. IDENTITY OF INITIATORS	21	Resident Alien Initiators ⓪ none or insignificant 1 pastoral migrants 2 foreign workers 3 foreign students 4 refugees 5 political exiles 6 foreign clandestine group 7 several of the above (ck.) 8 other _____
17–21	bbbbb no basis for judging		
17	Lower Classes 0 none or insignificant 1 farmers/peasants 2 rural wage laborers ③ urban wage laborers 4 unemployed 5 farmers, wage laborers 6 wage laborers, unemployed 7 farmers, laborers, unemployed 8 some, undifferentiable 9 other _____	22–26	Number of Initiators, Proximate 00000 (go to next heading) bbbb1 1 to 40 bbbb3 41 to 80 bbbb8 81 to 240 bbb16 241 to 400 bbb32 401 to 900 bbb64 901 to 1,700 bb128 1,701 to 3,500 bb250 3,501 to 6,500 bb500 6,501 to 14,000 ⓑ1000 14,001 to 27,000 b2000 27,001 to 55,000 b4000 55,001 to 110,000 bbbbb no basis for judging
18	Higher Classes ⓪ none or insignificant 1 students 2 petite bourgeoisie 3 professionals 4 students, bourgeoisie 5 students, professionals 6 bourgeoisie, professionals 7 all three		

Figure 11.3

Example of a recording form for aggregate data

Source: Ted Robert Gurr, *Politimetrics*, Englewood Cliffs, NJ: Prentice Hall, 1972, pp. 94–97. Reprinted by permission.

(continued on next page)

col. num.	contents of columns	col. num.	contents of columns
27–30	**Number of Initiators, Estimate** (0000) (previous heading coded) bbb4 less than 100 bb40 101–1,000, "hundreds," "many" b400 1,001–10,000, "thousands" 4000 10,001–100,000 bbbb no basis for judging other _____	37	**Conspiracy Events** (0) none 1 plot 2 purge 3 assassination 4 bombing 5 small-scale terrorism 6 small-scale guerrilla war 7 coup/putsch 8 mutiny
31–32	**II. GROUP AND SOCIAL CONTEXT** **Initiators Acting as Members of** b0 unstructured crowd b1 territorial group b2 ethnic/linguistic group b4 religious group b5 apolitical student group b6 political group (b7) economic group b8 governing hierarchy b9 clandestine group ____ ____ clash between two of above; <u>specify categories</u> other _____ bb no basis for judging	38	**Internal War Events** (0) none 1 large-scale terrorism 2 large-scale guerrilla war 3 civil war (secessionist) 4 private war 5 large-scale revolt 6 turmoil/conspiracy event is part of internal war
		39	**Summary of Form of Event** (1) turmoil 2 conspiracy 3 internal war 4 turmoil and internal war 5 conspiracy and internal war 6 other _____
33–35	**Social Area** bb1 rural village or county bb3 several villages, counties or a small town bb5 a large town b10 several towns, or a city, or a small state b20 large state, or part of the capital city (b40) several large states or several cities, or entire capital city b60 several states or cities and the capital city b80 almost the entire polity 100 the entire polity other _____ bbb no basis for judging	40	**Number of Actions** (1) single occurrence 2 two, "several" 3 three, "some" 4 4–6 5 7–11 <u>No. Reported</u> 6 12–20 7 21–35 1 8 36–60 9 61+
		41	**Incidence of Action** (1) single occurrence 2 multiple sporadic 3 multiple simultaneous
36	**III. TYPOLOGY OF ACTION** **Turmoil Events** 0 none 1 demonstration (2) political strike 3 riot 4 localized rebellion 5 banditry/raiding 6 political clash 7 nonpolitical clash	42–45	**Duration of Action** bbbb no basis for judging bbb1 1/2 day or less bbb3 1/2 to 1 day bbb5 1 to 2 days bb10 2 to 4 days (bb20) 4 days to 1 week bb40 1 to 2 weeks bb80 2 weeks to 1 month b160 1 to 2 months b320 2 to 4 months b640 4 to 9 months 1217 9 to 15 months 2000 15 months to 2 years 4000 2 to 4 1/2 years other _____

Figure 11.3

(continued)

col. num.	contents of columns	col. num.	contents of columns

IV. ACTION DIRECTED ACT

46–48 bbb no basis for judging

46 <u>Property Targets</u>
(0) none or negligible
1 foreign public
2 foreign private
3 all foreign
4 domestic public
5 domestic private
6 all domestic
7 foreign and domestic

47 <u>Political Actor(s)</u>
0 none or negligible
(1) major domestic
2 minor domestic
3 military/police, domestic
4 private political group
5 several of the above (ck.)
6 undifferentiable domestic
7 foreign public
8 foreign military
9 domestic, foreign actors
   (ck.)

48 <u>Nonpolitical Actor(s)</u>
(0) none or negligible
1 random actors
2 ethnic actors
3 religious actors
4 communal actors
5 economic actors
6 several of the above (ck.)
7 undifferentiable
8 foreign nonpolitical
   actors
9 other _____

V. STATED OR APPARENT MOTIVES

49–51 bbb no basis for judging

49 <u>Political Motives</u>
0 none or minor
1 retaliation
2 seize political power
3 increase pol. participation
4 injure/suppress competing
   political group
(5) promote/oppose specific
   domestic policy
6 promote/oppose specific
   domestic political actor
7 oppose foreign nation's
   policy or actors
8 several of the above (ck.)
9 diffuse political motives
   other _____

50 <u>Economic Motives</u>
0 none or minor
1 retaliation
2 seize economic goods
(3) change distribution
   patterns
4 oppose economic actor
5 several of the above (ck.)
6 diffuse economic motives
7 other _____

51 <u>Social Motives</u>
(0) none or minor
1 retaliation
2 promote/oppose belief
   system
3 promote/oppose community
4 increase social goods
   (status, education, etc.)
5 several of the above (ck.)
6 diffuse social motives
7 other _____

VI. PUNITIVE ACTION

52 <u>Role of Punitive Forces</u>
0 not committed or committed
   after end of action
1 victims
2 present but passive
3 defensive action
(4) moderate suppressive action
5 extreme suppressive action
6 provoked action
b no basis for judging

53 <u>Type of Punitive Forces</u>
0 none
1 police
2 domestic military units
(3) police and domestic military
4 foreign military units
5 domestic and foreign
b no basis for judging

54 <u>Number of Punitive Forces</u>
0 none
1 1 to 10
2 11 to 100
(3) 101 to 1,000
4 1,001 to 10,000
5 10,001 to 100,000
6 100,001 to 1,000,000
b no basis for judging

55 <u>Arrests and Detentions</u>
0 none
1 1 to 10   No. Reported
(2) 11 to 100   a dozen
3 101 to 1,000
4 1,001 to 10,000
5 no basis for judging

Figure 11.3

(continued)

200

col. num.	contents of columns	col. num.	contents of columns
56	**Executions** ⓪ none 1 1 to 10 2 11 to 100 3 101 to 1,000 4 1,001 to 10,000 b no basis for judging No. Reported _____	69–72	**Number of Injuries** bbb0 none, none likely (bbb4) 10 or less, "few" bb40 11 to 100, "scores, many" b400 101 to 1,000, "hundreds" 4000 1,001 to 10,000 bbbb no basis for judging No. Reported _____ Other _____

VII. EXTENT OF VIOLENCE

col. num.	contents of columns	col. num.	contents of columns
57–58	**Damage in Affected Area** (00) none or presumed negligable 01 slight 03 moderate 07 extensive 10 massive bb no basis for judging		**VIII. EXTERNAL SUPPORT** bbbb no basis for judging (0000) none apparent
59	**Who are Casualties?** 0 none, none likely ① initiators 2 victims 3 punitive forces 4 initiators, victims 5 initiators, punitive forces 6 victims, punitive forces 7 all three 8 some, unspecified b no basis for judging	73	**Degree of Support for Initiators** 0 none apparent 1 arms and supplies 2 provision of refuge 3 provision of facilities, training 4 military advisors, mercenaries 5 military units
		74	**Degree of Support for Regime** 0 none apparent 1 nonmilitary aid 2 military material 4 personnel, facilities 5 military units
60–64	**Number of Deaths, Proximate** 00000 (go to next heading) (bbbb0) zero, none likely bbbb1 1 to 2 bbbb3 3 to 6 bbbb8 7 to 16 bbb16 17 to 32 bbb32 33 to 64 bbb64 65 to 130 bb128 131 to 250 bb256 251 to 500 bb500 501 to 1,000 b1000 1,001 to 2,000 b2000 2,001 to 4,000 b4000 4,001 to 8,000 b8000 8,001 to 16,000 other _____ bbbbb no basis for judging No. Reported _____	75	**Number of Nations Supporting Initiators** (identify) ____ (USA; China; USSR; UK; No. ____; ____; ____; ____.
		76	**Number of Nations Supporting Regime** (identify) ____ (Metro. power; France; No. USA; UK; ____; ____; ____.
65–68	**Number of Deaths, Estimate** (0000) (previous heading coded) bbb4 10 or less, "few" bb40 11 to 100, "scores, many" b400 101 to 1,000, "hundreds" 4000 1,001 to 10,000 bbbb no basis for judging No. Reported _____	77	**Reliability of Report** ⓪ unclassified 1 unknown 2 questionable
		78–80	**Event Identification** G F T
			COMMENTS, OTHER INFORMATION

Figure 11.3

(continued)

Conclusion

In closing, we want to encourage beginning researchers not to overlook the potential of aggregate data as a *supplement* to other forms of data. There are countless studies that can be based exclusively on aggregate data, but it is also often the case that aggregate data can be used to check the accuracy of results obtained from other forms of data. For example, students of voting behavior are sometimes faced with the problem that is created when people who are eager to associate themselves with a winner falsely report, in interviews conducted after the election, that they have voted for the successful candidate. In this case, aggregate voting data can be used to estimate the level of misreporting present in a sample. If responses from a sample show that 75 percent of a district has voted for the winner of a recent presidential election but voting statistics show that only 25 percent of that district actually voted for the winner, we have to consider that district's survey responses to be at least potentially an invalid indicator of support for the winner in that district.

In addition to this use, aggregate data can often be relied on to provide additional indicators of concepts so that the multiple indicator approaches to validity discussed earlier can be employed. For instance, in a study of neighborhood stability, we might ask residents about their commitments to stay in the neighborhood and, as an additional indicator, seek aggregate data on the frequency of turnover in home ownership in the neighborhood in recent years. When the findings of a study are confirmed by data collected by such diverse methods, confidence in those findings is greatly enhanced.

Summary Points

- Aggregate data are grouped and lack individual-level information.
- The ecological fallacy occurs when researchers draw individual-level behavioral connections from grouped data.

Suggested Readings and References

A bold and controversial claim for the usefulness of aggregate data is made in Gary King, *A Solution to the Ecological Inference Problem* (Princeton, NJ: Princeton University Press, 1997). Difficulties with analyzing groups using individual-level data, as well as using aggregate data to study individuals, are addressed in Chistopher H. Achen and W. Phillips Shively, *Cross-Level Inference* (Chicago: University of Chicago Press, 1995).

It is rare to find textbooks that are solely devoted to aggregate data analysis. Most of the material is scattered among the literature-reporting studies that have employed the various techniques of aggregate data analysis. Drawn primarily from texts produced many years ago, the best general discussions of how to use aggregate data for beginning political scientists are probably Ted Robert Gurr, *Politimetrics* (Englewood Cliffs, NJ: Prentice Hall, 1972), and Richard L. Merritt, *Systematic Approaches to Comparative Politics*, ch. 2 (Skokie, IL: Rand McNally, 1970). David W. Stewart and Michael A. Kamins, *Secondary Research*, 2nd ed. (Newbury Park, CA: Sage, 1993), offers some practical tips and an excellent review of the issues surrounding use of aggregate data. More advanced discussions of the problems and techniques of using aggregate data and some examples of its use are found in Charles L.

Taylor, ed., *Aggregate Data Analysis* (Paris: Mouton, 1968). Additional examples of studies based on aggregate data are collected in Edward R. Tufte, ed., *The Quantitative Analysis of Social Problems,* ch. 3 (Reading, MA: Addison-Wesley, 1970).

Research operationalizing multiple measures is found in Patricia A. Hurley and Kim Quaile Hill, "Beyond the Demand-Input Model: A Theory of Representational Linkages," *Journal of Politics* 65 (May 2003), pp. 304–326. The standard reference for the multiple measurement approach and its role in research is found in David C. Leege and Wayne L. Francis, *Political Research* (New York: Basic Books, 1974). Some sophisticated techniques for using multimeasures are presented in Part II of Hubert M. Blalock, Jr., ed., *Measurement in the Social Sciences* (Chicago: Aldine, 1974).

A particularly imaginative use of content analysis of publications as aggregate data is found in Philip L. Steward et al., "Political Mobility and the Soviet Political Process: A Partial Test of Two Models," *American Political Science Review,* 66 (December 1972), pp. 1269–90. Richard F. Hamilton, *Class and Politics in the United States* (New York: Wiley, 1972), provides an example of the use of survey results as aggregate data on groups within a nation (social classes in this case). A major example of the use of judgmental data is Arthur S. Banks and Robert B. Textor, *A Cross-Polity Survey* (Cambridge, MA: MIT Press, 1963). An instructive example of the use of demographic data and organizational statistics is Michael S. Lewis-Beck, "The Relative Importance of Socioeconomic and Political Variables for Public Policy," *American Political Science Review,* 71 (June 1977), pp. 559–66.

A useful discussion of index construction is found in Tapani Valkonen, "Individual and Structural Effects in Ecological Research," in Matti Dogan and Stein Rokkan, eds., *Social Ecology* (Cambridge, MA: MIT Press, 1968), pp. 53–68. Some valuable hints on data transformations (and on the collection and use of aggregate data generally) are offered in Eugene J. Webb et al., *Unobtrusive Measures,* rev. ed. (Thousand Oaks, CA: Sage 2000).

Referenced work: Richard L. Merritt, *Systematic Approaches to Comparative Politics* (Skokie, IL: Rand McNally, 1970), pp. 27–36.

Research Exercises

1. The *Municipal Yearbook* provides data on the number of business establishments devoted to manufacturing, retailing, and services in each U.S. city. Use the data reported on this variable in a recent issue of the *Yearbook* to determine the proportion of firms devoted to manufacturing in the cities of Detroit, Houston, Pittsburgh, and Seattle. Write down the proportions for each city. Which of these cities would you say is the most industrialized according to this measure?

2. Using measures from the *Congressional District Data Book,* devise indices to represent (a) the level of party competition in and (b) the socioeconomic status of congressional districts. Then use the data reported in the *Data Book* to assign scores on each of these indicators to every district in the state of Indiana.

3. Select a research question and state a hypothesis relating to it that you can test using aggregate data. List the variables involved in the hypothesis and identify the units of analysis to which the hypothesis applies. Then use library resources to locate sources for at least three indicators for each variable in the hypothesis. Write a description of each measure, indicating the source in which it is found and the variable it is to represent.

4. Devise a definition for the concept *act of political terrorism* that can be used to identify terrorist acts from newspaper stories. Use the index to *The New York Times* to obtain a count of the number of acts of political terrorism taking place in Turkey, Germany, and Israel for any single year between 1994 and 2004. Which nation suffered the most terrorist acts? Can you devise a means of classifying terrorist acts by their level of violence? By this classification, were the acts in any one nation typically more violent than those in the others?

Key Terms

aggregate data	additive index
summative indicators	multiplicative index
syntality indicators	weighted index
areal groups	data transformations
demographic groups	standardized measure
ecological fallacy	data specifications
raw data	coding manual (or codebook)
index construction	recording form

CHAPTER 12

Comparative Research

- Why should we use comparative research?
- How are comparative studies designed?
- What kind of data can be used in comparative research?

All of the research strategies we have dealt with thus far could easily be carried out without ever setting foot outside our country. On most questions we can obtain more than enough data from our own nation's experience to help us explain political life. But an exclusive focus on one nation has some limitations. If we want to improve our ability to explain and predict political events, then one way is to take a comparative approach. This offers a broader range of information about the issues we want to study and in fact allows us to pose some kinds of questions that data from a single country might not answer. Thus, whether the question is about the causes of political violence, the reasons people become alienated from government, the effects of different kinds of political organization on public policy, or something else, comparative research can increase the chances of our reaching valid conclusions.

Research Across Borders

Why Comparative Research?   Why should there be any limitations in studying only one country? First, our results are likely to be *culture-bound*. That is, each nation has certain unique traits that can bias the findings. Suppose, for example, we want to explore the connection between socioeconomic class and voting choice. If we look only at data from the United States, we are likely both to conclude that class and voting are only modestly related and to question the notion that political preferences are shaped by the socioeconomic conditions in which voters must live and work. If, on the other hand, we expand our sample to include other Western countries—say, Britain, France, or Germany—we are likely to find a far stronger link, partly because of differences in the historical development of social classes in those countries. Thus, the United States might not be a representative example.

To take another case, suppose that we focus on voter turnout in national elections. For the United States, we will find that close to half of all eligible voters simply stay home on election day. We may explain this by arguing that democratic elections, especially at the national level, tend to discourage voter participation, because the large number of voters makes any individual ballot almost meaningless. But that conclusion, too, will be quite different if our sample includes other nations. Electoral turnout averaged 82 percent of eligible voters in Norway during the 1970s, and more than 90 percent in Italy during the same period, even though the large numbers of voters still dwarfed the effect of any single ballot in those countries (Powell, 1986).

Thus, there must be other reasons for the lower rate of participation within the United States, and these come into sharper focus when we add data from other nations. A comparative analysis shows that electoral competitiveness, and institutional features such as electoral laws and the existence of a two-party or multiparty system go a long way toward explaining different rates of voter turnout (Jackman, 1987). These examples suggest that there are specific features in the U.S. system—or in any system—that can distort our conclusions about political relationships.

Focusing on only one country also limits us in another way: it prevents our drawing conclusions about *system-level* traits. In other words, there are some variables, such as type of political system or type of territorial organization, that describe whole countries, and their effects can be studied only by comparing two or more nations. Consider, for example, the impact of federalism. We might argue that federal arrangements—in which power is shared between two or more levels of government—make for an inequitable distribution of public funds among localities. When regions or localities have power independent of the national government, they are likely to have different views about how much public money to spend and how to spend it.

In order to test this, we need to study at least one unitary system (in which regions and localities have no formal power independent of the national government) as a standard of comparison. Only if we found significant differences between nations with federal systems and those with unitary systems could we conclude that federalism was an important variable influencing the distribution of public funds. Similarly, we might make a case that economic growth in newly industrializing countries hinges on a government's ability to coerce and control the labor force. Our test of this proposition requires a sample that includes countries with varying degrees of control over labor. Of necessity, then, any concern with system-level attributes implies a cross-national study.

Cross-national research can also be a valuable tool for those committed to political reform. Studying other nations can offer insight into the advantages and disadvantages of alternative political "rules of the game." It thus helps to pinpoint the potential costs and benefits of political reform at home. Some analysts in the United States, for example, advocated reforms in the 1950s along the lines of the British system in order to encourage more unity within each major political party and a clearer choice between parties for the average voter. Others have been intrigued by proportional representation (as in France), giving out legislative seats to each party in proportion to the number of votes it receives, so that many different parties and groups have a legislative voice equal to their electoral support. In each case, the experience of other countries speaks volumes about both the benefits and the problems that flow from such political arrangements.

Requirements in Comparative Research   Comparative analysis is an important part of political research, because it allows us to generalize beyond the sometimes narrow confines of a single culture and because it permits us to test for the effects of system-wide characteristics. Needless to say, it should meet all the standards for good research that we have discussed in other chapters. But cross-national studies also require sensitivity to some additional issues. The first lies in conceptualizing what we want to address: *We need to ensure that the questions we pose actually* *permit cross-national study.* The second lies in operationalization: *Each variable we use must be an equivalent measure of the same concept for every culture in our sample.* The choice of a sample raises a third issue: *Countries should be chosen to minimize cultural biases that can affect our conclusions.* Finally, the sample must also satisfy another rule: *Observations must be independent from one country to another.*

The following sections explain each of these requirements in turn, describing how they can influence the results we obtain and offering examples of questions that invite comparative analysis.

Finding Questions that "Travel"

The first requirement in cross-cultural research is to pose questions that *apply* from one culture to another. Stated so baldly, this might seem too obvious to require comment. But its simplicity can be deceptive, because many of the questions we raise in political science are applicable only to a very select group of countries. Take, for example, the case of explaining electoral behavior—one of the mainstays of political science research. Our long-standing interest in the reasons why people cast a ballot and in the factors that influence their choices has produced a rich body of theory and a set of sophisticated methods that should be applicable in any setting, domestic or otherwise.

Yet questions about why and how people vote do not "travel" well, because they restrict us to studying countries that have regular, competitive, free, and fair elections—a qualification that automatically eliminates many of the world's nations. We would, for example, be likely to exclude consideration of single-candidate or single-party elections, since there would be little variation in electoral behavior and basically no choice other than to abstain. Without variation, there is not much to explain. The factors that lead people to cast a ballot in a certain way in a country with competitive voting appear to make no difference in a noncompetitive election.

Thus, by choosing to analyze elections, we have set up a research question in terms that are specific to certain countries. This in itself might not seem too big a drawback, because we still have a large number of countries in our potential sample. But there is a second problem, one that relates to our ability to draw more general conclusions from voting data. If we assume, as many researchers do, that ballots reflect support for, or alienation from, the political system or reflect a preference for a certain candidate, party, or policy, then we have, in effect, equated elections with political expression. We are treating votes as measures of the more general concept of political participation. Almost by definition, this excludes the possibility that countries without regular and competitive elections provide their populations with a way to express satisfaction with, alienation from, or preferences for the government. Do they? Or are we unnecessarily limiting ourselves by framing our research around competitive electoral behavior? Will we come to different conclusions if we redefine what we want to study?

An Example   If we start by asking about the more general topic of how people express satisfaction, alienation, or choices among leaders or policy options, we will find that average citizens in countries without competitive elections may have alternative means of participation and can transmit their preferences to the government in ways that we normally associate with the casting of a ballot in more democratic countries.

Voting may be a formality, but citizens might view other forms of participation in a much more favorable light. Thus, many people who took an active role in Soviet public organizations (such as housing commissions or trade union committees) in the Brezhnev era felt themselves to be influential in the organization and in Soviet society at large, even though the single-candidate elections of the time were largely a political ritual. And many activists in public life felt that their participation made a difference, though they were not necessarily satisfied with the system as a whole (Bahry and Silver, 1990, Friedgut, 1979).

Obviously, the system of citizen participation changed dramatically with Mikhail Gorbachev's Perestroika, and the emergence of fifteen new countries in the former Soviet Union. Gorbachev campaigned for more open elections, increased citizen participation, and broader civil liberties. Still, there are some striking continuities in citizen politics from the pre-Perestroika days. Citizens continued to contact public authorities, predominantly on bread-and-butter issues such as housing, and many people active in new, informal political organizations were the activists engaged in "old" public organizations of earlier years. Had we focused strictly on voting as a measure of participation, these continuities in the transition to more democratic rule would have been overlooked. The important point here is that each country may offer its citizens *different* modes for expressing preferences or complaints about what the government does, and this is something we overlook if we design our research to deal only with behavior in competitive electoral systems.

Another Example   We might want to explore the patterns of court cases among different countries as a means to test for the connections between democratic political institutions, the frequency of litigation, and the outcomes of court decisions. Here, too, the question of courts and litigation might not travel well, because societies can have very different modes of resolving disputes. In some countries, the emphasis may be on mediating conflicts through local notables rather than bringing them before a formal court, and such countries would be omitted from our analysis of formal court activities. If, like most political scientists, we are interested in drawing valid conclusions that are not culture-bound, then our initial research question must be phrased to allow us to generalize beyond one or a few countries.

Our initial question must also be appropriate to the countries included in the study. Suppose that we are studying the development of women's rights. One approach might be to explore how workplace grievances are resolved, since questions about pay equity and working conditions are a central concern for many women's groups. Yet, if we focus on jobs alone, we overlook a critical issue. In some countries, especially those with strong traditions of social democracy, campaigns for women's rights may focus much more on social policies—parental leave, child care, or other benefits—rather than on individuals at work. Thus, the more appropriate question for us to pose is, *What kinds of women's rights issues are on each nation's political agenda?* Our original question needs to be recast in terms that are appropriate to the countries we study.

In this brief discussion, we have not touched on all the possible biases that might color our initial research questions. We have, for example, dealt only with cases involving advanced industrial societies, in which government is embodied in the work of large, highly specialized bureaucracies. Clearly, the modes of political expression, and the provision of public goods and services, take quite different forms in societies without such institutions (such as many of the developing countries), and these are things we need to consider when we form the questions that will guide our research. Whatever the issue, and whatever the countries we study, we need to be sure that our research is constructed in a way that permits us to generalize about our conclusions and in a way that fits the context of the countries we want to explore. In effect, our design should be able to travel and to focus on questions appropriate to the sample we ultimately choose.

Using Equivalent Measures

Once we have settled on a question that allows cross-national study, we will need **equivalent measures** in each country we observe. In other words, comparative research should measure the same concept from one culture to another. There are two ways we can do this: first, by using the same variable everywhere, and second, by choosing variables that are specific to each country. At first glance, this might appear to be a lopsided choice, for nothing should ensure equivalence between countries better than using the same variable in each one. But this is true only if our "identical" variable means the same thing in every country we study.

Using Identical Variables Suppose that we want to compare levels of tolerance for minority rights across nations. We might adopt one of two approaches. In one, we might compare the degree to which people in each nation are willing to grant political rights to particular groups such as a religious sect. Based on this measure, we are likely to conclude that citizens of some nations are more tolerant than others. But if people in the nations under study are more or less hostile to the specific group in question, this measure may be revealing how the group under study is perceived by people in different nations and *not* how tolerant those people are of minority rights. This means that our "identical" measure of tolerance does not have the same meaning in each nation.

Alternatively, we might ask people about their willingness to grant political rights to the groups *they most dislike*. This would allow us to control for differences in the acceptance of different groups across nations. This raises another question, however. In some nations, the most disliked groups are larger and more powerful than in other nations, where they may be tiny minorities with little power. If so, the degree to which people are willing to grant political rights to a group may reflect the degree of threat the group poses to the majority. In that case, our measure may reflect fear of a given group rather than citizens' general level of political tolerance. Thus, for comparisons to be valid, *we need measures that tap the same underlying concept* whatever the countries we include in our sample.

Similar problems may arise no matter what question we take up or what countries we study. Suppose, for example, we want to compare the relative commitment to social welfare between nations at different levels of development. We might predict that the more developed a country, the more resources it will commit to social programs. Our measure of commitment to welfare should be relatively easy to define: we can look at expenditures on social welfare programs (such as pensions and aid to the disabled and poor) as a share of a country's total government spending or a share of all the goods and services it produces (as measured by its gross national product). With this measure, we are likely to discover that our prediction holds true: more developed countries devote a greater share of resources to welfare.

Yet here, too, our measure may not be equivalent for all the countries we might want to study. By defining it in terms of formal programs such as government pensions and aid to the disabled and poor, we may be underestimating the degree of non-institutional, local effort that aids the most needy in countries where formal government programs either do not exist or are limited in scope. If farmers and local villagers in less developed countries organize to contribute food, shelter, and other kinds of assistance to their indigent relatives and neighbors, then they are, in effect, redistributing community resources in the same basic sense that welfare programs do in more developed systems. Thus, different communities may rely on different methods of providing for the needy, so that a measure based only on formal programs may well exclude informal but significant redistribution. If this is the case, then our measure of welfare provision is more a reflection of a society's degree of institutionalization than of its commitment to aiding the indigent.

Using Country-Specific Variables   Both examples illustrate how the use of identical measures in all countries can lead to serious problems when our variables take on different meanings from one country to another. As an alternative, we may decide on measures that are *country specific;* that is, we may use a different variable for each nation we study, with the choice depending on the local culture. In this case, we need to be sure that every indicator reflects the same underlying concept. As with the selection of identical or common indicators, this can create a problem, since there is no guarantee that our choices will in fact be equivalent.

As evidence of this, consider the issue of political protest. Clearly, if each political system has somewhat different rules governing political life, then protest against the system may take different forms from one country to another. While one government may permit open dissent or demonstrations, another may impose severe penalties for the same behavior, forcing people to vent their dissatisfaction by other means. Thus, where open dissent is costly, we may anticipate that people protest through indirect methods, such as evasion of government demands and regulations. The discontented may avoid overt ways of expressing anti-system attitudes and may turn instead to beating the system by misappropriating funds, evading taxes, or bending bureaucratic rules. Thus, in order to compare the extent of anti-system activity between countries, we may look at open dissent in one place and noncompliance or evasion (assuming that we can measure it) in another.

We can thus make a plausible case that the two are equivalent measures of protest, but we cannot prove it conclusively. Another researcher may argue that the two activities really reflect different things: Open dissent may actually be a good barometer of our underlying concept, whereas white-collar crime is not. People may misappropriate funds, evade taxes, or bend bureaucratic rules for any number of reasons, none of them directly related to protest against, or dissatisfaction with, the political system. If this is the case, then our two measures are not equivalent, and we are not really tapping the same thing in each country. In other words, white-collar crime may not be a valid indicator here, because it may not reflect what we want to measure. Our use of country-specific variables, then, is not necessarily a guarantee that we have comparable data for all the nations we include in our sample.

This suggests that both of our options for choosing variables—the use of identical or country-specific indicators—have their limitations. Neither guarantees equivalence. But we can offer some ways to minimize the problem. First, we clearly need a good, basic knowledge of the culture of each country we study, so that we can determine when a given measure is appropriate. Second, we need multiple measures or indicators. If we can define several different ways of measuring protest, for example, and if those ways tend to produce the same conclusions, then we can have some confidence that we are in fact tapping the right dimension. Using these strategies can help to give us equivalent or comparable data for all the countries we study.

Choosing Cases to Study

Given an appropriate question and a sensitivity to the problem of equivalence, we need to be sensitive as well to the problems involved in selecting a sample. Ideally, we should not have to choose among countries: the best way to keep our results from being culture-bound is to include data from every possible nation. But in practice, our range of options is much narrower, because the data available to us are limited. If, for instance, we rely on data provided by each individual country, we are limited by the fact that many nations publish little or no information about the issues we want to study. In some countries, accurate and timely publication of political, economic, and social data remains a luxury. And even where resources are available, some topics may be considered too sensitive (such as data on political unrest) or not salient (such as statistics on domestic violence) to warrant publication. Countries that do provide information often use different ways of defining and reporting data, so that published information may not really be useful for comparison. If, on the other hand, we want to collect our own data—as, for example, in the case of survey research—the costs of research abroad can be prohibitive and the amount of data collected will be limited.

Most-Similar-Systems Design   These constraints mean that for most questions we study, we have to work with a sample of a few select countries, chosen expressly to minimize bias. Our choice thus has to be made with some care because it can have a significant effect on what we find. We might follow one of two strategies common in comparative research. The first, called a **most-similar-systems design,** focuses on countries that are very similar, on the grounds that the characteristics they share can thus be held constant. Then, if the countries differ in some other trait, we can eliminate the shared characteristics as explanations for the variation.

To visualize how this might work, imagine that we have decided to explore differences between countries in the scope of government activity. Why do governments play a much larger role in the economic and social life of some nations than of others? There are several possible explanations, ranging from differences in levels of economic development to differences in cultural norms about politics. Cultural norms, though, are sometimes difficult to measure precisely. Accordingly, we might control for their effects by looking at variations in the scope of government action among countries with similar cultures, such as the United States and Britain. Whatever differences we find in the reach of political institutions cannot be attributed to cultural factors, because such factors are, in effect, roughly constant across our sample. To put it another way, focusing on countries that have similar traits means that we can safely rule out these specific factors in explaining the differences we find.

Most-Different-Systems Design   Alternatively, we might adopt the opposite strategy: choosing countries that are different in as many ways as possible. This is referred to as a **most-different-systems design**. In this case, if we find a common characteristic across our sample, we can rule out the differences between countries as explanations. As an example, consider our earlier question about social welfare. We might choose a set of countries at different levels of economic development and with different types of political systems but, using an equivalent measure for each, discover that they devote roughly the same share of resources to welfare. If so, the differences between them must not affect what each country spends to help needy citizens. Thus, choosing countries that differ on several characteristics allows us to eliminate these characteristics while explaining some shared trait.

Which of the two options should we choose? The answer depends in part on how well we have developed the theory that guides our research. For example, the most-similar-systems approach is appropriate when we can identify all of the important factors that might influence what we find and can locate a set of countries that share them. But because few countries are likely to be so well matched, it is normally much easier to find a sample that differs on the important dimensions. In that case the most-different-systems design is likely to be more suitable. This design also makes it less likely that we will find a common pattern between widely different countries. It thus gives more credibility to the results when we do find a common pattern. In effect, a most-different-systems approach offers us somewhat better control over the factors that might influence or bias what we find, as well as more assurance that our results are valid.

Finding Independent Observations

In choosing a sample, we are usually guided by the notion that the more countries we can include, the more confidence we can have in our results. A large sample increases the chance that we have included a representative range of values for key variables and lends more weight to whatever statistical procedures we might employ. This is true, though, only when each observation is *independent*. The advantages of a large sample hold only when data from one country are not influenced by events in another. If the two are not independent, then we really do not have two separate pieces of information backing up our results.

Consider a historical example from the Soviet bloc. When the Soviet party leader Joseph Stalin died in 1953, both the USSR and its East European satellites experienced major changes: leadership changed hands in most countries, and policy priorities imposed by Stalin were revised. The main priority in each country up until

1953 had been almost exclusively to develop heavy industry, even if it meant taking resources away from building houses or making consumer products. In the wake of Stalin's death, most Soviet bloc countries began to place more emphasis on improving the lot of the average consumer. We could argue that these changes in leadership and in policy were part of a natural progression or trend in communist political development and that communist countries experience such changes when they reach a certain stage of development; the evidence from the different countries seems to bear this out.

Yet the observations in our sample are not independent, because both leadership and policy changes in the bloc were set in motion—if not controlled outright—by the USSR. Thus, our conclusion that a developmental trend caused the changes in Eastern Europe would be incorrect, for the changes were actually initiated by events in only one country—the Soviet Union.

Diffusing Culture

The process whereby events in one country affect the life of another is referred to as *diffusion,* and testing for its effects on cross-national research is referred to as **Galton's problem** after the author who first described it. It suggests that we may see a strong causal connection between two variables—such as a country's reaching a certain stage of development and its experiencing shifts in policies—where none really exists, all because several countries in our sample are jointly influenced by another country. If so, having a large sample is of no real value, because all the extra observations really add no new information.

Actually, we would be hard-pressed to find a sample in which all of the data are completely independent. It is almost inevitable that some degree of diffusion influences virtually everything we study in cross-national research. If this is true, we need strategies that can minimize diffusion's effects. One, of course, is to look for explicit signs that one country in our sample has been influenced by another and to exclude it from our analysis. Another is to adopt a most-different-systems design, choosing countries that are as divergent as possible and choosing observations from different time periods. If it can be assumed that diffusion effects wane with distance and time, this strategy can help to increase the chance that each piece of data in our sample is independent of the others.

Finding Data

Each issue that we have discussed corresponds to a stage in comparative research, from developing the appropriate question to deciding how best to choose measures and select a sample. In theory, at least, the last stage is to locate the actual data (though sometimes the whole sequence is reversed). If our goal is to find consistent and comparable information, we will need to take several issues into account.

Aggregate Data   There are substantial variations in the scope and quality of aggregate information from one country to another, and even more variation in the availability of data on different topics. Not surprisingly, more developed countries generally have better infrastructure and resources for assembling and publishing national data. They are also likely to face more domestic demand for such information. Thus, comparable aggregate data are far easier to find on the United States, Western Europe, and other developed states than on poorer countries. The CIA's *World Factbook* (www.odci.gov/cia/publications/factbook), for example, offers comprehensive country-by-country overviews of political structures and economic conditions such as GDP per capita and percentage of the population living in poverty. But the data are much more complete for wealthier states than for poor ones. Even for wealthier countries, we are likely to encounter differences in definitions and coverage of ostensibly identical data. To take our earlier example of public spending on social welfare programs, each country may include different types of expenses or programs in its national statistics, and some may include state and local spending, while others may not.

Data availability also differs by topic. Data on election results, for example, have become increasingly easy to locate and are accessible online (one good source is the *International Foundation for Electoral Systems* at www.ifes.org). Other types of information can be more difficult to collect. As one example, consider the question of whether democratization breeds greater income equality. To answer it, we would need data on the timing of democratization and on the distribution of incomes during and after the shift from authoritarian rule. For measures of democratization, we might tap data from *Polity IV* (www.cidcm.umd.edu/inscr/polity), a data set housed at the University of Maryland with country-by-country evidence on regime changes extending back to the 1800s, or *Freedom House*'s annual ratings of civil liberties and political rights (www.freedomhouse.org). But comparable measures of income inequality are far harder to locate. Even if the data exist, they may be issued sporadically, making it difficult to determine how inequities respond to changes in the political system.

Survey Data   Limitations arise in using survey data. Such data are generally far easier to find for wealthier countries, where resources, logistics, and political stability facilitate individual interviews. Many major cross-national survey projects have thus focused predominantly on more developed states. And, as with aggregate data, coverage varies by topic. It can be much easier to find cross-national surveys on elections and partisan choice, or on core attitudes and values than on individual political behavior, or on interethnic relations. Thus, we are generally limited to the topic and questions defined by other researchers.

The alternative, collecting new survey data, does give us control over the choice of sample and variables employed. But as with aggregate data, the more countries and time periods we include, the more difficult it becomes to guarantee that we are measuring the same thing in each one. In fact, collecting data on individuals in other cultures can be an extremely complicated task. Assuming that we have the resources to carry out a cross-national study—say, a survey of political alienation or of participation—and that we have the cooperation of the government in each of our sample countries (which should not be taken for granted), we need to consider several issues.

The first concerns how to ensure that our survey is *linguistically equivalent*— that is, how to be sure that the questions we use in one language are translated accurately into others. This clearly requires fluency (or translators who are fluent) in the language of each individual we interview, as well as back-translations to ensure that the questions are indeed equivalent. Even the most fluent researcher, though, may still have some difficulty in expressing some concepts. Certain ideas or terms derived from one culture may simply have no counterpart in another. Take, for example, the notion of an interest group (that is, a collection of like-minded individuals who attempt to influence government policy) and the notion of pluralism (a political order in which different groups compete and cooperate to influence the government's actions). Because the two notions are products of Western democratic theory, both may have equivalents in Western democratic systems. But in other cultures, neither idea may even exist because each derives from the experience of highly institutionalized political systems that give rise to formally organized groups. When such differences occur, our survey questions will have to be rewritten in terms that allow equivalent translations between cultures.

In addition to the possibility of differences in concepts and language from one country to another, there is the possibility that *cultural traits* may influence the way people respond. Thus, for example, respondents in some countries may view the survey as a game in which their role is simply to string along an interviewer, whether their answers are accurate or not. Others may place a high value on cooperation or deference to authority and thus may be inclined to give the responses they think the interviewer wants to hear. Finally, some may not acknowledge having certain reactions or values, because they go against what local society prescribes (for example, racial or ethnic stereotyping). In each case, culture produces a bias that influences the responses we obtain.

As with other aspects of the equivalence problem, part of the solution lies in in-depth research on each country to help identify factors that might influence the way people answer. Another lies in the use of multiple measures of what we want to study. If other types of evidence support our survey results, then we have more reason to believe that our findings are valid.

Conclusion

This very short overview identifies neither all of the data sources available for cross-national research nor all of the problems we might encounter in using them. But it does suggest that each source has different strengths and weaknesses, and these are things that we need to recognize in any comparative study.

Given the state of our theories about politics and our access to information, we obviously do not have perfect solutions for each of the problems that comparative research might raise. Yet we still need to take each one into account when we design a study and interpret its results. The more clearly we recognize and control for possible biases, the more confidence we can have that our conclusions are right.

Summary Points

• Comparative analysis is a necessity if we want to develop generalizations that apply beyond national borders and if we want to study system-level traits.

• Cross-national research must be designed in accordance with several considerations, including the framing of truly comparative questions, the use of equivalent measures, the choice of an appropriate sample, and the inclusion of observations that are independent from one country to another.

• The availability and accessibility of comparative data differ from country to country. Generally, it is easier to find data for industrialized rather than developing nations. Increasingly, however, international organizations provide access to comprehensive country-by-country overviews through the Internet.

Suggested Readings and References

Several authors present a more detailed discussion of issues and problems in comparative research, and many more take up some aspect of the various examples we have discussed in the text. For a general discussion of comparative methods, consult Adam Przeworski and Henry Teune, *The Logic of Comparative Social Inquiry* (Melbourne, FL, Krieger Publishing Co., 2000); David Collier, "The Comparative Method: Two Decades of Change," in Dankwart A. Rustow and Kenneth Erickson, eds., *Comparative Political Dynamics: Global Research Perspectives* (New York: HarperCollins, 1991), pp. 7–31; B. Guy Peters, *Comparative Politics: Theory and Methods* (New York: New York University Press, 1998); and Todd Landman, *Issues and Methods in Comparative Politics: An Introduction* (London: Routledge, 2000). For an excellent general overview of the choices to be made in comparative research design, see Gary King, Robert O. Keohane, and Sidney Verba, *Designing Social Inquiry: Scientific Inference in Qualitative Research* (Princeton, NJ: Princeton University Press, 1994).

For more details on specific methodological questions, read David Collier and James E. Mahon, Jr., "Conceptual 'Stretching' Revisited: Adapting Categories in Comparative Analysis," *American Political Science Review*, 87 (December 1993), pp. 845–55, on choosing the appropriate research question and using categories that travel; William Chandler and Marsha Chandler, "The Problem of Indicator Formation in Comparative Research," *Comparative Political Studies*, 7 (April 1974), pp. 26–46, on equivalent indicators; and Marc Ross and Elizabeth Homer, "'Galton's Problem' in Cross-National Research," *World Politics*, 27 (October 1976), pp. 1–28. On the choice of cases to compare and the implications of selection bias, see Theodore Meckstroth, "'Most Different Systems' and 'Most Similar Systems': A Study in the Logic of Comparative Inquiry," *Comparative Political Studies*, 8 (July 1975), pp. 132–57; Barbara Geddes, "How the Cases You Choose Affect the Answers You Get: Selection Bias in Comparative Politics," *Political Analysis*, 2 (1990) pp. 131–150; and David Collier and James Mahoney, "Insights and Pitfalls: Selection Bias in Qualitative Research," *World Politics*, 49 (October 1996) pp. 56–91.

Referenced work: G. Bingham Powell, Jr., "American Voter Turnout in Comparative Perspective," *American Political Science Review*, 80 (March 1986), pp. 17–43. Robert W. Jackman, "Political Institutions and Voter Turnout in the Industrial Democracies," *American Political Science Review*, 81 (June 1987), pp. 405–24. Donna Bahry and Brian D. Silver, "Soviet Citizen Participation on the Eve of Democratization," *American Political Science Review*, 84 (September 1990) pp. 821–848. Theodore Friedgut, *Political Participation in the USSR* (Princeton, NJ: Princeton University Press, 1979).

Research Exercises

1. Choose four countries to include in a *most-similar-systems design* to study each of the issues listed below and explain why you would choose each. Choose four countries to include in a *most-different-systems design* for each issue and explain your choices.

   a. The relationship between poverty and extent of protest against the government

   b. The effect of economic development on political democratization

2. To get a sense of the types of information that different countries make available, you might examine a United Nations publication such as the *Statistical Yearbook*. Do all countries provide data in all categories listed in the yearbook? Answer the following questions:

   a. How does the level of economic development or the type of political system influence the amount of information that some countries report?

   b. Does each country's definition of a category match others, say, for the percentage of the population living in urban areas or the percentage unemployed? What effect might differences in definitions have on comparative analysis?

3. Imagine that you are about to set up a study to explain why the scope of government varies from one country to another. Select three possible indicators you might use to measure the extent of government activity. Would these necessarily be equivalent measures in a study that includes countries at different levels of development and with different types of political systems?

Key Terms

equivalent measures
most-similar-systems design

most-different-systems design
Galton's problem

CHAPTER 13

Social Network Analysis: Finding Structure in a Complex World

- What are social networks?
- What are the principal facets of such networks?
- What are the basic techniques for analyzing social networks?
- What types of data are useful in social network analysis?
- What different forms can such networks take?

A Concept of Social Networks

A **social network** is a group of actors—people, organizations, governments—who are linked together by some common actions, common membership, shared communication, or some other form of exchange.

An Example   The world is filled with social networks, some highly visible and others hidden. The directors of corporations, for example, often are members of the same trade or business organizations, such as the National Association of Corporate Directors, or read the same magazines, such as *Corporate Board Member Magazine*—patterns that might increase their cohesiveness as a group. At the same time, many corporate directors serve on the boards of more than one company, which can produce communication flows and even perhaps common perspectives across those companies.

Similarly, those who may be at odds with business leaders also form organizations with overlapping memberships. Environmental and other activist groups participate in coalitions with overlapping membership and frequently share directors or advisors with other organizations. The result can be information sharing, commonality of perspective, or even coordinated action. Networks of donors to political campaigns often give to the same candidates, political action committees, or advocacy organizations. Activist foundations of the left and right contribute funds to advocacy groups that may themselves form activist networks.

Participants in criminal conspiracies are, by definition, members of a network, and demonstrating the nature of that network is often an important part of prosecuting them. Even terrorist organizations such as Al Qaeda are constructed in the form of networks through which such resources as money, plans, and instruction flow.

The Key Facet of Networks   Not all of these networks have the same structure and not all function in the same ways. But at their core is a common fact: they are based on patterns of exchange—money, information, influence, leadership, programmatic objectives, and the like—that can be usefully summarized in the form of maps of these various relationships. Social network analysis is the method by which such maps are produced and analyzed.

This chapter provides some very basic information about the development and analysis of social network maps. The introductory treatment here is restricted to some very basic graphic and generally non-mathematical applications of the technique. In point of fact, social network analysis is a highly developed quantitative methodology based, among other things, on the analysis of matrices. If you are interested in more sophisticated applications of social network analysis, the bibliography at the end of the chapter includes references to several key works.

Social Network Data

The data employed in social network analysis consist of two types: nodes and links. **Nodes** are the actors or participants in a network. For example, if we are studying networking structures associated with the Republican Party, our nodes might include the Republican National Committee (RNC), the Senate and House Republican Caucuses, the Republican Governors' Conference, the Ripon Society (a group of moderate to liberal Republicans), the Federalist Society (an influential conservative group with ties to the Republican Party), and the Log Cabin Republicans (an organization of gay and lesbian Republicans). Nodes can be of different types. The RNC, for example, is a direct arm of the party itself, while the Federalist Society is not.

Links are the connections among the actors. In the present example, this might include such elements as shared members or leaders, the flow of funds to or from each organization, and the sources and movement of policy proposals.

Links may also have different intensities. The ties between the Republican Governors Conference and the RNC, for example, are likely to be much stronger than those between the RNC and the Log Cabin Republicans. Strength can be measured in a variety of ways, such as the number of personnel interlocks, the value of dollar flows between the nodes, and the number of messages or policy proposals. When constructing a map of such a network, then, we have a number of choices to make: *which nodes we want to include* (all? only those that share a particular characteristic?), *which resource flows we want to include* (money? information? interlocking directorships? direct membership?), *the extent or intensity of the flows* (we can represent this in our map by the size or number or color of the links), and *the direction in which those resources flow* (only toward one or another key participant? only from that participant? both? or do we simply ignore the direction of flow?). As we make each of these choices, we begin to develop the appearance of our network map and, in the process, shape both the information it conveys and the analysis it supports.

Social Network Matrices   All social network analysis begins with a data matrix that represents both the nodes of the network and the relationships, or links, among them. While these tables contain detailed information, the data will also be placed into more intuitive figures below. Examples of matrices are provided in Tables 13.1(a), and 13.1(b). In the tables, the letters represent the nodes in a five-member

Table 13.1

(a) Matrix of symmetrical relationships

	A	B	C	D	E
A		1	1	1	1
B	1		0	0	1
C	1	0		1	1
D	1	0	1		1
E	1	1	1	1	

(b) Matrix of asymmetrical relationships

	A	B	C	D	E
A		1	1	1	1
B	0		0	0	1
C	0	0		1	1
D	0	0	1		1
E	0	1	1	1	

(c) Matrix of symmetrical relationships showing intensity

	A	B	C	D	E
A		1	3	1	5
B	1		0	0	1
C	3	0		1	1
D	1	0	1		4
E	5	1	1	4	

network. Where the nodes have some form of relationship with one another, the corresponding cell in the table shows a "1"; where there is no connection, the cell shows a "0."

The matrix in Table 13.1(a) is known as a **symmetrical matrix**. That means that the relationships represented in the table are reciprocal—if A is linked with B, then B is also linked with A. For example, if the connection between Company A and Company B is provided by Jane Smith, who serves on the board of directors of each company, then Ms. Smith also provides a linkage in the opposite direction, i.e., between Company B and Company A. In the table, this means that if there is a "1" in cell AB (row A, column B), there must also be a "1" in cell BA (row B, column A). In a basic symmetrical matrix, the direction of exchange is not an important consideration.

The matrix in Table 13.1(b) is known as an **asymmetrical matrix**. Here the relationships are not necessarily reciprocal, though some of them may be. For example, if the Progressive Policies Foundation gives money to Environmentalists to Save the World, but the environmental group does not give money to the foundation, then the flow of money is in one direction only, which is to say non-reciprocal. In this instance, if the foundation was represented in the matrix by "A" and the environmental group by "B," then the table would have a "1" in cell AB, but a "0" in cell BA. In a basic asymmetrical matrix, the direction of exchange is an important consideration.

Finally, consider the matrix in Table 13.1(c). This is a symmetrical matrix that is similar to that in Table 13.1(a) in all ways but one—the entries in the cells are not all equal to "1." Rather, they take on different values that represent the amount or intensity of the connection between each pair of nodes. Suppose, for example, that A and C are activist organizations that share five members in common, while D and E share four members, A and C share three members, and the other combinations of activist groups share either one or no members in common. If our objective is to analyze patterns of political activism, that information might be well worth capturing. Table 13.1(c) captures it by assigning different values to the cells depending on the number of shared members. These entries could be actual counts of members in common (and, hence, interval data) or simply a ranking from lowest to highest overlap (and, hence, ordinal data). Though not illustrated here, asymmetrical matrices can also capture variable degrees of interconnectedness among the nodes.

Mapping a Network   Working from a matrix like those we have just constructed, it is then a simple matter to draw a map of a given network. As specified in the matrix, the nodes are represented as points in space and the links as lines that connect them. Figure 13.1 illustrates network maps that correspond, respectively, with the matrices in Table 13.1.

Notice that in Figure 13.1(a), there are five nodes, corresponding to the five participants in the network, and that lines have been included to connect each pair for which a "1" appeared in the matrix in Table 13.1(a). So, for instance, A is shown as being connected with each of the other participants, while B is connected—or *linked*—only with A and E.

In Figure 13.1(b), we have the same five nodes, but rather than using simple lines to represent the relationships among the nodes we have employed arrows.[1]

Recall that in the asymmetrical matrix in Table 13.1(b) the exchanges were in one direction only. The arrows capture that additional directional information.

Finally, in Figure 13.1(c), we return to a symmetrical network, but one in which some relationships are stronger (or larger and more important) than others. In this instance, we capture the additional information by increasing the thickness of the connecting lines, or links. If the links were of different types—say, money, common programs, and interlocking directors—we could also capture their variations by using multiple lines (in different forms, e.g., solid, dashed, or dotted), each of which could vary in thickness.

---

[1] Often symmetrical networks are shown with arrows in both directions rather than with simple lines. We have chosen not to do so here in the interests of clarifying the basic dynamics of network analysis.

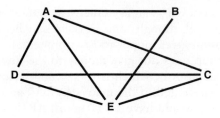

(a) Network map of symmetrical relationships

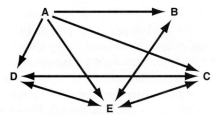

(b) Network map of asymmetrical relationships

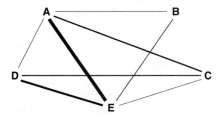

(c) Network map of symmetrical relationships of varying intensity

Figure 13.1

Types of Networks

Networks can be very simple and straightforward, or they can be very complex and convoluted. The more members (nodes) we include, the more types of linkages we incorporate and the further out we extend our notions of connectivity (e.g., including other networks in which our principal nodes may participate), the more complicated things become. But at the same time, networks tend to display certain structural characteristics that can help us to analyze and understand them. Figure 13.2 illustrates some of these basic configurations.

The first type of network structure shown in Figure 13.2(a) is the **chain** or **linear network.** In this structure, each participant has contact with only two others. Typically, this would be an asymmetrical arrangement in which one participant passes resources or instructions to another (hence the arrows). Although Participant A has a natural power advantage here as the initiator of all exchanges, a network of this type is highly decentralized—indeed, there is no central, controlling authority—and the members do not actually know who their co-members are at more than one degree of separation. And because Participant A has no direct links to any participants

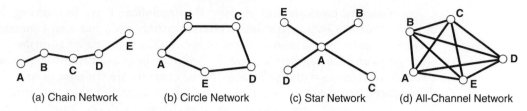

(a) Chain Network   (b) Circle Network   (c) Star Network   (d) All-Channel Network

Figure 13.2
Basic network configurations

beyond B, and thus no way to monitor or adjust subsequent exchanges, even A's power is limited.

As an example, consider a terrorist network in which plans and goals are set by A and sent into the network. By the time D and E have their exchange, both plans and goals may have been modified in ways unknown to, and inconsistent with the wishes of, Participant A. At the same time, should some portion of the network be compromised, the fact that no participant can identify more than two other participants—if certain precautions have been taken in communicating (e.g., through blind drops), each participant may actually only know the identity of the next participant downstream—provides a measure of security against the network being fully dismembered.

A variant on the chain network is the **circle network** shown in Figure 13.2(b). Here the flow remains asymmetrical, but Participant E closes the loop with Participant A. This structure can provide some measure of feedback to A, who can then make adjustments as necessary. But in the example above, because it requires that E possess some means of exchanging with A, it can also compromise the security of the network at the highest level.

A **star network** shown in Figure 13.2(c) is one in which a central actor—Participant A—is linked with every other actor, but none of the other actors is linked with one another. This is very much the opposite of the chain network, because here there is a single, centrally located participant who controls, and is a party to, every exchange that takes place. In fact, in a star network the identities of the other participants may be entirely unknown to any of them. Each deals only with A. Modifying the above example, a terrorist network organized in a star pattern would have substantial security at its periphery because no individual cell has any contact of any kind with any other. And such a network could be easily and effectively controlled because each cell depends on the central participant for its resources and instructions. But, should Participant A ever be compromised, the entire network would be destroyed for the simple reason that, because each participant other than A operates in virtual isolation, no combination of other participants could communicate with one another.

Finally, there is the **all-channel network** shown in Figure 13.2(d). Here, every participant is linked with every other participant in a thoroughly decentralized structure. In this form of networking, rather than limiting, masking, or controlling exchanges, every member interacts more or less openly and more or less extensively with every other member.

Consider the previous example using the Republican Party. Broadening the range of connections to include not only common membership but also communication between organizations, support for common policies, campaign contributions, and other types of financial support, you can see that the organizations in question have a variety of contacts with one another. Some contacts are stronger or more frequent than others. Some are of one type, some of another. But the participants in the Republican network know and engage in exchanges with one another more or less independently of any central authority. Similarly, we can think of the nations of the world as participants in an all-channel network. They all belong to international organizations like the United Nations, but they also retain direct diplomatic relations with one another. Not all of these channels will be equally important, but together they do very closely resemble a large-scale version of an all-channel network.

Roles of Participants

In addition to documenting the overall structure and functioning of the network *per se*, researchers are often interested in the functions of individual participants. The most basic question, of course, is which individuals, organizations, or other kinds of entities are members of a given network and, conversely but also often equally as interesting, which ones are not. This is important, for example, in determining which actors are likely to have influence on the actions of others within the network and which are not.

Analyzing Influences   Similarly, an examination of the particular role(s) played by a participant within a social network can often help us to understand the behaviors and influence possessed by that particular actor. In the star network depicted in Figure 13.2(c), for instance, there is a clear difference between the roles of Participants A and D. A is more centrally located, more influential, and presumably more important in determining the actions of the network.

In the circle network depicted in Figure 13.2(b) and the all-channel network in Figure 13.2(d), on the other hand, every participant appears to have roughly co-equal influence. Factors determining a particular participant's role and influence would be such things as the participant's number of network links relative to other nodes, the types of exchanges in which the participant engages (e.g., a participant may be involved in exchanges of money but not information), and the direction in which resources flow (e.g., whether a given participant is a major source of funds for the network or, alternatively, a major recipient of funds from others; whether a participant originates most of the plans for the network or receives direction from others). In effect, then, social network analysis provides a tool for gauging and characterizing the relative power of each participant.

Outside Links   It may also be worth noting which nodes in a network provide links to other networks. Some participants may be relatively isolated, interacting only with other members of the original network. Others may provide connections to outside sources of money, information, or other resources. And some may be highly integrated into a large number of networks, which would permit them to serve as conduits through which networks might exchange resources with one another, in effect creating a network of networks. Participants that perform this external integrative function may not be powerful within the structure of any given network, yet may exercise considerable power through their ability to control the flow of exchanges *between* networks.

Example: Networking for the Environment   We can illustrate the use of social network analysis by examining some of the relationships among environmental activists, social responsibility investors (those who invest based on the social policies of companies as well as their financial prospects), and religious organizations. This is accomplished in Figures 13.3–13.5. For purposes of this example, we will not show the underlying matrix of relationships. It is important to note, however, that compiling such a matrix was the first step in the analysis.

We begin by examining three organizations, the Coalition of Environmentally Responsible Economies (CERES), the Social Investment Forum (SIF), and Co-op America. CERES is a prominent group of environmental organizations and others that has created a set of environmental business practices that its members ask companies to follow. Using the Internet to research CERES (see Chapter 4 for research techniques), we can easily learn that CERES was established in 1988 and was originally begun at the initiative of another group, SIF. SIF, in turn, is a part or project of yet another organization, Co-op America, a relatively little-known environmental group. Applying this information, Figure 13.3 illustrates the networking origins of CERES. The network is directional because each group acted in turn to create the next. Figure 13.3 is a basic chain network.

Next, let us consider the membership of CERES itself. CERES is a coalition of more than eighty organizations, including well known environmental advocates, social responsibility investment companies, and others. You will find these members listed on the group's Web site. The star network illustrated in Figure 13.4 shows a few of these members. Since all are members of CERES rather than the reverse, we have again included directional links. To help facilitate the analysis, we have organized the network into clusters. On the left are the two companion organizations (Co-op America and SIF) that founded CERES. On the bottom are several of the more prominent social responsibility research and investment companies. At the top are several of the better known environmental activist groups. To the right is yet another organization, the Interfaith Center for Corporate Responsibility (ICCR). Organizing the network in this manner helps us begin to understand the nature and role of CERES, about which we will say more below.

Figure 13.3
Origins of CERES

Figure 13.4
CERES members

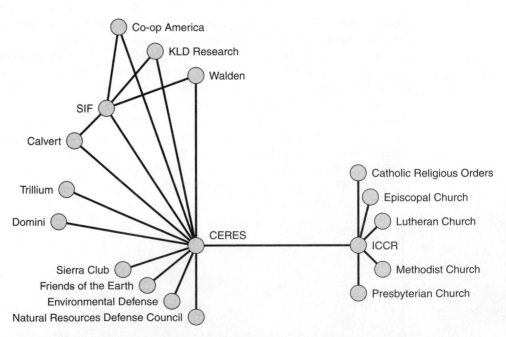

Figure 13.5
Network interlocks including CERES, ICCR, and SIF

Figure 13.5 adds two new sets of information, both, again, based on readily available information from the Internet. ICCR is a coalition of approximately 275 faith-based organizations and others that tries to influence corporate policies. We have included a few of the organization's church-based members to represent its membership. We have also added links from three of the social investment companies to the Social Investment Forum. Each of these three companies is represented on the organization's board of directors. (Because the network is now becoming more complex, we have eliminated the arrows to reduce visual clutter.)

What can we discern from Figure 13.5? We can see that CERES has been constructed as a diverse coalition that includes policy-oriented environmental groups, investors who value environment-friendly business practices, and faith-based activists who share an interest in corporate policies. As political scientists, this might suggest to us that the group relies on the environmentalists for its policies, on faith-based activists for its moral authority, and on social responsibility investors for its financial clout. If we were to take such additional steps as including more members of each coalition in the network, examining patterns of cross-membership (one group belonging to two or more coalitions) more extensively, examining different kinds of links (money, leadership, and so forth) and examining other affiliations of the members of this particular network (that is, links to other outside networks), we could learn a great deal more still.

Conclusion

To the extent that power relationships drive politics, a set of techniques that systematically characterizes patterns of exchange among groups of political actors clarifies these relationships. Social network analysis advances political science research by focusing on the structure and character of political relationships.

This form of analysis addresses such research questions as:

1. Does a network exist among some group of political actors, be they individuals, organizations, or governments? Who are the members? What do they have in common?

2. What form does the network take? What resources flow through it? How extensive is it?

3. What is the respective role of each participant? Which participants, if any, are positioned to have greater influence within the network? How and why?

4. What does the network's structure indicate about the relative and absolute relationships among the participants?

5. Which key actors have been excluded from the network? What, if any, light does this shed on the nature of the relationships?

6. Does the presence of actors holding membership in multiple networks effectively link the networks to one another? How many (and which) members have such dual linkages? What are the implications of either the isolation of individual networks or their linkage one to another?

The examples in the discussion above have only begun to suggest the types of networks that could be explored using this analytic approach. Networks of activists of various stripes, funding networks, terrorist or criminal networks, governmental networks in the international system, networks of political organizations with governments or political parties, networks of parties and interest groups, networks of citizens joined together through memberships in organizations or through their exposure to the same television broadcasts or magazines—these are but a few of the potential sets of relationships that can be studied using social network analysis.

Summary Points

• Social networks are linkages connecting individual actors or groups.
• Networks may involve individual citizens, interest or advocacy groups, party organizations, agencies of government, or even national governments.
• Relationships or exchanges between the participants in a network may be described using a network matrix and transformed into maps that convey the linkages' direction, extent, and significance.
• In addition to the value of the network dynamic itself in contributing to our understanding of the behaviors of various political actors, the individual networking roles of the actors themselves—including their possible connections to still other networks—can yield important insights.

Suggested Readings and References

A thorough and concise conceptual overview of social network analysis is provided by Peter R. Monge and Noshir S. Contractor in *Theories of Communication Networks* (New York: Oxford University Press, 2003). Manuel Castells offers a sweeping, even visionary, account of the increasing importance of networks in *The Rise of the Network Society*, 2nd ed. (Oxford: Blackwell Publishers, 2000). An early and influential work on political networks is David Knoke, *Political Networks: The Structural Perspective* (New York: Cambridge University Press, 1990).

Applications   John Arquilla and David Ronfeldt, *Networks and Netwars: The Future of Terror, Crime and Militancy* (Santa Monica: RAND, 2001); Mario Diana and Doug McAdam, eds., *Social Movements and Networks: Relational Approaches to Collective Action* (Oxford: Oxford University Press, 2003); Margaret E. Keck and Kathryn Sikkink, *Activists Beyond Borders: Advocacy Networks in International Politics* (Ithaca: Cornell University Press, 1998); and Jarol B. Manheim, *Biz-War and the Out-of-Power Elite: The Progressive Left and the Attack on the Corporation* (Mahwah, NJ: Lawrence Erlbaum Associates, 2004). Those interested in understanding the mathematics associated with social network analysis will want to consider Philippa Pattison, *Algebraic Models for Social Networks* (New York: Cambridge University Press, 1993).

Software   An example of the specialized software that facilitates large-scale and complex social network analysis is UCINET 6, a package developed by Steve Borgatti, Martin Everett, and Linton C. Freeman. UCINET is available online from Analytic Technologies (http://www.analytictech.com), which offers student pricing. Accompanying the software in electronic form is an excellent introduction to the technique, *Introduction to Social Network Methods*, by Robert A. Hanneman. Figures 13.3–13.5 were prepared using the UCINET software.

Internet   A number of Web sites now feature social network analysis. For an example, visit http://www.govcom.net. Look under the "Maps" heading to find examples of networks that range from very simple to highly elaborate.

Research Exercises

1. Identify five to ten popular authors, all of whom are generally considered either liberal or conservative in their views. Go to http://www.amazon.com and find the page devoted to the most recent book written by each author. Further down on the page, you will find references to other authors whose books are being purchased by customers who purchased the book you have selected. Make note of these for each author. Then develop a matrix and network map of the reading habits of liberals or conservatives. Which authors appear to be the most influential?

2. Identify the members of the following international organizations: NATO, the European Union, and the Group of Eight. Draw a network map of the organizations and their members. Can you draw any conclusions about the world role of the United States? Russia? France?

3. Collect news stories about the terrorist organization Al Qaeda for the last six months. You can do this by using indexes at the library or, if your university provides access to the service, using search procedures on *LexisNexis*. Using the techniques of content analysis, identify all references to ties or linkages between any two individual members, or between Al Qaeda and other organizations (including governments). Use these references to build a matrix of relationships and to prepare a map of the Al Qaeda network. Can you identify two or three individuals whose capture might significantly disrupt the network?

4. Examine the network illustrated in Figure 13.5. Using the Internet research skills you learned in Chapter 4, locate the information on which this network diagram was based. How would the network change if you included other members of CERES, such as the AFL-CIO? Other members of ICCR? What do these changes tell you?

5. Examine the chain network illustrated in Figure 13.3. Using the Internet research skills you learned in Chapter 4, can you take the network back in time one or more steps by gathering information about Co-op America?

Key Terms

social network
node
links
symmetrical matrix or network
asymmetrical matrix or network

chain or linear network
circle network
star network
all-channel network

CHAPTER 14

Data Preparation
and Data Processing

- Why are proper data coding techniques an important research concern?
- What are the key characteristics of useful data coding formats?

We have reached the stage of the research process when we have our data in hand and we must decide upon the most efficient and effective strategy for analyzing them. It is at this stage that we begin to create a finished record of our effort—in the form of charts and graphs, statistics, and other elements of our final research report; these are the products of our research that will be seen and read by others. Yet there remains one far less visible set of operations that we must undertake before we may analyze our data: the preparation and processing of data. These topics serve as the focus of this chapter.

How do we assign numerical values to the information we have gathered so that it may be analyzed thoroughly? How can we use these numbers to communicate in some meaningful way with computers, without which our masses of data would often prove unmanageable? What, for that matter, can computers tell us about our data? These and related questions must be resolved before we can proceed to the analysis of data and the reaching and presentation of conclusions.

Coding: What Do All Those Numbers Mean?

The process of assigning numerical values to our observations is termed **coding.** Coding is to measurement what the alphabet is to speech: a mechanism for making a precise and lasting record of information. Just as each letter or combination of letters in the alphabet represents a certain sound, each number or combination of numbers in a code represents a particular characteristic or behavior of a research subject. And just as letters allow those who know the alphabet to communicate complex ideas with one another without speech, numbers allow those who know the codes to communicate complex ideas to one another in a much abbreviated form. But numerical **codes** allow the researcher to go one step farther, for coded information, precisely because it is in numerical form, can be transformed and manipulated according to the rules of mathematics so that the findings may yield meaningful conclusions that might remain obscure were there no resort to numerical representations. Proper coding, in other words, allows us to learn more from our research than might otherwise be the case.

The Role of Coding In research, particular numbers are assigned to represent each value of a given variable. Thus, if we measure the educational achievement of members of a given population in which each respondent is scored either as not having

Figure 14.1
Coding in research

completed high school, as having completed high school but not college, or as a college graduate, we might assign the numbers 1, 2, and 3, respectively, to represent the three levels of achievement. Alternatively, if we wish to score each respondent on the number of years of schooling completed, we might assign to each a numerical code equivalent to that number (for example, the code 7 might represent seven years of schooling). Both coding schemes accurately summarize the findings of our study, though each conveys a meaning different from the other. Once we have assigned one or another set of such numbers, we may process and analyze the data to our heart's content before reconverting our codes into verbal expressions as we prepare our research report. This process of translation from concept to number and back may be summarized as shown in Figure 14.1.

The most important thing to keep in mind as we develop codes for our data is that our numerical representations must always be consistent with the measurement characteristics of the variables we are researching. That is, nominal-level variables should have nominal codes, ordinal-level variables should have ordinal codes, and interval-level variables should have interval codes. The numbers may *look* very much the same in each instance, but their meanings will differ substantially. Once we convert from words or concepts to numbers, we may be tempted to analyze or manipulate our data in ways that simply cannot be supported by their underlying level of measurement (this problem becomes more apparent in later chapters, when we focus more directly on techniques of analysis). Such temptations must be resisted if we are to preserve the usefulness of our research, for, as we learned in Chapter 5, not all numbers are created equal.

Choosing Codes   The mechanics of encoding (or decoding) data are really quite simple. We begin from the values (categories) of each variable in our study. In the case of *nominal* variables, when our numbers need distinguish only between mutually exclusive categories without respect to rank, we merely assign scores in whatever manner is convenient. If, to choose a relatively typical example, our subjects' religious affiliation is to be classified as Protestant, Catholic, or Jewish, we might assign codes according to any of the following schemes:

1 Protestant	1 Catholic	1 Jewish	43 Protestant
2 Catholic	5 Jewish	2 Protestant	17 Catholic
3 Jewish	8 Protestant	3 Catholic	27 Jewish

In each instance, a unique numerical value is used to represent one value or category of the variable. Since religious affiliation is a nominal characteristic, the order and magnitude of the codes have no significance whatsoever. We can use 1-, 3-, or even 10-digit numbers in our codes if we so desire. It is, of course, best to keep the codes as simple and manageable as possible, and we will generally opt for the lowest numbers and the fewest digits we can, but this is a function of our concern for **parsimony** rather than of any mathematical requirement.

It is possible to use slightly more sophisticated nominal coding schemes in order to convey more complete information. Suppose, for instance, that we wish to further categorize our Jewish and Protestant subjects by their specific denominations. Here we might use a two-digit code that builds on our earlier classification. The first digit would be selected as above (for example, 1 representing Protestants; 2, Catholics; and 3, Jews). The second would add the new information. Consider the following scheme:

10 Protestant	20 Catholic
11 Baptist	30 Jewish
12 Methodist	31 Orthodox
13 Presbyterian	32 Conservative
14 Lutheran	33 Reform

Here our codes preserve (in the first column) the gross differences between the categories but allow as well (in the second column) for some fine-tuning. The result is a more complete record of our subjects' characteristics, which still preserves the essence of the less precise variable with which we began.

Were we to list all of the Protestant denominations, of course, the "10" codes (those from 10 through 19) would soon be exhausted and we would be forced to modify our scheme. Either of the following alternatives can easily meet this challenge, though the desirability of choosing one or the other may vary depending on one's analytical requirements.

10	*Protestant*	100
11	Baptist	101
12	Methodist	102
13	Presbyterian	103
14	Lutheran	104

15	Episcopalian	105
16	Church of Christ	106
17	Latter-day Saints	107
18	Church of God	108
19	Christian Science	109
20	Wesleyan	110
21	Assembly of God	111
30	*Catholic*	200
40	*Jewish*	300
41	Orthodox	310 (or 301)
42	Conservative	320 (or 302)
43	Reform	330 (or 303)

In the first instance we simply expand the number of decades (sets of 10 codes) assigned to the Protestants; in the second we add a digit. Again, since the variable in question is nominal, neither the specific numbers nor the number of digits has any significance. As long as our coding system is parsimonious, and as long as the coding categories are mutually exclusive, any numbers will suffice.

When we code *ordinal* variables, we are a bit more constrained. Because ordinal measurement does not include equal, or even known, intervals between values, we remain free to employ numbers of any magnitude. But because ordinal measurement requires that we preserve in our codes the relative positions (rankings) of these values, we must, at the very least, take care that our numbers are properly ordered. Thus, for the variable *level of political development* or any variable entailing differences of level, degree, or likelihood, any of the following coding schemes might be equally correct (and equally meaningful):

1 Lowest	1 Lowest
2 Low	6 Low
3 High	7 High
4 Highest	9 Highest

Each preserves the order inherent in the variable. None is in any way more precise than the others, because precision is a function not of the numbers themselves but of the underlying ordinal measurement. As was true earlier, our concern with parsimony might well lead us to select the first of the two schemes, but beyond that, our choice is strictly arbitrary.

In contrast, neither of the following schemes is appropriate:

1 Lowest	1 Highest
9 Low	2 High
6 High	3 Low
7 Highest	4 Lowest

Though the relative magnitude, or ordering, of numerical codes (and therefore the direction of their ordering) has no significance for nominal measurement, it is very important when we work with ordinal data. In the first of the two examples just given, the ranking of the numbers has been mixed; in the second, it has been reversed. As a result, neither coding scheme satisfactorily preserves the relative position and magnitude of the values on the variable. Thus, the codes are an inaccurate translation of our observations. Either they deprive us of the opportunity to rank our cases one against another, or they mislead us about the nature of any ranking we develop. Accordingly, such schemes are to be avoided with ordinal data.

Developing codes for interval measures may prove the easiest. Here numbers take on more precise meanings, and our options in assigning them are substantially reduced. A dollar is a dollar, a year is a year, and the difference between 47 percent and 43 percent is the same as that between 73 percent and 69 percent. In interval measurement, not only are values mutually exclusive and indicative of rank, but also the distances between any two sets of adjacent categories are constant and equal. The coding of interval variables must preserve these characteristics.

In order to code scores on an interval variable, we must find a set of numbers such that each is mutually exclusive of the others, each corresponds to a value of the variable, each is equally distant from its nearest neighbors, and the distance between any two adjacent values is known. Finding such numbers is generally an easy task, for unlike most nominal or ordinal scales, for which the researcher must, in effect, invent numerical equivalents for observations, many interval codes are naturally occurring. That is, interval codes are far more likely than those at lesser levels of measurement to derive *directly* from the operational definitions of variables. If we define a person's income as the number of dollars earned in a given period, then each specific quantity of dollars earned constitutes not only a value of the variable income but also a code for that value as well. As a result, the emphasis in the coding of interval data is generally less on *creating* meaningful codes than on recognizing and preserving them.

As we pointed out in Chapter 5, situations occur in which the researcher may, in order to enhance the manipulability or the explanatory power of a data set, wish to collapse interval/ratio data into ordinal categories. It may, for example, be both easier and more meaningful for us to compare respondents according to their general level of income than to focus on each dollar of difference. In such instances, it may be that the initial coding of the data will preserve their interval character and that these categories will subsequently be reaggregated according to the needs of the researcher (for example, we might record the actual number of dollars earned by respondents and then later group these earnings into larger categories), or the design may be to collapse the data at the time of acquisition (as when we simply classify respondents into general income categories [e.g., $20,000–$49,999] and make no record of their specific earnings). Each method entails both advantages and disadvantages, which should be weighed in the context of the research question at hand. Whichever is selected, however, researchers should be sure that their ultimate coding scheme meets the measurement requirements of the indicator in question.

As should be evident by now, the assignment of appropriate codes to data is inseparable from the process of operationalizing variables. Indeed, *codes are nothing more than numerical manifestations of our operational definitions.* For that reason, it is somewhat misleading to have placed our discussion of coding so late in this book. Decisions about what codes to associate with values on a variable must be made early in the research process. Such decisions are merely one more important part of proper planning. Yet the real usefulness of codes does not become apparent until later in the research process, for it is when we begin to analyze our data that codes come to bear most directly on our enterprise. It is here that coding provides for the transition first from observation to data processing and then from data processing to interpretation. To understand how this transition takes place, let us now consider the structures and uses of several code-related mechanisms.

The Codebook and the Coding Sheet

The first such device we must examine is the codebook. A **codebook** is simply a listing of each variable to be employed in a study, of each value the variable might take on, and of the numerical scores—the codes—associated with each of these values.

An Example Suppose that on July 1, 2003, the governments of Libya, Iran, and Cuba hired public relations firms to improve their images in the U.S. press, and that we wish to design a study to determine the effect these efforts have had on news and editorial content. In such a study we might compare the periods immediately before and immediately after the starting date of these campaigns to see whether, after the contracts took effect, (1) the amount of coverage of each nation increased or decreased significantly and (2) the various nations were presented more or less favorably than they had been in the earlier period. (In reality, we would also have to control for such additional factors as regular seasonal variation in coverage, as in the case of countries that get more press attention during the tourist season or the occurrence of newsworthy events such as political upheavals or natural disasters, but for purposes of illustration let us assume these are not concerns.)

To assess the effects of these image-enhancing efforts, we can turn to any of a number of indexes of news coverage and either analyze the index entries, which will be in the form of either titles or abstracts of various news articles and may, in fact, convey a good deal of information, or use them to identify the actual articles themselves. For purposes of illustration, let us design a project using index entries in Infotrac *Expanded Academic ASAP* (which indexes the contents of a large number of popular magazines) under the headings "Iran," "Libya," and "Cuba." Our independent variable is the introduction of professional public relations activities or, more correctly, their absence (before July 1, 2003) or presence (after that date).

Following on the two questions identified, we will have two sets of dependent variables. The first set will measure the *quantity* of news coverage and might include the number of index entries each month in the pretest and posttest periods, and the proportion of such entries (as evidenced by their titles or index classifications) that refer to the political, economic, or social system, respectively, of each country. We might further classify these as focusing on domestic or international concerns. The second set of variables will measure the *quality* of news coverage through judgments on such matters as whether the article (again, as evidenced by its title) suggests progress or decline in the nation's fortunes. Finally, in any such study we should include codes identifying each individual article, the country to which it refers, the date of publication, its length, and the specific publication or type of publication in which it appears.

Table 14.1
Abbreviated codebook for a hypothetical study of public relations of foreign nations

Column	Variable	Values	Code
1–4	Article (case) ID number		—
5	Nation referenced	Libya	1
		Iran	2
		Cuba	3
6–7	Month of publication	July 2003	01
		August 2003	02
		January 2004	07
		May 2005	23
		June 2005	24
8	Reference to political system in title (including references to government, political leaders or events, political parties, public policies)	No reference	0
		Reference present	1
9	Reference to economic system in title (including references to industry, the currency, the workforce, production, markets, trade, economic opportunity, etc.)	No reference	0
		Reference present	1
10	Reference to social system in title (including references to cultural, religious or social institutions, social events or actors, social structure, etc.)	No reference	0
		Reference present	1
11	Reference to domestic or international context	Exclusively domestic	1
		Both domestic and international	2
		Exclusively international	3
		Does not apply, NA	9
12	Reference to progress or decline	Reference exclusively to progress	1
		Reference to both progress and decline	2
		Reference exclusively to decline	3
		Does not apply	9
13–15	Number of pages in article		—
16	Type of magazine	News weekly (*Newsweek, U.S. News & World Report,* or *Time* only)	1
		Other, primarily political (including opinion magazines and featuring primarily political news and analysis)	2
		Other, primarily nonpolitical (including general audience magazines and those with specialized but primarily nonpolitical coverage)	3

Creating a Codebook   An abbreviated codebook for this hypothetical study is illustrated in Table 14.1. As you can see, the codebook summarizes the indicators to be used in the study and their associated values. It is, in fact, little more than a formal statement of the operational definitions with which any piece of research begins. Here, however, these definitions are set out in complete detail, including instructions for their interpretation, and are organized not with respect to our hypotheses *per se* but with an eye toward facilitating the actual gathering of information. The codebook provides step-by-step guidance to what we are looking for and how we can recognize it when we find it.

The codebook identifies the computer columns in which data will be stored and provides a description of the information to be found in each location. It also tells what codes were used to represent nonnumeric data. For example, the codebook depicted in Table 14.1 indicates that a number 1 found in computer column 16 signifies that the type of magazine in which the article in question was found is a news weekly (like *Time* or *Newsweek*). Having this information in a central location helps researchers correctly record data and accurately interpret the results of data analysis when it is completed. It also makes it possible for others who use the data set to see how data are organized and to interpret the results of data analysis without relying exclusively on the original researcher.

Creating a Coding Sheet   Once the codebook has been prepared, it is a quick and easy step to the next stage of data preparation—the development of a coding sheet. A **coding sheet** is a data recording device whose structure is based on the codebook and whose form will aid in computerizing our information once it has been gathered. The survey questionnaire and the recording form for structured observation described in earlier chapters, for instance, are both examples of coding sheets, as is the form presented in Figure14.2 for our study of coverage of foreign nations in the American press.

In Figure 14.2 the column labels correspond to the indicators developed in the codebook. A column is reserved on the coding sheet for *each digit* in a given code;

Coding sheet number _____

Date coded   _____

Coded by   _____

Figure 14.2

Coding sheet for studying effects of public relations of foreign nations thus, a two-digit code (such as that for month of publication) requires two columns on the coding sheet. Similarly, each row represents one case, and each numerical entry represents a value on the indicator in question for that particular case. Thus, we see that case number 0001 is an article about Iran that appeared in a news weekly in January 2004, focused exclusively on the political system, and made reference to the nation's declining fortunes and to certain weaknesses in its domestic situation. Such scores might derive, for example, from an article in *Time* entitled "Iran in Chaos: Leaders Unable to Halt Executions, Stability Threatened." In this manner, relevant characteristics of each article title we encounter can be recorded on the coding sheet, with each case taking up one row or line. Thus, if we study, or *code,* 821 cases, we can expect to end up with 821 rows of data. In each instance, corresponding data about the various cases will appear in the same column(s) on the coding sheet.

Finally, all coding sheets should be numbered (to ensure that none has been lost), dated (dates are often useful, for example, if we are forced to alter a definition or add a variable in midstream and must recode or add codes to all previous cases), and signed or initialed by the coder (as a basis for measuring intercoder reliability, as discussed in Chapter 10). If more than one coding sheet is required for each case, as when the number of indicators to be measured is quite large, all sheets for the same group of cases should be both stapled together and numbered identically. This minimizes the chances of their being separated and mixed up during processing.

Data Entry and Data Processing

Once the recording of data has been completed, we turn our attention to processing or manipulating our numbers to arrive at our findings. You can well imagine that in a study with large numbers of indicators and cases, the jumble of numbers can be absolutely overwhelming. To deal with this problem and to increase the ease, accuracy, and sophistication of our analysis, we rely on statistics software.

Many software packages are available for performing statistical analysis. One of the most established programs found at many universities and research companies is Statistical Package for the Social Sciences (SPSS), which provides a fairly intuitive click-and-drag interface for analyzing and graphically displaying data. Other common statistical programs are, for example, SAS, Statistica, Genstat, or Minitab. Software packages with full statistical programming languages like S-Plus, STATA, or SHAZAM can provide more flexibility for creating graphics and using new statistical methods. In the end, choosing a program will depend on the analyses you want to do, your statistical background, and which programs are readily available.

Entering Data   All of these statistics programs allow the user to enter data into a spreadsheet or data-editing screen. When using such a spreadsheet to enter data, you should first define and label one column for each variable of interest. Then, you enter the data, with each row representing a different case or observation. If, for example, you would like to analyze ten characteristics (your variables) of 200 newspaper stories (your cases), you would use one line of data for each of the 200 newspaper stories. In this example, each line of data would use ten columns, one for each of the ten variables. In addition to the columns that represent the variables in your analysis, you should also add one column for a case identification number in order to keep track of your data. All of that should sound familiar, for it is directly analogous to the coding sheet described above.

While manual data entry has become easier due to the availability of spreadsheet-like data entry systems, other methods of data entry are available. Optical scan sheets, with which most students probably are familiar ("fill in the bubbles with a number two pencil . . ."), are also popular due to the increased availability of optical scanners and new software that allows the creation and scanning of questionnaires to produce data files. Optical scan sheets are especially useful for recording large amounts of data that have been recorded on predesigned, standardized forms, thus avoiding the arduous task of entering this data manually. There are, however, a few disadvantages of using optical scan sheets for data entry. First, scan sheets only allow data to be entered in a predetermined way. Notes in the margins of the scan sheet, for example, will not be recognized by the scanner and therefore will not appear in the final data file. Second, optical scanners often do not recognize markings on scan sheets that do not conform with the predesigned option. Thus, scan sheet bubbles that are not completely filled, or are smudged or wrongly marked will probably not be recognized correctly by the scanner. Finally, some people might find it difficult to record data on scan sheets because of their often generic layout or the difficulty in identifying the appropriate space for marking the data on the sheet.

Once the data have been entered into the computer, the next step is to check them carefully for errors, a process that is also called "data cleaning." Manual data entry can easily lead to errors because of typos, incorrect reading of the codes, or simply a tired person entering the data. The easiest way to check data for erroneous entries is to print out the distribution for each of the variables in your data set and then look for inappropriate codes. For example, you might have decided to code the variable *party identification* as 1 for Republicans, 2 for Democrats, and 3 for Independents. If you see in the printed distribution that one of the cases has been coded as 5, it is obvious that an error has been made during the data entry. After identifying an error, simply review the original questionnaire responses and find the correct codes.

Conclusion

Before we conclude, three final points are in order. First, it is not unusual for those without prior statistical software experience to be both overwhelmed and intimidated by these programs. Such feelings are understandable, but they should not be allowed to stand in the way of learning. With the manuals and help menus now available, using this software is much simpler than it used to be.

Second, don't be ashamed if you make mistakes. Careful data entry and proofreading eliminate many errors, but as with any new skill you will invent ways to make more. This is a common pattern and should not trouble you. When you think about it, making and correcting mistakes represent two of the most important ways that we learn. Track down your own errors when you can, get help when you must, and keep trying.

Finally, don't get carried away. Computers are inherently stupid; they process information and they follow instructions precisely, but they do not think. By using the software packages we have described here, you can easily get a computer to perform the most elaborate statistical analyses imaginable on data of such low quality that the results, though impressive looking, are meaningless. Accordingly, it is quite important that you think through and understand the statistical and analytical procedures that you call upon the computer to perform, and that you select only those that fit your needs and your data. Those procedures are the subjects of the next several chapters.

Summary Points

• The type of data analysis you may perform is governed by your data's measurement and coding format.
• The most useful data coding schemes are detailed and highly systematic.

Suggested Readings and References

For a more detailed discussion of coding procedures, see Kenneth Janda's classic, *Data Processing: Applications to Political Research,* 2nd ed. (Evanston, IL: Northwestern University Press, 1969).

Examples of coding schemes, and their authors' rationale, may be found in the appendices of the quantitative data analysis articles in the current issues of the political science journals listed in Chapter 3. In recent years, several massive projects have coded large numbers of factors linked to international conflicts. The Correlates of War project covers the breadth of history, while the International Crisis Behavior Project is a more temporally constrained study that analyzes conflict in the twentieth century. The latter study includes a CD-ROM, and is found in Michael Brecher and Jonathan Wilkenfeld, *A Study of Crisis* (Ann Arbor, MI: University of Michigan Press, 1997).

An example of an automated coding technique is Gary King and Will Lowe, "An Automated Information Extraction Tool For International Conflict Data with Performance as Good as Human Coders: A Rare Events Evaluation Design," *International Organization*, 57 (July, 2003), pp. 617–642.

Two excellent books with step-by-step data analysis instructions for new or even advanced users of SPSS are Marija J. Norusis, *SPSS 12.0 Guide to Data Analysis* (Upper Saddle River, NJ: Prentice Hall, 2004) and Earl R. Babbie, Fred Halley, and Jeanne Zaino, *Adventures in Social Research: Data Analysis Using SPSS 11.0/11.5 for Windows*, 5th ed. (Thousand Oaks, CA: Pine Forge Press, 2003).

Research Exercises

1. a. Prepare a codebook for a hypothetical study using survey research or content analysis.
   b. Develop a coding sheet to correspond to your codebook.
   c. Either gather data on twenty-five cases or make up imaginary data on twenty-five hypothetical cases. Enter these data on your coding sheet.
   d. Find out what software packages are available at your computer laboratory. Obtain and peruse the manual for at least one of these packages.
   e. Enter your data into the computer, using the rules stated in the manual. Be sure to proofread and correct any errors.
   f. Experiment with writing a set of instructions to analyze the data you have entered.

2. Find the Web site of the Inter-university Consortium for Political and Social Research (ICPSR) at the University of Michigan (www.icpsr.umich.edu) and access its online archive of social science data. Choose one of the listed topics and examine the available abstract and codebook. (*Note*: the codebook is listed together with the dataset.)

Key Terms

coding   codebook
codes   coding sheet
parsimony

CHAPTER 15

Describing the Data: The Construction of Tables and Charts

- How may information be visually communicated?
- What are the standard guidelines for visual information presentation?

The problem we face at this point in the research process is how best to share with others the results of our work. We seek a style of presentation that is clear, precise, concise, and, above all, true to our data. Yet at the same time, we must help others to understand the meaning or significance of what we have found. That is, we must present our results so they may be readily interpreted. In part, the successful presentation of data involves statistical analyses, which we shall discuss in the next chapter. But in large measure, the effective communication and interpretation of research data depend on the quality of tabular and graphic presentation, on the tables and charts that one chooses, and on the appropriateness and clarity of their construction.

Computer-Generated Graphics

Available Software   The variety of types of tabular and graphic presentations is vast, especially given the ever-expanding graphics capabilities of software packages for the analysis and presentation of data. Common programs such as Microsoft Word, Excel, or Powerpoint, for example, all have interactive tools and templates to create a wide range of presentation-quality tables and charts. Similarly, statistical programs such as SPSS make it very easy to display data in the form of bar or pie charts, histograms, or scatterplots, to name but a few options. In most of these programs you must first enter the data for the table or chart into a worksheet or spreadsheet and then create the table or graph through a graphical menu or wizard. Once your chart or table is created, modifications can be made interactively by changing the data or the graph or table itself. For example, you can insert or delete graphical elements, change colors and textures, rotate three-dimensional graphs, and adjust lines and surfaces.

Interactive Tables   Another nice feature of interactive table and chart tools is that they allow you to visually identify the clearest presentation format by changing the order of the variables or the way the data are displayed. The fact that data can now be examined so easily by reorganizing the layout of a graph or viewing different levels of detail has added a new dimension to the art of data analysis that should not be underestimated. While graphs might be useful to display complex information in a simple and easy-to-understand way, the introduction of interactive graphs has created an entirely new technique for exploratory data analysis.

In the limited space available here, we are unable to describe all or even the most common software packages that allow the tabular or graphical presentation of data. Rather, by examining a few typical examples, we suggest the kinds of concerns you need to take into account when either reading or preparing tables and graphs and the like. In the process, we deal with such questions as, When should you employ a graphic representation? Which is better, a table or a chart? What should tables and charts look like (what is their structure)? How can tabular and graphic presentations help you to better understand your findings?

The Simple Table

We begin our discussion of these issues by looking at a device with which you are probably already familiar—the simple table. A **simple table** is little more than a tabular presentation of research data in what is essentially the form of a list.

An Example   Table 15.1, for example, summarizes the Democratic presidential vote and its gender components for the period 1980 to 2000.[1] Each column in the table represents a different variable (there are four variables in all). The fact that the table is ordered by the variable year, which appears in the first column, provides a cue for the interpretation of the data. It suggests that the table has been constructed to answer the question, *How has the Democratic presidential vote varied from year to year?*

While the findings reported in Table 15.1 are easy to digest, you should not expect such clearly distilled results directly from a statistics program such as SPSS or even Excel. For example, the data in this table came from ten separate crosstabulations, drawing on five different surveys. That is to say, after obtaining your data analysis, often you will need to compile new summary tables that condense data from several sources into a simple presentation. When combining, though, great care must be used to accurately represent your data.

A close examination of Table 15.1 reveals a number of points about the proper format for tabular presentation. As in the example, all tables should be numbered consecutively. In a lengthy paper with several numbered sections (or in a thesis or book with several chapters), these numbers may take the form Table 3.1, Table 3.2, and so forth, or Table III:1, Table III:2, and so forth. In a shorter or more simply structured paper, single-numbered listings (Table 1, Table 2) are quite sufficient. When tables appear in the same work with charts, graphs, or other illustrations, they are usually numbered separately. Graphic presentations are generally referred to as, for example, Figure 1 or Figure 3.1.

Titling Tables   Each table should have a title that accurately summarizes the nature of the data it reports. This title should give the reader enough information to decide whether to examine the table in detail, but it should not go so far as to save the

---

[1] Just as gender is commonly used in the literature to denote differential partisan voting by females in the term "gender gap," sex and gender are used interchangeably here, although sex is a biological characteristic and gender a social construct.

Table 15.1
Size and gender composition of the U.S. Democratic vote, 1980-2000[*]

Year	Democratic Vote (%)	Male Democratic Vote (%)	Female Democratic Vote (%)
1980	44	40	47
1984	42	37	45
1988	47	44	50
1992	58	55	61
1996	58	51	64
2000	53[†]	47	57

SOURCE: Data reported in this table are drawn from the quadrennial surveys of the National Election Study (NES).

[*] Data on minor party voting have been excluded from the present analysis.

[†] In the regionally divided electorate of 2000, this national survey somewhat overstates the Democratic vote percentage.

reader the trouble of doing so. Thus, a title for Table 15.1 such as *Data Showing That Democrats Polled More Than Half of the Votes Three Times in 1980-2000 and Did Better Among Women Than Men* would be inappropriate. In general, a title should simply indicate the major variables for which data are reported in a given table. When, as in Table 15.1, these data represent a geographic or political subdivision (e.g., the U.S.) or cover a particular time period, those characteristics should be incorporated into the title as well. When a table is drawn in whole or in part from another source, the reference should be placed immediately below the table (e.g., the National Election Study). Explanatory references pertaining to the table as a whole (the first footnote in the example) should be indicated with superscript lowercase letters or other symbols following the title. Those pertaining to parts of the table (the second footnote in the example) should be placed appropriately within the table. The footnotes themselves should be located immediately below the table and should follow a source identification when one is present.

Other points to keep in mind when preparing tables:

1. The table number and title should be separated from both the preceding text and the table itself by open space. Place each table on a separate page at the end of the research report, after the list of references. At the point in the text where the table is discussed, skip a line, type <Table 3 about here> in the center of the page, skip another line, and continue the text.

2. If possible, it is best to avoid drawing vertical lines to separate cells within the table. Make sure you take advantage of the table function available in most graphics, word processing, or database programs. Microsoft Word, for example, allows you to create tables quickly and automatically format them with a variety of borders, fonts, and shading. This feature is especially useful for "hiding" vertical lines in tables and giving all of your tables a consistent look.

3. Labels and data within the table should be double-spaced to facilitate reading, except that titles and category labels that will not fit on one line may be single-spaced. Category labels should describe as briefly as possible the variables or

values in question, but they should always be sufficiently complete to make clear the meaning of the data simply by reading the table.

As a rule of thumb, no table should be included in a research report unless it can generate at least a page of discussion. That discussion should not merely repeat the contents of the table. Nor should one overload the discussion with percentages or other quantitative terms, though these can be used sparingly. Rather, the discussion of a table should make clear any relationships demonstrated in the table and should focus the reader's attention on the highlights and particularly noteworthy findings. The discussion may also be used to report the results of any statistical tests one has performed on the data in the table (see Chapters 16–18).

An Example A discussion of Table 15.1, for example, would probably touch on the overall level of and changes in the Democratic vote during the period in question and on the relative contributions of male and female voters to that vote. Additionally, the discussion of alternative explanations for this gender-based vote disparity might lead to the next table or chart that explores other hypotheses. Specific points to be discussed might include the range of variation and the consistency (if any) in the pattern of variation for the variables, any notable inconsistencies in the data, and even the reliability of the source from which the data have been obtained.

The Line Graph

Sometimes we may wish to augment or replace tabular presentations with visually simpler graphics. This may be done either to clarify the presentation (consider the difficulty of interpreting Table 15.1 if it covered the period of 1896 to 2000) or to illustrate some particular aspect of the data.

An Example One of the simplest graphical presentation formats is the line graph, as illustrated in Figure 15.1. A **line graph** connects with a continuous line all the data points for a given indicator and provides for a comparison of data points across indicators by representing each in a separate corresponding line, often in a contrasting style. Line graphs are especially useful for representing trends.

The chart in Figure 15.1 reports the same data as does Table 15.1 but in graphic form. In contrast to the table, which requires a thorough reading, a quick glance at Figure 15.1 is sufficient to tell us that between 1980 and 2000 Democrats polled, in general, between 40 and about 60 percent of the vote in presidential elections; that they did better in 1992, 1996, and 2000 than in 1980, 1984, or 1988; that the pattern of male and female voters' support for the party followed very much the same path as its overall fortunes (males and females deserted the party in 1980 and 1984, but returned strongly in 1992); that support for the Democratic party among female voters was consistently higher than among males. The fine detail available in Table 15.1 is less evident in Figure 15.1, but the overall lessons of the data emerge much more readily.

In general, graphs should be formatted similarly to tables. Each figure should be numbered separately and titled appropriately. Both the vertical and horizontal

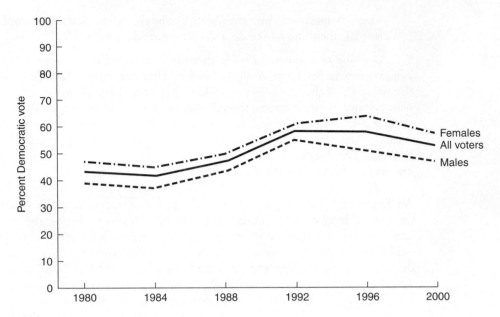

Figure 15.1
Line graph: Size and gender composition of the Democratic vote, 1980–2000

axes, when present, should be labeled. Vertical-scale labels should be placed to the left of the vertical scale numbers. Horizontal-scale labels should be placed below the figure. If the horizontal-scale numerals are years (as in the example), further labeling is optional. In the case of a complex line drawing, a **key** (an itemized explanation) to the lines should be placed below the figure. Alternatively, explanatory labels may be placed on the graph.

   Just as great care should be exercised to ensure that each figure you create is properly and consistently scaled, attention should also be given to scaling when reading others' charts. Improperly or inconsistently scaled axes can confuse the reader, or even the researcher, by either overstating or understating orders of magnitude or degrees of change. Indeed, truncated graphs (those whose lower values are not included) or stretched graphs (those on which the scale is smaller for one range of values and larger for another) may be deliberately employed to misinform a careless reader. Fortunately, use of these devices is less common in the academic research literature than in advertisements or commentaries.

The Pie Chart and the Bar Chart

Both the simple table and the line graph are useful primarily for describing and summarizing information. With some slight transformation of the data, however, it is possible to use graphic techniques to analyze or interpret these numbers as well. Suppose, for example, we are interested in highlighting the relative importance of women and men voters to the fortunes of Democratic presidential candidates. In particular, we might be interested in such questions as whether females' or males' support is more crucial to Democratic victories and whether (as was widely argued at the time) women voters put Bill Clinton in the White House in 1992. Let us suppose further, to keep our argument simple, that in each of the six election years we are considering, 47 percent of all voters were males and 53 percent females. In reality, since the 1980s, women typically do account for roughly 53 percent of voters, but turnout rates vary from one election to the next (Center for American Women and Politics 2004). Combining this pattern of turnout with the data presented in Table 15.1, we can identify the components of the Democratic vote in each election in terms of their proportional support.

With regard to 1992, for example, we know that 55 percent of male voters supported the Democrats and that 47 percent of all voters were male. Taking 55 percent of 47 percent, we find that 25.85 percent of all voters were males who voted Democratic. Similarly, we know that 61 percent of women voters supported the Democrats and that 53 percent of all voters were female. Taking 61 percent of 53 percent, we find that 32.43 percent of all voters were women who voted Democratic. Together these figures account for the roughly 58 percent of all voters who went Democratic in 1992. (The total figure is actually 58.28; these numbers are fractionally different from those in Table 15.1, because of rounding error and because the actual turnout rates that underlie the data in the table only approximate 53 percent for women and 47 percent for men.)

Let us carry this calculation a step further. We know that these male and female voters constituted some 58 percent of the two-party vote in 1992. What proportion of its support did each contribute to the Democratic party? To ascertain this we simply divide each individual figure by 58 percent (25.85 ÷ 58 and 32.43 ÷ 58) to find that in 1992 some 44 percent of Democratic votes came from males and some 56 percent from females. Similar calculations for each of the five other elections show females have contributed 58 percent, 58 percent, 56 percent, 58 percent, and 58 percent of all Democratic votes in 1980, 1984, 1988, 1996, and 2000, respectively; males contributed 42 percent, 42 percent, 44 percent, 42 percent, and 42 percent. These figures may be illustrated graphically by a pie chart, as shown in Figure 15.2.

Using Pie Charts   A **pie chart** is a figure in which a circle (or in this case, a series of circles) representing a given population has been segmented to show the distribution of particular attributes. In Figure 15.2, each circle represents 100 percent of the *Democratic* presidential vote in a given year. The shaded area represents the proportion of that vote provided by women voters. Note that the title and key to the figure are similar in style and placement to those in Figure 15.1 and that each circle, or pie, is labeled individually at the bottom of the figure. Percentages of the pie taken up by each segment may be labeled either within the graph as in Figure 15.2(a) or outside it as in Figure 15.2(f), whichever is clearer. Alphabetic labels (a, b, c, and so on) for separate elements within the figure often make it easier for the researcher to discuss the chart in the text and for the reader to follow the discussion.

Limitations of Pie Charts   Looking at Figure 15.2, one may be struck by the seeming lack of change in the proportion of Democratic votes contributed by women between 1980 and 2000, which is consistently about 58 percent. Using Figure 15.2 (and assuming the accuracy of the underlying data), one might thus be tempted to argue in answer to one of the questions posed earlier that in fact Bill Clinton was

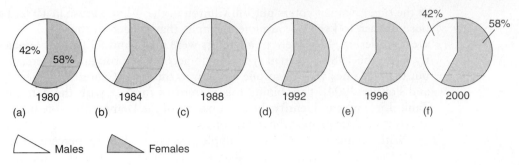

Figure 15.2
Pie Charts: Gender components of the Democratic coalition, 1980–2000

not put into office by women's votes. Indeed, substantiation for this argument is apparent from even the most cursory inspection of the pie charts. Unfortunately, in the present instance, the pie charts, although quite accurate, offer evidence that is incomplete and that consequently may prove misleading. This is true because the size of the Democratic vote varied from election to election (47 percent one year, 58 percent the next) while the size of the circles in the chart, representing 100 percent of that vote regardless of size, remains constant. Thus, in order to be not only accurate but also complete, the pies themselves should vary in size to account for variations in the overall Democratic vote.

The visual interpretation of sectored circles of differing sizes, however, is difficult at best. People are simply not good at it. Accordingly, such charts can defeat the goal of effective communication of our research results. Some alternative must be found, but before we find it, we want to emphasize that our point here is not that pie charts are always misleading and should never be used. On the contrary, pie charts may be the most effective graphic device for putting across an argument. Rather, the point is that *any* form of chart must be used with care. We must understand the data that underlie a graphic presentation, and we must be sure that the graphic is appropriate for the data *in the context in which they will be used.* Only in this way can graphics make a positive contribution to the interpretation of our data and the presentation of our research.

Using Bar Charts　An alternative graphic device that can illustrate the proportion of women's votes for the Democrats in a given year while at the same time making clear the fluctuations in the overall level of Democratic votes is a segmented bar chart like that illustrated in Figure 15.3. A **bar chart** is a graphic representation in which the height, and occasionally the width, of a series of bars illustrate a set of observations on one or more variables. In a **segmented bar chart,** each individual bar is subdivided to illustrate an additional set of observations relating to the distribution of attributes among the population represented by the bar itself. Note once again that the format is similar to those of Figures 15.1 and 15.2 except that in a bar chart, the key is typically found *above* rather than below the chart itself. (Occasionally, bar charts are drawn horizontally beginning at the left margin rather than vertically as in Figure 15.3. In such instances, the key should be placed either below the chart or to the right.)

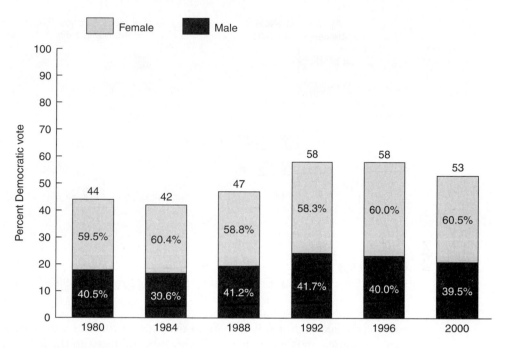

Figure 15.3
Bar chart: Gender components of the Democratic vote, 1980–2000

In Figure 15.3, the female vote is again represented by the shaded area of the chart. The bars, however, vary in size according to the overall percentage of the Democratic vote. This percentage is evident both in the scale along the left-hand margin of the chart and in the labels atop each individual bar. As a result, the impression one gets from the figure is rather different from that suggested by the pie charts, for here we see that though the female Democratic vote did shift up and down a bit, it did so within a relatively narrow range. Instead, it was the overall Democratic vote that proved most volatile, expanding and contracting in concert with the party's fortunes. Returning to our research question of whether female or male support is more crucial to the Democrats, we are now able to answer that the party wins when both genders are mobilized. The data used to arrive at this conclusion are essentially the same as those reported in Figure 15.2, but they are more complete. As a result, the conclusions we may draw from them are both more sophisticated and more satisfying.

The Bilateral Bar Chart

Another type of chart commonly found in the research literature of political science is the **bilateral bar chart**—a two-directional figure that is used to illustrate variation above or below some norm as represented by a center line. Two typical bilateral bar charts are illustrated in Figure 15.4. In Figure 15.4(a), the center line represents the average (mean) percentage of males who voted Democratic in presidential elections from 1980 to 2000 (46 percent). The bars represent variations around that average in

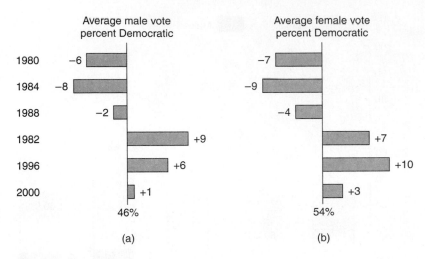

Figure 15.4
Bilateral bar chart: Variations in presidential voting by gender, 1980–2000

each of the six elections, with bars to the right of the line signifying above-average support among male voters for the Democrats and those to the left signifying below-average support. The length of the bars represents the degree of variation from the average, and the numerals indicate the precise degree of difference. For example, the average of 46 percent minus the variation of 6 percent in 1980 yields the 40 percent support by men noted in that year in Table 15.1. Figure 15.4(b) presents a similar analysis of women's votes, based on an average level of Democratic support of 54 percent.

These figures add yet another dimension to our analysis of the data reported in Table 15.1, for taken together they suggest that while both men and women put Bill Clinton into office in 1992, men's support waned in 1996. In contrast, women supported President Clinton at the polls even more strongly in 1996 than they had in 1992. When we combine this new information with our earlier findings, we get a more thorough picture of the role of female and male voters in the Democratic party during these years. And more generally, we can see that the type of information available from a bilateral bar chart complements and supplements that which can be developed by using other graphic devices.

The Crosstabulation

One other form of tabular presentation deserves attention before we move on to a discussion of statistics. Indeed, it is perhaps the single most common form of table used in contemporary political science research and provides the basis for a number of the statistical calculations we examine in the next chapter. This form of presentation is known as the **crosstabulation (or crosstab)** and is illustrated in Tables 15.2 and 15.3.

In format and structure, the crosstabulation resembles the simple table presented earlier, but its substance is different. Crosstabs are based more directly upon hypotheses and are structured so as to facilitate an examination of the relationships between variables. Table 15.2, for example, summarizes the relationship between gender and

Table 15.2
Gender differences in presidential voting, 1980

Presidential Vote	Gender		
	Male	Female	All Voters
Percent—Democratic	39	47	44
Percent—Republican	61	53	56
Total percent	100	100	100
Number of cases	(394)	(483)	(877)

Table 15.3
Gender differences in presidential voting, 1996

Presidential Vote	Gender		
	Male	Female	All Voters
Percent—Democratic	51	64	58
Percent—Republican	49	36	42
Total percent	100	100	100
Number of cases	(470)	(564)	(1034)

the presidential vote for 1980; Table 15.3 summarizes the comparable data for 1996. In each instance, the data are drawn from the National Election Study, and the sample sizes are noted in the table. These tables are organized so as to permit us to examine the hypotheses that women, for one reason or another, are more likely than men to vote Democratic in any given year.

Each entry (exclusive of totals) in each table is termed a *cell*. The tables may be described by the number of rows and columns that they contain, where each row represents a particular value on one variable and each column a particular value on the other. Thus, Tables 15.2 and 15.3 are each referred to as a 2 × 2 (two-by-two) table, since each table has two rows of cells and two columns of cells, excluding totals.

Crosstabs are always arranged so that the data total on the independent or explanatory variable's column or row. In the present instance, that variable is gender (in the columns). This means that if the table contains percentages, they will be based upon and sum to 100 percent along the independent variable. Thus, Table 15.2 tells us that in 1980, 39 percent of males voted Democratic—not that 39 percent of all Democrats were male. It would be possible to calculate our percentages in the other direction, but in the present instance this would tell us nothing of explanatory value because one's party preference *invariably* is acquired later than one's gender. The sum of all of the percentages in column 1 of the table accounts for all (100 percent of) male voters, in column 2 for all female voters, and in column 3 for all voters. The row labeled "number of cases" reports the number of respondents to our survey who were classified as members of each group. These numbers constitute a *frequency distribution* (discussed in the next chapter) and because of their position in the table, are often referred to as the *marginals*. The independent variable in a crosstab may be in either the rows or columns, but it is conventionally the *column variable*, as in both Tables 15.2 and 15.3.

In examining tables such as these, it is often possible to tell in general terms whether or not your hypothesis is supported by the data. In both Table 15.2 and Table 15.3, for instance, it is evident that women did vote consistently more Democratic than males. Although a majority of women voted Republican in 1980, even in that year female voters were 8 percentage points more likely to vote Democratic (47 – 39). In 1996, a majority of both genders voted Democratic, but women more strongly supported Bill Clinton's candidacy. Still, such eyeball measures are rough at best, and when tables are more complex than these, as is often the case, they are generally unreliable. In the next chapter we consider some statistics that enable us to state more precisely the degree of harmony between hypothesis and data.

Conclusion

In conclusion, let us restate for emphasis three important points about the use of tabular and graphic presentations.

First, these devices should be used both imaginatively and constructively. As part of the research process itself, they can be extremely helpful in developing our concepts to the fullest and in bringing us to a firm understanding of what our data tell us. Flexibility and an openness to new forms of analysis can contribute greatly to expanding our knowledge of political phenomena, and even techniques as simple as these can help us to give shape to our discoveries.

Second, tabular and graphic devices should be used appropriately. As may be evident from even this brief treatment, it is possible to present research results deceptively through the subtle abuse of these techniques, and it is equally possible to fool oneself by their careless misuse. Researchers have both an ethical obligation to others to report their findings not only accurately but also fairly and an intellectual obligation to themselves to examine them rigorously. Together, these obligations are the cornerstones of research.

Finally, in the presentation of research, tables and graphics should be used parsimoniously. Too many such materials in a research report clutter the text and detract from its readability. The author's decision to include a table or chart is taken by the reader as an indication of the importance the author attaches to the particular information contained therein. The author has an obligation to make those choices and not simply to offer the reader a smorgasbord of information. Not only does such discretion enhance authors' reports; it forces them to think more clearly and decide what is important, thus directly contributing to the research effort.

A final suggestion: the best way to learn data presentation is through hands-on use and experimentation. If you run into difficulty, programs such as Excel or SPSS have useful help functions, offering step-by-step instructions for constructing charts and tables.

Summary Points

• Different facets of your data are revealed by using photographs, charts and tables, or text.

• Your audience's understanding of visual information will be improved by simplification, enlargement, and using methods appropriate to the data type.

Suggested Readings and References

Useful texts on the practical aspects of graphic presentations include William S. Cleveland, *The Elements of Graphing* (Summit, NJ: Hobart, 1994). Another good introduction to the graphical display of statistical data is Gary T. Henry, ed., *Creating Effective Graphs: Solutions for a Variety of Evaluation Data* (San Francisco, CA: Jossey-Bass, 1997).

More theoretical discussions of the use of graphics can be found in William G. Jacoby, *Statistical Graphics for Univariate and Bivariate Data* (Thousand Oaks, CA: Sage, 1997); William G. Jacoby, *Statistical Graphics for Visualizing Multivariate Data* (Thousand Oaks, CA: Sage, 1997); and Gary T. Henry, *Graphing Data: Techniques for Display and Analysis* (Thousand Oaks, CA: Sage, 1995). Edward R. Tufte offers both a discussion of the conceptual approaches to graphic representation and a collection of examples covering some three centuries in *The Visual Display of Quantitative Information* (Cheshire, CT: Graphics Press, 1997). In a companion volume, *Envisioning Information* (Cheshire, CT: Graphics Press, 1995), Tufte provides many examples of the use of graphics to summarize data. Tufte's latest book, *Visual Explanations: Images and Quantities, Evidence and Narrative* (Cheshire, CT: Graphics Press, 1997), examines the logic of depicting quantitative information and explores how visual evidence influences design strategies. For insights into the subtleties and potential abuse of graphic presentation, see Gerald E. Jones, *How to Lie with Charts* (San Francisco, CA: Sybex, 1995). One of the best examples of the use of graphic techniques for the presentation and analysis of political science data is Sidney Verba and Norman Nie, *Participation in America: Political Democracy and Social Equality* (Chicago, IL: University of Chicago Press, 1987).

References: Center for American Women and Politics (CAWP), *Fact Sheet: Sex Differences in Voter Turnout* (Eagleton Institute of Politics, Rutgers University, 2004).

Research Exercises

1. Using the list of political science journals presented in Chapter 3, find three examples of graphic presentations from three separate articles. Reproduce each and write a brief summary of the information it conveys.

2. Using the list of political science journals presented in Chapter 3, find three examples of crosstabulations from three separate articles. Reproduce each and write a brief summary of the information it conveys.

3. Consult the most recent editions of the *State and Metropolitan Area Data Book* (published by the U.S. Census Bureau online at: www.census.gov), and the *UNESCO Statistical Yearbook* (online resource at: www.uis.unesco.org). Examine and compare the structures of the tables in these sources. Are these simple tables or crosstabs?

Table 15.4
Crosstab format

	I	II	III	IV
I				
II				
III				

4. Using data from the *State and Metropolitan Area Data Book*, arrange the fifty states of the United States into three groups according to their population ranking in the 2000

census. Prepare a crosstab comparing the three groups of states according to their respective per capita income levels in the same year. This will require that you develop ordinal categories of per capita income, determine which is your independent variable, count the number of cases in each cell of the resulting table, and calculate the appropriate percentages. In doing so, you may wish to use as a worksheet a grid similar to the one shown in Table 15.4.

Key Terms

simple table

line graph

key

pie chart

bar chart

segmented bar chart

bilateral bar chart

crosstabulation (or crosstab)

CHAPTER 16

Statistics I: Summarizing Distributions on One Variable

- What are the three measures of central tendency?
- Which level of measurement is most associated with each?
- How is a variable's dispersion measured?

Often in political science research, charts and tables alone do not tell us enough about our data to permit a satisfactory answer to our research question. In part this is a problem of complexity (our variables may have either too many values or too many cases—or there may even be too many variables involved—to lend themselves to ready analysis) and in part a question of precision (degrees of difference or subtle variations among variables may be important, and they are often difficult to assess accurately by simply eyeballing a table or chart). In instances such as these, as well as others that call for highly sophisticated analysis, political scientists employ *statistics*.

In this context, **statistics** are numbers that summarize either the distributions of values on, or the relationships between, variables. They are a form of mathematical shorthand capable of telling us at a glance and with great precision what our data show (or, in many cases, what they do not show). What is the political ideology of the typical college student? Do Hispanic voters differ systematically in their party preferences from African Americans? What kinds of actions or situations in the world community are most likely to give rise to armed conflict? If the proper data are applied for analysis, statistics can answer these questions and many more.

Statistics can be extremely complex. It is equally true, however, that many of the primary concepts and techniques of statistical analysis are extremely simple, can be learned in a short time, and can get you a good deal further into the subject than you might imagine. In fact, your knowledge of high school algebra arms you with just about all the mathematics you will need, and you may be surprised at how intuitive many statistical concepts really are.

We should make clear that this chapter and the two that follow will not teach you all there is to know about statistics, nor even all there is to know about the particular statistical measures we discuss. Still, by the time you complete these chapters, you should have a good sense of what statistics are and of how you can use them, you should have some understanding of the concepts that lie behind the numbers and the calculations, and you should have a reasonable facility in the use of several specific statistics. Together, these skills will enable you both to employ statistical analysis in your own research and to comprehend more fully and more critically what you read in scholarly journals and in other reports of political science research.

In this chapter we examine statistics that answer the following types of questions about a given set of data: How are the cases distributed among the values of each of our variables? What does the typical case look like? How typical is it?

Statistics and Level of Measurement   In each instance, we examine a different statistic for each level of measurement: nominal, ordinal, and interval/ratio. You will recall from Chapter 5 that these levels differ from one another in that the first merely differentiates categories, the second ranks them, and the third assumes constant degrees of difference between them. In effect, then, *nominal*, *ordinal*, and *interval/ratio* numbers are different kinds of numbers with different qualities. In a sense, nominal numbers are soft numbers; they don't tell us very much. Because they merely separate objects into groups and serve as no more than labels for those groups, they cannot even be added or subtracted. Accordingly, we cannot use very sophisticated statistical methods in analyzing nominal data. On the other hand, interval numbers are much harder, or more rigorous, in that they convey a great deal more information about the data they represent. They can be added, subtracted, squared, and variously transformed. As a result, they offer much more flexibility and an opportunity for far more sophisticated analysis. It is for this reason that different techniques are applied to different levels of measurement. For the same reason, of course, one must take care to use each technique appropriately.

Measures of Central Tendency and Dispersion

Two types of statistics are used to describe the distribution of cases over the values of a single variable. The first—the measure of **central tendency**—helps us to identify the most typical value: the one value or score that best represents the entire set of cases on that variable. Suppose we were told that the average American female employee is a white-collar worker, is a high school graduate, and has 1.7 children. Clearly not every American woman fits these categories, but when we look at all American females in some summary manner, this set of characteristics might well come closest to a general description of what we find. It is this same notion of an average, or typical, case that we employ in calculating a measure of central tendency. Indeed, it was precisely such measures that identified these particular traits of American females in the first place.

As we have noted, however, not every member of the female population fits this description. Many are blue-collar or professional workers or perhaps even unemployed, some have finished only grade school while others hold advanced degrees, and some may have 10 or 20 children while others are unmarried and childless. In other words, the "typical" American female may well represent the *tendencies* within the population, but she does not accurately reflect each individual case. For this reason, once we have identified such a typical case, we must ask a follow-up question: How typical is it? How good a job does this average score do of summarizing the distribution of scores for all the cases on a given variable? We answer this question by using a second type of statistic—the measure of dispersion. The measure of **dispersion** tells us whether the variation around the average value we have identified is limited, in which case we can have confidence that our average is a meaningful one, or whether that variation is so great that the most typical case is not really very representative of the population after all.

This raises an important point, which should be explained before we proceed any further. Statistics are powerful tools of analysis; they can tell us a great deal

Table 16.1
Frequency distribution: Type of occupation of respondents

Code	Value	Number of Cases
1	Blue-collar	25
2	White-collar	23
3	Professional	22
4	Farm	20
5	Unemployed	10

about our data that we could not otherwise ascertain. But statistics, on their own, are mindless. One can calculate and report *any* statistic on *any* set of numbers and in the process appear to be wringing the last drop of knowledge from one's data. For two reasons, however, many of these "results" may be meaningless. The first reason is one we have discussed already and whose logic should become more evident as we go on. Put most simply, the level of sophistication of our statistics may exceed the level of sophistication of our data. If our statistic requires us to add two numbers, but our data are based on nominal-level measures for which the whole concept of addition is inappropriate, we could in fact go through the mechanical process of combining the coded values, but the result would be worthless. Thus, if the score 1 represented blue-collar workers; 2, white-collar workers; and 3, professional workers, we could add 1 and 2 and get 3, but would we really want to argue that one blue-collar worker plus one white-collar worker *equals* one professional? Certainly not.

The second reason that statistical results may be less than meaningful is that one statistic, by itself, often cannot tell the whole story. If the single *most* typical level of education of American females is completion of high school, but only 28.6 percent of the population has both reached that level and stopped there, how much does this average really tell us? Not much. And how many people do you know who actually have an average of 1.86 children? Thus, while we can calculate and report these figures accurately, they should not be allowed to stand alone. Each measure of central tendency should be qualified or evaluated with an accompanying measure of dispersion. And similarly, as we shall argue later, whenever we are dealing with a sample, each measure of association between two variables should be accompanied by a measure of statistical significance, which is an indication of how likely that finding is to represent a substantive relationship between the variables in question. Thus, statistics must be not only appropriate to the level of measurement of the data but substantively meaningful as well if they are to prove of much value.

All measures of central tendency and dispersion are based on a summary of values and cases termed a *frequency distribution*. A **frequency distribution** is simply an ordered count of the number of cases that take on each value of a variable. For example, suppose we ask 100 people to tell us their present occupation and then we classify their responses according to type. For the variable *type of occupation*, we might arrive at the frequency distribution shown in Table 16.1. The frequency distribution simply lists each value on the variable and reports the number of cases that take on that value. The same information may be communicated by a bar graph,

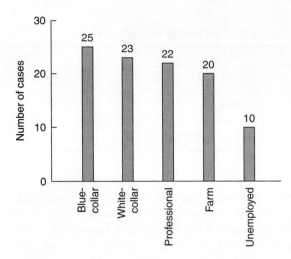

Figure 16.1
Histogram: Type of occupation of respondents

which, when used for this particular purpose, is often called a **histogram**, as illustrated in Figure 16.1. Using this information, we may identify the most typical case and determine its descriptiveness.

Measures for Nominal Variables

As we suggested earlier, different measures of central tendency and dispersion are appropriate for different levels of measurement. Since *type of occupation* is a nominal variable, let us begin to examine these calculations by focusing on statistics appropriate for nominal-level measures.

The Mode   At this level, where numbers represent merely category labels without regard to order, the only available measure of central tendency is the mode. The **mode** is simply *the most frequently occurring value*—that which is taken on by the greatest number of cases. In the example, this is category 1, or the value *blue-collar*. We refer to this as either the mode or the modal category. (A distribution in which two categories tie for the greatest number of cases is said to have two modes, or to be *bimodal*, and it is possible to have a tie between even more than two categories.) Blue-collar employment, then, is the single most typical type of occupation among our sample of 100 persons.

But clearly, most people in this sample (in fact, fully 75 percent) are not blue-collar workers, so even though we can identify the most typical value in this distribution, that information may not be very meaningful. We can be more precise in judging just how meaningful it is by calculating the appropriate nominal-level measure of dispersion—the **variation ratio**—the formula for which is as follows:

$$v = \frac{\sum f_{\text{nonmodal}}}{N}$$

$$or \; v = 1 - \frac{f_{\text{modal}}}{N}$$

where $\sum f_{\text{nonmodal}}$ = the sum of all cases *not* falling into the modal category

f_{modal} = the number of cases in the modal category

N = the total number of cases.

In effect, this statistic tells us the *percentage of all cases that do not fit into the modal category.* In the example,

$$v = \frac{23 + 22 + 20 + 10}{100} = .75$$

or in the simplified form,

$$v = 1 - \frac{25}{100} = .75$$

The variation ratio ranges between 0 (when all cases take on the same value) and $1 - 1/N$ (when each case takes on a different value). In general, the lower the variation ratio, the more typical or more meaningful the mode. In the case of bimodal or multimodal distributions, one modal value is arbitrarily selected for purposes of calculation, and v is determined precisely as above.

Measures for Ordinal Variables

When dealing with ordinal-level data, we have a bit more information, since our codes represent not only categorization but relative position or ranking as well. Our selection of measures of central tendency and dispersion should both reflect and take advantage of this fact.

The Median   The appropriate measure of central tendency for ordinal data—the median—does precisely this. The **median** is simply *the value of the middle case in a distribution*—the case above and below which an equal number of other cases lie. Obtaining the median, then, requires only that we count from either end of the distribution toward the center until we find the middle case and then ascertain the value associated with that case. When we have an odd number of cases, we will be able to locate one middle case (for example, for 99 cases, the 50th case from either end of the frequency distribution will have 49 cases both above and below it). The value of this case is the median. When N (the number of cases) is an even number, two middle cases will emerge (for example, for 100 cases, the 50th and 51st cases from either end together constitute the midpoint of the distribution). If both of these

Table 16.2
Educational achievement in three samples

Code	Value	Sample 1 (*n*)	Sample 2 (*n*)	Sample 3 (*n*)
1	Grade school	25	25	10
2	Some high school	23	23	40
3	High school graduate	22	22	35
4	College graduate	20	20	10
5	Advanced degree	9	10	5
Total *n*		99	100	100

cases take on the same value, that value is the median. If they take on different values, the median is said to be the midpoint between those two values. An example may help to make this clear. Let us consider the distribution of educational achievement in three samples (Table 16.2).

In the first, we identify the middle case (the 50th from either end), note its value, and determine the median level of education to be 3, or *high school graduate*. In the second, we identify two middle cases (the 50th and 51st from either end), note that each takes on the same value, and determine the median once again to be a score of 3. In the third sample, however, the middle cases split between the *some high school* and *high school graduate* categories. Here the median is the midpoint between the two values in question, or $(2 + 3)/2 = 2.5$. Because fractional values have no meaning in ordinal measurement, this figure merely tells us that the midpoint of the distribution lies somewhere between 2 and 3.

Using Quantiles   Any of several measures of dispersion for ordinal variables, termed **quantile ranges,** tells us how tightly the various cases cluster around the median or, again, how typical or representative the median is of the whole distribution. A **quantile** is a measure of position within a distribution. For example, a percentile divides a distribution into 100 equal parts such that the first percentile is the point or value in that distribution (counting from the lowest score up) below which 1 percent of all the cases lie, the second percentile that point or value below which 2 percent of all the cases lie, and so forth. Or, to use what may be a more familiar example, the prospective college student who scores in the 85th percentile on the SAT has achieved a test score that is higher than the scores of 85 percent of all who took the test. Similarly, a decile divides the distribution into tenths (for example, the third decile would be the point below which 30 percent of all the cases lie), a quintile into fifths, a quartile into fourths. Any of these can be used to indicate dispersion around the median, though the decile and quintile ranges are most commonly found in the literature.

An Example   Let us use the quintile range to illustrate the procedure. The quintile range (q) is defined as follows:

$$q = q_4 - q_1$$

where q_4 = the fourth quintile (the value below which 4/5, or 80 percent, of
the cases lie)

q_1 = the first quintile (the value below which 1/5, or 20 percent, of the
cases lie).

The narrower the range of values separating these two points in the distribution, the more tightly clustered the cases are about the median and the more truly representative of the distribution the median will be. In sample 2 in Table 16.2, for instance, where $n = 100$, we calculate q by locating the 81st case (below which 80 percent of the cases lie) and the 21st case (below which 20 percent of the cases lie), starting our count within the frequency distribution from the lowest scores. We then subtract the value associated with the 21st case from that associated with the 81st ($q = q_4 - q_1 = 4 - 1 = 3$) to obtain the quintile range. In sample 3, the equivalent computation yields a quintile range of 1 ($q = 3 - 2 = 1$), suggesting by comparison that this distribution is better typified by its median of 2.5 than is sample 2 by its median of 3. An examination of the two frequency distributions will confirm the validity of this conclusion.

One difficulty in interpreting quantile ranges is that they are extremely sensitive to variation in the number of categories on a given variable. The more categories there are, the greater the range is likely to be. For this reason, quantile ranges can prove difficult to interpret for comparison between variables that differ in their number of categories. For similarly coded variables, for longitudinal or cross-sectional comparisons of the values of any single variable, or for some absolute indication of variability around the median, however, they are generally quite adequate.

Measures for Interval/Ratio Variables

Interval/Ratio data, of course, provide us with the most complete information of all, including categorization, rank, and distance. Interval values can be subjected to any arithmetic manipulation. Consequently, our measures of central tendency and dispersion for interval/ratio data can and should take this added information and capability into account.

The Mean The measure of central tendency for interval/ratio data is the **mean**—a measure that locates *the central point of a distribution* in terms of both the number of cases on either side of that point and their distance from it. The mean of a distribution is the statistic many people commonly associate with the term *average*.

Let us visualize the nature of the mean by using Figure 16.2. If all the cases in a distribution are represented by equal weights, and if they are arranged on a board at fixed intervals so that those with the most extreme values are farthest from the center in one or the other direction and those with equal values are placed at the same point on the board, the mean value of the distribution will be the fulcrum point—the value at which the combined weights and distances to one side precisely balance those to the other. As illustrated in the figure, both weight (number of cases) and distance (extremity of the scores) are important in ascertaining the mean.

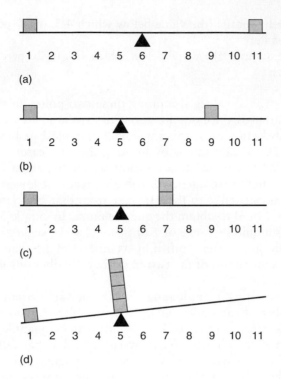

Figure 16.2
The mean as a point of balance

The mean of a distribution, designated $\overline{X}$, is calculated by taking the sum of the values of the individual cases and dividing by the number of cases. This procedure is summarized in the following equation:

$$\overline{X} = \frac{\sum_{i=1}^{N} X_i}{N}$$

where X_i = the value of each individual case

N = the number of cases

$\sum_{i=1}^{N}$ = an instruction to take the sum of all the individual values of cases 1 to N.

Note, too, however, as illustrated in Figure 16.2(d), that precisely because it is sensitive to distance, the mean is subject to distortion in a distribution that has one or a few very extreme cases. That is, a small number of cases with very extreme scores can cause the mean to be less than a truly typical value. Let us see how this might occur.

Consider a group of 11 persons, 10 of whom earn $10,000 a year and 1 of whom earns $1 million. The mean income for this group equals $100,000,

$$\frac{(10 \times \$10,000) + \$1,000,000}{11}$$

but 10 of the 11 members of the group actually earn one-tenth of that amount. Thus, the mean, while correctly calculated, is not as representative as, say, the median, which in this case is $10,000.

It would seem at first glance that to determine how typical of a distribution a given mean is, all we need do is measure the distances of all cases from that point (taking account of direction), add these together, and divide by N (the number of cases). In effect, we would calculate the mean of the distances around the mean as in the formula

$$\text{Dispersion} = \frac{\sum_{i=1}^{N} (X_i - \overline{X})}{N}$$

The greater the dispersion for a given distribution, then, the *less* typical the mean; and the less the dispersion, the *more* typical the mean.

But when we try this with, for example, the three cases illustrated in Figure 16.2(c), a problem emerges. Applying the formula to the example, we find

$$\text{Dispersion} = \frac{(1-5) + (7-5) + (7-5)}{3}$$

$$= \frac{-4+2+2}{3} = 0$$

Even in a distribution with such clear divergence as our income example, we find

$$\text{Dispersion} = \frac{10(10,000 - 100,000) + (1,000,000 - 100,000)}{11}$$

$$= \frac{-900,000 + 900,000}{11} = 0$$

Indeed, for *any* mean in any distribution the result is the same. The reason is a simple one. We have, in effect, *defined* the mean as precisely that point where these weights and distances cancel out, or the point or value about which all variations are balanced. Therefore, once we have calculated the mean, we should hardly be surprised to find exactly the effect we have intended. Yet the notion that we ought to be able to measure dispersion by comparing the closeness of cases to, or their remoteness from, the mean retains its appeal. Enter the standard deviation.

Calculating the Standard Deviation The **standard deviation** (*s*) employs a mathematical device to accomplish our purpose. In effect, it is a procedure that eliminates the tendency of opposing distances to cancel one another out by the simple expedient of squaring those distances (thereby eliminating all negative signs), averaging the *squares* of the distances around the mean, and then taking the square root of the result so as to return to the original units of distance. The formula by which all of this is accomplished resembles the rejected formula except for the use of the squared distances and the square root of the result. That formula is

$$s = \sqrt{\frac{\sum\limits_{i=1}^{N} (X_i - \overline{X})^2}{N}}$$

where X_i = the value of each individual case

$\overline{X}$ = the mean

N = the number of cases

$\sum\limits_{i=1}^{N}$ = an instruction to take the sum of the individual values for cases 1 to N.

Thus, in the example from Figure 16.2c,

$$s = \sqrt{\frac{(1-5)^2 + (7-5)^2 + (7-5)^2}{3}}$$

$$= \sqrt{\frac{16+4+4}{3}} = \sqrt{\frac{24}{3}} = \sqrt{8} = 2.8$$

It is expressed in the same units as the original data.

When two variables are measured by the same or comparable scales, the standard deviation provides a basis for comparing the representativeness of the means: the greater the standard deviation, the less representative the mean. But when scales differ substantially or when a single variable is being analyzed, the interpretation of the standard deviation is less clear.

The Normal Distribution One exception to this applies to variables whose values closely approximate a **normal distribution,** or one in which there is *a single mode in the very center of the distribution and in which the frequencies decline symmetrically as the values become more extreme in each direction.* (The bell-shaped curve with which you may be familiar is simply a graphic representation of a normal distribution.) In these cases, we know (through procedures that lie beyond the scope of the present discussion) that 68.3 percent of all cases will lie within +1 and −1 standard deviation from the mean, 95.5 percent will lie within +2 and −2 standard deviations from the mean, and 99.7 percent will lie +3 and −3 standard deviations from the mean. In fact, for such distributions, we can locate the exact number of standard deviation units any particular value lies above or below the mean, then use this information for comparing the relative position of two cases on the same variable or, alternatively, the relative scores on two variables for the same case. The measure that allows us to do this is called the **standard score** (or *z*-score), and it is calculated by simply subtracting the mean ($\overline{X}$) from the score (X) and then dividing by the standard deviation (s):

$$z = \frac{(X_i - \overline{X})}{s}$$

What makes the standard scores so useful is the fact that they allow us to compare scores that are based on very different units of measurements (for example, age measured in number of years and height measured in inches). Since *z*-scores all have a mean of 0 and a standard deviation of 1, each score simply tells us how many standard deviation units a variable (age, height, etc.) is above or below the mean.[1]

Suppose, for example, that we have data showing the per capita spending by each state for education, the number of teachers per 1,000 students each employs, and the number of high school degrees per 100,000 population awarded by each in a given year, and that values on these variables are distributed among the states in a manner approximating the normal curve. Suppose further that we wish to use these data to examine educational policy in, say, Arizona and Virginia. We first calculate the mean ($\overline{X}$) and standard deviation (s) for each variable for all fifty states and then determine the respective standard scores (z) on each variable for the two states in which we are interested. The result will be two sets of scores in standard units (no longer dollars, teachers, and certificates but the number of standard deviations about the mean) that can be used to construct indices of educational policy, determine an average position for Arizona or Virginia among the states, or provide for standardized comparisons across substantively different measures. As the basis for the standard score, then, the standard deviation may be an especially useful statistic.

Conclusion

In this chapter we have focused on statistics that summarize the distribution of scores on one variable. Because these statistics describe the characteristics of individual variables, they are often called **univariate statistics.** We have seen that different univariate statistics are appropriate for variables with different levels of measurement: nominal, ordinal, and interval/ratio. In the next chapter we examine what are termed **bivariate statistics**—those that summarize the relationship between *two* variables.

Summary Points

- Central tendency may be measured with the mode, median, or mean.
- The mode is typically used with nominal variables.

---

[1] Table A.6 in Appendix A summarizes the area between the mean and *z*, as well as the area beyond *z* in the distribution, for standard scores between 0 and 4, which is to say, for all values between the mean and a distance of four standard deviations in either direction around it. The values in the table can be used to locate (for purposes of comparison) any number of cases relative to the means on different variables.

- The median is most appropriate with ordinal data.
- The mean works best with interval/ratio information.
- The standard deviation measures the dispersion of interval/ratio variables—literally, the deviation of the values from the mean.

Suggested Readings and References

At the end of Chapter 18 we suggest several books you might read to begin learning about statistics in more detail. For the present, it might be more useful to start with books that can put you at ease about using statistics and at the same time help you grasp some important basic concepts. These books may seem somewhat dated, but the information is still relevant and the writing is more engaging than any other works. For this purpose, we suggest Darrell Huff and Irving Geis, *How to Lie with Statistics* (New York: Norton, 1993), a classic and lighthearted examination of the uses and abuses of statistics, or what the authors term "statisticulation," and Jerald G. Shutte's rather complete *Everything You Always Wanted to Know About Elementary Statistics (But Were Afraid to Ask)* (Englewood Cliffs, NJ: Prentice Hall, 1977). Another humorous and very readable book that looks at the use of statistics with examples from everyday life is Jefferson Hane Weaver, *Conquering Statistics: Numbers Without the Crunch* (New York: Plenum Trade, 1997). For those who prefer to absorb their statistics through the medium of cartoon drawings, we recommend Larry Gonick and Woollcott Smith, *The Cartoon Guide to Statistics* (New York: HarperPerennial, 1993).

Research Exercises

1. For each of the following frequency distributions, determine the mode and variation ratio, the median and quintile range, and the mean and standard deviation. Think about your results.

Value	Sample 1	Sample 2	Sample 3
1	0	50	14
2	0	0	14
3	0	0	14
4	100	0	16
5	0	0	14
6	0	0	14
7	0	50	14

2. Both of the following frequency distributions approximate the normal (bell-shaped) curve. For each one, calculate the mode, median, and mean.

Value	Sample 1	Sample 2
1	5	0
2	10	5
3	20	20
4	30	50
5	20	20
6	10	5
7	5	0

3. Consider again the frequency distributions in Exercise 2. Both have the same mean, and both approximate a normal curve.

a. Draw a bar graph summarizing each of these distributions. Which would you expect to have the smaller standard deviation! Why?

b. Calculate the standard deviation for each of these distributions. Did you find what you expected?

Key Terms

statistics

central tendency

dispersion

frequency distribution

histogram

mode

variation ratio

median

quantile ranges

quantile

mean

standard deviation (s)

normal distribution

standard score (z)

univariate statistics

bivariate statistics

CHAPTER 17

Statistics II: Examining Relationships Between Two Variables

- How is association defined?
- What does Chi² represent?
- How does one know which measure of association is most appropriate when comparing variables with different levels of measurement?

In political science research, we are generally less concerned with describing distributions on single variables than we are with determining whether, how, and to what extent two or more variables may be related to one another. It is these bivariate (two-variable) and multivariate (more-than-two-variable) relationships that usually cast light on the more interesting research questions.

When examining the relationship between two variables, we typically ask three important questions. The first is whether and to what extent changes or differences in the values of one variable—generally the independent variable—are associated with changes or differences in the values of the second, or dependent, variable. The second question examines the direction and form of any association that might exist. The third considers the likelihood that any association observed among cases sampled from a larger population is in fact a characteristic of that population and not merely an artifact of the smaller and potentially unrepresentative sample. In this chapter we introduce some of the statistics that are most commonly used to answer these questions, and we explain when it is appropriate to use them and what they tell us about relationships.

Measures of Association and Statistical Significance

An **association** is said to exist between two variables when knowing the value of one for a given case improves the odds of our guessing correctly the corresponding value of the second. If, for example, we examine the relationship between the size of a country's population and the proportion of its adults who are college-educated, we may variously find (1) that larger countries generally have a greater proportion of college-educated adults than smaller ones, (2) that smaller countries generally have a greater proportion of college-educated adults than larger ones, or (3) that there is no systematic difference between the two—that some countries from each group have relatively high proportions of such people but that some from each group have low proportions as well. If our research shows that either case 1 or case 2 holds, we can use our knowledge of values on the independent variable, *size of population*, to guess or predict values on the dependent variable, *proportion of adults who are college-educated,* for any given country. In the first instance, for any heavily populated country, we predict a relatively high proportion of college-educated adults, and for a less populous nation, we predict a lower proportion. In the second, our prediction is precisely reversed. In either event, although we may not guess every case correctly, we will be right fairly often because of the underlying *association* between the two variables. Indeed, the stronger the association between the two variables (the more the individual countries tend to align on each in precisely the same order), the more likely we are to guess correctly in any particular instance. If there is total correspondence in the alignments on the two variables, high scores with high scores or, alternatively, high scores on one with low on the other, we can predict one from the other with perfect accuracy. This contrasts sharply with the third possibility, which permits no improved prediction of values on the education variable based on our knowledge of populations. In such instances, when cases are, in effect, randomly distributed on the two variables, there is said to be no association.

To get a mental picture of what a strong association might look like, consider the two maps presented in Figure 17.1, which relate to the murder rate in Washington, DC, during the "crack wars" of the 1980s. Figure 17.1(a) shows the location of known drug markets in the nation's capital; Figure 17.1(b) shows the location of homicides. Both are based on information provided by the D.C. Metropolitan Police Department. The apparent similarity in the locations of clusters of drug dealing and murders suggests an *association* between the two phenomena.

Measuring Association   Clearly there can be more or less association between any two variables. The question in each instance then becomes, *Just how much association is there?* The answer is provided by a set of statistics known as coefficients of association. A **coefficient of association** is a number that summarizes the amount of improvement in guessing values on one variable for any case based on knowledge of the values of a second. In the example, for instance, such a measure would tell us *how much* our knowledge of a country's population size helps us in guessing its proportion of college-educated adults. The higher the coefficient, the stronger the association and, by extension, the better our predictive or explanatory ability. In general, coefficients of association range from 0 to 1 or −1 to 1, with the values closest to unity indicating a relatively strong association and those closest to 0 a relatively weak one.

In addition to the magnitude of association, it is also useful to know the direction or form of the relationship between two variables. Take another look at the earlier example about level of education of a nation's adults, and most particularly at options 1 and 2. We have already suggested that the closer we get to either case, the higher will be our coefficient of association and the better our chances of guessing a particular country's proportion of college-educated adults based on our knowledge of its population size. It should be obvious, however, that our predictions in the cases are precisely opposite. In the first instance, higher values of one variable tend to be associated with higher values of the other, and in the latter instance, higher values of one tend to be associated with *lower* values of the other. Such relationships are said to display differences in *direction.* Those like the first, in which

(a)
Drug Markets

Military Rd.

16th
St.

N.
Capitol
St.

R.I.
Ave.

N.Y.
Ave.

E. Cap St.

PA.
Ave.

Figure 17.1
Drug markets and homicide locations, Washington, DC, 1988
SOURCE: Reprinted from the *Washington Post*, January 13, 1989, p. E1, with permission of the publisher.

(b)
Homicide Locations

Military Rd.

16th
St.

Wisconsin
Ave.

N. Capitol
St.

R.I.
Ave.

N.Y.
Ave.

PA.
Ave.

Figure 17.1
(continued)

both variables rise and fall together, are termed *direct,* or *positive,* associations. Those like the second, in which scores move systematically in opposing directions, are termed *inverse,* or *negative,* associations. This additional bit of information, which is represented by a plus or a minus sign accompanying the coefficient of association, makes our guessing even more effective. Thus, a coefficient of −.87 (negative and relatively close to 1) might describe a relatively strong relationship in which the values on the two variables in question are inversely related (moving in opposite directions), whereas a coefficient of .20 (positive—the plus sign is usually omitted—and rather close to zero) might describe a weak direct association.

Defining Statistical Significance   Finally, we should say a word about tests of *statistical significance,* though our discussion of the topic will be purposely limited.[1] You will recall from our discussion of levels of confidence and sampling error in Chapter 7 that when we draw a presumably representative sample and use that sample to develop conclusions about the larger population from which it is drawn, we run some risk of coming to incorrect conclusions. This is true because there is a chance that the sample is not in fact representative and that the actual error in our measurement exceeds that specified for a given sample size (Tables A.2 and A.3 in Appendix A). The *chance* of such improper generalizing is known, but we cannot tell whether or not it has occurred in any particular instance. For a level of confidence of .95, that chance is .05, or 1 − .95. For a level of confidence of .99, it is .01. These values represent the likelihood that any generalization from our sample to the larger population, even allowing for the estimated range of sampling error, is simply wrong.

Tests of **statistical significance** perform the same function in evaluating measures of association. They tell us just how likely it is that the association we have measured between two variables in a sample might or might not exist in the whole population. Let us see if we can clarify this point.

An Example   Suppose, to continue our example, we have a population of 200 nations for which we *know for a fact* that the coefficient of association between population size and the proportion of adults with a college education is 0. There is, in reality, no relationship between the two variables. But suppose further that we take a sample of only 30 of these countries and calculate the association between these two variables. It might come out as 0, but this is actually unlikely, because the strength of association is now based not on all the countries but on only 30 and will probably reflect their particular idiosyncrasies. In other words, the coefficient itself is determined by *which* 30 countries we pick. If, by chance, we pick 30 countries that are truly representative of all 200, we will in fact find no association. But chance might also lead us to pick 30 countries for which the association between population size and education level is unusually high, say, .60. In that case, our coefficient of association measures a characteristic of the particular sample in question, but if we generalize to the larger population, our conclusions will be incorrect. Knowing this, of course, we reject our measure of association based on this particular sample.

---

[1] A full explanation of statistical significance is beyond the scope of this text; to pursue a deeper understanding of significance testing, you are encouraged to consult one of the statistics texts listed at the end of Chapter 18.

Figure 17.2
Normal distribution of coefficients of association for samples of 30 cases

The problem is that in the real world we seldom know the underlying population parameter, which is the true degree of association in the whole population (as defined in Chapter 7). Indeed, the reason we draw samples in the first place is exactly because we often simply *cannot* study whole populations. It follows, then, that more often than not the *only* tests of association we will have will be those based on our sampling. Moreover, these calculations will usually be based on only *one* sample. Thus, the question becomes one of how confident we can be that a test of association based on a single subgroup of a population accurately reflects an underlying population characteristic. The job of the test of statistical significance is to pin a number on that confidence—that is, to measure the probability or likelihood that we are making an appropriate, or, conversely, an inappropriate, generalization.

To see how this works, let us continue our example. Suppose that we draw not one sample of 30 nations from our population of 200, but 1,000 separate and independent samples of the same size and that for each we calculate the coefficient of association. Because the true coefficient for the entire population is in fact 0, most of the coefficients for our 1,000 samples will also be at or relatively near 0. Some particular combinations of 30 countries may yield relatively higher values (that is, we might by chance happen to pick only countries scoring either high-high or low-low on the two variables), but the majority will be nearer to the population parameter. Indeed, the closer one gets to the true value, the more samples one finds represented. These distributions, in fact, often resemble the normal curve we mentioned earlier. This is illustrated in Figure 17.2, where the height of the curve at any given point represents the number of samples for which the coefficient of association noted along the baseline has been calculated. As you can see, most of the sample coefficients cluster around the true population parameter.

What, then, is the likelihood that any particular coefficient is simply a chance variation around a true parameter of 0? Or in other words, if we take a sample from some population and find in that sample a strong association, what are the chances that we will be wrong in generalizing so strong a relationship from the sample to the population? The normal curve has certain properties which enable us to answer this question with considerable precision.

Suppose, for example, we draw from our 200 nations a sample of 30 for which the coefficient of association is −.75. How likely is it that the corresponding coefficient for the population as a whole is 0? From Figure 17.2, the answer must be a resounding *Not very!* The area under the curve represents all 1,000 (actually any number of) sample coefficients when the true parameter is 0. The much smaller shaded area at and to the left of −.75 represents the proportion of such coefficients that are negative in direction and .75 or stronger in magnitude. Such cases constitute a very small proportion of the many sample coefficients. For this reason, the odds of drawing such a sample in any given try are quite slim. If 5 percent of all samples lies in this area, for instance, then only one time in 20 will we be likely to encounter a sample from a population with a true coefficient of 0 for which we find a coefficient in our sample of −.75. Yet that is precisely what we have found in this instance.

In other words, we have just drawn a sample with a characteristic that has a 5 percent likelihood of being an erroneous representation of a population in which the two variables in question are not associated with each other. Thus, if we claim on the basis of our sample that the two variables are in fact associated in the larger population (that is, if we generalize our results from the sample), we can expect to be wrong 5 percent of the time. That means, of course, that we will be right 95 percent of the time, and those are not bad odds. Indeed, levels of statistical significance of .05 (a 5 percent chance of erroneous generalization), .01 (a 1 percent chance of such error), and .001 (a 1/10 of 1 percent chance of such error) are commonly accepted standards in social science research.

If we look again at Figure 17.2, it should be apparent that more extreme values such as −.75 are less likely to give rise to this kind of error in generalization than are those closer to the center (for example, a greater proportion of samples from such a population will, by chance, show coefficients of −.50 or stronger, and so forth). It seems, then, that we can never be very confident of the trustworthiness of weaker associations, since we can never eliminate the heavy odds that they are simply chance occurrences in a population with a true coefficient of 0.

We can increase our confidence in our sample simply by increasing our sample size. If instead of 30 cases per sample we draw 100 or 150, each will be more likely to cluster around 0. In effect, the normal curve will be progressively squeezed toward the middle, as illustrated in Figure 17.3, until ultimately there is only one possible outcome—the true parameter. In the process, with a set of sufficiently large samples, even a coefficient of association of .10 or .01 can be shown to have acceptable levels of statistical significance. We can conclude, then, that some combination of sufficiently extreme scores and sufficiently large samples allows us to reduce to tolerable levels the likelihood of incorrectly generalizing from our data.

(a) (b) (c)

Figure 17.3
Sampling distribution for differing numbers of cases in a population of 200

In the balance of this chapter we present a brief discussion of the most common measures of association and significance for each of the three levels of measurement. Although the procedures employed in calculating each of these measures differ, the purpose in each case, as well as the interpretation of the result, will remain relatively consistent, for each coefficient of association is designed to tell us to what extent our guessing of values on one variable is improved by knowledge of the corresponding values on another. Each test of significance tells us *the probability that any observed relationships in a sample result from bias in the sample rather than from an underlying relationship in the base population.*

The examples we use to illustrate these statistics involve comparisons of variables that are operationalized at the same level of measurement. However, researchers often want to look for relationships between variables that are at *different* levels of measurement (as in the case of an ordinal-level independent variable such as socioeconomic status and a nominal-level dependent variable such as party identification). To select the correct statistic in these situations, you need to be aware of a simple rule: you can use a statistic designed for a lower level of measurement with data at a higher level of measurement, but you may *not* do the reverse (because doing so would produce statistically meaningless results). It would, for example, be legitimate to use a statistic designed for the nominal level with ordinal-level data, but illegitimate to use an ordinal-level statistic with nominal-level data. This means that when comparing variables that are measured at different levels of measurement, *you must choose a statistic suitable to the lower of the two levels.*

Measures of Association and Significance for Nominal Variables: Lambda

A widely used coefficient of association for two nominal variables where one is treated as independent and the other dependent is λ (lambda).[2] **Lambda** measures the *percentage of improvement* in guessing values on the dependent variable on the basis of knowledge of values on the independent variable when both variables consist of categories with neither rank, distance, nor direction.

An Example Suppose we measure the party identification of 100 respondents and uncover the following frequency distribution:

Democrats   50

Republicans   30

Independents   20

Suppose further that we want to guess the party identification of each individual respondent, that we must make the same guess for all individuals, and that we want to make as few mistakes as possible. The obvious strategy is simply to guess the mode (the most populous category), or Democratic, every time. We will be correct 50 times (for the 50 Democrats) and incorrect 50 times (for the 30 Republicans and

---

[2] Actually, the statistic we shall describe here is λ_a, or lambda asymmetrical, a measure that tests association in only one direction (from the independent to the dependent variable). A test of mutual association, the true λ, is also available.

Table 17.1
Paternal basis for party identification

Father's Party Identification	Respondent's Party Identification			
	Dem.	Rep.	Ind.	Totals
Democratic	45	5	10	60
Republican	2	23	5	30
Independent	3	2	5	10
Total	50	30	20	100

20 Independents), not an especially noteworthy record but still the best we can do. For if we guess Republican each time, we will be wrong 70 times, and a guess of Independent will lead to 80 incorrect predictions. The mode, then, provides the best guess based on the available information.

But suppose we have a second piece of information—the party identification of each respondent's father—with the following frequency distribution:

Democrats	60
Republicans	30
Independents	10

If these two variables are related to each other—that is, if one is likely to have the same party identification as one's father—then knowing the party preference of each respondent's father should help us to improve our guessing of that respondent's own preference. This will be the case if, by guessing for each respondent not the mode of the overall distribution, as we did before, but simply that person's father's party preference, we can reduce our incorrect predictions to fewer than the 50 cases we originally guessed wrongly.

To examine a possible association between these variables, we construct a crosstab summarizing the distribution of cases on these two variables. In Table 17.1, the independent, or predictor, variable (father's party identification) is the row variable, and its overall distribution is summarized to the right of the table. The dependent variable (respondent's party identification) is the column variable, and its overall distribution is summarized below the table. The numbers in the cells have been assigned arbitrarily, though in the real world they would, of course, be determined by the research itself.

With this table we can use parental preference to predict respondent's preference. To do this, we use the mode just as before, but we apply it *within each category on the independent variable* rather than to the whole set of cases. Thus, for those respondents whose father is identified as a Democrat, we guess a preference for the same party. We are correct 45 times and incorrect 15 (for the 5 Republicans and 10 Independents). For those whose father is identified as a Republican, we guess Republican. We are correct 23 times and incorrect 7. And for those whose father is identified as an Independent, we guess a similar preference and are correct 5 out of 10 times. Combining these results, we find that we are now able to guess correctly

73 times and are still wrong 27 times. Thus, knowledge of the second variable has clearly improved our guessing. To ascertain the precise percentage of that improvement, we use *the general formula for a coefficient of association:*

$$\text{Association} = \frac{\text{Reduction in error in guessing}}{\text{Amount of original error}}$$

$$= \frac{\begin{array}{c}\text{Amount of} \quad\quad \text{Amount of} \\ \text{original error} - \text{remaining error}\end{array}}{\text{Amount of original error}}$$

In the present instance, this is

$$\text{Association} = \frac{50 - (15 + 7 + 5)}{50}$$

$$= \frac{23}{50} = .46$$

By using father's party identification as a predictor of respondent's party identification, we are able to improve (reduce the error in) our guessing by some 46 percent.

The formula for calculating λ, which will bring us to the same result though by a slightly different route, is

$$\lambda = \frac{\sum f_i - F_d}{N - F_d}$$

where f_i = the maximum frequency *within each subclass or category* of the *independent* variable

F_d = the maximum frequency in the *totals* of the *dependent* variable

N = the number of cases.

Lambda ranges from 0 to 1, with higher values (those closer to 1) indicating a stronger association. Because nominal variables have no direction, λ will always be positive.

Our next step is to decide whether the relationship summarized by λ arises from a true population parameter or from mere chance. That is, we must decide whether the relationship is statistically significant.

Chi-Square The test of statistical significance for nominal variables is χ^2 (**chi-square**). This coefficient tells us whether a nominal-level association between two variables, such as the one we have just observed, is likely to result from chance. It does so by comparing the results we actually observe with those that would be expected if no real relationship existed. Calculating χ^2, too, begins from a crosstab. Consider Table 17.2, which resembles Table 17.1 in that the marginals for each variable are the same as those of Table 17.1, but Table 17.2 does not include any distribution of cases within the cells.

To begin the determination of χ^2, we ask ourselves what value we *expect* in each cell, given these overall totals, if there is *no association* between the two

Table 17.2

Paternal basis for party identification: marginal values

Father's Party Identification	Respondent's Party Identification			
	Dem.	*Rep.*	*Ind.*	*Totals*
Democratic				60
Republican				30
Independent				10
Total	50	30	20	100

variables. Of the 60 cases whose father was a Democrat, for instance, we might expect half (50/100) to be Democrats, almost a third (30/100) to be Republicans, and one in five (20/100) to be Independents, or, in other words, 30 Democrats, 18 Republicans, and 12 Independents. Similarly, we might arrive at expected values for those with a Republican or Independent father. These expected values are summarized in Table 17.3.

The question then becomes, are the values we have actually observed in Table 17.1 so different (so extreme) from those that Table 17.3 would lead us to expect if there were, in reality, no relationship between the two variables that we can be reasonably confident of the validity of our result? Chi-square is a device for comparing the two tables to find an answer to this question. The equation for χ^2 is

$$\chi^2 = \sum \frac{(f_o - f_e)^2}{f_e}$$

where f_o = the frequency *observed* in each cell (Table 17.1)

f_e = the frequency *expected* in each cell (Table 17.3)

We calculate χ^2 by filling in the values in Table 17.4 for each cell in a given table. The ordering of the cells in the table is of no importance, but f_o from Table 17.1 and f_e from Table 17.3 for any particular line must refer to the same cell. The rationale for first squaring the differences between f_o and f_e and then dividing by f_e is essen-

Table 17.3

Paternal basis for party identification: expected values

Father's Party Identification	Respondent's Party Identification			
	Dem.	*Rep.*	*Ind.*	*Totals*
Democratic	30	18	12	60
Republican	15	9	6	30
Independent	5	3	2	10
Total	50	30	20	100

Table 17.4
Values used in deriving χ^2

f_o	f_e	$f_o - f_e$	$(f_o - f_e)^2$	$\dfrac{(f_o - f_e)^2}{f_e}$
45	30	15	225	7.50
5	18	−13	169	9.39
10	12	−2	4	.33
2	15	−13	169	11.27
23	9	14	196	21.78
5	6	−1	1	.17
3	5	−2	4	.80
2	3	−1	1	.33
5	2	3	9	4.50

tially the same as that for the treatment of variations around the mean in determining the standard deviation. Chi-square is determined by adding together all the numbers in the last column. In the example, this yields a value of 56.07.

Degrees of Freedom   Before we can interpret this number, we must make one further calculation, that of the so-called degrees of freedom. The **degrees of freedom** (df) in a table simply consist of the number of cells of that table that can be filled with numbers before the entries in all remaining cells are fixed and unchangeable. The formula for determining the degrees of freedom in any particular table is

$$df = (r - 1)(c - 1)$$

where r = the number of categories of the row variable

c = the number of categories of the column variable.

In the example, $df = (3 - 1)(3 - 1) = 4$.

We are now ready to evaluate the statistical significance of our data. Table A.4 in Appendix A summarizes the significant values of χ^2 for different degrees of freedom at the .001, .01, and .05 levels. If the value of χ^2 we have calculated (56.07) exceeds that listed in the table at any of these levels for a table with the specified degrees of freedom (4), the relationship we have observed is said to be statistically significant at that level. In the present instance, for example, in order to be significant at the .001 level (that is, if when we accept the observed association as representative of the larger population we run a risk of being wrong one time in 1,000), our observed χ^2 must exceed 18.467. Since it does so, we are quite confident in our result.

Measures of Association and Significance for Ordinal Variables: Gamma

A widely used coefficient of association for ordinal variables is G, or **gamma**, which works according to the same principle of error reduction as λ, but focuses on predicting the ranking or relative position of cases rather than simply their membership in a particular class or category. The question treated by G is that of the degree to which the ranking of a case on one ordinal variable may be predicted if we know its ranking on a second ordinal variable.

When we examine two such variables, there are two possible conditions of perfect predictability. The first, in which individual cases are ranked in exactly the same order on both variables (high scores with high scores, low scores with low), is termed *perfect agreement*. The second, in which cases are ranked in precisely the opposite order (highest scores on one variable with lowest on the other and the reverse), is termed *perfect inversion*. Therefore, predictability is a function of how close the rankings on these variables come to either perfect agreement (in which case G is positive and approaches 1) or perfect inversion (where G is negative and approaches -1). A value of G equal to 0 indicates the absence of association. The formula for calculating G is

$$G = \frac{f_a - f_i}{f_a + f_i}$$

where f_a = the frequency of agreements in the rankings of the two variables
f_i = the frequency of inversions in the rankings of the two variables.

G is based on the relative positions of a set of cases on two variables. The cases are first arranged in ascending order on the independent variable. Their rankings on the dependent variable are then compared. Those for which the original ordering is preserved are said to be in agreement, and those for which the original order is altered are said to be in inversion. Limitations of space do not permit us to consider this procedure in detail or to discuss the calculations of G when the number of cases is relatively small and/or no ties are present in the rankings. Rather, we shall focus on the procedures for calculating G under the more common circumstances, when ties (more than one case with the same rank) are present and the number of cases is large.[3] Here, as before, we work from a crosstab, such as that depicted in Table 17.5.

To measure the association between these two variables, we determine the number of agreements and inversions relative to each cell in the table. An agreement occurs in any cell *below* (higher in its score on the independent variable) and to the *right* (higher in its score on the dependent variable) of the particular cell in question. Thus, agreements with those cases in cell *a* include all cases in cells *e*, *f*, *h*, and *i*, since these cases rank higher than those in cell *a* on *both* variables. An inversion occurs in any cell *below* (higher in its score on the independent variable) and to the *left* (lower in its score on the dependent variable) of the particular cell in question. Thus, inversions with those cases in cell *c* include all cases in cells *d*, *e*, *g*, and *h*, since these cases rank higher on one variable than those in cell *c*, but lower on the other. The frequency of agreements (f_a in the equation), then, is the sum for each cell of the number of cases in that cell multiplied by the number of cases in all cells

---

[3] In such applications, G may be unreliable, but it is included here to facilitate the discussion of association as a concept. A related statistic, Kendall's *tau*, may be more reliable, but its determination may be less intuitive to the beginning political scientist.

Table 17.5
Centralized crosstabulation

Independent Variable	Dependent Variable		
	Low	*Medium*	*High*
Low	a	b	c
Medium	d	e	f
High	g	h	i

below and to the right ($a[e + f + h + i] + b[f + i] + d[h + i] + e[i]$). The frequency of inversions (f_i in the equation) is the sum for each cell of the number of cases in that cell multiplied by the number of cases in all cells below and to the left ($b[d + g] + c[d + e + g + h] + e[g] + f[g + h]$). The resulting totals are simply substituted in the equation.

If, for example, the variables in Table 17.1 were ordinal, we could calculate G as follows:

$$f_a = 45(23 + 5 + 2 + 5) + 5(5 + 5) + 2(2 + 5) + 23(5)$$
$$= 1{,}575 + 50 + 14 + 115 = 1{,}754$$

$$f_i = 5(2 + 3) + 10(2 + 23 + 3 + 2) + 23(3) + 5(3 + 2)$$
$$= 25 + 300 + 69 + 25 = 419$$

$$G = \frac{f_a - f_i}{f_a + f_i} = \frac{1754 - 419}{1754 + 419} = \frac{1335}{2173} = .61$$

This tells us that there is 61 percent more agreement than disagreement in the rankings of the cases on the two variables. If f_i exceeded f_a, the sign of G would be negative, in order to indicate the existence of an inverse relationship.

The test of the statistical significance of G is based on the fact that the sampling distribution of G is approximately normal for a population with no true association, as was the sampling distribution of the hypothetical coefficient of association we discussed earlier. Since this is so, we can determine the probability that any particular value of G has occurred by chance by calculating its standard score (z), locating its position under the normal curve, and assessing the probabilities. The actual calculation of z_G (**standard score of gamma**) will not be presented here, because the formula is complex and its understanding requires a more detailed knowledge of statistics than we have provided. Suffice it to say that when z_G exceeds ± 1.645 (when G lies at least 1.645 standard deviation units above or below the mean), G is sufficiently extreme to merit a significance level of .05, and that when z_G exceeds ± 2.326 (when G lies at least 2.326 standard deviation units above or below the mean), G achieves significance at the .01 level. The interpretation of these results is precisely the same as that in the earlier and more general example.

Measures of Association and Significance for Interval/Ratio Variables: Correlation

The measure of association between two interval variables is the Pearson product-moment correlation (r), also known as the **correlation coefficient.** This coefficient summarizes the strength and direction of a relationship using the same notion we have already presented—about proportionate reduction in error in guessing values on one variable on the basis of known values of another—though the procedure, like the data for which it is designed, is more sophisticated than others we have discussed to this point. Here, rather than using the mean of the dependent variable (usually designated Y) to predict the values of individual cases, we use its geometric relationship with the independent variable (usually designated X) for this purpose. More particularly, we focus on the degree to which the equation of a particular straight line can help us to predict values of Y based on knowledge of corresponding values of X.

Graphing the Variables   The determination of r begins with the examination of a **scatter plot,** which is a graphic summary of the distribution of cases on two variables, in which the base line, or X axis, is denoted in units of the independent variable; the vertical line, or Y axis, is denoted in units of the dependent variable; and each dot represents observations of one case on both variables. Such a plot is presented in Figure 17.4, in which the independent variable is age, the dependent variable is years of schooling completed, and the number of cases is 25. The circled dot thus represents one case—a person 30 years old with 10 years of schooling. The values in the figure have been arbitrarily assigned but would in reality be ascertained by the research itself.

The next step is to draw a straight line, called a **regression line,** through this field of dots so that no other line comes closer to touching all of the dots. This *line of best fit* for the relationship between two variables is analogous to the mean in univariate descriptive statistics. Just as the mean represents a most typical case in a frequency distribution, the regression line represents a most typical association between two variables. Just as we might use the mean to guess values of a variable in the absence of additional information, we can use the regression line to guess values of one variable on the basis of our knowledge of the values of another. If, for example, we know the value of X for a given case, we can project a vertical line from that point on the X axis to the regression line, then a horizontal line from there to the Y axis. The point of contact on the Y axis gives us a predicted value of Y.

But just as a mean may be the single most typical value yet not be a good summary of a particular distribution, a regression line may be the best possible summary of a relationship between two variables yet not be a very useful summary. Accordingly, just as we use the standard deviation (s) as a measure of dispersion or goodness of fit around the mean, we use the correlation coefficient (r), or, more correctly, for purposes of interpretation, the square of that coefficient (r^2), as a measure of the *goodness of fit* of the various data points around the regression line. It is, in effect, a measure of how typical that line is of the *joint* distribution of values of the two variables.

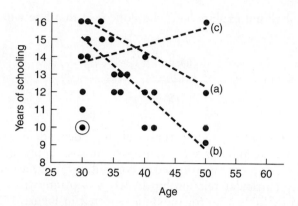

Figure 17.4
Scatter diagram showing relationship between age and years of schooling

Closeness of Association   Where all points actually fall directly on the line, as in Figure 17.5(a) and (e), the line provides a perfect description of the relationship between the two variables. Where the points are generally organized in the direction indicated by the line but do not all fall upon it, as in Figure 17.5(b) and (d), the line provides an approximation of the relationship between the two variables. And where, as in Figure 17.5(c), no one line is closer to the data points than any other, no association exists between the two variables. The problem, then, is twofold: First, what does this line of best fit look like? Second, how good a fit to the data does it in fact provide?

You may recall from your study of algebra that any straight line takes the form

$$Y_i = a + bX_i$$

where a = the value of Y when $X = 0$
b = the slope of the line
X_i = the value of a given case on the independent variable.

The regression line is simply the one set of guessed values of this form that provides for the most accurate prediction of values of Y based on knowledge of values of X.

(a) $r = 1.0$ (b) $0 \leqslant r \leqslant 1.0$ (c) $r = 0$ (d) $0 \geqslant r \geqslant -1.0$ (e) $r = -1.0$

Figure 17.5
Summary of regression lines and values of r

For reasons we shall not explore here, the slope b of that line will always take the form

$$b = \frac{\sum_{i=1}^{N}(X_i - \overline{X})(Y_i - \overline{Y})}{\sum_{i=1}^{N}(X_i - \overline{X})^2}$$

where X_i and Y_i are the corresponding values of the independent and dependent variables for case i, and $\overline{X}$ and $\overline{Y}$ are the respective means. Applying this formula and using a chart similar to the one we used in computing χ^2, we are able to ascertain the slope of any particular relationship between two interval variables. This process is illustrated in Table 17.6 for the data reported in Figure 17.4. For these data, $\overline{X} = 37.08$ and $\overline{Y} = 12.88$. Substituting these values in the equation, we find

$$b = \frac{-136.79}{1,151.93} = -.12$$

In a **linear relationship**—one described or summarized by a straight line—a particular change in the value of the independent variable X is always accompanied by a particular change in the value of the dependent variable Y. Moreover, in such a relationship the rate of change is constant; that is, no matter what the particular values of X and Y, each change of one unit in X will be accompanied by a change in Y of some fixed size determined by the slope of the regression line. Relationships in which slight changes in X are accompanied by relatively large changes in Y are summarized by lines that have a relatively steep slope ($b > 1$). Relationships in which large changes in X are accompanied by smaller changes in Y are summarized by lines that have a relatively flat slope ($b < 1$). Relationships in which one unit of change in X is accompanied by one unit of change in Y are summarized by lines for which b is equal to 1. Lines that slope upward from left to right, such as those in Figure 17.5(a) and (b), have a positive slope and represent relationships in which increases in X are accompanied by increases in Y. Those sloping downward from left to right, such as the lines in Figure 17.5(d) and (e), have a negative slope and represent relationships in which increases in X are accompanied by *decreases* in Y. Indeed, the slope of the line is simply the rate of change in Y for each unit of change in X. In our example, then, where b is equal to $-.12$, we know that the regression line will slope downward from left to right and will, if the two variables are drawn to the same scale, be relatively flat.

To arrive at the formula we used to compute the slope of the regression line, we had to assume that the line passes through the intersection of $\overline{X}$ and $\overline{Y}$—the means of the respective variables. This is a reasonable assumption, because the means represent the central tendencies of these variables and because we are, in effect, seeking a joint or combined central tendency. Because we know both means and have now determined the value of b, we can easily find the value of a (the point at which the regression line intercepts the Y axis) and solve the equation. The general equation of the regression line is

$$Y' = a + bX_i$$

Table 17.6
Values used in deriving the equation of the regression line

X_i	$(X_i - \overline{X})$	$(X_i - \overline{X})^2$	Y_i	$(Y_i - \overline{Y})$	$(X_i - \overline{X})(Y_i - \overline{Y})$
30	−7.08	50.13	10	−2.88	20.39
30	−7.08	50.13	11	−1.88	13.31
30	−7.08	50.13	12	−.88	6.23
30	−7.08	50.13	14	1.22	−7.93
30	−7.08	50.13	16	3.12	−22.09
31	−6.08	36.97	14	1.12	−6.81
31	−6.08	36.97	15	2.12	−12.89
31	−6.08	36.97	16	3.12	−18.99
33	−4.08	16.15	15	2.12	−8.65
33	−4.08	16.15	16	3.12	−12.73
35	−2.08	4.33	12	−.88	1.83
35	−2.08	4.33	13	.12	−.25
35	−2.08	4.33	15	2.12	−4.41
36	−1.08	1.17	12	−.88	.95
36	−1.08	1.17	13	.12	−.13
37	−.08	.01	13	.12	−.01
40	−2.92	8.53	10	−2.88	−8.41
40	−2.92	8.53	12	−.88	−2.57
40	−2.92	8.53	14	1.12	3.27
42	−4.92	24.21	10	−2.88	−14.17
42	−4.92	24.21	12	−.88	−4.33
50	−12.92	166.93	9	−3.88	−50.13
50	−12.92	166.93	10	−2.88	−37.12
50	−12.92	166.93	12	−.88	−11.37
50	−12.92	166.93	16	3.12	40.31
Totals	0	1,151.93		0	−136.79

and at the point where the line passes through the intersection of the two means

$$\overline{Y} = a + b\overline{X}$$

It must then follow that

$$a = \overline{Y} + b\overline{X}$$

Because all of these values are now known, we can determine that

$$a = 12.88 - (-.12)(37.08)$$
$$= 12.88 + 4.45 = 17.33$$

Thus, the equation of the regression line—the single best-fitting line—for the data reported in Figure 17.4 would be

$$Y' = 17.33 - .12X$$

Using this equation, we can predict the value of Y for any given value of X.

Once this equation has been determined, we may use the correlation coefficient (r) to assess the utility of the regression line. The formula for r_{XY} (the coefficient of correlation between X and Y) is

$$r_{XY} = \frac{N\sum XY - \sum X \sum Y}{\sqrt{[N\sum X^2 - (\sum X)^2][N\sum Y^2 - (\sum Y)^2]}}$$

where

X = each value of the independent variable (the subscript i has been omitted here to simplify the presentation)

Y = each value of the dependent variable

N = the number of cases

Although the assertion is certainly not obvious and although its algebraic proof lies beyond our present discussion, this working formula is derived from a comparison of the original error in guessing values of Y by using $\overline{Y}$ (the mean of the frequency distribution) with the error remaining when one guesses values of Y using Y' (the equation of the regression line). Thus, the procedure for computing r is analogous to that for computing both λ and G. It may best be accomplished by setting up a chart of the type with which we are now familiar in which the columns include X, Y, XY, X^2, and Y^2. The sums required by the equation are then provided by the column totals. Thus, for the data represented in Figure 17.4, whose regression line we have already determined, the chart is completed as in Table 17.7.

We substitute these totals in the equation

$$r = \frac{25(11{,}803) - (927)(322)}{\sqrt{[25(35{,}525) - (927)^2][25(4{,}260) - (322)^2]}}$$

$$= \frac{295{,}075 - 298{,}494}{\sqrt{(888{,}125 - 859{,}329)(106{,}500 - 103{,}684)}}$$

$$= \frac{-3{,}419}{\sqrt{(28{,}796)(2{,}816)}}$$

$$= \frac{-3{,}419}{\sqrt{81{,}089{,}536}}$$

$$= \frac{-3{,}419}{9{,}005}$$

$$= -.38$$

This tells us that the slope of the regression line is negative and that the points cluster weakly to moderately around it (because r ranges from $+1$ to -1, with the weakest association at 0).

Explained Variance   While r itself is not easily interpreted, r^2 may be interpreted as *the proportion of reduction in the variance of Y attributable to our knowledge of*

Table 17.7
Values used in deriving the correlation coefficient (r)

	X	Y	XY	X^2	Y^2
	30	10	300	900	100
	30	11	330	900	121
	30	12	360	900	144
	30	14	420	900	196
	30	16	480	900	256
	31	14	434	961	196
	31	15	465	961	225
	31	16	496	961	256
	33	15	495	1,089	225
	33	16	528	1,089	256
	35	12	420	1,225	144
	35	13	455	1,225	169
	35	15	525	1,225	225
	36	12	432	1,296	144
	36	13	468	1,296	169
	37	13	481	1,369	169
	40	10	400	1,600	100
	40	12	480	1,600	144
	40	14	560	1,600	196
	42	10	420	1,764	100
	42	12	504	1,764	144
	50	9	450	2,500	81
	50	10	500	2,500	100
	50	12	600	2,500	144
	50	16	800	2,500	256
Totals	927	322	11,803	32,525	4,260

X. In other words, r^2 is the proportion of variation in Y that is predictable (or explainable) on the basis of X. The quantity r^2 is often referred to as the percentage of *explained variance,* and the quantity $1 - r^2$ is often termed the percentage of *unexplained variance.* Thus, in our example, the r of $-.38$ means that differences on the independent variable *age* account for some 14 percent, or $(-.38)^2$, of the variance in the dependent variable *years of schooling* for the cases under analysis.

Computing Statistical Significance For reasons that lie beyond the scope of the present discussion, we are able to specify the statistical significance of r only when *both* the independent *and* dependent variables are normally distributed. This is accomplished by using Table A.5 in Appendix A, for which purpose two pieces of information are needed. The first is r itself, which, of course, is known. The second, analogous to the χ^2 test, is the number of degrees of freedom of the regression line because two points determine a line (in this case, the intersection of $\overline{X}$ and $\overline{Y}$ was the first and the intercept with the Y axis the second), all other data points may fall freely, so *df* will always equal $(N-2)$, where N is the number of cases. To use the table, then, we locate the appropriate degrees of freedom (in the example, $N-2 = 25 - 2 = 23$) and the desired level of significance (for example, .05), just as we did for χ^2; identify the threshold value of r necessary to achieve that level of significance; and evaluate our actual observation. In the present instance, this requires that we interpolate values in the table between $df = 20$ and $df = 25$. For $df = 23$, these values would be .3379, .3976, .5069, and .6194, respectively. Thus, our r of $-.38$ is statistically significant at the .10 level (it exceeds .3379) but not at the .05 level (it does not exceed .3976). The interpretation of this result is the same as those for other measures of statistical significance.

Conclusion

In this chapter we have introduced some of the more common statistics that are used to summarize the relationship between two variables. As in Chapter 16, we found that differing measures of association and statistical significance were appropriate, depending on the level of measurement that characterized the data being analyzed. Together with the techniques presented earlier, these various coefficients provide the researcher with some very useful basic tools with which to summarize research results. In the next chapter we outline some more sophisticated statistical techniques, which can further enrich our ability to analyze and understand what we have discovered.

Summary Points

- If knowledge of the values of a given variable improves your ability to predict the values of a second variable, the variables are associated.
- In a crosstab, chi^2 numerically assesses the deviation of cell counts from expected values—that is, the values that are expected if there were no association between the variables.
- When comparing two variables that have different levels of measurement, the most appropriate measure of association is the one indicated for the lower level of measurement. For example, if comparing a nominal to an ordinal variable, you may choose lambda.

Suggested Readings and References

A bibliography on statistics and related topics is found at the end of Chapter 18.

Research Exercises

1. Find a recent report of a Gallup poll or some other public opinion poll (try your local newspaper or *The New York Times*) in which a bivariate relationship is presented. What statistics might the pollsters have used to evaluate their findings? If sufficient information is present, construct a crosstab for the two variables in question, and then calculate and interpret the appropriate coefficient of association.

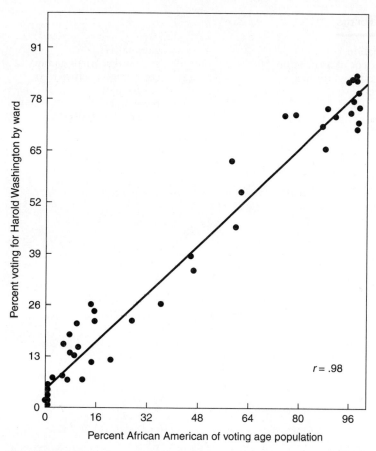

Figure 17.6
African American voting in the 1983 Democratic mayoral primary in Chicago
SOURCE: Reprinted from Kenneth Janda, "A Preliminary Analysis of the 1983 Chicago Mayoral Election," *Vox Pop,* Winter 1983, p. 7, by permission of the author.

2. Figure 17.6 reports the level of voting support—by ward (section of the city) in the 1983 Chicago Democratic primary—for Harold Washington, an African American candidate who was eventually elected mayor.

   a. What does the figure tell us about the relationship between the racial composition of Chicago wards and their voting patterns?

   b. What does the figure tell us about housing patterns in Chicago?

   c. The correlation coefficient (r) for the data reported in Figure 17.6 is .98. What proportion of the variance in voting behavior from ward to ward is explained by the racial composition of the respective wards?

3. Recalculate r and r^2 for the data in Figure 17.4, eliminating the data points at $X = 30$, $Y = 10$; $X = 30$, $Y = 11$; $X = 30$, $Y = 12$; and $X = 50$, $Y = 16$. How do you account for the difference in explained variance between this and our earlier result? Is the new value of r statistically significant?

Key Terms

association
coefficient of association
statistical significance
lambda (λ)
chi-square (χ^2)
degrees of freedom (*df*)

gamma (G)
standard score of gamma (Z_G)
correlation coefficient (r)
scatter plot
regression line
linear relationship

CHAPTER 18

Statistics III: Examining Relationships Among Several Variables

- What is the primary analytic advantage of multiple regression techniques?
- What limits the type of variables upon which regression analysis may be performed?

The univariate and bivariate statistics described in the preceding chapters are often important to our understanding of the subjects we are researching. However, univariate and bivariate analyses rarely can provide convincing tests of hypotheses or the theories from which they were derived. To test a hypothesis convincingly, we must be able to rule out major alternative rival hypotheses. Though a sound research design can sometimes allow us to dismiss alternative rival hypotheses, social scientists commonly find that they must rely on data analysis rather than research design to examine the validity of rival hypotheses. This requires the use of **multivariate analysis**, which is analysis of the simultaneous relationship among three or more variables.

Tabular Analysis

Many of the statistical tools we have already discussed can be employed in multivariate analysis. To illustrate, we can use a highly simplified example to suggest the way in which crosstabs and bivariate statistics can be adapted in order to conduct a multivariate analysis.

An Example   Suppose we want to explore the relationship between political ideology and attending college. If we reason that going to college gives people a stake in maintaining the status quo by preparing them to do relatively well within the existing socioeconomic system, we might begin with the hypothesis that those who have completed college will be more conservative than those who have not. To test this hypothesis, we might interview a sample of 50 people who have completed college and 50 people who have not completed college.

Imagine that we got the results shown in Table 18.1. The diagonal "loading" of cases in this table indicates that those who have attended college are more likely to be classified as conservative than those who have not attended college. By calculating a chi-square for this table, we find that the relationship between college and political ideology is statistically significant at the .01 level. All of these findings are consistent with our original hypothesis.

Table 18.1

Hypothetical relationship between college education and political ideology

Education	Ideology			
	Liberal		*Conservative*	*Totals*
College	40%	(20)	60% (30)	(50)
No college	60%	(30)	40% (20)	(50)
Totals	100%	(50)	100% (50)	(100)

Before we rush to submit this finding to *American Political Science Review*, however, we need to test some alternative rival hypotheses to be sure that our result is valid. One approach to doing this is to extend our bivariate analysis into a multivariate analysis that will allow us to "control for" the effects of other variables on the relationship between college and ideology. For example, one alternative rival hypothesis that merits examination derives from the observation that men are more likely to be conservative than women. If, by chance, more of the people in our sample who went to college were male than female, the results shown in Table 18.1 may reflect gender differences rather than an actual effect of college attendance on political opinions.

Controlling for Other Factors   To explore this possibility, we could examine the relationship between college and ideology separately for men and for women by constructing two crosstabs such as Tables 18.2 and 18.3. If the alternative rival hypothesis is valid, the statistical relationship between college and ideology shown in Table 18.1 will *not* show up in these new tables because the effect of gender on that relationship will be eliminated. This process of holding constant the influence of a third variable on the relationship between two other variables is referred to as **controlling** and is a major step in all forms of multivariate data analysis.

In this case, Tables 18.2 and 18.3 actually show that the relationship between college and ideology is essentially the same for men and women. Although the women in our sample are, as predicted, less likely than the men are to be classified as conservative, the "loadings" in these two tables are highly similar to each other, and calculation of the chi-square for each table shows that the relationships they represent are statistically significant. In such a situation, researchers say that the original relationship has "survived control" and that an alternative rival hypothesis

Table 18.2

Hypothetical relationship between college education and political ideology for males

Education	Ideology			
	Liberal		*Conservative*	*Totals*
College	33%	(5)	57% (20)	(25)
No college	67%	(10)	43% (15)	(25)
Totals	100%	(15)	100% (35)	(50)

Table 18.3

Hypothetical relationship between college education and political ideology for females

Education	Ideology			
	Liberal		*Conservative*	*Totals*
College	43%	(15)	67% (10)	(25)
No college	57%	(20)	33% (5)	(25)
Totals	100%	(35)	100% (15)	(50)

can be "ruled out" as an explanation of the original findings. If a relationship survives enough such controls, it will be accepted as valid.

We have thus conducted a very simple multivariate analysis using techniques designed for bivariate analysis. We could extend this logic to evaluate more alternative rival hypotheses by controlling for two or more additional variables *at the same time*. To illustrate, one of our alternative rival hypotheses might contend that racial differences between whites and nonwhites in terms of both political values and the likelihood of attending college created the apparent relationship between college and ideology shown in Table 18.1. To hold constant the effects of both race and gender on the relationship between college and ideology, we would have to set up four crosstabs tables showing the relationship between college and ideology: one for white males, one for white females, one for nonwhite males, and one for nonwhite females.

Limitations of Tabular Multivariate Analysis   Under many circumstances, generating separate tables can be a quite useful multivariate approach to evaluating hypotheses. However, it has important limitations. First, it becomes very cumbersome to use and its results become difficult to interpret if the variables involved have many possible values. This makes it impractical for analysis of interval/ratio-level data and difficult to use with many nominal and ordinal variables. For instance, to compare an independent and dependent variable each having 5 values while controlling for a third variable with 10 values would require an analysis of 10 tables with 25 cells each. In that situation, unless we have an exceptionally large and diverse sample, many of the cells in the tables will have no cases in them, which can make it impossible to calculate some measures of association and significance. We might try to avoid this by collapsing certain categories of the variables in order to create fewer values and hold down the number of tables and cells needed (as when we reduce the measure "years of education" to a dichotomy of "less than 12 years" and "12 years or more"). However, it would mean giving up potentially important information contained in our original measures and may produce misleading results. Moreover, the same problem will appear, even after collapsing categories, if we tried to apply several control variables at once in order to examine the *combined effects* of different variables. Second, even if we can complete such an analysis, its results may be difficult to report because the patterns are likely to be complex and there are no overall statistics with which to summarize the results.

Fortunately, there are a variety of statistical procedures that are designed specifically for multivariate analyses, that can be used in a wide range of situations, and that provide easily interpretable results. The procedures are important because of their value in hypothesis testing (allowing us to examine the relationship between two variables while holding the effects of other variables on each constant), but their greatest value may come from the ways in which they help us understand the complex and subtle networks of relationships within which social phenomena are usually embedded. In this chapter we introduce you to two of the most commonly used multivariate techniques so that you can know when and how to apply them in your research and can judge the skill with which others have applied them when you are reading research reports. We selected these techniques from among the many that are available because (1) they are very widely applicable, (2) they illustrate many basic principles of multivariate analysis, and (3) they are based on the same basic mathematical techniques and can therefore be explained more quickly than techniques that rest on different mathematical foundations.

Multiple Regression

The bivariate correlation and regression procedures described in Chapter 17 can be extended to cases in which you want to explore the relationship between one dependent variable (DV) and several independent variables (IVs). The purpose of **multiple regression** is to provide (1) an estimate of the *independent* effect of a change in the value of each IV on the value of the DV and (2) an empirical basis for predicting values of the DV from knowledge of the joint values of the IVs.

Analysis begins with your statement of an equation that you feel accurately describes the causal influences you are investigating. Because this equation can be viewed as a **model** of the process in which you are interested, this step is referred to as **model specification**. It involves translating your verbal theory of the phenomenon into a mathematical equation. The general form for a **multiple regression equation** is

$$Y' = a_0 + b_1X_1 + b_2X_2 + b_3X_3 \ldots + b_nX_n + e$$

which you should recognize as an extension of the bivariate regression equation explained in Chapter 17. Understanding this equation is simplified by the introduction of a concrete example.

An Example   Let us say that we are interested in assessing the validity of the argument that election to the U.S. Senate can be "bought" by heavy spending on a media campaign. We might do this by attempting to explain the percentage of the vote that candidates get as a function of (1) the amount they spend on media advertising and (2) the percentage of the electorate in their state that has the same party identification as the candidate. We might begin with the following simple model of the electoral process:

$$Y' = a_0 + b_1X_1 + b_2X_2 + e$$

where Y' = the predicted percent of the vote received by the candidate

a_0 = the average value of Y when each IV equals 0

b_1 = the average change in Y associated with a unit change in X_1 (the amount spent on advertising), *when the effects of other variables are held constant*

X_1 = the amount the candidate spends on advertising (in units of $1,000)

b_2 = the average change in Y' associated with a unit change in X_2 (the percentage of the electorate that shared the candidate's party identification), *when the effects of other variables are held constant*

X_2 = the percentage of the electorate that shares the candidate's party identification

e = an "error term" representing any variance in Y that is not accounted for by variance in the IVs in the model.

We might test the accuracy of this model by collecting appropriate data on 100 races for U.S. Senate seats. Successful application of multiple regression techniques to this or any other task, however, requires that our model and the data with which we hope to test it conform to five assumptions that underlie the regression procedure:

1. The model is *accurately specified* (it accurately describes the actual relationships in question). This includes the assumptions that (a) the relationship among variables is linear, (b) no important IVs have been excluded, and (c) no irrelevant IVs have been included.

2. There is *no error in measurement* of the variables.

3. Variables are measured at the *interval/ratio level*.

4. The following are true of the error term, *e:*

   a. Its mean (the expected value for any given observation) is 0.

   b. The error terms for each observation are *un*correlated.

   c. The IVs are *un*correlated with the error term.

   d. The variance for the error term is constant for all values of the IVs.

   e. The error term has a *normal distribution*.

5. None of the IVs is perfectly correlated with any of the other IVs or with any linear combination of other IVs. If this is true, there is *no perfect multicollinearity*.[1]

If our study comes *close enough* to meeting these assumptions,[2] we can substitute actual values from our research for Y', X_1, and X_2 and solve the regression equation representing our theory for the unknown terms a, b_1, and b_2 using the logic of least squares estimation. One hypothetical result of such a solution could be

$$Y' = 10 + .1X_1 + 1X_2$$

---

[1] For an explanation of these assumptions and an extended general discussion of multiple regression, see Elazar J. Pedhazur, *Multiple Regression in Behavioral Research: Explanation and Prediction*, 3rd ed. (Fort Worth, TX: Harcourt Brace, 1997).

[2] Studies seldom meet these requirements fully, and it is often impossible to know in advance of analysis whether or not they are met in a given data set. In this context, "close enough" means that the effect of any violation of assumptions can be corrected for or at least estimated and taken into account in drawing conclusions. See Pedhazur, op. cit.

Interpreting Multiple Regressions Results

The *least squares procedure* for multiple regression works in a manner similar to bivariate regression in that it passes a line through a plotting of the values of cases on several variables in such a way as to minimize the sum of the squared distance of each point from that line. The difference is that the "line" in the case of multiple regression is a set of mathematically estimated points on a plane that cannot be represented in a two-dimensional scatterplot. The *a* or intercept term is generally of little practical interest, because the values of the IVs are rarely 0. However, the substantive interpretation of an *a* of 10 in the equation is that even if the candidate spent no money on advertising and 0 percent of the voters in the state shared the candidate's party identification, the candidate would receive 10 percent of the vote just by being on the ballot.

Interpreting Coefficients   It is far more important to understand the b_i terms. They are referred to as **partial regression coefficients** and describe the unique contribution of each IV to the determination of the IV. In our electoral example, a b_1 of .1 would be substantively interpreted as meaning that every additional $1,000 spent on advertising increases the candidate's portion of the vote by one-tenth of a percentage point, and a b_2 of 1 would indicate that for every 1 percent increase in the percentage of voters that share the candidate's party identification there is a corresponding 1 percent increase in the share of the vote that goes to that candidate. In calculating these coefficients, regression statistically holds constant the effect of any variables that influence both the individual IV and the DV through use of the formula

$$b_i = \frac{\sum (X_n - X'_n)(Y - Y')}{\sum (X_n - X'_n)^2}$$

This statistical control simulates the control we might have obtained in an experimental setting and is thus valuable in two important respects. First, as we will explore shortly, it allows us to assess the *relative* importance of different IVs in determining the value of the DV. Second, it allows us to rule out the alternative hypothesis that the relationship between the DV and any given IV is spurious. If we are willing to assume that we have included all important causes of change in the DV in our model and we find that the partial regression coefficient for any given IV is significantly different from 0, we can conclude that the relationship between that IV and the DV is *not* spurious. If, however, the *b* is near 0 or statistically insignificant, we must conclude that there is no independent relationship between that IV and the DV. In that case, we would drop the IV from our model in order to make it conform more closely to observed reality. Clearly, then, multiple regression can be a valuable tool in refining and improving our theories of political phenomena.

Interpreting R^2   We can assess the completeness of our theory by calculating a **coefficient of determination**, or R^2 (sometimes referred to as the *multiple R*), using the formula

$$R^2 = \frac{\sum(Y' - \bar{Y})^2}{\sum(Y - \bar{Y})^2} = \frac{\text{Regression sum of squares}}{\text{Total sum of squares}}$$

This coefficient tells us how close all the data plots came to touching the "line" projected by our model and is commonly interpreted as the *proportion of the variation in the DV that is "explained"* (accounted for) *by variation in all of the IVs.* For example, an R^2 of .57 would be interpreted as showing that the IVs in the model from which it was calculated explain 57 percent of the variance in the DV. R^2 can range between 0 and 1; the closer it is to 1, the more complete the model is. The size of R^2 can almost always be increased by adding additional IVs to the model, but the researcher must ask if additional variables make the model too complex or add anything of value to our understanding of the phenomenon in question. In the case of our electoral example, for instance, we could probably increase the R^2 by adding the number of letters in the candidate's last name to the equation, but to do so would be to forget that research is a quest for more complete and useful understanding of the world and not a competition to see who can produce the most impressive statistics.

Solving Common Problems in Multiple Regression

Neither data nor reality always conforms to the conceptual model underlying multiple regression analysis. Relationships are not always linear, measurement error is almost always present, and so on. Fortunately, statisticians have devised ways for us to adapt multiple regression in order to compensate for some of these problems. In this section we discuss adaptations to three of the most commonly encountered problems so that you can (1) learn how to cope with these issues in your applications of multiple regression and (2) get a sense of the flexibility of multiple regression as an analytic technique.

Noninterval Data   In the social sciences, important variables often are not (and sometimes cannot be) measured at the interval/ratio level, thus violating the assumption of interval-level measurement. Noninterval data can, however, be used in multiple regression under two conditions.

First, if the measure is (or can be converted into) a *dichotomy,* it can be entered directly into the regression by simply coding the value of the dichotomy as 1 and the other as 0. For example, in a study of international trade, goods might be classified as "foreign" or "domestic," with a code of 1 being assigned to the value "foreign" and a code of 0 assigned to the value "domestic." Regression would treat this scheme as if it were interval, because dichotomies have special mathematical properties. As a result, we can interpret the partial regression coefficient computed for any variable coded as a dichotomy just as we would if it were measured at the interval level.

Second, noninterval variables that have multiple categories can be incorporated into multiple regression by use of a system of *dummy variables.* For example, consider the case in which occupational status is measured only as "high," "medium," or "low" in a study that seeks to predict the number of political organizations to which a person belongs as a function of education (number of years of schooling) and occupational status. We can use the ordinal data on status in multiple regression if we create two dichotomous dummy variables to represent the variable occupational status. The equation would be

$$Y' = a + b_1X_1 + b_2X_2 + b_3X_3 + e$$

where Y' = the number of organizational memberships

X_1 = the number of years of schooling

X_2 = a dummy variable scored 1 if occupational status = "low" and 0 otherwise

X_3 = a dummy variable scored 1 if occupational status = "medium" and 0 otherwise.

Why use only two dummy variables to represent a noninterval variable with three categories? Because the value of the third dummy variable would be an exact linear function of the values of the other two, thus violating the assumption of no perfect multicollinearity and making it impossible to obtain a unique estimate of the various coefficients.

Whenever we use dummy variables, we must follow the rule of creating *one fewer dummy variables than there are categories in the noninterval variable* being represented. In practice, it is usually advisable to leave out the category in which you expect the fewest cases. In our example, the "high" category was not represented by a dummy variable because there are relatively few high-status jobs.

Interaction Effects   Conventional least squares regression assumes that the effects of different IVs on the DV are independent of one another and can be added together to determine the total effect of a set of variables. In practice, the effects of many variables reinforce or amplify the effects of some other variable. Whenever the impact of one IV depends on the value of another IV, an *interaction effect* exists. To return to the electoral example used earlier in this chapter, we might argue that the effect of advertising expenditures is different for incumbents (who tend to be well-known) and challengers (who need to make voters aware of their qualifications).

Multiple regression can be adapted to this situation by including the interaction between advertising and incumbent status as a separate variable. If we let incumbent status be represented by a dummy variable (X_3) coded 1 for challengers and 0 for incumbents, the new regression model would be:

$$Y' = a + b_1X_1 + b_2X_2 + b_3(X_1X_3) + e$$

where X_1X_3 is an interaction variable created by multiplying X_1 by X_3. This procedure allows us to interpret b_1 as the unique contribution of advertising expenditures to vote percentage by breaking off the *joint* effects of advertising and incumbency into b_3, and it can yield more accurate predictions of Y.

Multicollinearity   Regression analysis requires that no IV be perfectly correlated with any other IV or any linear combination of other IVs. It is usually easy to meet this strict requirement because few social science variables can be perfectly predicted from knowledge of any other variable or set of variables. However, many important variables are highly correlated with each other. (Consider urbanization and indus-trialization, education and income, or party and ideology in Western Europe.) This condition is referred to as **multicollinearity.** If the correlations among IVs in a regression model are high enough, estimations of the coefficients become inaccurate and we cannot place any confidence in the results of the regression analysis. Significant multicollinearity can cause such large variances in the estimation of par-tial regression coefficients that it becomes impossible to compare the relative effects of different IVs on the DV. In addition, coefficients may fail to attain statistical significance even where there is a substantial relationship, leading us to falsely identify bivariate relationships as spurious.

It is therefore essential that researchers make a serious effort to determine if multicollinearity is present and to make the adjustments necessary to correct for it. Multicollinearity is usually indicated by one or more of the following symptoms:

1. A high R^2 for the equation but statistically insignificant regression coefficients (b's).

2. Dramatic changes in regression coefficients (b's) for given variables when other IVs are dropped from or added to the equation.

3. Regression coefficients that are *far* larger or smaller (either in absolute terms or in relation to the coefficients for other IVs) than theory and knowledge of other research results would lead us to expect.

4. Regression coefficients that have the wrong sign—that are negative when we have good reason to expect them to be positive or positive when we have good reason to expect them to be negative.

When any of these symptoms is noted in a regression analysis, it is important to test for multicollinearity. This is done by *regressing each IV on all other IVs.* We would, for example, test the equation

$$Y' = a + b_1X_1 + b_2X_2 + b_3(X_3) + e$$

by running the following equations:

$$X_1 = a + b_2X_2 + b_3X_3$$
$$X_2 = a + b_1X_1 + b_3X_3$$
$$X_3 = a + b_1X_1 + b_2X_2$$

If the R^2 for any of these equations were higher than, say, .8, we could conclude that substantial multicollinearity existed.

There are several possible approaches to correcting for multicollinearity. If we have the option of adding cases to our sample (as when we are collecting data from published records and can simply go back and resample), then increasing the sam-ple size will sometimes eliminate multicollinearity. A second strategy would be to determine *which* of the IVs are highly related to each other and then combine them into a single indicator. If, for example, we had originally measured expenditures on radio, television, and newspaper advertising separately in our study of senatorial elections and found these three indicators to be highly correlated, we could combine the three into a single measure called *media expenditures* in order to eliminate the destabilizing effects of multicollinearity. Clearly, any such combining of variables works only when it is theoretically justified. We could not, for instance, solve a problem of multicollinearity by combining the incumbent status of the candidate with the regional location of the state since these are theoretically distinct concepts. Finally, we can attempt to cope with multicollinearity by discarding one or more of the highly intercorrelated variables. This can produce specification error, but by dropping first one and then the other correlated IV and comparing the results of different regressions, we can at least get a firm estimate of the damage done by both multicollinearity and misspecification.

Comparing IVs   It is often important to know which of several IVs exerts the most influence on a DV. If we wanted to encourage people to wear seat belts, for instance, we might want to know which of several factors that could lead to this behavior actually has the most impact on the decision to buckle up so that we can invest our resources in the most efficient way. Multiple regression analysis is well-suited for this purpose since it provides estimates of the unique contribution of each IV to variance in the DV in the form of its partial regression coefficients. Unfortunately, determining the relative effects of different IVs is not a simple matter of comparing the size of their regression coefficients.

When IVs are measured in different units (number of dollars versus percentage of voters, for instance), regression coefficients do not reflect the relative influence of IVs on the DV. One way to cope with this is to *standardize* the variables—so that they are measured in the same units—and obtain new estimates of the regression coefficients. Standardization of a case's score is achieved by converting the raw score into units of standard deviation from the mean value of the variable using the formula

$$X^* = \frac{X - \overline{X}}{s_X}$$

where the * indicates that the variable is standardized, X is the score for a given case, $\overline{X}$ is the mean score on that variable for all cases, and s is the standard deviation of the distribution of values on variable X (see Chapter 16).

When standardized scores are substituted for raw scores in the regression equation, the a term drops out because standardization forces it to 0, and the equation takes the general form

$$Y'^* = \beta_1 X_1^* + \beta_2 X_2^* \ldots \beta_n X_n + e$$

where β represents a *standardized partial regression coefficient*, referred to as a **beta weight** or **beta coefficient**. A beta weight corrects the unstandardized partial regression coefficient by the ratio of the standard deviation of the IV to the standard deviation of the DV and can be calculated by the formula

$$\beta_i = b_i \frac{s_{Xi}}{s_Y}$$

A beta weight can be interpreted as representing *the average standard deviation change in Y associated with a standard deviation change in X* when the effects of other IVs are held constant. Thus, a β of .5 would indicate that one standard deviation change in the value of an IV would be associated with a change of one-half standard deviation in the DV.

Standardizing thus allows us to compare the influence of different IVs *within a single sample.* However, when we are seeking to compare the influence of variables *across samples,* it can be misleading. If we wanted to compare the effects of campaign spending on the electoral success of candidates in the United States and Mexico, for example, we would find that there were substantial differences in the variance (and thus the standard deviation) of key variables because media campaigns cost more in the United States and election outcomes are usually significantly closer in one nation than in the other. Since the size of β is a function of variance (the larger the variance, the larger the β, other things being equal), we could be misled into thinking that spending had much more effect in one nation than in the other simply because of mathematically determined differences in β. To avoid this error, it is important to use the *un*standardized partial regression slopes (*b*'s) for a variable whenever we are seeking to compare the effects of an IV in different samples if *the variance for that variable differs considerably from sample to sample.*

Path Analysis

Regression analysis can be quite useful in testing specific hypotheses and assessing the relative impacts of different IVs. Regression, however, assumes a model of causation that does not always reflect the complexities of the real world—it assumes that all IVs *directly* effect the DV. In reality, variables may often act indirectly through other variables.

An Example If we wanted to investigate the determinants of racial segregation in public school systems, for instance, we could hypothesize that school segregation was caused by segregation in housing (since most schools draw on a given geographic area), which was in turn caused by racial differences in income. A causal diagram or model of these relationships developed according to the advice given in Chapter 2 is shown in Model 1.

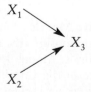

Model 1

(X_1 = *racial differences in income,* X_2 = *housing segregation,* and
X_3 = *school segregation*)

This simple diagram is typical of the causal model assumed by conventional regression analysis because it indicates that the IVs exert their influence on the DV independently. In real social situations, however, IVs often influence *one another* as well as the DV.

To return to our example, the least bit of knowledge about our subject would suggest that income differentials affect housing segregation as well as school segregation, because more and less expensive houses each tend to be geographically clustered. Taking this into account would require that we revise our model. We might propose a developmental sequence in which one IV exercises its influence on the DV exclusively by causing changes in another IV. This would be diagramed as in Model 2.

$$X_1 \longrightarrow X_2 \longrightarrow X_3$$

Model 2

A more sophisticated understanding of our subject might lead us to realize that racial differentials in income affect school segregation directly as well as through housing segregation, because more affluent people can place their children in private schools. This information would be incorporated into the model by creating an arrow directly from X_1 to X_2 as in Model 3.

Model 3

Path analysis is a statistical technique by which we can evaluate the accuracy of such models by empirically testing the direct *and indirect* effects of one variable on another. It has been widely used in the social sciences because it is applicable to a great many research questions and has the advantage of allowing us to test large pieces of a theory at once rather than one hypothesis at a time. Our objective in this section is to introduce you to the basic procedures of path analysis and to teach you to read the path diagrams you are likely to encounter in the literature. We do not attempt to address the many issues involved in more sophisticated applications of the technique, so you would be wise to do additional reading before attempting to apply path analysis to complicated research questions.

Recursive and Nonrecursive Models   Path analysis begins with a conceptual model that specifies the causal relationships the researcher thinks are at work in the world. For purposes of path analysis, Model 3 would be redrawn as Model 4, where the R's represent the variance in the variable with which they are associated that is *un*explained by variance in other variables in the model.

$$R_u \longrightarrow X_1 \longrightarrow X_2 \longleftarrow R_v$$
$$\downarrow$$
$$X_3 \longleftarrow R_w$$

Model 4

The model is then stated as mathematical equations. However, any model in which the IVs are not independent of each other (as they are in Model 1) cannot be represented in a single equation, but must be described by a set of *structural equations*. Model 4 would be represented by the following set of equations:

$$X_1 = p_{1u}R_u$$
$$X_2 = p_{21}X_1 + p_{2v}R_v$$
$$X_3 = p_{32}X_2 + p_{31}X_1 + p_{3w}R_w$$

The p's in these equations represent *path coefficients* that summarize the amount of influence one variable has on another when the effects of all other variables are held constant. The standard way of writing path coefficients is as p_{ij}, which indicates the path *to* variable i *from* variable j. The set of equations just given, then, tells us that X_1 is caused entirely by factors outside the model, X_2 is caused by X_1 and factors outside the model, and X_3 is caused by X_1, X_2, and factors outside the model. Variables like X_2 and X_3 that are determined at least partially by other variables in the model are referred to as *endogenous*, and variables that are determined entirely by factors that are left out of the model are called *exogenous*.

Models are classified as *recursive* or *nonrecursive*. A model is **recursive** if all of its variables can be ordered so that the first one is determined only by factors outside the model, the second is determined only by factors outside the model and the first variable, the third is determined only by factors outside the model and the first and second variables, and so on. In essence, this means that *all causal influence must flow in one direction*, with no "feedback." Model 4 is an example of a *recursive model*.

If there is feedback (reciprocal causation) among any of the variables in the model, it is referred to as **nonrecursive**. For example, we might add the variable "occupation" (X_4) to our model of school segregation and argue that segregated schooling leads to racial differences in occupational attainment that in turn cause income differentials, so that the model would look like Model 5. The model no longer contains any variable that is determined entirely by factors outside the model and is now nonrecursive. Such models require special analysis techniques that are well beyond the scope of this book. Recursive models, however, can be successfully examined by using the ordinary least squares regression techniques described earlier in this chapter. When variables are stated in standardized form, the path coefficients can be estimated as the *standardized regression coefficients* produced by regression.

Model 5

Using Path Analysis   We can test the empirical accuracy of the predictions implied in a model by running a series of regressions in which each endogenous variable is regressed on all variables that are theorized to influence it. To take a purely hypothetical example, we might work with the five-variable recursive model in Model 6 (eliminating the residual terms for simplicity of presentation). To test this model, we would regress X_5 on X_1 through X_4; X_4 on X_1 through X_3; and X_2 on X_1. X_1 and X_3 are considered exogenous. If any of the path coefficients (standardized regression coefficients) produced by this process approaches a value of 0 or is statistically insignificant, we know that we have misspecified the model by anticipating a relationship that is not actually found in the data.

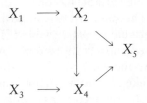

Model 6

In addition, we would test the validity of our assumptions about the *absence* of effects by regressing endogenous variables on others to which they are *not* supposed to be related. For example, in testing Model 6, we would regress both X_3 and X_4 on X_1 to see if the arrows we omitted should have been drawn in. If the resulting path coefficients are substantially different from 0 ($\geq$.2, for instance) and statistically significant, we would conclude that the model (and our theory about the events it represents) should be modified by adding a path.

One of the major advantages of path analysis is that it facilitates *theory elaboration* by bringing theory and data analysis into a fruitful interaction in which each informs the other. A path analysis of this type will tell us not only whether or not the variables in our model are related in the way we hypothesize but also *what relative influence each variable has on other variables in the model*. The *total effects* of one variable on another are equal to the value of the direct path between the two plus the indirect paths by which they are linked. An indirect path is equal to the products of the direct paths of which it is composed. For example, in Model 6, the total effect of X_2 on X_5 is equal to

$$p_{52} + (p_{42} \cdot p_{54})$$

and the total effect of X_1 on X_5 would be

$$(p_{21} \cdot p_{52}) + (p_{21} \cdot p_{42} \cdot p_{54})$$

As long as we are using *standardized* regression coefficients, we can use this procedure to compare the total effects of different variables in the system. Such knowledge can be of great practical significance because it can help citizens and policy makers to focus their energies where they will be most effective. For instance, if we were trying to encourage students to resist drugs, we could find out if one of several factors that contribute to that decision has a disproportionate impact and invest our resources in changing that variable.

Path analysis can also be used to compare the effects of variables in different settings. To return to the school segregation example, we might gather data on, say, Atlanta, Los Angeles, and Detroit and test the accuracy of Model 4 in each city. If we do not standardize our data and we use *unstandardized regression coefficients*, we can compare the effects of, say, housing segregation on school segregation in each of these cities to see if the causal processes we are interested in differ from city to city. It is necessary to use the unstandardized coefficients because standardizing makes the size of the path coefficient dependent on the variance of the variable in the sample. If, for example, there is a great deal more school segregation in one city than another, the relative size of the standardized regression coefficients will reflect that difference in variance rather than reflect any real difference in the relative strength of the influence of variables in the different cities.

The general rule is to use *standardized* coefficients when comparing the effects of different variables in the same sample and to use *unstandardized* coefficients when comparing the effects of the same variable in different samples. It is the unstandardized coefficients that are viewed as representing the "causal laws" that drive social processes.

Conclusion

We end this chapter with two notes of caution. First, it is important to recognize that we have discussed only a fraction of the many multivariate statistics that are available for the analysis of both interval and noninterval data. Each of these techniques is applicable to different analytical tasks. Among the most important commonly used techniques that we have *not* discussed here are *discriminant analysis,* which seeks statistically significant differences in dichotomous groups and is therefore especially applicable to experimental and quasi-experimental designs; *analysis of variance (ANOVA),* which is used to test hypotheses about differences of means in various groups and can be especially valuable in identifying the effects of some "treatment" or intervention on the degree to which cases manifest a concept; and *factor analysis,* which is used to identify common factors that reflect the relatedness of apparently independent indicators. Explanations of when and how to use these and other techniques can be found in the readings suggested at the end of this chapter.

With such a wide variety of statistical techniques to choose from, the task of selecting the statistical procedure that is most appropriate to your data and research question can be quite challenging. Asking a series of data and analytic questions to help researchers select the correct statistical procedure from among almost 150 options, *A Guide for Selecting Statistical Techniques for Analyzing Social Science Data* (Andrews, et al., 1981) makes the task of choosing the appropriate technique less overwhelming. This book also provides a useful way of learning about the properties of the most commonly used statistics in the social sciences.

The second caution to bear in mind is that the overview of statistical techniques in this text has only introduced you to data analysis—it has not prepared you to actually execute more sophisticated data analysis techniques. Fortunately, you need not be a statistician to learn about and use the most common methods, since statistical analysis programs such as SPSS or SAS will carry out the calculations for you if the analysis is correctly set up. Statistics software programs have "help" functions that will enable you to learn both the statistics and the analytic requirements. Therefore, an aversion to math or statistics need not be an insurmountable barrier to relatively sophisticated data analysis and empirically grounded research on important political issues.

Summary Points

• Multiple regression permits the use of additional independent variables as controls.
• To successfully perform regression analysis, the interval or ratio variables and error terms must satisfy a set of assumptions.

Suggested Readings and References

Some of the many texts that provide a general introduction to statistics appropriate to the social sciences are James T. McClave and Terry Sincich, Statistics, 9th ed. (Upper Saddle River, NJ: Prentice Hall, 2003); George W. Bohrnstedt and David Knoke, *Statistics for Social Data Analysis,* 3rd ed. (Itasca, IL: F. E. Peacock, 1994).

A highly regarded, comprehensive examination of regression techniques is provided by Sanford Weisberg, *Applied Linear Regression*, 3rd ed. (New York, NY: John Wiley and Sons, 2005). A detailed introduction to the types of statistics most often used in hypothesis testing is found in Barbara G. Tabachnick and Linda S. Fidell, *Using Multivariate Statistics,* 4th ed. (Needham Heights, MA: Allyn & Bacon, 2001). Procedures for analyzing noninterval data are covered in detail in Jean Dickinson Gibbons, *Nonparametric Methods in Quantitative Analysis,* 3rd ed. (Columbus, OH: American Sciences Press, 1997). A highly readable introduction to path analysis, as well as a graduate-level examination of the procedure, is found in Chapters 5 and 6 of Rex B. Kline, *Principles and Practice of Structural Equation Modeling,* 2nd ed. (New York: Guilford, 2005).

Detailed and generally quite readable explanations of many specific analysis techniques can be obtained in the Sage series: *Quantitative Applications in the Social Sciences.* There are dozens of these monographs, each focusing on a specific social science quantitative procedure. The analytic procedure is described using empirical examples of the techniques being described.

A broad-based introduction to SPSS, complete with screen-shots and extensive statistical explanations is in Marija Norusis, *SPSS 12.0 Guide to Data Analysis* (Upper Saddle River, NJ: Prentice Hall, 2004).

While examples of political science research using multivariate analysis may be found in nearly every issue of the major journals listed in Chapter 3, path analysis is less common. The continued utility of path analysis in public opinion analysis is demonstrated by the modeling of factors related to different death penalty attitudes in different states in Barbara Norrander, "The Multi-Layered Impact of Public Opinion on Capital Punishment Implementation in the American States," *Political Research Quarterly,* 53 (December 2000): 771–793.

References: Frank M. Andrews, Laura Klem, Terrence N. Davidson, Patrick M. O'Malley, and William L. Rogers, *A Guide for Selecting Statistical Techniques for Analyzing Social Science Data* (Ann Arbor, MI: Institute for Social Research, 1981).

Research Exercises

1. Does spending more on public education reduce the amount of poverty? Select a sample of thirty of the states in the United States and use *Statistical Abstracts of the United States* to gather data on three variables for each state: (1) whether it is above or below the national average on the amount it spends on public education per student, (2) whether it is above or below the national average on the percentage of its population that is below the poverty line, and (3) the political party that controls its legislature. Set up a crosstabulation to show the relationship between variables 1 and 2. Set up a crosstab to show the same relationship *controlling for variable 3*. Use the formulas given in Chapter 17 to compute lambda and chi-square for each of the tables. Write an interpretation of your findings.

2. Devise a theory to explain differences in the rate of growth in the gross national product of Third World nations that includes four IVs. Write a single multiple regression equation that summarizes this theory, and explain what each term in the equation represents.

3. Draw a path diagram illustrating the theory you developed for Exercise 2, being sure that at least two of the IVs are endogenous. Then write the structural equations necessary to represent this model in a path analysis, explaining what each term in the equations represents.

Key Terms

multivariate analysis
controlling
multiple regression
model
model specification
multiple regression equation
partial regression coefficients

coefficient of determination (R^2)
multicollinearity
beta weight or beta coefficient (β)
path analysis
recursive
nonrecursive

Introduction to Qualitative Methods

- What is qualitative methodology?
- How does it relate to quantitative methodology?
- How do qualitative and quantitative researchers view each other's work?
- Are qualitative and quantitative methods compatible with each other?

While other sections of this book do not have separate introductions, we provide an introduction to this section because its chapters represent a departure from the material presented in prior sections. We feel that you can better understand the ideas covered in this section if we offer some general background comparing quantitative to qualitative research before describing specific methods.

Limitations of Quantitative Research

From the time scholars began using scientific methods to study social phenomena, some academics (as well as some public officials and political activists) have seen limitations in quantitative methods. These critics typically raise three types of concerns.

First, some believe that since research methods were developed in the physical sciences, with their stress on treating all cases alike and reducing complex concepts to numeric representations, these methods can never fully capture important dimensions of human thought and interaction. To these critics, even the most carefully executed quantitative research does not provide an adequate understanding of the actions of humans who are each unique in many ways and may see very different meanings in the same phenomena.

Second, some argue that quantitative research methods require that we remove subjects from their natural setting and pay attention only to limited aspects of who or what they are. People, they argue, may not behave in real contexts in the same way as they behave in, for example, the artificial setting of a survey interview. Moreover, they contend that actions can only be fully understood by understanding the context in which they occur, for it is their context that gives them meaning.

Finally, some view quantitative methods as so inherently politically biased that they are inappropriate for the study of some subjects and populations. For example, these critics argue that applying the methods of the physical sciences can never capture crucial aspects of the lives and thinking of marginalized groups—people who, because of some personal characteristic, are excluded from political, social, and economic power. They often argue that quantitative methods are a cultural artifact of the same processes that created the currently dominant social and political culture. Accordingly, they believe that we cannot employ quantitative research to gain a valid understanding of the deep cultural roots of contemporary political or social behavior.

Defining Qualitative Research   Scholars who share these concerns have sought alternative means of gaining an understanding of the empirical world through the development of a very diverse set of research approaches described collectively as **qualitative methods**. To their advocates, these means of inquiry provide a more complete, meaningful, and useful understanding of social phenomena by studying them *in their entirety, in the context in which they occur*, while *considering the meanings those being studied give to their actions and to the actions of others*. Catherine Marshall and Gretchen Rossman capture the distinct features of this approach when they write that qualitative research "entails immersion [of the researcher] in the everyday life of the setting chosen for study, values and seeks to discover participants' perspectives on their worlds, views inquiry as an interactive process between the researcher and the participants, is both descriptive and analytic, and relies on people's words and observable behavior as the primary data." (Marshall and Rossman, 1999, p. 7)

This indicates that there can be some fundamental differences between qualitative research and the type of inquiry we have described so far. There are, however, substantial similarities between the way many qualitative and quantitative researchers approach their studies. In the chapters in this section we will focus only on those aspects of qualitative research that have a good deal in common with quantitative methods. Our decision to do this does not reflect any lack of appreciation for the more fundamentally distinctive qualitative approaches. Rather, we choose to describe only qualitative approaches that require the least additional explanation simply to limit the scope and length of our text. In addition, we have selected qualitative methods that are most self-evidently *empirical*, even though not quantitative, in order to highlight the fact that *empirical research can be either quantitative or qualitative* so long as its purpose is to characterize real-world phenomena rather than to interpret them in some normative context.

At the end of this section introduction, we provide some suggestions for readings which can help you explore other types of qualitative research.

Comparing Qualitative and Quantitative Methods

It is useful to frame a comparison between qualitative and quantitative research by highlighting their differences in each of the major steps in the research process. In making this comparison, we will speak of qualitative and quantitative researchers as if they were two different groups. Please remember, however, that the same scholar may employ both types of methods—sometimes even within the same study. In addition, it is important to recognize that the distinctions discussed are generally more matters of degree than absolutes. The two types of methods often require only different *forms* of work, but are working toward similar objectives.

Empirical Focus of Research Questions   Both qualitative and quantitative research begins with a research question. While scholars using each of the approaches tend to pursue rather different research questions, both approaches are designed to produce knowledge of the empirical world. Both rely on concepts that are, at least in principle, observable with the ordinary human senses. Thus, qualitative researchers are just as obligated to represent accurately the reality that they observe as are those using strictly quantitative methods.

Theorizing   Qualitative researchers are less likely than those using quantitative methods to be interested in testing pre-formed theories. Rather, they are more likely to attempt to gain insights into some phenomenon as they develop their conceptual understanding. Qualitative researchers seek to be "taught by the world" to a far greater extent than quantitative researchers. They often elaborate their theories as they make their observations.

This, they argue, makes their theories more firmly grounded in reality. By contrast, their critics worry that this practice may open the door to unintentionally shaping a theory that fits observations, leading to an untestable theory. These critics also contend that such "theories" apply only to the cases actually observed and, as a result, are of limited usefulness.

Research Design   It is important for those using qualitative methods—just as it is for those using quantitative methods—to be clear about their research question and to know what they are seeking to learn from their study. However, qualitative researchers are far less likely to base their research design on the logic of the experiment than are quantitative researchers. Qualitative research rarely emphasizes control groups, pretests, or any of the other elements of experimental and quasi-experimental designs that allow researchers to "hold constant" some factors in order to make causal inferences.

A qualitative research design will generally focus on who or what is to be observed, in what settings they are to be observed, how observations are to be conducted, what methods will be used to secure the information needed, and how data (often referred to in qualitative research simply as "information") will be recorded. There is far less concern with being able to establish cause and effect relationships and more concern with viewing the people or events as they "naturally" occur. Only in this way, qualitative researchers argue, can one fully and accurately describe and understand behavior, beliefs, values, social interactions, and the like.

Sampling   Qualitative researchers also differ from their quantitatively oriented colleagues in that they are less concerned with generalizing conclusions to large populations and more concerned with gaining insights into specific cases from which they can construct an understanding (rather than a statistical explanation) of broad phenomena. As a result, they use very different sampling methods than we have described in earlier chapters.

In quantitative research, sampling is often based on the logic of probability and designed to produce statistical representativeness. It is usually done in advance of data collection. By contrast, the sample for a qualitative study will often "emerge" as the study progresses. That is, researchers will select an initial case to observe and then let what they learn from those observations determine who or what they observe next. This strategy reflects their belief that we can determine where to look for the answers we seek only after having gained a partial understanding of the subject by direct experience with it. This is consistent with qualitative researchers' view that each case is unique and should not be treated in a standardized way (as is done in quantitative research).

Qualitative researchers are also often far less concerned with observing "representative" cases than they are with observing cases that will yield the insights they seek. To illustrate, a qualitatively oriented scholar might try to understand the fundamental assumptions that constitute a "political culture," not by surveying a representative sample of "ordinary" citizens, but by conducting in-depth interviews with a few people who do not share these assumptions and reject the dominant political culture. By understanding the political thought of these "outsiders," the researcher would hope to see how accepting the assumptions of the prevailing political culture influences the majority's thinking about politics.

Due to a lack of concern with statistical representativeness and the highly time-consuming nature of their methods, qualitative studies are usually based on far fewer cases than are quantitative studies.

Data Collection   Some of the most dramatic differences between qualitative and quantitative methods appear in the data collection stage. On the surface, there is the fact that data in qualitative research usually consist of words (or sounds and images translated into words) rather than numbers. This calls for the use of different procedures and instruments for data collection.

There is a more fundamental difference, however. For qualitative research, data collection usually involves extended observation of (or even participation in) the phenomenon under study. Rather than standing apart from the people or events to be studied, the researcher often is intimately engaged with them. Only in this way can researchers probe for the information they need to understand, for example, why people act as they do, how complex processes unfold, or what impact some specific event had on those who experienced it.

While some qualitative research attempts to avoid the problem of reactivity by concealing the observer or the purpose of the research from the subjects (as we explain in Chapter 19), much qualitative research takes a very different approach to reactivity. Since researchers have to interact with those they are studying, they depend not on deception or concealment, but on trust (and their own perceptiveness) to avoid artificial reactions.

The goal of qualitative research is for the researcher to build a strong enough relationship with those being observed that they will reveal their true feelings or reasoning and will act "naturally" because they feel that the researcher will not judge or harm them. At a minimum, the researcher will learn enough about the subjects and their context to know when they are not being truthful or are modifying their behavior because of the researcher's presence. Effective use of this approach to control reactivity obviously requires a great deal of effort and skill.

Data Analysis   The distinction between data collection and data analysis is far less clear for qualitative studies than for quantitative ones. In quantitative studies, data analysis is planned in advance so that data can be obtained in the necessary form. The analysis is then carried out after all the data are gathered. In studies using qualitative methods, data collection and analysis generally proceed together. Since data collection in qualitative research consists primarily of observing and recording those observations, the very act of deciding what to pay attention to and how to record it involves some analysis.

To illustrate the interaction between observation and analysis, consider a qualitative researcher who seeks to understand the political power structure in a voluntary organization by observing its meetings. This observer will see, hear, and feel a great deal at each meeting—for example, the temperature in the room, noises from outside, whether or not people bring small children to the meeting—but may regard most of it as irrelevant to the research. However, some seemingly irrelevant things may be important in understanding the power structure. Deciding whether to record and how to describe such things as what clothes different people wear to the meeting, the order in which they arrive, or the tone of voice they use in asking questions involves deciding what each of these things means in the context of the study. That requires analysis on the spot as well as when writing up the notes later.

Failing to recognize the importance of an event when it is observed or transcribed can lead to a failure to understand accurately the subject under study. Thus, some level of analysis must begin immediately. As a result, qualitative researchers often modify their data collection techniques in the course of the project as a result of new insights they gain from this early analysis.

Another distinction between qualitative and quantitative research is the use of computerized data analysis. With large numeric datasets, computers are central to most quantitative analysis. Qualitative researchers are far less likely to make much or any use of them because the form of data they have (narratives) does not lend itself to computerized manipulation. A number of computer programs have been developed to assist in the analysis of qualitative data, so this distinction is not as stark as it once was. However, it is highly unlikely that computerized analyses will ever be used as extensively in the interpretation of qualitative data as they are in quantitative research.

Standards of Evidence   Quantitative researchers are usually able to employ some well-established rules of analysis in deciding what is valid evidence for or against their theory. These include such tools as measures of statistical significance and statistical tests of validity, as well as formal logic. Qualitative researchers generally lack this type of commonly agreed to "objective" tool.

Rather, they must rely on their ability to present a clear description, offer a convincing analysis, and make a strong argument for their interpretation to establish the value of their conclusions. Advocates of qualitative methods argue that this is an inevitable result of seeking to deal with the richness of complex realities rather than abstracting artificially constructed pieces of those realities for quantitative analysis. Critics of their approach contend that the vagueness and situational nature of their standards of evidence make it difficult (if not impossible) to achieve scientific consensus and, therefore, to make progress through the accumulation of knowledge.

Reporting the Results   Reports of quantitative research usually rely heavily on presentations of numerical data to make the case for the interpretations offered, whereas reports of qualitative research usually consist primarily or entirely of narratives describing and interpreting what was observed.

More substantively, reports of qualitative projects often include long quotations from the people being studied, or present the "stories" they told the researcher about their "lived experience." This is necessary not only to capture the full complexity of the subject matter, but also to give readers a way to judge the validity of the researcher's interpretations (as explained in the discussion of rules of evidence above). Accordingly, the process of writing the report is even more crucial to qualitative projects than to quantitative ones. Qualitative researchers must be highly concerned with avoiding even unconscious bias in deciding what evidence (quotations, observations, etc.) to include in the report if they are to give other scholars a chance to critically evaluate their conclusions.

Research Ethics   Qualitative and quantitative research projects must meet highly similar ethical standards. However, because qualitative methods generally require far more extensive interaction between researchers and subjects, the use of qualitative methods often raises more ethical questions and often raises them in more complex forms. We will explore this challenge to qualitative methods in the following chapters that describe specific approaches.

Different Methods for Different Questions?

There are disagreements about many aspects or applications of all types of research methods. In most cases these disagreements arise from a sincere desire to make research as accurate and valuable as possible. Such debates usually have the positive effect of making all researchers examine their methods and conclusions very carefully, and thus produce better science.

The differences scholars have over qualitative versus quantitative methods are generally more extensive and profound than differences within either of the research traditions. This conflict calls for a brief examination of these differences in this section introduction.

Most empirical researchers work primarily with either qualitative or quantitative methods but recognize value in the other approach. The differences between the two traditions can often be resolved by using the insights provided by both to gain a more complete understanding of a subject, or by using results obtained with one type of method to generate questions to be explored using the other. In some cases, the two types of methods can even be used as complements to each other in a single study, with the results from each approach providing a form of validation for findings generated from the other. Scholars who take this position do not feel that qualitative and quantitative methods are fundamentally at odds.

However, there are researchers who view the differences between the two traditions as so profound that they cannot accept the validity of research based on the tradition they reject. Some quantitatively oriented scholars regard most qualitative work as so dependent on the perceptions of the individual researcher and so focused on specific cases as to be unverifiable and essentially useless. In contrast, some qualitatively oriented scholars judge quantitative methods to be so incomplete in their representation of reality as to be empirically misleading and politically biased in favor of existing power arrangements.

Scholars on both sides of this divide sometime see themselves as defending "scientific truth" against misguided ideas. As a result, their criticism of the other approach can be quite strident. The sharpest conflicts, however, usually occur when research touches most directly on normative issues. If the distinction between empirical and normative inquiry is not recognized (or respected), intense debates from the world of politics can be introduced into scholarly research. Since some qualitative research is intended to be at the boundary between normative and empirical inquiry, it can evoke strong disagreements.

You will want to gain more experience with social science research before you are in a position to fully understand or take a position on this debate. However, we do want to alert you to the depth of the differences here so you are not surprised to read or hear strongly worded criticisms of certain research from some scholars. You may also find cases in which research results are challenged as strongly on the basis of methodology and political values as they are on substantive grounds. We hope this quick review of the divisions among qualitative and quantitative researchers can help you put these cases into context if you encounter them.

Summary Points

• Qualitative methodologies are a complex set of techniques used to gain insight into how the social world works with little or no resort to translating observations into numbers.
• Qualitative methods differ from quantitative methods in the nature of the theories they examine, the ways they collect, record, and analyze data, the standards of evidence they apply, and the ways they present their results.
• Qualitative and quantitative methods may be compatible with each other and can also complement one another to provide a more complete understanding of the political world.

Suggested Readings and References

One entry-level text that provides a broad overview of qualitative methods is Bruce L. Berg, *Qualitative Research Methods for the Social Sciences*, 5th ed. (Allyn & Bacon, 2003). Norman K. Denzin and Yvonna S. Lincoln, eds., *Handbook of Qualitative Research*, 2nd ed. (Thousand Oaks, CA: Sage, 2000) provides a collection of readings that illustrate the various paradigms for doing qualitative work, the strategies developed for studying people in their natural setting, and a variety of techniques for collecting, analyzing, interpreting, and reporting qualitative findings.

Sharan B. Merriam, ed., *Qualitative Research in Practice: Examples for Discussion and Analysis* (San Francisco, CA: Jossey-Bass, 2002) offers examples of how qualitative methods are used in actual research. Joseph A. Maxwell, *Qualitative Research Design: An Interactive Approach*, 2nd ed. (Thousand Oaks, CA: Sage Publications, 2004) explores the nature of research design in qualitative research, and David Silverman, *Interpreting Qualitative Data: Methods for Analyzing Talk, Text and Interaction*, 2nd ed. (Thousand Oaks, Ca: Sage Publications, 2001) examines the challenges of analyzing qualitative data.

Books that describe how qualitative and quantitative methods can be successfully combined include John W. Creswell, *Research Design: Qualitative, Quantitative, and Mixed Methods Approaches*, 2nd ed. (Thousand Oaks, CA: Sage Publications, 2002), and Abbas Tashakkori and Charles Teddlie, *Mixed Methodology: Combining Qualitative and Quantitative Approaches* (Thousand Oaks, CA: Sage Publications, 1998).

Examples of software that can be used in the analysis of qualitative data include *Atlas.ti* developed by Scientific Software Development (www.atlasti.de), *HyperRESEARCH*™ from ResearchWare (www.researchware.com) and *NVivo* developed by Qualitative Solutions and Research (www.qsr.com.au).

Those interested in pursuing qualitative research will find like-minded individuals in the Organized Section on Qualitative Methods of the American Political Science Association (APSA). The Section publishes a quarterly newsletter, which features discussion of current topics in the field as well as research notes utilizing qualitative methods. Information on membership in the Section may be obtained from the APSA (www.apsanet.org).

Reference: Catherine Marshall and Gretchen B. Rossman, *Designing Qualitative Research,* 3rd ed. (Thousand Oaks, CA: Sage, 1999).

Key Term

qualitative methods

CHAPTER 19

Direct Observation

- When might researchers need to observe political events directly as they occur?
- Can this be accomplished with scientific validity?
- What are the advantages and limitations of direct observation?
- What ethical issues are posed by direct observation and how might they be addressed?

In the other data collection techniques we have discussed in this text, researchers must rely to some degree on others' experience with the political events they are seeking to understand. For example, with aggregate data, we usually rely on information collected by public or private agencies to represent the events we are studying; we do not actually observe coups, agricultural production, the distribution of income, or any of the other phenomena represented by the figures with which we work. Even when we conduct surveys, we are relying on respondents' memories of their experiences or perceptions of their surroundings—we do not actually observe their actions or the setting in which those actions occurred. Although there is a great deal to be learned through these data collection methods, there are times when researchers need to see and hear events for themselves in order to gain a full understanding of them.

New phenomena may be best studied directly. For example, the alternative political parties that developed in the authoritarian states of Eastern Europe in the 1990s were a new phenomenon—political parties seeking to gain power through elections in previously non-democratic Soviet bloc nations. To understand their functioning, we could try to apply theories of political party behavior that have been developed by observation of parties in democratic nations of the West. However, there are good reasons to suspect that these new parties will operate according to very different rules because they exist in a dramatically different context from, say, Canadian or French political parties. To formulate theories about their operation, we may need to observe them firsthand.

A second situation calling for direct contact with the subject of research is one in which we cannot be confident of the usefulness of others' reports of some ongoing behavior. In some cases, even though we could interview participants in the events we are interested in, we may feel they would be unable to give us the understanding we need because they do not share our conceptual framework. We might, for instance, be looking for the effects of institutionalized ideology on the decisions of U.S. embassy personnel in handling requests for political asylum. If we ask the officials how they make decisions, they will quite sincerely cite the written rules they follow. But if we saw for ourselves the procedures followed, we might be able to identify unofficial ideological criteria at work.

Another situation in which we might not be willing to rely on others' accounts of events is one in which those who can supply the information might have an interest in misleading us. Real estate agents, for example, would have legal and professional reasons for giving the impression that they always comply with federal equal housing opportunity laws even if they knew that their practices often did not satisfy the requirements of that legislation.

In these and other circumstances, researchers may need to turn to **direct observation.** When we collect data by personal contact with the events we are studying *as they happen,* we are employing direct observation.

Direct Observation and the Scientific Method

Despite its rich potential for providing insight, the use of direct observation is not common in political science. One reason for this is that many of the subjects political scientists study are too large in scale to allow direct observation. Elections, for example, happen all over a nation simultaneously and therefore cannot be physically observed directly as complete events. Individual researchers must rely on indirect observation.

A second reason for the infrequent use of direct observation in political science is that we often do not have access to events that could be fruitfully studied by this method. Spontaneous popular uprisings such as those that unseated the Milosevic government in Serbia in 2000, for example, occur too rapidly to allow us to plan a research project. Similarly, even ongoing phenomena may be inaccessible to us. We would be unlikely to get permission to observe the White House staff making national security decisions, for instance.

A third set of reasons why we do not see more use of direct observation relates to the nature of the method. First, it is usually a very time-consuming technique that may take months or years to produce results and can be quite expensive to carry out. Second, it often demands a great deal of the researcher, who may have to become immersed in the study to the exclusion of other activities, and it can seldom be carried out by assistants.

Political scientists, however, often choose not to use direct observation, even when it is appropriate and possible, because they question its scientific validity. This is usually a result of either or both of two concerns. First, there is often a perception that direct observation produces highly *subjective data* reflecting the unique insights and, perhaps, biases of the observer. Second, direct observation often produces *qualitative* data. Because some researchers think that only quantitative data can be scientific, they may view data collected through direct observation as "soft" (subjective and subject to challenge). Neither of these concerns is totally without foundation. Improperly done direct observation *can* produce highly subjective results that are influenced by the researcher's preconceptions. Even well-executed observations depend a great deal on the skill, energy, and insight of the observer and may be difficult to reproduce. In addition, much of the data that come from direct observation *are* qualitative in nature and do not lend themselves to standard data analysis techniques.

There are at least five reasons why these concerns should not deter social scientists from using direct observation under the right conditions.

1. Research has different purposes at different stages of the study of a topic and, as discussed in Chapters 1 and 6, the requirements for scientific precision differ with the purpose of research. Direct observation is especially well-suited to the exploratory and descriptive stages of research, when we are seeking to *develop* theories rather than to test them. Descriptive research can be crucial to the scientific process in that it can provide an accurate picture of how a social or political process unfolds. A description of the process can serve as a foundation for using inductive logic to devise testable theories that provide a scientific understanding of the phenomenon in question. When used at the proper stage of the research process, direct observation is not only adequate to the task but often far superior to other methods of data collection.

2. Many of the fears about subjectivity in reporting results can be overcome by proper execution of direct observation. If researchers follow correct procedures in making and recording observations, it is possible for others to verify their conclusions or at least judge the degree of confidence that should be placed in them.

3. Even qualitative data can be analyzed in rigorous and objective ways if the analyst employs the right techniques. The fact that direct observation may produce primarily qualitative data, therefore, need not be taken as a major limitation on its applicability.

4. Under the right conditions and with the right approach, direct observation can even be used to *test* theories and should not be ruled out as a potential data-gathering technique in explanatory research.

5. Against any of the limitations associated with the method, we must weigh the fact that direct observation has the distinct advantage of providing a very high level of *external validity* for our research. Because we observe *actual behavior* (not oral reports, written accounts, or simulations of it) and observe it *in the context in which it naturally occurs*, we can obtain a realistic view of events and can get highly valid measures of our concepts. Moreover, in some types of direct observation, *reactivity may be less of a problem than with more obvious data-gathering techniques*.

In the rest of this chapter, we explore the potential of direct observation and suggest some methods for using it to its full potential.

Approaches to Direct Observation

Direct observation can take several forms. First, we can distinguish between *obtrusive* and *unobtrusive* approaches. **Obtrusive research** occurs anytime the persons being studied are aware of being observed. It always carries some risk of provoking reactivity and, thus, producing at least partially invalid results. In **unobtrusive research**, subjects are unaware of being observed and, therefore, unlikely to alter their natural behaviors in response to the research itself. This has the advantage of increasing the chances of obtaining valid data.

Obtrusive Observation   In *obtrusive* observation, the researchers or trained assistants request permission to observe subjects and are identified as observers at the time of the data collection. An example of this approach is the case in which an investigator attends meetings of a committee of the state legislature and observes its decision-making processes. Committee members are aware of the observer and know the general purpose of the study.

Unobtrusive Observation   In *unobtrusive* observation, the researcher is either concealed from those being studied or is visible, but the purpose of the observation is unknown to the subjects of the study. In the first type of study, the observer might be concealed from view or might use a hidden camera. An example would be a project in which the researcher is given permission to study the behavior of public personnel by observing the interaction of welfare clients and welfare agency caseworkers from behind a two-way mirror when neither the caseworkers nor the clients know they are being observed. In the second type, the observer may be in full view, but the purpose of the study is concealed. There are two versions of this type of unobtrusive observation.

The first is **passive observation.** It can be exemplified by a case in which a researcher attends all public meetings of a city council and openly sits with other citizens in the audience but carefully watches the debate to analyze patterns of influence on the council *without the knowledge of the council members*. A second form of unobtrusive observation is known as *participant observation*. When researchers actually become part of the events under study, they are engaging in **participant observation.** The researcher studying a given political organization who joined that group as any other citizen might, attended its meetings, served on its committees, took part in its fund-raising efforts, voted on its policies, and otherwise acted as a member *without the other members of the organization knowing that they were being observed as part of a study* would be using unobtrusive participant observation.

The obvious advantage of unobtrusive observation is that it virtually eliminates the possibility that subjects will alter their behavior in reaction to being studied so that it can yield highly valid information. However, unobtrusive observations can be very difficult to arrange and conduct and, as we discuss later in this chapter, often pose serious ethical questions for the scholar.

A second division of approaches to direct observation is made between *structured* and *unstructured studies*. This distinction is made on the basis of the degree to which the researcher organizes or *structures* the process of observation by imposing a preconceived set of concepts and categories.

Structured Observation   In a **structured observation,** we use our understanding of the events under scrutiny to construct an **observation protocol** to guide the observer. The protocol tells the observer what to look for, the order in which to make observations, and the way to record the results. This approach is especially suited for gaining accurate descriptions of events.

As an illustration, we might want to study the ways in which members of the U.S. Congress use debate on the floor of the House of Representatives to gain support from interest groups and constituents. If we have a strong enough theory of how this is done, we could develop a checksheet listing the techniques that we expect to be used. We could then observe floor debates and use the checksheet to record whether or not each representative used the given techniques to send messages to potential supporters. The protocol would restrict our attention to a limited range of what was happening when representatives made public statements but would provide more objective data than a survey and would facilitate comparisons of the behavior of different House members.

Unstructured Observation   By contrast, if we were in an earlier stage of our study of this subject, we might be unwilling to restrict our observations to a list of items on a protocol. Such a situation would call for use of **unstructured observation,** in which we attempt to pay attention to all that goes on in a debate, to take careful notes, and to analyze the notes in an effort to discover patterns that can provide a basis for theorizing about how representatives use floor debate to influence potential supporters.

Structured and unstructured observation can be combined in a single research project. In fact, it is quite common for researchers using direct observation to mix the two approaches. A study may start with unstructured observation to gain a broad understanding of an event and formulate concepts with which to analyze it. The researcher may then use these insights to structure subsequent observations of the same phenomenon in order to test the utility of the conceptualizations. Alternatively, the two approaches may be combined by structuring portions of the observational task while leaving other parts unstructured.

It is important to recognize that the distinction between structured and unstructured observations is *not* a true dichotomy, with "pure" types of observation on either side. It is a continuum ranging from the least structured to the most structured methods of observation. Even the least formally structured observation involves an element of structure in that the researcher approaches the task with a set of questions about the event under study and with perceptions of how the event might work. Similarly, even in a highly structured observation, an alert researcher often notices unexpected qualities of the phenomena under study and may learn more than what is anticipated by the observation protocol. In this sense, the two approaches to observation are almost always blended to some degree.

We can offer some guidelines for the effective use of structured and unstructured techniques in both obtrusive and unobtrusive research.

Techniques of Unstructured Observation

Unstructured observation is used to develop a full understanding of the behaviors and relationships under study. It requires that investigators be open to discovering new dimensions to the behavior and willing to devise new ways of thinking about the topic. Observers are seeking to be taught by the world and want to get as close to the reality of the events as possible without being so constrained by preconceived notions of how things work that they overlook some important patterns.

The procedure for unstructured observation begins with identifying the set of behaviors that have to be observed in order to acquire a full understanding of the events in question. Refining the research question so that it provides a better guide to observation may require doing some background reading, talking with others who have had contact with the subject, and engaging in some very preliminary theorizing about what processes might be at work.

Next, the researcher needs to gain access to the subjects for purposes of observation. How this is done depends on whether he or she is using obtrusive or unobtrusive methods, and varies with the details of the project. It can be one of the most challenging portions of the work. Clearly, some subjects will be less willing to be observed than others, and most subjects will find some objectives in the study to be more acceptable than others. For example, revolutionaries conducting a guerrilla war will not be open to outsiders under almost any circumstances. By contrast, bureaucrats who may be willing to cooperate with research described as "a study of chains of command in public agencies" may be quite unwilling to participate in "a study of corruption in the management of public agencies."

This early step in the research process may very well present an ethical dilemma: Do you tell people they are being observed and, if so, do you tell them the real purpose of the study even if doing so risks losing their cooperation or at least creating a serious problem of reactivity? We address this and other ethical issues of direct observation later in this chapter. For now, assume that the ethical questions are resolved in favor of taking an obtrusive approach and that we can move to the third stage in the process.

The primary activity here is to observe and take careful notes on all that is seen and heard. The *written record of observations* is referred to as **field notes.** Though field notes are not as structured as interview notes, there are definite general rules for proper taking of field notes.

1. You should *clearly define the objectives of the research* so that you know what you want to learn about the events under observation. From that you can develop a list of the types of things you are looking for, so as to focus your attention on those features of the events that are most important to observe. Having such a list is not inconsistent with keeping an open mind and being willing to change your focus as you gain a better understanding of the behaviors in question. It merely simplifies the task of reducing all that you will observe to a manageable number of entries for your notes.

   This list will be nothing more than a set of broad categories of information you hope to obtain about the events you are observing. For example, if you were observing meetings of opposing teams of negotiators who represented two sides of a civil war, you might want to note such things as (1) how often each side initiates proposals, (2) how eager each side seems to be to continue the talks as opposed to breaking them off, (3) how willing each side is to make concessions, and (4) whether each negotiating team is united or seems divided into factions. As you learn more about the process, you will want to refine these broad, overlapping categories into a more focused list of things to look for, with each observation building on what you learned in the prior one.

2. *Avoid taking detailed notes in the presence of those who are being observed.* The primary reason for this is that open note-taking can make your subjects even more aware of your presence and cause them to alter their normal behavior. Your objective is to put the subjects so at ease that they act exactly as they would if you were not present. This requires that you develop the skill of

making *mental notes* of all that you see that is relevant to the study so that you can write up detailed notes later. This is a difficult task, so in advance of going to the field, it is wise to practice mental note-taking by observing activities similar to those you are to study and then trying to re-create the events on paper later. If the practice subjects agree and you have the necessary equipment and setting, you can check on your accuracy by recording or filming the events observed and comparing the recordings of the events with the impressions conveyed by your field notes.

Though you should not take detailed notes in the presence of subjects, it is sometimes possible to keep a small note pad concealed so you can inconspicuously jot down key words or phrases that will later serve to jog your memory of events when writing up field notes.

3. *Always write up field notes as soon as possible after actual observation* so that your memory of the events is clear. This is often difficult, because you may be tired at the end of several hours of observations and there may not be a convenient place to sit to write your notes. However, it is *essential* that you find a way to get the observations on paper as soon as possible so that you have a detailed and accurate record. Some investigators expedite this process by using a tape recorder to record their field notes verbally and then transcribe them later. If you choose this approach, it is crucial to check the tape immediately to ensure that it worked properly; in that way, you will avoid discovering several days later, when you may find it difficult to re-create them from memory, that notes from an observation session have been lost.

It may take up to half as much time to make notes on observations as it took to actually make the observations, but this is time well spent because *field notes are the foundation of a direct observation project.*

4. *Make field notes as complete and detailed as possible.* Especially in the early stages of a project, it is important to put in almost everything that was observed. Facts that at first seemed unimportant may turn out to be crucial as you acquire a fuller understanding of the topic.

5. *Always distinguish clearly in your notes between descriptions of actual behavior and your speculation about the meaning or importance of that behavior.* It should be clear to you, even after your memory of the events has faded, what was actually said and done by the subjects and what you *inferred* about their behavior at the time.

Because the content of field notes is dictated by the objectives of an individual project, it is difficult to state rules for what to include. In general, however, it is better to include too much than to risk leaving out useful information. Excessive detail in field notes may complicate the task of analyzing them, but this problem can be dealt with. There is no way to remedy the problem of not having information if you failed to put it in at the time of the observation. Remember that one of the major objectives of direct observation is the creation of a complete and accurate description of a political phenomenon. More detail, therefore, is usually preferable to less.

Figure 19.1 provides an example of the kind of information that is recorded in field notes. It presents observations from a hypothetical study of several community

Figure 19.1
Example of transcribed field notes from
hypothetical study of community organizations

October 24, 2004. Observation of a demonstration by members of the Waterside Neighborhood Improvement Association to protest the announcement by the city government of plans to open a landfill on some abandoned property in the Waterside neighborhood.

Background: The Waterside community is composed of large old homes that were left behind as members of the upper class abandoned the city for the suburbs in the 1950s and 1960s. Today it is a fairly poor area with few remaining local businesses and inhabited almost exclusively by Hispanics. The neighborhood organization was formed in 1985 to combat problems of crime, unemployment, and poor public services in the area.

Observations: The demonstration was held on the steps of city hall during the noon hour, when a large number of people were entering and leaving the building. The organization had obtained a permit from the police department, and all members remained on a grassy area beside the main entrance so that they did not block pedestrian traffic. Thirty-three members of the Waterside Association took part in the demonstration. In addition, there were two officials of the Catholic Church, the president of a statewide Hispanic political organization, and a member of the city council, who represents the neighborhood. The event was covered by two reporters from the local paper, a camera crew and reporter from each of the two local TV stations, and a reporter from National Public Radio.

The demonstration began promptly at noon and consisted of the following activities: (1) Throughout the demonstration, twelve of the participants waved handmade signs with slogans condemning the landfill. They were careful to face the TV cameras at all times. (2) The association president, the city councilman, and the state political leader (in that order) each stood on an old oil drum the demonstrators had brought to the site to make speeches lasting about 10 minutes each. (3) Between each speech, a very energetic member of the group used a megaphone to lead chants about the injustice of the landfill decision. The chants were defiant in tone (e.g., "We won't take your trash!"), and one accused the mayor of "selling out." All members of the association who attended the demonstration were very active during the action, shouting, cheering, clapping, calling out to passersby, and shaking their fists in the cameras. The demonstration ended with a short speech and prayer by one of the priests. The signs and chants were in English, but the speeches were primarily in Spanish. Each speaker referred at least once to the fact that Waterside was a Hispanic community. Each asked at least once why the landfill was not put in Carlton (an affluent, predominantly white neighborhood at the edge of the city that had been recommended by a consultant's study as the most logical site).

When she was not speaking, the president of the Waterside association was moving among the demonstrators, encouraging them to wave their signs, shout, and otherwise show their feelings. She pulled reporters into the middle of the group on three occasions and coached the camera crews on what to shoot. Comments made by the other speakers revealed she had personally invited them to attend and speak. While the group was returning to the neighborhood on a church bus borrowed for the occasion, the president made a statement about how she was sure that the event had made a difference and how important it was for Hispanics to stand up for their rights. She then went down the aisle and personally thanked everyone on the bus for taking part in the demonstration, using a lot of handshaking, backslapping, and hugs. Everyone else had carried out the tasks assigned to them, but no one seemed to share responsibility for making the demonstration work.

Comments: This group has a well-organized, highly disciplined core of active members and a good deal of support from other community institutions. The president, however, appears to be the main moving force. She seems to come up with most of the ideas and to mobilize others with her energy. The members seem to be motivated by a combination of ethnic pride and social solidarity. Much of what they do is predicated on their minority status, but they also seem to have developed a sense of comradeship in which each one carries on partly because they do not want to let the others down. The president apparently encourages both of these tendencies—perhaps because she knows that she can't promise the members much in the way of material rewards. I can't help but wonder how the organization would survive if she stepped down. She takes on so much responsibility that no one else seems to be getting any leadership training. Her strength may be the organization's weakness.

organizations in which the investigator is seeking to understand how leaders of these organizations persuade residents of a neighborhood to join and remain in the group. Note the detail in which events are recorded. Notice also how notes on actual events are set off from interpretations or analysis of those events.

The next stage in the direct observation project is to analyze the field notes. With other methods there is a clear distinction between data collection and data analysis. This is not true of direct observation because the process of making field notes blends both data collection (writing down descriptions of what happened) and analysis (noting your impressions about the reasons for or importance of what happened). *Data analysis begins with the making of field notes.* Moreover, in direct observation, the researcher must *not* wait until all the data are in to begin analysis. It is vital that investigators review field notes from time to time during the period in which they are making observations. The purpose of this is to begin to look for patterns in what has been observed so as to be alert to the most important aspects of events in the next observation session.

Once all observation has been completed, you will formally shift to data analysis. With direct observation data, this means *using inductive reasoning to discover patterns among the many discrete facts recorded in the field notes.* The first step is usually to review the notes in order to find some meaningful categories to use in distinguishing among the events observed.

An Example   Consider a hypothetical study of legislative committees designed to investigate the degree to which they are subject to influence by organized interest groups. You might observe the meetings of several committees and then ask: Are there any systematic differences in the way these groups function? After examining your notes, you may decide that the groups differ along two important dimensions: the degree to which power is centralized in the formal leaders versus being widely shared among the members, and the degree to which the groups are businesslike and rule-driven in transacting their business versus being more collegial and relying on personal interaction. If we break these two dimensions in the middle and juxtapose them, we get the typology of committee operating styles presented in Figure 19.2, and we have a way of classifying committees for analysis.

The next step in analysis would be to examine the field notes for evidence of differences *between* and *within* categories or types. For example, we might ask if committees of different types responded differently to interest groups and if the same type of committee treated different types of interest groups differently. We might ask if it seems to be easier for interest groups to gain access to some types of committees than to others or if the ease of access depends more on the characteristics of the

Style of Operation	Power Configuration	
	Decentralized	Centralized
Collegial	Populist	Machine
Rule driven	Democratic	Authoritarian

Figure 19.2
Hypothetical typology of congressional committees

interest group (such as how well financed it is, how professional its lobbying staff is, or how politically active it is in the representatives' home districts).

The major challenge in both taking and analyzing field notes is to avoid the natural tendency to see only what you expect to see. If you are to gain a truly accurate understanding of these events, it is crucial to be open to the possibility that things do not work as you expect and *to avoid imposing patterns* that are not there. One technique for keeping an open mind about your subject and ensuring that you are not overlooking important relationships is to occasionally ask trusted colleagues who are *not* involved with your research project to read over portions of your field notes and share with you their impressions of what is going on. They may be able to see patterns that your preconceived theory of the events has hidden from you.

Techniques of Structured Observation

If unstructured observation is used to gain a more refined and accurate understanding of political behavior so that we can develop theories of it, structured observation is used to verify the utility of our understandings and to test hypotheses derived from our theories. Conducting a structured observation requires that we have a clear idea of what we expect to see when we observe and what specific behaviors we are looking for. We are interested primarily in *recording specific behaviors*, not in finding the meaning our subjects attach to their behaviors or patterns in those behaviors. It is similar to carrying out a survey or a content analysis in that we are guided by an instrument that makes our observation very systematic and facilitates recording what we see in ways that make comparing cases easier. In direct observation, this instrument is known as an *observation schedule*.

Designing an Observation Schedule   An **observation schedule** is a detailed list of specific things to be observed and a system for recording them. The content and design of observation schedules depend on the nature of the research project and can vary widely, so that it is difficult to provide firm guidelines for their construction. Our objective here is merely to suggest some very general rules to follow and techniques to use in designing useful observation schedules.

Before we turn to a discussion of those rules, it is important to mention three features of structured observation that set the context for development of an observation schedule. First, recall that structured observations may be either obtrusive or unobtrusive. However, because the observer must pay attention to a great many details and is most concerned with precision in recording events, *it is essential that observations be recorded as they are made*. As a result, structured observations run a greater risk of creating reactivity than unstructured ones do when they are done obtrusively. Subjects who see an observer busily taking notes on their actions are very likely to be keenly aware that they are being studied and may alter their behavior as a result. Structured techniques, then, are probably most effective when used unobtrusively.

An additional implication of the need in structured observation to record events as they happen is that *it is almost never possible to use structured techniques in a participant observation*. It would be virtually impossible to keep detailed records of behaviors while acting as a participant and would almost certainly give away your purpose in being there.

The second contextual feature of structured methods to consider before discussing the construction of observation schedules is that structured observations are often made by someone *other than the principal investigator*. Because the observations are more routine and often more numerous than those involved in unstructured methods, researchers commonly hire assistants to carry out the observations. This means that the observation schedule must be detailed and informative enough that it (1) can be used by an assistant *as the researcher intends it to be used* and (2) leaves very little discretion to the observer, so that the observations recorded by different assistants can legitimately be compared.

Finally, it is important to recognize the basic design of a structured observation in order to understand what is needed in an observation schedule. This design involves first identifying a *unit of analysis* for the study. In direct observation, units of analysis usually consist of recurring events. Examples include reaching a compromise at a negotiating session, debating a motion before the U.N. Security Council, and arguing between members of opposing groups at a demonstration in front of a clinic providing abortions.

After identification of a unit of analysis, the next step is to *designate the aspects of that event to be observed*. Here is where the observation schedule comes in. An observation schedule is far more than a simple checklist in several ways: (1) It often provides more than simple *yes* or *no* options for recording behaviors. Observers are usually asked to record events in degrees or frequencies. (2) It usually contains instructions on *how* to conduct the observations by telling the observer what procedures to follow. (3) It generally includes some fairly detailed definitions of the behaviors to be observed so that observers know what to look for.

That last feature is vitally important. An observation schedule *is always based on operational definitions of the behaviors in question*. If it is to be useful, it must reduce a set of potentially complex events to basic elements, so that the observer can be sure when the event has been observed and can distinguish it from other, similar behaviors or events. To do this, an observation schedule breaks events into discrete variables, gives the observer an operational definition of each, and provides a scheme for recording observations of each variable.

An Example   Returning to the example of the study of the operating styles of congressional committees, one unit of analysis for such a study might be a public disagreement among members of the committee. The researcher would need to define what constitutes a disagreement and then identify the features of the event (the variables) to be observed—that is, the dimensions along which to classify each disagreement. These dimensions can be highly specific or quite broad. In the committee study, we might want to know something as specific as how often the parties to the disagreement interrupted each other, whether or not certain words were used by either side, and who spoke last. Alternatively, the dimensions may be as broad as whether the tone of the argument was hostile or cordial, whether or not it seemed to be conducted within mutually accepted norms, or what role the committee chair played in mediating the argument.

Which approach is better depends on the specific research project. However, *the broader the dimensions to be observed, the greater the discretion the observer has in classifying events*. More narrow dimensions may seem to trivialize the subject, but they have the advantage of limiting observers' discretion and, thereby, producing data that are more standardized and more comparable from observation to observation. Researchers are usually well-advised to be *as specific as possible* in constructing an observation schedule.

A major reason for this is that one of the most important rules for designing an observation schedule is that *the categories used to classify events must be exhaustive and mutually exclusive.* It must be possible to place all observed events in some category. However, it must not be logically possible to place any single observation in more than one category. The best way to achieve this mutual exclusivity of categories is to be very specific—to break larger variables down into smaller ones. For example, rather than asking the general question about whether or not a disagreement seemed to be governed by mutually accepted norms, we might ask if the parties to the argument interrupted one another, raised their voices, or yielded the floor promptly when asked to do so by the chair.

Figure 19.3 is a segment of a hypothetical study of community organizations in which the meeting is the unit of analysis. Note that some items require only that the observer record objectively verifiable information about the meeting (when it started, how many people were in attendance, etc.), whereas other items require a judgment on the part of the observer (whether the members paid attention to the chair when he or she spoke, if the members were cordial and friendly to each other before the opening of the meeting, etc.). This mix is almost inevitable, but the investigator should provide observers with clear instructions on how to make a judgment about those matters that require judgment. It is wise to check their understanding of these instructions by having the assistant record observations of an event that the researcher also observes and then comparing the assistant's classification of events with those of the investigator.

Assessing Reliability and Validity   Those who use structured observation to gather data have to be just as concerned with the validity and reliability of their measurements as those who use other data collection techniques. It is therefore important to build into the data-collection effort ways to check on this. When data from an observation schedule are quantitative, they can be analyzed with standard statistical techniques and are subject to the same tests of validity and reliability discussed in Chapter 5.

However, the observation schedule almost always gives observers some degree of discretion about how to record events. Therefore, if more than one observer is used, it is also especially important to pay attention to **interobserver reliability**—the degree to which different observers classify similar events in the same way on the observation schedule. This is essentially the same as the problem of intercoder reliability in content analysis and can be verified by procedures similar to those discussed in Chapter 10. It is crucial, however, that investigators build into the instrument and data-collection procedure the means of collecting the information they will need to verify the validity and reliability of their measures.

It is also a good idea to *pretest the observation schedule and procedure* before beginning actual field work. A pretest involves the researcher and/or assistants using the schedule to record an event like the one you are studying to be sure that the categories are exhaustive and mutually exclusive, that the instructions on the form are

---

COMMUNITY ORGANIZATION OBSERVATION SCHEDULE

1. a. Name of organization _____
    b. Date and time of meeting _____
    c. Location of meeting _____
    d. Nature of meeting: *(1) regular business*
                              (2) annual meeting
                              (3) special or emergency
                              (8) other _____
    e. Purpose of meeting: *(1) routine business*
                              (2) to elect officers
                              (3) to discuss a problem
                              (4) social gathering
                              (5) to recognize members/accomplishments
                              (8) other _____

2. Premeeting socializing: *(1) less than half participated*
                              (2) about half participated
                              (3) most members participated

3. a. Was there a written agenda for the meeting?   YES   NO
    b. If yes, was it distributed to the members?   YES   NO
    c. If yes, when was it distributed?   *(1) before the day of the meeting*
                                          (2) just prior to the meeting
                                          (3) after the meeting

4. How many people attended the meeting? _____

5. a. Was the meeting open to the public? YES   NO
    b. How many persons who were apparently not members attended? _____
    c. Were any nonmembers on the formal program? YES   NO
    d. If yes, who (city council member, police officer, etc.)? _____

6. Who presided at the meeting (by office)? _____

7. What other persons had a formal role in the meeting (made a presentation, gave a report, etc.)? _____
    _____
    _____

8. Did the presiding officer say that members were encouraged to speak during the meeting? YES   NO

9. How many members made comments or asked questions during the meeting? [Use tic marks to keep
    track.]
    _____

10. How closely were parliamentary procedures followed in managing the meeting?
    _____   *(1) not at all*
    _____   *(2) loosely*
    _____   *(3) fairly closely*
    _____   *(4) strictly*

Figure 19.3
Partial observation schedule for a hypothetical study of community organizations
(continued on next page)

---

11. What were the main topics discussed during the program?

    a. _____

    b. _____

    c. _____

    d. _____

    e. _____

12. a. How many formal votes were taken? [Use tic marks to keep track.]

    b. How was voting done?   *(1) show of hands*

                                (2) voice vote

                                (3) paper ballot

                                (8) other _____

    c. What was the issue and outcome on each vote taken?

                ISSUE   OUTCOME

    Vote 1: _____

    Vote 2: _____

    Vote 3: _____

    Vote 4: _____

    Vote 5: _____

                         (CONTINUE ON BACK IF NEEDED)

Figure 19.3

Partial observation schedule for a hypothetical study of community organizations

easy to follow, and that the explanations of how to classify are clear enough that different observers can agree on the coding for the same or highly similar behaviors and events.

Sampling Procedures in Direct Observation

After identifying a set of behaviors to treat as a unit of analysis, we must decide which of these units to study. Because we cannot observe all instances of the behaviors that serve as our units of analysis, we are forced to select a sample of them.

Representative Sampling   The objective of this sampling—as in survey research or other methods of data collection—is *to examine a representative group of cases.* We want to understand how the events in question *usually* happen and do not want to be misled by observing atypical episodes. However, what we are sampling is not people or nations or publications, but events and behaviors. The important point about this is that we can seldom predict in advance when (and sometimes where) these events will take place. As a result, it is often impossible to apply standard random sampling procedures to the type of events that are most often studied through direct observation.

    The sampling procedure that *is* used depends on the nature of the study. If the events reoccur on a regular basis and occur frequently enough, it may be possible to take a random sample of these events to study. For instance, if we were studying the way a large administrative agency processes citizens' complaints, and we knew that formal complaints were accepted in a specific office every workday between the hours of 2 P.M. and 5 P.M., and that the agency heard an average of fifteen complaints a day, we could set up rules for drawing a random sample of the anticipated complaints. In the room where complaints were received, we could station observers on random days with instructions to record the details of the handling of the eighth complaint brought each day until some statistically-determined minimum number had been observed. We could have a good deal of confidence in the representativeness of this sample because of the number and regularity of the events.

However, if there are far fewer instances of our units of analysis or if we cannot predict when or where they will occur, then standard sampling procedures cannot be relied on to yield a good sample. To illustrate this, let us change the above example to say that the agency scheduled the hearing of complaints *only once a month* at a regular time and heard an average of only four complaints at each session. We could sample by way of the procedure just described, but would have to observe the organization over *many* months before our random procedure had produced a representative sample (because random procedures are not dependable with small numbers of cases). We may not be able to stretch our research out over such a long period.

To modify the example again, assume that the agency accepted complaints at a window in its offices *at any time of any workday.* Because we cannot predict when citizens will show up with complaints, it is impossible to apply standard sampling procedures to select complaints. However, if we had reason to believe that complaints were fairly evenly spaced throughout the day and the week, we could divide the workweek into hours and sample certain *time periods*. Observers could watch the window at preselected hours of specified days of the week and record any complaints filed at those times. With a sufficiently large number of complaints, this could provide a representative sample. However, if the number of complaints is small (only one or two each day, for instance), most observation periods would not include a complaint, and it would again take a *very* long time to observe enough complaints to have confidence in our sample. This would be both time-consuming and extremely expensive.

When we turn from events that occur with some regularity to more sporadic events, sampling problems become even greater. To stay with our administrative example, say that we are concerned with complaints made only by certain types of citizens (elderly persons, minority-group members, etc.) or only with a certain type of complaint (like those that involve allegations of nonenforcement of a specific rule, or gender discrimination in service delivery). We have no way of knowing when and if such complaints will arise and cannot effectively sample them using some variant of random sampling.

Judgmental Sampling   When we are studying a behavior that occurs infrequently or without warning, we almost always have to rely on a *judgmental sample* as described in Chapter 7. We use what we know about the nature of the event to select a set of occurrences that will be *typical* of the behavior of interest if not representative in a strictly statistical sense. The task in judgmental sampling is to select for observation events that informed readers of the research can be persuaded are likely to be representative.

To illustrate, say that our study of complaint-handling was focused entirely on complaints about nonenforcement of agency rules and that we knew from agency records or prior research that complaints of this type came almost exclusively from low-income communities. We might choose to observe only complaints filed at those agency offices serving low-income neighborhoods in the hope of locating enough complaints of the desired type. If background research makes it possible to build a statistical profile of the events we want to study (when and where they happen most often, what types of people participate, how long they last, etc.), this information can assist in the judgmental selection of typical cases.

Coping with Method Effects in Direct Observation

In Chapter 6 we pointed out that researchers must always be alert to the possibility that their data collection efforts have, in some way, influenced the data that are obtained and have produced an inaccurate picture of the reality they hope to understand. For example, because people tend to give what they feel are socially acceptable answers to survey questions regardless of their true feelings, one effect of using the personal interview to gather data is a tendency to *understate* the occurrence of behaviors and attitudes that are contrary to dominant social norms. This impact is referred to as a **method effect**.

Minimizing Reactivity   The possibility of a method effect is especially high in direct observation for at least two reasons. First, in most direct observations, researchers are in closer and more extended contact with the subjects than with other methods, so there are more opportunities for the observer's actions or presence to influence subjects' behavior. We call this effect *reactivity*. Second, because observers exercise so much discretion in determining what to record and how to record it, direct-observation data are heavily influenced by observers' values and expectations. We call this effect *bias*. If we fail to minimize these method effects, we lose the main advantage of direct observation—the high degree of external validity it provides our research.

Which strategies are appropriate for minimizing method effects depends on the character of the specific project. We can, however, offer some general guidelines. The most effective means of coping with reactivity is to employ *unobtrusive observation,* because subjects who are not aware they are being observed do not react to being studied. Investigators should always consider the possibility of arranging an unobtrusive observation. However, as we explained earlier, it is often impossible to use unobtrusive methods and, as we will soon discuss, it may sometimes be judged unethical to do so.

Moreover, one particular technique of unobtrusive study—participant observation—may not get around reactivity problems even when it is possible. Even if the observer's identity and purpose are concealed from members of the group, the observer's actions *as a member of the group* can cause other members to act differently from ways they otherwise would. If a researcher posing as a member of a political organization takes part in the group's debate about what action to take in response to some new threat to its interest, for example, that participation may sway the decision. Similarly, the researcher's work on one of the organization's projects may lead to its success when it otherwise would have failed or to its failure when it otherwise would have succeeded.

This sort of effect is difficult to avoid if the investigator is to retain credibility as a devoted member of the organization, but observers have to be very sensitive to it and attempt to strike the delicate balance between losing credibility and actually shaping the events they are trying to study. It is also important to attempt to judge the degree to which researcher participation influenced outcomes, so that this effect can be discounted in attempting to form an accurate picture of the processes under investigation.

When obtrusive methods are the only possibility, researchers can still take steps to minimize reactivity. The key to success in this lies in investigators' ability to *control their relationship to the subjects and the subjects' perception of the researcher.* Researchers must consciously manipulate subjects' perception of their character, values, and purpose in order to put the subjects so at ease that they behave as they normally would. Subjects must come either to ignore the observer as harmless, or to trust the observer enough to reveal their true feelings and behavior patterns. To accomplish the first end, observers must **blend in;** to accomplish the second, they must **fit in.**

Blending In   Observers can use several tactics to *blend in.* (1) They can physically stay in the background or at the margins of any action they are observing so that subjects easily forget their presence when focusing on the activity. (This practice often has the added advantage of placing observers in a location that provides a good vantage point from which to view the entire scene at once.) (2) Observers can adopt a passive manner, which makes it easy for others to overlook them or to consider them unthreatening. In this mode, they will certainly want to avoid commenting on what they see or confronting subjects in any way. (3) Observers can exercise patience and perseverance by showing up again and again so that they become commonplace and subjects begin to relax in their presence. The objective is to make the process of observation seem normal to the subjects—part of everyday life. This can take a great deal of time to accomplish. (4) Observers can blend into the group physically by grooming themselves and dressing in a manner that is inconspicuous under the circumstances. Wear what the subjects wear, but be careful to avoid violating any dress codes that may exist in the group by, for instance, wearing something recognized as a symbol of rank in the group or something reserved for persons with special status in the group. (5) Researchers can blend in socially by learning to converse comfortably with the subjects. This involves talking about things that are common topics of conversation among the subjects, using a personal style that is appropriate to the norms of the group (loud and outgoing or reserved and introspective, openly sharing feelings or putting up a front, frequently touching the subject or keeping your hands to yourself, etc.), and respecting any clear role definitions within the group such as a norm that says that women don't talk about politics or that younger members don't volunteer information about themselves unless asked by an elder. It is important not to carry this too far by trying to imitate subjects' speech patterns, mannerisms, or dress if it seems unnatural for the observer to act that way. An observer with a strong New England accent probably should *not* dress like a cowboy in an effort to study the political culture of western bars. Unnatural behavior will only attract attention and may be seen as an insult to the group.

Fitting In Observers can *fit in* by using some of these same tactics. However, fitting in demands much more interaction between observer and subjects than blending in. It is a much greater concern in participant observation than in nonparticipant observation. Fitting in requires that the researcher consciously project an image as one of the group. This is done primarily by expressing values consistent with those of the subjects (perhaps a disregard for authority, prejudice toward some other group, or acceptance of a given political ideology). Behaving like one of the subject group may be necessary to build trust, but it has its dangers.

There is sometimes a risk that adopting the identity of a group member will make observers lose their objectivity about the study. Coming to see the world as subjects see it is known as **going native.** Investigators must be alert to this prospect because going native can prevent researchers from gaining scientifically useful insight into the behaviors under study. This is not a simple matter, because there is a fine line between going native and "getting inside" subjects to understand their motivations, values, and the like. Successful researchers can get close to subjects without losing sight of their objectives and interpretive framework.

Observers who seek to fit in also face ethical problems if they find that they must deceive subjects. They are very likely to have to lie about how they feel, what they have done, how they live, their background, and so on. We address this problem in the last section of this chapter.

Avoiding Personal Bias Another method effect associated with direct observation is the bias that can result when observers' values or expectations influence their perception and interpretation of what they see. Direct observation is especially subject to this danger because, with this method, *the observer is the primary instrument of measurement.* Bias can result from a researcher's rigid adherence to preconceptions about the phenomena under study or from a researcher's uncritically accepting the perspective and interpretations of the subjects (going native). Avoiding bias requires being both open-minded about and detached from the subject of our studies. Several strategies can help achieve this end.

First, in obtrusive research when observer and subjects can interact, observers can avoid letting their preconceptions lead them to wrong conclusions by periodically *checking their interpretations of what they see with the subjects.* For example, rather than simply assuming we know what motivates subjects to take a particular action, we can ask subjects why they did what they did. Their understandings of the situation or their values may be so different from the researcher's that their motivations are just the opposite of what the researcher had thought. Someone from an industrialized nation might think the harsh punishment of a Third World child by its parents is motivated by spite and the desire to inflict pain. In fact, the parents may act as they do because they love the child and want to make it strong enough to survive the hardships of life in a harsh environment. Similarly, researchers may assign meaning to events that subjects do not. An example would be the case in which an observer interprets as a danger signal a group of teenagers "hanging out" on a block, but a local resident knows the youths and views them as protecting the block from intruders by their presence.

It is wise to ask subjects how they interpret events before making assumptions. However, it is important to be subtle in asking these questions, phrasing them in terms familiar to the subjects, and presenting them as concerned inquiries, not demands for explanations. After observing a heated verbal exchange, for example, an observer should not ask, "Why were you so hostile toward her?" but may ask, "Do you think she will be mad about this?" to find out if the actor saw the exchange in the same terms as the observer. This does *not* mean that observers should let subjects determine their analysis of events, but only that they should check to see if subjects are thinking what the observers believe they are thinking.

Second, observers can avoid the mistake of seeing events too much as subjects see them by (1) periodically discussing with someone outside the study what they have seen and how they interpret it and (2) soliciting the views of persons who are marginal to the group, such as the lone environmentalist on a city planning commission generally unconcerned about environmental issues, or people who have recently moved back into a community after living elsewhere. Such persons can be a valuable resource for researchers, because they have the insight born of close association with the events in question but can still take a critical perspective on those events.

Third, it is often useful to blend direct observation with some other form of data collection so the other data can be used to verify impressions formed from direct observation. A direct-observation study of the effect of crime on citizens' behaviors might be augmented by a survey in which the same people who had been observed are asked direct questions about how fearful they are and how their behavior has changed as a result of their fear. The survey would not provide as much detailed data as the direct observation and may have less external validity. It could, however, be used to verify impressions gained from direct observation by asking such questions as, "Do respondents see the actions that observers attributed to fear (e.g., staying off the streets at night) as being motivated by fear of crime or do they have other explanations for this?" A wide variety of data sources (content analysis, public records, etc.) can serve this verification function.

These and other means of *cross-validating* the conclusions drawn from observation can reduce the degree of subjectivity involved in the method and add significantly to the degree to which results are accepted as valid.

The Ethics of Direct Observation

Any research project can raise questions of what is ethically right or fair. The unique features of direct observation make it even more likely that researchers will confront questions of ethics. The two areas in which ethical issues are most likely to arise concern *the relationship of the researcher to the subjects* and *the reactions of the researcher to what is observed*.

Ethics in Relationships   Problems can arise in the relationship of the observer to the observed, because there is often a fundamental tension between being honest and obtaining scientifically valid information. If subjects know they are being studied or know why they are being studied, they may refuse to cooperate or may alter their behavior in ways that make it impossible to secure a valid answer to a research question. Yet, getting around these problems by using unobtrusive observation or by concealing the true purpose of the study from subjects involves some degree of deception. Investigators are most likely to face choices about whether or not to use deception with regard to (1) *the grounds on which they gain access to opportunities to observe* and (2) *the development of trust between themselves and their subjects.* We can examine these issues in turn.

If it is possible to observe subjects without their knowledge, observers first face the question of whether or not to tell subjects they are being studied. The issue here is whether the researcher has a right to watch and possibly report people's actions when they have not given their consent and cannot control what the observer sees or reports. Researchers confront a similar situation when they tell subjects they are being studied but deceive them as to the purpose of the study. Are such actions an invasion of privacy and a denial of the fundamental human right to control of our lives?

This is seldom a simple issue. It is often possible to argue *in favor* of deception in a given project for any of several reasons: (1) Subjects will not be harmed in any way by being observed, given the purposes of the study. (2) Researchers will keep subjects' identity secret in any reports from the study, so no one will be hurt. (3) Subjects would agree to the study if they were given the opportunity to do so but cannot be asked in advance without risking reactivity. (4) The good that will come from the findings of the study outweighs any harm that may be done to subjects through the deception. Researchers, funding agencies, sponsoring agencies, and critics must decide whether these are valid arguments in any given case by careful examination of the facts of the situation.

Ethical questions can arise with respect to the issue of trust between observer and observed. First, in order to gain subjects' trust, observers may have to lie about who they are, why they are there, how they feel about events, and so forth. Moreover, once trust is established, do researchers have the right to use what is told them in confidence to advance the purposes of the research or to report such information in a write-up of the project? Can deception be justified in the name of science when we abhor its use for personal, political, or financial gain? Deception at this stage can sometimes be justified by the same kind of arguments previously cited.

Ethics in Personal Feelings   Another arena in which ethical issues may arise deals with the observer's reactions to what is observed. Those who investigate behaviors that are potentially illegal or morally repugnant to society put themselves in situations in which they may witness actions that outrage or disgust them. Some actions may impose a moral obligation to report the events to some authority. At other times, observers may witness actions in which their own moral code demands that they intervene to stop.

Consider the example of a researcher engaged in participant observation of the politics of Neo-Nazi skinheads. What if the skinheads shout insults at and spit on minority children? What if they vandalize a synagogue? What if they beat up an elderly Jewish man? Researchers who react as their value system dictates would "blow their cover" and put an end to the project. (To keep the case as simple as possible, assume that such reactions would not endanger the researcher.) What are the researcher's obligations in this situation? Can the need to understand what motivates people to join such groups and how the groups function outweigh the obligation to express personal moral outrage? Can it negate the obligation to report violations of the law? Can it possibly justify allowing someone to be physically harmed? How do we balance long-term objectives against the short-term need for justice? How do we balance benefits to society (in this case, added knowledge about how to control a problem) against the welfare of individuals who may be harmed if we do not act?

These questions have to be answered in the context of a specific research project and situation. The value of some projects will justify actions that could not be justified by others. On rare occasions it is possible to come up with creative arrangements that allow researchers to minimize ethical dilemmas. For instance, it may be possible to observe without informing subjects but to tell them later, show them how the observations of their behavior will be used, and give them the right to veto use of the data. In most cases, however, investigators must confront ethical questions head-on and make hard choices between unattractive alternatives.

The important point is that it is vital that those who plan to use direct observation consider *in advance* the ethical implications of their decision. Before putting themselves in situations that pose ethical dilemmas, researchers should think through the problems that are likely to arise, and they should weigh the relative value of the good of the project against the rights of subjects or social and moral obligations. Most important, they must *be very clear about their own values* and, if at all possible, *decide in advance where they will draw the line in cases of ethical conflict.*

Scientific knowledge may be of such great value to society that acquiring it sometimes justifies exceptions to normal rules of conduct. However, it is very clear that science must always be viewed as a means to the end of improving the human condition, not as an end in itself. Some values are so basic that they should never be sacrificed even in pursuit of knowledge.

Conclusion

Direct observation techniques of information gathering are an important tool for social science inquiry. They can offer unique access to aspects of interesting phenomena that cannot effectively be studied using other methods. Both quantitative and qualitative researchers should actively consider these methods as a possible way of seeking answers to the questions they are investigating. However, direct observation must not be undertaken without a full understanding of its processes, serious consideration of its potential drawbacks, and careful planning and preparation.

This is true because direct observation techniques place field researchers in situations that can be both professionally and personally risky. They rely to a greater degree than most other methods on the judgment and skills of individual researchers, and can, in some circumstances, cause researchers to directly confront the most difficult questions of personal and professional ethics. Against these risks, researchers must balance the exceptional potential for gaining valid insights that direct observation can offer and the personal and professional growth that can result from meeting its unique challenges.

As you read research reports based on direct observation, you should keep all dimensions of this method in mind. To look carefully for evidence that biases have been introduced into the findings of the research by the peculiar features of direct observation you will need to know as much about the research design and its implementation as possible. Always ask what steps the researchers(s) took to get around the potential pitfalls described in this chapter, and be cautious about accepting its conclusions until you are satisfied.

Summary Points

• When researchers are seeking to develop a theory or gain a complex and subtle understanding of a phenomenon, they may use direct observation techniques.
• Direct observation makes special demands on the researcher if it is to reach valid, intersubjective conclusions, but it can produce empirical analyses.
• The major advantage of direct observation is that it can provide a very high level of external validity by observing events in "real world" settings, and it (potentially) minimizes research reactivity.
• The disadvantages of direct observation include the intensive demands it makes on the researcher, the time and resources it requires, and an enhanced risk that subjective factors will affect the validity of conclusions.
• Direct observation methods are divided into obtrusive and unobtrusive, structured and unstructured, and passive and participant observation techniques.
• Because it requires intensive contact with subjects in "real world" settings, direct observation can pose numerous ethical challenges for researchers. To meet these challenges, researchers need to be clear about their own values, weigh the importance of the research against other values, and try to anticipate ethical issues they may confront in specific projects.

Suggested Readings and References

General introductions to direct observation methods include Jennifer Mason, *Qualitative Researching*, 2nd ed. (Thousand Oaks, CA: Sage, 2002) and Gretchen Rossman and Sharon Rallis, *Learning in the Field: An Introduction to Qualitative Research* (Thousand Oaks, CA: Sage, 2003). Principles of direct observation are addressed in Raymond M. Lee, *Unobtrusive Methods in Social Research* (Philadelphia, PA: Open University Press, 2000). Participant-observation techniques are discussed in Kathleen Musante Dewalt and Billie R. Dewalt, *Participant Observation* (Lanham, MD: Rowman & Littlefield, 2002). Issues in the analysis of data obtained from direct observation are addressed in David Silverman, *Interpreting Qualitative Data Methods for Analyzing Talk, Text and Interaction*, 2nd ed. (Thousand Oaks, CA: Sage, 2001).

Research Exercises

1. Develop a research question that can be answered through direct observation about one of the politically oriented student groups on your campus—groups like Progressive Student Alliance and College Republicans. (For example, you might ask if the role of female members is different in liberal and conservative groups or what common values members of the group share beyond their political ideals.) Write out a list of the things you would have to observe in the group to answer this question.

2. Attend a meeting of the student group and observe it according to the list you developed for the previous exercise. Keep mental notes and write up formal field notes immediately afterward. Then write a short essay on what you learned that you had not expected to.

How did what you saw and heard differ from the way you thought things would work? How would you modify your list of things to look for in light of what you actually observed?

As an extension of this exercise, have another student in your class observe the same meeting and write up a set of field notes independently. Then compare your notes with the other student's and write a description of the ways in which they differ and the points on which they agree.

3. Devise a simple prediction about the operation of your city council. (For example, "Economic issues will produce more serious disagreements than social issues.") Develop an observational schedule that fully operationalizes the concepts involved in the prediction and any strong rival interpretations you feel you would have to be able to rule out before having confidence in the original prediction. Observe at least two meetings of the council and use the observation schedule to record what you see. Write an essay both on what you concluded about your prediction and on how you would change the observation schedule after having had some experience with it. What shortcomings did you find?

Key Terms

direct observation
obtrusive research
unobtrusive research
passive observation
participant observation
structured observation
observation protocol
unstructured observation

field notes
observation schedule
interobserver reliability
method effect
blending in
fitting in
going native

CHAPTER 20

Focus Group Methodologies

- What is focus group methodology and when should it be used?
- What are the advantages and limitations of focus group methodology?
- How are focus groups conducted and how are the data analyzed?
- How can focus group methodology be used with other methods?

Researchers sometimes want to study questions that others have not investigated, or they may want to gain a fresh perspective in an area where past research has failed to resolve major questions. In such cases, they will be unable to rely on prior theories or empirical studies to guide their efforts. If the phenomenon in question is new (or at least new to social science researchers), there may not even be firsthand knowledge of the events in question. In these situations, scholars may need to gather information through the use of focus groups.

At the most basic level, **focus group** methods involve bringing together small groups of carefully selected individuals for an in-depth discussion of some topic, guided by a **moderator,** in order to learn how people think about that topic. Focus groups can be used for different purposes at different stages of the research process. They can help formulate hypotheses for future studies, develop indicators to be used in data collection, improve the interpretation of data collected by other means, or produce data that are directly useful in answering a research question.

This chapter explains why and when researchers might use focus group methods either as their primary methodology or in support of other data-collection methods. It then describes some of the basic rules for conducting focus groups and using the information they produce.

Why Use Focus Groups?

Focus group methods were developed in the 1940s by researchers who wanted to get as realistic a view of people's thinking as possible. Government agencies, political advisors, and social scientists have been making more use of focus groups in recent years, but the approach has been used most extensively in *market research* to help businesses explore aspects of consumer behavior as part of their effort to develop and sell products. Businesses often use focus groups to gain insights into such questions as how consumers will react to a new product, how effective a proposed advertising campaign might be, and why consumers prefer one product over another.

Limitations of Surveys Survey research or individual interviews can often be used for these purposes, but early researchers recognized at least five limitations to survey-based methods.

1. Respondents can give us only the information we know to ask for, and many problems may have aspects that researchers will not think to ask about. For example, in a survey, we might ask a random sample of voters to rate two opposing candidates on each of five dimensions that we feel will determine how voters decide among candidates. We might then be surprised to find that the candidate who earned the higher rating did not win the election because voters used a different set of criteria in making their actual choice. Even if voters answered our questions honestly, we had asked the wrong questions.

2. Even if one uses open-ended questions, respondents may be influenced by the style in which questions are asked or by subtle aspects of their interaction with the interviewer and may not give valid answers.

3. Surveys are very expensive and time-consuming. If we don't have a clear understanding of what we want to know and how to ask questions in order to get that information from respondents, we run the risk of making a large investment to obtain useless data.

4. Survey results are not always "self-explanatory" because it is always possible that respondents interpreted questions differently from the interpretations the researchers intended and that respondents' answers meant something different to them than they meant to the researchers.

5. People do not make decisions in isolation but are influenced by others' opinions and reactions. A survey interview, however, asks people to act in isolation from their social context in expressing opinions or making judgments. As a result, the data produced by a survey or interview may not accurately reflect social reality.

Limitations of Direct Observations   To avoid these limitations of interview-based data collection, researchers could turn to direct observation. While that approach may be very valuable for certain research questions, it may be inappropriate for others. Scholars who are interested in a fairly narrow subject may face four problems with direct observation.

An Example   To illustrate the challenges of direct observations, let us use the subject of how heterosexuals perceive the goals of the gay rights movement. First, it may be difficult to find a site at which to observe interaction on this topic. Where can researchers go to be sure they will hear a discussion of the gay rights movement by non-gays? Second, in a natural setting, it may be necessary to observe *many* hours of discussion of other topics in order to hear a few minutes of conversation about gay rights. Third, even if the subject comes up, the discussion may not address the aspects of the issue that are of interest to researchers since, in direct observation, researchers have no way to guide the discussion. Finally, even in natural settings, discussion may be artificially constrained. For example, people who work together may avoid expressing political disagreement for fear that they will damage relationships in the workplace. Properly designed and executed focus groups can help overcome all of these problems.

Advantages of Focus Groups   The central feature of focus group methods is that they *rely on interaction among the participants to generate insights into the subject under study.* As you will see when we describe the technique, focus groups enable their members to interact in a "safe" environment with very little direction from the researcher. As a result, participants have a chance to express their true feelings on the topic under study and can bring up any aspect of that topic that they feel is important. The group process may also allow them to come to understandings about the topic that none of them could have achieved alone.

This means that focus groups have three substantive advantages: they *may* provide more accurate insights into what people actually think than do other techniques that involve more influence from the researcher; they can produce results that reflect social realities more accurately than methods that ask people to act in isolation; and they give us the ability to study *group dynamics* in ways that other techniques do not. In addition, focus groups offer some practical advantages: First, though they are *not* inexpensive, focus groups typically cost far less than a large survey and take far less time than direct observation. Second, because focus groups do not require elaborate measuring instruments and procedures, they can usually be conducted with far less preparation than interview-based research or even direct observation. This saves time and money.

Limitations of Focus Groups   Like other methods, focus group research has its potential drawbacks. We will describe four common limitations and suggest ways to cope with them. Each of the limitations may affect any given focus group session, but they do not all affect every focus group project equally. This is because there are many different ways to structure focus groups and because focus groups are held for many different purposes. If recognized and properly addressed, the limitations of focus groups need not damage the usefulness of the method.

First, focus group research may yield *subjective interpretations*. The primary product of a focus group is a *transcript* of what was said. To contribute to our understanding, this transcript must be interpreted by someone. Since the transcript does not consist of numerical data that can be subjected to statistical tests, its interpretation inevitably involves more subjectivity than do the analyses associated with other methods. As a result of differences in their own background or values, different observers may reach different conclusions about what "lessons" are to be learned from the focus group.

Remember that the interpretation of quantitative data can also be subject to debate. We are saying only that focus groups are more prone to the interpretation problem than some other methods are, and *not* that focus groups have this problem when other approaches do not.

Since subjectivity is inherent in the interpretation of focus group sessions, the only protection against being misled by it is some combination of the following steps: Researchers must be honest with themselves about their biases and try to be as objective as possible. They can bring in disinterested but qualified persons to do independent interpretations of the focus group results. They can also share their work with other scholars who can judge the validity of their interpretation and suggest alternatives before they consider their conclusions final. In addition, when writing up the study, researchers can faithfully describe enough of what was said to allow others to draw their own conclusions.

A second limitation is that the small number of people that can be involved in any focus group offers *limited representativeness* of any larger population. As a result, we cannot generalize to the larger population with the same precision or confidence that we can when larger samples are used. Additionally, there is always the chance that even carefully selected groups may be atypical of the population and thereby lead us to incorrect conclusions. Moreover, even if the focus groups are quite typical of the larger population, we have no objective measures to tell us this is the case in advance (as we do with probability sampling). We must wait until we can verify focus group results through some other method.

The appropriate responses to this problem consist of the researcher's awareness of the potentially unrepresentative nature of the results of focus groups and the researcher's avoidance of making unwarranted generalizations. Clearly it would be unwise to attempt very precise predictions of popular behavior on the basis of focus group results. For example, one could not, on the basis of focus group results, justifiably claim that "68.6 percent of citizens will vote against higher taxes to be used to retrain defense industry workers for civilian jobs." However, by observing focus groups, scholars might be able to reach conclusions like, "the participants tend to see the retraining of defense industry workers as a personal rather than a public responsibility."

A third limitation is that the *artificial setting* of a focus group may unpredictably affect subjects' behavior. The major purpose of focus groups is to get people to express themselves freely and reveal their true thinking without the restrictions imposed by a survey or interview. They often do this very well. However, we must recognize that the focus group is *not* a natural setting. Even if the moderator succeeds in creating a "permissive environment" that encourages self-expression, responses may be sincere but still unlike what they would have been in a different setting. As a result, we may not be able to generalize from the results of the focus group to the way people will behave in other social settings.

For example, the composition of the group may be unlike that of any group with which the participants are likely to interact in their daily life. If we have intentionally selected participants of mixed socioeconomic backgrounds but who seldom cross socioeconomic lines in their daily life, the group dynamic that develops may not be typical of any that would occur in the real world. Similarly, the permissive environment of the focus group may allow people to express ideas they would never verbalize in naturally occurring groups that have more restrictive norms. As a result, a consensus may emerge that is unlike any that would be produced by a real-world interaction.

In addition, each focus group develops its own dynamic as a result of some chance factors such as who happens to express an opinion first or the direction or tone of the first set of comments. The same members might behave differently on another evening or if placed in another group. As a consequence, the results of any given focus group may be unrepresentative both of real-world outcomes and of the thinking of the group participants as individuals.

In short, even a carefully designed and well-run focus group may create false impressions because it is not itself a natural setting. There are two main avenues to coping with these issues. First, researchers can run a number of groups and form conclusions based on *patterns* rather than isolated results. Second, they must be sensitive to both the ways in which focus groups may differ from natural settings and the effects these differences may have on the outcome of the sessions, and they must incorporate that awareness into their analysis of the focus group observations.

A fourth limitation is that this technique may produce *method effects*. Most observational research methods carry the risk of influencing subjects' responses in some way. (Recall, for example, our discussion in Chapter 8 of biased question wording and resulting survey responses.) Focus groups are no exception. *Method effects* can arise from biases introduced by the behavior of the moderator, who could have preconceived notions about what the focus group will or "should" reveal and who may unconsciously steer the discussion in that direction. Moderators who conduct several focus groups on the same subject may have had early experiences that cause them to lead discussions in subsequent groups in the direction of being consistent with the early groups. Similarly, unintentional cues given to participants before the group session (through a description of the purpose of the group or simply the naming of its sponsor, for example) may shape the outcome.

When Are Focus Groups Useful?

Researchers must weigh the strengths and weaknesses of focus groups in the context of specific research situations and tasks. Focus groups can be of great value under some conditions and of little use under others. There are five general situations in which focus groups often represent an appropriate method.

Conducting Exploratory Research When researchers venture into an area that is so completely unexplored that they do not even know how to go about studying it or when they want a fresh perspective on an old but unresolved research question, focus groups can help them formulate ideas about both what questions to ask and what methods to use. An example of this can be found in study of the transformation of Eastern European nations from authoritarian to democratic political systems following the fall of communism after 1989. Researchers might want to know how citizens who have been denied any opportunity for meaningful participation in politics approach the tasks of democratic citizenship when they are given the chance. Because the transition from communism to democracy has never happened before, we have no prior theories or studies to guide us. Moreover, Western scholars have generally been unable to conduct surveys in those nations for decades and have little knowledge of how their citizens thought about politics before the transition. In this case, focus groups consisting of citizens of the changing nations could help researchers discover what is to be explained and develop hypotheses to guide research.

Refining Data Collection Instruments Even when researchers know enough about an area to formulate hypotheses, they may be unsure about the best way to operationalize concepts. For example, standard question wording on a survey may not communicate effectively with unusual respondents. In the case of the Eastern European nations, we cannot even be sure that their citizens think about politics in the same terms as citizens of Western nations do. A series of focus groups could provide information that would assist in the development of appropriate wording for survey questions to be used with this population. Alternatively, researchers who plan to use direct observation to study political participation in Eastern European nations could use focus groups to learn the meaning of different expressions or actions so that they would know what significance the people being observed attached to their own words and deeds.

Interpreting Quantitative Findings   When researchers have used other methods to collect data that show clear patterns, they may still be unsure about how those patterns developed or what the patterns mean to the people who exhibit them. Again, focus groups can often provide answers. For example, many studies of environmental politics have found that women are far more likely than men to express concern about environmental hazards and to regard technologies as risky. Focus groups in which men and women discuss environmental issues may help researchers understand differences in the way the sexes tend to judge environmental hazards: what standards they use, how they process information, whom they trust as an authority, and so on. Scholars could then make more sense of the statistical relationships observed in their data.

Studying Group Processes   Whether they are legislative committees, juries, military units, law enforcement task forces, workplace teams, street gangs, or any of dozens of other collections of people, small groups make many of the decisions in our society. Understanding the processes by which groups influence their members' perceptions and reach decisions can, therefore, help us understand social phenomena or formulate public policies. Social scientists have long recognized that one behaves differently when in a group than when alone, and that the only way to understand *group* behavior is to study *group dynamics*. If our interest is in some aspect of group dynamics, then focus group methods offer an excellent way to observe efficiently and to avoid raising some of the ethical issues involved in direct observation.

Designing and Evaluating Public Policy   Focus groups can often help public officials and policy analysts to gain an understanding of how citizens see problems, evaluate services, and are likely to react to new programs. Such insight can then be used to create new policies that address problems or to evaluate how well existing policies are working. To illustrate, public housing officials could conduct focus groups to help them anticipate how residents of a public housing development would react to a system of tenant management that gave the residents a voice in running the housing project. Based on what they learn, they could try to build into the tenant management program a realistic set of incentives for participation rather than guess at what might motivate residents to take part.

An even more practice-oriented use of focus groups is to design and evaluate specific communication materials and strategies. To illustrate, imagine that public health officials want to convey to an immigrant community that has its own distinctive subculture certain information on a serious health hazard. The officials might use focus groups composed of members of the immigrant population to determine such things as what channels of communication would be most effective in reaching those residents and whether or not a given message would successfully capture residents' attention and be properly interpreted.

This use of social science methods to achieve very practical ends is commonly referred to as **applied research,** and focus groups constitute one of the most commonly used methods in "applied" settings. Such groups have, for example, proven especially valuable in designing election campaigns because they help campaign managers identify voters' most powerful concerns, thus enabling managers to get a feel for the ways that different appeals will be interpreted by voters.

Planning and Conducting Focus Groups

Once researchers have decided that focus groups are an appropriate method to use in a given study, they will confront several basic choices in planning and conducting the focus group sessions. We can explore these choices as responses to a series of questions.

The Role of Goals   The first step is to determine exactly what is to be learned from the focus groups. Objectives can range from the very general to the very specific. A relatively general goal might be "to gain insight into the impact of a localized environmental hazard on the lives of residents in order to formulate hypotheses about what determines how residents respond to the hazard." A more specific goal might be "to find out which of five possible sources of information about the hazard citizens are most likely to trust in order to devise a plan for conveying believable information to the public."

It is only once you are clear about what you hope to learn that you will know what to listen for in the focus group discussions. From a practical standpoint there are at least three reasons to identify goals as clearly as possible.

1. The goals will affect *the selection of participants and composition of groups*. If, for instance, you wanted to find out how the controversies surrounding a local environmental hazard had affected social relations within the community, you would want to be sure to include in the groups people on both sides of any issues. The statement of goals should help researchers identify important characteristics to be considered in recruiting participants and assigning them to groups.

2. The goals will influence *the degree of moderator involvement*. Some goals will require that members of the focus group perform a task while others do not. You may, for example, want the group to reach a formal consensus, solve a hypothetical problem, or make a recommendation about how to address some issue. If so, you will need to have the moderator be more active in guiding the discussion to be sure that the task is completed. If the goals are very general, moderator involvement can be minimized. Selecting goals is therefore the first step in the planning of focus group sessions and the instructing of the moderator.

3. The goals will direct *the development of a "guide" for the moderator*. Even in largely unstructured focus groups, researchers will want the moderator to have a **guide** which sets forth some rules for the discussion and provides a very general outline of how the session should proceed in order to be sure that all of the important points are raised and addressed. A focus group guide is not as detailed as an interview schedule in survey research or even an observational schedule in direct observation. Each guide will be different and will reflect the objectives of the study. Most will cue the moderator to step in at appropriate times to move the discussion along or bring it back to the main issue if it strays

too far. Most guides list the main points to be addressed in some appropriate order, suggest phrases to use in making the transition from one subtopic to another, and may even set time limits for the discussion of subtopics or lay out procedures to be used in performing tasks (for example, "Have the group break into three subgroups of equal size . . .").

Choosing How Many Sessions   It is almost always necessary to conduct more than one focus group session to rule out the possibility that there was something atypical about the participants or the group dynamic that developed in any one group. If similar patterns appear in more than one group, we can have more confidence that those patterns accurately reflect reality. Since two groups may give exactly opposite impressions or reach opposing conclusions, many practitioners consider *three* to be the minimum number of group sessions that should be held. Two other considerations, however, will weigh heavily in the choice of the number of sessions.

First, on the substantive side, your research objectives may dictate that you hold separate sessions for different subgroups within a general population or in different geographic locations. In the environmental contamination example, you may want to have separate sessions for citizens who choose to move away and for those who will stay in the contaminated community, or you may want to hold groups in various towns facing different types of environmental hazards so you can compare the groups' reactions. You would need to hold several sessions *for each subgroup* to have confidence in the results. These design considerations may dictate a larger minimum number of sessions.

Second, from a practical standpoint, focus group are expensive and time-consuming to plan, arrange, conduct, and analyze. The amount of time and money and the number of personnel available for the project may impose a limit on the number of sessions that can be held. The costs of *each* focus group session generally vary from $1,500 to $4,000 depending on such variables as whether a professional firm is hired to conduct the sessions, how much money participants must be paid, how transcription is done, and transportation costs.

Choosing an Appropriate Number of Participants   Experience has shown that focus groups rarely work well with fewer than six or more than ten participants. With smaller numbers of participants, especially strong personalities tend to exert too much influence on the outcomes, and individuals may feel too much pressure to carry a share of the conversation. With larger numbers, it is both difficult to give all members enough time to express their thoughts and hard to keep the discussion focused.

Again, the time and money available for the project will play some role in determining how many participants to include, given the decision to hold a certain number of sessions. One reason this is true is that it is frequently necessary to pay participants. The appropriate fee varies with the prevailing wage scale in a given area and with the characteristics of the participants. A group of, say, physicians or business executives may require far higher compensation than those who earn less. Occasionally, people can be persuaded to volunteer their time if the purpose of the research is one they value or if the sponsor of the research is one that commands respect and support. Local public health officials, for example, may be willing to take part in a study sponsored by their professional association and conducted for the purpose of improving public health services in the community.

Selecting Participants   Once the number of participants has been determined, the task of recruiting them begins. The first issue here is what kind of people you want to attract. The key is that you want people who are typical of the population group under study. Depending on the focus of the study, you may be able to work from a telephone book if any of the residents of a given community will do, or you may need more specialized lists of people such as welfare recipients, public school teachers, or members of local civic organizations. Once you have a list to work from, it is common to conduct a **screening interview** to determine whether specific individuals are suited for the study and are willing to take part. This is usually done by phone and followed with a written invitation and a follow-up call to confirm prospective participants' acceptance.

In the recruiting process, researchers must be alert to several additional issues. First, there is a tendency for people with unusually strong feelings about a subject to be more willing to participate than those with less emotional involvement in the issue. To keep this from distorting results, researchers should make a conscious effort to recruit some people with little initial interest in the subject. Second, unless friendship ties, work relationships, or family roles are a specific part of the research focus, it is usually better to recruit people who do not know one another. Strangers are usually less inhibited in their responses. Finally, researchers need to consider the effects of placing people who have different *social roles* in the same focus group. If the topic to be discussed relates to the expectations and interests associated with different social roles, participants in "mixed" groups may change their behavior as a result. Generally, it is unwise to put into the same focus group people with significantly different but interacting roles (like managers and workers or regulatory agency officials and members of the regulated industry) if those roles are relevant to the topic of the discussion. Unless interaction between people in different social roles is specifically part of the research objectives, it is better to select *relatively homogeneous groups* in order to have a sufficient basis for communication among the participants.

Selecting a Physical Setting   Since the main product of a focus group session is a transcript of what was said, it is important to arrange to make a high-quality audio recording of the event for later transcription. Audio equipment should be tested in advance to be sure it picks up comments from all positions in the room, and the moderator should have a backup system on hand in case the primary recording equipment fails. Well-funded projects use professional technicians for the recording of the session. In some cases, it may also be desirable to videotape the sessions in order to capture the nonverbal communication that may occur. This advantage has to be weighed against the possibility that video cameras may make respondents self-conscious and that hidden cameras can seldom be positioned properly so as to pick up all the action.

In any case, it is important both to tell participants they are being recorded and to get their permission. Professional ethics require that such recordings and any transcripts made from them be kept strictly confidential by the project staff and not be used for any purpose beyond the research.

Focus groups are best conducted in a room large enough to allow participants to sit around a single table (or at least in a circle) but small enough to feel intimate. The room should be furnished and decorated in a manner that puts people at ease. Sometimes researchers want to observe the sessions in person and need a place to sit to the side. Other times they may not want to be seen and thus need a room with a one-way mirror so they can observe without affecting the dynamics of the group. Actual discussions usually last about one and a half hours, but it is wise to allow two hours per session in case participants are late arriving, technical problems arise, or the discussion simply runs longer than anticipated.

Working with the Moderator   No single factor is more important to the success of a focus group than the competence of the moderator. The moderator is responsible for putting participants at ease, ensuring that all relevant topics are covered in the discussion, keeping more aggressive speakers from dominating the conversation, and helping to characterize the results of the session in a set of notes for the researchers. Accordingly, it is important to hire an experienced and skilled moderator if the budget allows or to invest substantial time in training someone to serve as moderator if an experienced one cannot be hired. It is generally unwise for a researcher to serve as the moderator because a researcher may unintentionally bias the results.

Moderators should usually share enough characteristics with focus group participants to help participants feel free to talk and to understand well enough what they *mean* by their remarks so as to respond properly. This is especially true with distinctive groups (for example, farmers, unemployed industrial workers, or female state legislators) and when the topic is one that touches on tensions between social groups.

An *assistant moderator* is almost always necessary. The assistant sits to the side and takes more detailed notes on the session than the moderator can take while interacting with the participants. The assistant may handle mechanical tasks such as greeting participants when they first arrive or distributing any written materials to be used in the session. Assistants can also serve as a backup since they often are familiar enough with the focus group process to step in if for some reason the moderator cannot attend a session. The assistant's most important function, however, may be to serve as a check on the moderator's perception of the sessions. The assistant works with the moderator in writing up an accurate set of notes after the session. If the two disagree on an event, both opinions should be included in the notes for the researcher to consider.

Once moderators are hired or trained, they must be instructed. As explained earlier, much of the moderator's role is dictated by the objectives of the project and outlined in the focus group guide. Even in those cases when moderators are expected to take a fairly active role in moving the discussion along, it is vital that they not influence the outcome. Doing this requires that they strike the proper balance between empathy and detachment, being accepting of all opinions expressed but not rewarding any particular type of statement. The emphasis must be on *having the participants express their opinions.*

At the end of the session, the moderator should write up a set of **field notes** summarizing themes or conclusions that emerged from the discussion, and pointing out any facts about the session that might influence the researcher's interpretation of the transcript. The moderator might note such issues as a high level of tension in the group, the exceptional influence of one or more participants over the group, or an apparent reluctance of some participants to express opinions. Moderators might also compare the results of different sessions they have conducted.

This raises the issue of whether to use *one or more than one main moderator.* Using the same moderator for all sessions offers more consistency in the way the sessions are run and provides a better basis for comparing sessions. It also allows a moderator to develop some insight into the topic and may help a moderator to anticipate problems and do a better job of running sessions subsequent to the first one or two.

However, researchers may want to use more than one moderator in several circumstances. One is the situation in which very different social groups are represented in different sessions and it is necessary to use different moderators to match participants' characteristics. For instance, if race relations is the topic and groups are racially homogeneous, it would be wise to select a moderator of the same race as the participants in each session. A second situation that calls for more than one moderator is one in which researchers want the results of each session or group of sessions to be totally independent of each other and there is some fear that a moderator might influence the outcomes on the basis of expectations developed in early sessions. Finally, logistical considerations such as geographically separated research sites or the need to conduct several sessions at once in order to meet a deadline or avoid "contamination" of the groups by news reports appearing between sessions might dictate the need for multiple moderators.

Conducting Sessions   Focus group meetings usually open with the moderator explaining the general purpose and the ground rules for the discussion. This is commonly followed by an opening statement by each participant. Such statements usually tell a few basic facts about the individual. Having each person speak helps participants feel as if they have been introduced and makes the discussion more relaxed. It also encourages less outgoing individuals to speak up later in the session. The key objective of the opening moments of a session is to make it clear that the moderator wants to hear each member's story in each member's own words and that the purpose of the exercise is for the moderator and the session's sponsors to learn from the participants. Thereafter, the moderator should ask general questions like, "How do you feel about X?" "Has anyone had any experience with Y?" and "Does anyone want to respond to that?" This keeps things focused and moving. Most of the discussion will involve the participants reacting to one another.

One variation on this procedure is to ask participants to fill out a questionnaire before and/or after the session. Such questionnaires can be used to gather background information on the participants that might not be evident from the discussion but that influences interpretation of participants' comments. They also show how participants' views changed as a result of the focus group discussion if the same questions are asked both before and after the session. Finally, they elicit from participants their assessments of the focus group process in order to improve the running of subsequent sessions. Pre-session questionnaires must be very carefully constructed so as not to influence the direction of the session by asking questions that suggest positions on issues or set up expectations about how the session will go. As a result, pre-session questionnaires should be used only if the benefits outweigh any threat of distorting the results of the sessions.

Analyzing Focus Group Results   As a qualitative method, focus groups do not produce numerical data that can be analyzed using statistics to identify patterns and relationships. Focus groups produce a very large volume of verbal data in the form of transcripts, recordings of sessions, and moderators' field notes. The tasks of reducing all of this information to a readable summary and of drawing some justifiable conclusions from it can be daunting. We can provide no step-by-step guide for focus group analysis both because there is so much variation in project objectives and focus group procedures and because qualitative analysis relies heavily on insight and creativity. We can, however, suggest some general guidelines that will help you recognize a good analysis.

The first principle of focus group analysis is that researchers should always begin with a clear picture of what they hope to learn from the data. This step should have been taken in the identification of the purpose for the study as the first step in designing the project. Returning to that objective helps identify relevant information from the sessions and eliminate marginal information. It gives a benchmark as to how detailed the analysis must be. For example, if the purpose was largely descriptive (such as finding out what terms ordinary people use to discuss some political issue), only a summary may be needed. If the purpose was more analytical (such as determining why people were opposed to nuclear power), the analysis would have to be much more complex, and certain subtle features of the discussions might take on importance.

Once the objective has been established, researchers face the task of organizing the data for analysis. One approach is to read through the transcripts and literally cut out sections addressing specific topics. Researchers can then physically reassemble the sections so that all the comments relevant to a given subtopic are together. If the transcript is on an electronic medium, a word processor can speed the process. This approach can help reveal themes more clearly and can reduce the volume of data to be considered at any one time. It must be done skillfully to avoid taking comments out of their context and, thereby, concealing their *actual meaning*.

In analytical studies, it is especially important to listen to the recordings of the sessions in order to be sure that the context of members' comments is taken into account and their *meaning* understood. Transcripts can be produced so as to reflect some of the subtle texture of oral communication by means of certain conventions such as typing in all capitals those words that speakers stressed or putting interpretive comments in parentheses. For example: "Oh, I *never* believe what *my* mayor says" (*laughing*). However, even these practices may conceal subtle differences in meaning that only listening to the tape can reveal. Taken in context, for instance, the comment about the mayor may have been sarcastic, indicating that the speaker *does* believe the mayor. Researchers therefore rely on moderators to report significant *nonverbal communication* (body language) that went on in the group and that may influence the interpretation of verbal comments.

One potentially productive approach to interpreting focus group data is to use *content analysis* to help identify themes in the discussions. For example, if focus group participants were asked their reasons for opposing a hazardous waste incinerator, they would probably offer many different answers. A sophisticated content analysis of the transcripts might help by grouping those answers into a smaller set of related arguments that identified themes in the responses and indicated which occurred most often.

In all this, the researcher's job is to form an impression of how the participants felt about the topic and to produce a summary statement of their expressions. The object is not to explain why participants feel as they do in the scientific sense of explanation discussed in Chapters 2 and 6. Analysts might, however, draw on existing theories or their knowledge of the subject in order to offer interpretations of what participants meant by various comments, why participants said what they did in the manner in which they said it, or even how they developed these attitudes. Often the most useful insights derived from analyses of focus group results come from linking what was observed to larger theories or processes in order to highlight the *larger significance* of what was said in the focus groups. For instance, if focus groups reveal that residents of racially divided communities are denying the problem, a researcher may turn to theories of social psychology to interpret those residents' remarks as examples of coping mechanisms.

Reporting Focus Group Results   Reporting focus group results can be as challenging as analyzing them. Whereas quantitative data can be reduced to measures of association and presented in tables, it is difficult to reproduce the richness of qualitative data for simple presentation. It is worth putting a good deal of time into meeting this challenge because the report is very important to the success of a project.

Richard Krueger, in his book *Focus Groups* (1994) suggests that reports perform three primary functions. First, and most obvious, a report communicates to a given audience information about the results of a study. Only if it is easy for the intended audience to understand, and clear in its message, will it actually have an impact on how that audience sees the topic of the study and thereby influence scholarship or public policy. Second, the act of writing a report assists researchers in developing their own personal understanding of a project and the subject it was designed to address. Third, a report provides a usable historical record of the results of a project. Because focus group data are so complex, it is especially important to have a compact summary if the results are ever to be used as background for future studies.

Researchers usually choose among three basic approaches for reporting focus group results: (1) They can *present enough carefully selected quotations* from the participants to convey an accurate picture of the discussions. This amounts to providing a representative sampling of what was said so readers can draw their own conclusions. (2) They can *summarize statements* by participants to point out major themes, using quotes only for illustrative purposes. This is a descriptive approach in which researchers assume responsibility for deciding what is important enough to report but also in which they offer little analysis. (3) They can *interpret what was said* so as to provide understanding, using description and quotes only to support their conclusions or illustrate points. Which strategy is appropriate depends on the purpose of the focus group project and the nature of the intended audience for the report.

To know what kind of report is called for, researchers must ask who will receive it and what use will be made of it. To understand the significance of this, recall the list of conditions under which focus groups are useful that was presented earlier in this chapter. If the focus groups were used to supplement another data collection technique, then the primary users of the report will be the researchers themselves. They will use understandings gained from the focus groups to formulate hypotheses, develop indicators, or assess their interpretation of data gathered by other means. Others may never see any more about the focus groups than a brief statement in a subsequent report to the effect that focus groups were used to frame the research question, design the project, or verify interpretations. In those cases, the report on the focus group results may be closer to the representative sampling of quotes just described, because the intended audience has the capability to draw informed conclusions from raw data.

If the focus groups were used to evaluate some aspect of public policy, assist in policy development, or design a campaign strategy, the audience for the report is likely to be persons who are less interested in the details of the sessions and more interested in the lessons to be learned from them. Such persons are, however, still also likely to want a strong sense of the thrust of the sessions. In this case, the report will probably rely heavily on summarized statements and a description of the key themes. Finally, if focus groups were used as a primary source of data collection (as in a study of small-group dynamics) and the results will appear in an academic publication, the report will have to be briefer and will have to stress interpretation of the sessions.

Conclusion

We want to highlight the point we made at the outset of this chapter. Focus groups can make a contribution at several stages of the research process. Not only can they serve as the primary data collection method for more qualitative studies, but they can also be integrated with quantitative methods. In the early stages of research, they can help clarify research questions or suggest new approaches to old problems. Once under way, they can help design measuring instruments to be used in interviews or direct observation. In the analysis stage, focus groups can improve our interpretation of quantitative data by shedding light on the meanings people attach to responses or actions.

Summary Points

• Focus group methodologies are a form of qualitative research that relies on brief but intense observation of carefully selected small groups of people to gain insights into social phenomena.

• Focus groups are especially appropriate for studying new subjects and for formulating new theories. Additionally, this method may provide insights that more structured methods cannot, as well as allowing researchers to explore people's thinking in detail.

• Focus groups are not statistically representative of larger populations, and produce data that must be subjectively analyzed.

• Focus groups are brought together in a room and guided through a recorded discussion of a subject by a trained moderator. The transcripts and other records of focus groups are analyzed along with the report of the moderator, by researchers seeking to identify patterns, themes, and new insights.

• Focus group methodologies can be used to develop research designs using other methods and to verify the results of studies done with other methods.

Suggested Readings and References

Two general introductions to focus group methods are Holly Edmunds, *Focus Group Research Handbook* (McGraw-Hill, 2000), and Gloria E. Bader and Catherine A. Rossi, *Focus Groups: A Step-By-Step Guide,* 3rd ed. (The Bader Group, 2002). Three books that explain the use of focus groups in social science research are Michael Bloor, et al., *Focus Groups in Social Research* (Thousand Oaks, CA: Sage, 2001), Lia Litosseliti, *Using Focus Groups in Research* (Continuum International Publishing Group, 2003), and Richard Krueger, *Focus Groups: A Practical Guide for Applied Research* (Thousand Oaks, CA: Sage, 1994). Jarol B. Manheim, *Strategic Public Diplomacy and American Foreign Policy* (New York: Oxford University Press, 1994) illustrates the use of focus groups in politics by providing an account of their use to design the presentation to the American public of the George H. W. Bush administration's rationale for U.S. involvement in the first Gulf War.

Research Exercises

Note: Before conducting any of these exercises, ensure with your instructor's assistance that your college or university's institutional review board will authorize a waiver for this type of educational illustration of human subject research.

1. Much attention has recently been focused on the idea that the words we use to discuss people and events reflect our attitudes about the subjects of those discussions and help determine the status of those people and events in society. By that reasoning, means of expression are political and can be judged as more or less consistent with some set of values and, therefore, as "correct" or "incorrect."

    Some commentators are worried that political correctness is being so strongly enforced that it threatens to stifle meaningful discussion of ideas, especially on college campuses. Others argue that there is no such danger and that advocates of "politically correct" language are simply calling attention to the biases inherent in much of what has come to be accepted as everyday speech. Who is right?

    Form teams within your class to conduct a focus group to learn how college students perceive and are affected by the issue of "political correctness." First, write a statement of objectives for a focus group, stating what you hope to learn about political correctness from the group. Develop a "guide" to the focused discussion, in which you identify some questions about political correctness that you want explored in a focus group composed of college students. You may want to know, for example, whether students are even aware of the issues raised by the idea of political correctness, whether they are receptive or hostile to the idea of politically correct language, whether they feel pressured to be politically correct, or how political correctness might be enforced (if at all) in their social circles. Then devise a set of standards by which you would select participants for such a focus group.

Recruit six to ten students who are not in your research methods class to take part in the group. Conduct the group using one of your team as the moderator and having the other members observe and take notes. Tape-record the session if possible. After the group leaves, go over the notes as a team, come to agreement about what was observed, and write a summary of the session. Analyze the discussion and ask yourself if it offered answers to the questions around which you designed the focus group.

Ideally, you can divide your entire class into several teams, have all the teams conduct focus groups with different students, and then compare results at the end to see how input from several groups may change the conclusions drawn from one group alone.

2. This exercise shows how focus groups can be used to enrich the information gathered through other means. It is also best done by a team.

Part A: Draw on what you learned from Exercise 1 above and from Chapter 8 on survey research to devise a brief questionnaire designed to measure people's opinions about *political correctness*. Write an explanation of the ways in which the things you learned in Exercise 1 influenced the questions you chose and the way you phrased those questions.

Part B: Administer the questionnaire to at least ten students from diverse backgrounds. Total the responses and look for simple patterns (for example, different answers from men and women or from people with different majors). Shortly after that, get at least six of those students to participate in a focus group that will review their reactions to the questionnaire. Try to find out what they thought was being asked with each question, how they chose their answer, what other issues they felt each question was related to, and how responding to the questionnaire made them feel. Review the notes from this focus group and make a list of all the things that surprised you—things that were revealed by the focus group that you had not thought of when you devised the questionnaire or that might affect your interpretation of the responses you received.

Key Terms

focus group	guide
moderator	screening interview
applied research	field notes

CHAPTER 21

Elite and Specialized Interviewing

- How can we study events that only a select few people know about or gain insight into processes involving people who are outside the mainstream?
- How is specialized interviewing conducted and what specific challenges does it produce?
- How can we ensure the validity of information obtained in such a personally interactive way?
- How do these qualitative interview methods differ from quantitative methods?

Intensive interviewing techniques involving in-depth, one-on-one conversations with respondents are a primary instrument of qualitative research. They are used, not to obtain precise measures of concepts for testing theories, but as a means of gaining *in-depth understanding* of a phenomenon and discovering aspects of that phenomenon that you did not anticipate.

As you read this chapter about elite and specialized interviewing, be alert to the ways in which effective use of this technique requires attention to a different set of concerns than survey interviewing or any other quantitative data collection method. Pay special attention to the distinct "mind-set" required for qualitative inquiry. You will find that you will be less concerned with carrying out a precisely planned research design and measuring process than you are when conducting quantitative research, and more concerned with being open to learning what your subjects can uniquely teach you about the subject.

Elite Interviewing

Many important research questions in political science can be answered only if we can learn how certain individuals or types of individuals think and act. For example, whereas we can always speculate about reasons for the passage of a specific piece of legislation, we can learn the actual reasons only by finding out what the legislators thought. Answering these types of questions requires **elite interviewing** rather than surveys of the general population.

Defining Elites   In this context, people are referred to as *elite* if they have knowledge that, for the purposes of a given research project, requires that they be given individualized treatment in an interview. Their elite status depends not on their role in society but on their access to information that can help answer a given research question. While people who get elite treatment in research *are* often persons of political, social, or economic importance, they need not be. In a study of "extremist" groups like the Ku Klux Klan, for example, "elite" respondents (those with special knowledge of the organization), may not be persons of wealth or public notoriety.

Elite Interviewing Versus Surveying   A central difference between sample survey interviewing and elite interviewing is the degree to which the interview is *standardized*. In sample surveys, each respondent is treated as much like every other respondent as possible. This is because the purpose of the interview is to obtain specific information that can be used to make quantitative comparisons between respondents in an effort to generalize to some larger population. In elite interviewing, each respondent is treated differently to the extent that obtaining the information possessed by that individual alone requires unique treatment. The purpose of elite interviewing is generally not the collection of pre-specified data but the gathering of information to assist in reconstructing some event or discerning a pattern in specific behaviors.

A second major difference between elite interviewing and survey interviewing is that, whereas survey interviews are generally highly **scheduled interviews,** elite interviews are largely **unscheduled interviews.** An interview is highly *scheduled* if the questions to be asked and the order of their appearance are predetermined and inflexible. Highly scheduled interviews produce standardized data because they require that all respondents answer the same questions and select from the same options in answering. This has the advantage of allowing comparisons between respondents and facilitates data processing. Strict scheduling, however, has the disadvantage of restricting the information gained from interviews to that which the researcher has already decided is necessary for understanding the phenomena under study. Scheduling limits the researcher's opportunities to learn what respondents consider relevant or important and to gain new theoretical insights.

In a totally *unscheduled* interview, the interviewer is guided only by a general objective (for example, to find out how a given decision was made in a particular state agency) and has no predetermined set of questions to ask. Unscheduled interviews produce data that are difficult to condense and summarize and that may not allow precise comparisons among respondents. The asset accompanying this liability is a greater opportunity to learn from respondents and to acquire unexpected information that can lead to truly new ways of understanding the events being studied.

Unscheduled interviews are especially suited to elite interviewing, because in elite interviewing the researcher is interested in learning what the respondent perceives as important and relevant to the research and lets the respondent's observations suggest what questions should be asked in order to gain useful information. The interviewer is concerned with discovering facts and patterns rather than with measuring preselected phenomena.

Elite interviews can provide crucial information about political events that is otherwise unavailable. Elite interviewing involves some very real scientific risks, however. It generally means asking people who are deeply involved in a political process to shape the researcher's definition of the process. This may threaten the scientific validity of the information obtained if respondents (1) have so narrow a view of the events in question that they do not understand which aspects are important in explaining them; (2) have inaccurate information (either because they misperceived events in the first place or because they have forgotten important elements); (3) have convinced themselves, in order to rationalize their own actions, that things are one way when they are actually another; or (4) intentionally lie in order to protect themselves or others. For example, interviews with ranking members of George W. Bush's administration about the timing of their knowledge of the prisoner abuse at Abu Ghraib prison in Iraq might produce instances of invalid information for each of these reasons.

Seeking Validity

Though researchers cannot control what respondents say, they can guard against drawing invalid conclusions from elite interviews by following some general guidelines. First, never treat what interviewees say as factual data, but rather *treat the fact that they said it as data.* For an understanding of political behavior, it is often as important to know what people believe or claim to be true as it is to know what is true. For example, if you want to know why residents of a given community have organized to demand the closing of a nearby chemical plant, finding out how much of a safety hazard the plant actually poses may be less useful than finding out how much of a safety hazard residents *believe* the plant poses.

Second, never rely on a single respondent for information about any event, but obtain information about each event from as many respondents as possible before drawing conclusions.

Third, always seek ways of verifying information from elite interviews by comparing it with information from outside sources. If we interview party leaders to learn why a given candidate has been selected as the party's nominee in an election and respondents refer to "the obvious public support for the candidate" as their reason for supporting him or her, we will want to look for public opinion polls that supply evidence of the degree to which the public actually did support the candidate.

Fourth, learn enough about the subject to be able to recognize incorrect statements or to perceptively analyze responses for possible sources of invalidity. We should be able to answer questions such as the following before engaging in elite interviewing: Is there any reason why respondents might want to believe something other than the truth or want to have others believe something other than the truth? Do they stand to gain economically or politically from given statements? What answers are plausible given the facts we know about the subject from other, reliable sources?

So serious are the threats to validity in elite interviewing that Lewis Anthony Dexter, one of the original authorities on the method, wrote in *Elite and Specialized Interviewing*:

> no one should plan or *finance* an entire study in advance with the expectation of relying chiefly on interviews for data *unless the interviewers have enough relevant background to be sure that they can make sense out of interview conversations or unless there is a reasonable hope of being able to hang around or in some way observe so as to learn what is meaningful and significant to ask. . . . Any planning for a study assuming a heavy reliance upon elite interviews should have a contingency plan . . . so that if elite interviews prove basically uninformative some other technique can be substituted.* (Dexter 1970, 17)

Despite these drawbacks, elite interviewing has tremendous potential for shedding light on important political phenomena and can often be a valuable supplement to studies relying principally on other data collection techniques, as well as providing the sole basis for important conclusions. It is crucial to remember, however, that information from people with inside knowledge is no substitute for a sound theoretical understanding of the subject. In order to reach scientifically valuable conclusions, political scientists must always impose their own analytic categories and conceptual schemes on the information gathered from elites.

Techniques of Elite Interviewing

One of the first questions faced in elite interviewing is whom to interview. In survey interviewing, all of the respondents are treated as equally able to contribute information that can be used in answering the research question, and sampling methods determine whom to interview. Elite interviewers have to assume that potential respondents differ in how much they can contribute to the study and that each respondent has something unique to offer. Often, background research will identify the entire population of those likely to have relevant information. If we are studying the decisions of the presidential commission created to investigate the terrorist attacks of September 11, 2001, for instance, background research would identify the members of the commission, their staff personnel, and the people called to testify. By contrast, if we are doing a "community power study" to determine who controls public policy in a certain city, we will not find any official list of people who exercise political influence in the city. Finding out whom to interview in this case is one of the objectives of the interviews themselves.

Once a group of potential interviewees has been identified, the question of what order to see them in arises. It is tempting to see first those people who should be most willing to talk and most sympathetic, or to want to see first the person believed to have the most information. Two things should be kept in mind, however. First, elite interviewing is a process of discovery. We seldom come to the interviews knowing everything important to ask. Early interviews may teach us things that help us get the most useful information from subsequent interviews. Often it is best to interview the most central figures late in the study.

Second, in elite interviewing, we are generally not dealing with isolated and uninvolved individuals. Each respondent is likely to have a unique (perhaps self-interested) view of the situation under study and may intentionally or unintentionally give inaccurate advice about who should be interviewed. Under no circumstances should the researcher let early interviewees' suggestions *determine* the choice or order of subsequent interviews, although those suggestions can provide partial data on which to base such decisions. Sometimes the fact that early interviewees have suggested certain other persons is evidence in itself, as it may reveal alliances, communication patterns, or shared perceptions.

In addition, because elite respondents are likely to know one another and be involved with the subject matter, the researcher must be cautious that early interviews do not jeopardize the study by identifying it with a particular group among the potential respondents. If possible, it is best to avoid interviewing the most unusual persons first—the mavericks, opposition leaders, persons thought to have extreme views, or leaders of any dominant coalition. If word is passed to other interviewees that you have already spoken with those perceived to be outside of the norms or in positions of power, it may bias your other interviews.

Considering all this, researchers may find that the best initial interviews may be with people who are somewhat marginal to the situation but who are viewed as neutral or "mainstream" by most participants. In a study of politics in a state legislature, for example, it may be best to interview members of the legislative council (a general service agency used by all members of the legislature) first, rather than starting with key legislators. It is also wise to explain to the first respondents that the interview is preliminary and exploratory and that you may want to see them again. This is because you may learn what other questions to ask or how to interpret answers only after subsequent conversations.

Arranging Interviews   It may be difficult to schedule interviews with elites, because such individuals are often busy people and this type of interview generally demands large amounts of their time (an hour or more is common). The following tips will generally help in securing interviews, *though it will sometimes be impossible or inadvisable to follow them in particular situations.*

1. Always call or write in advance to arrange for the interview rather than simply showing up, as is done in survey interviewing.

2. Be sure to request the interview by speaking with *the person to be interviewed* rather than a secretary or aide. You want to be certain the respondent understands the purpose of the meeting so he or she will not feel you are being deceitful.

3. Avoid highly detailed explanations of the purpose of the interview, because these can bias responses or cause potential respondents to refer you to a staff person who has "expert" knowledge of the subject.

4. Always try to determine the reasons for refusals and try to see whether you can remove the cause. For example, if scheduling is a problem, you may offer to interview after work hours; if confidence is a problem, you may be able to secure references from people the potential respondent trusts, or agree to have a third party sit in on the interview as insurance against subsequent false claims.

5. Always have on hand materials that identify you and the sponsor of the research, in case questions arise. If possible, give contact information for someone who can verify the purpose and legitimacy of your study.

Conducting Elite Interviews

Once an interview has been arranged, it should *not* proceed by the rules given for survey interviewing. Dexter (1970) says that "the most nearly universal rule for elite and specialized interviewing is that *the best way to interview in a concrete situation depends upon the situation* (including the skills and personalities of the interviewers)." Elite interviewers have to be more flexible and have a wider range of interviewing styles than survey interviewers, but there are some general guidelines that will fit most situations:

1. Always introduce yourself and restate the broad purpose of your study at the beginning of each interview rather than assuming that the respondent remembers these facts from a letter of introduction, phone call, or even a prior interview session with you.

2. The setting of an interview can be crucial. It is generally best to arrange a private interview away from potential distractions. Interviews over meals in restaurants or in the presence of the respondent's family usually do not go well. Occasionally, however, it is useful to have an interview in an unorthodox place (a city park, the Lincoln Memorial, a bus) if it serves to put respondents at ease or jog their memory of past events.

3. Though group interviews can sometimes help produce a consensus on facts or reveal personal relationships, it is normally best to interview only one person at a time.

4. The tone of the interview should be reflective and conversational. Avoid firing questions in rapid succession. Do not be afraid of pauses as you or the respondent processes information and collects thoughts.

5. Plan initial questions carefully. Though the bulk of the interview will be unscheduled, the first few questions can be so important in focusing respondents' attention, stimulating their memory, and clarifying their perception of what you want that they should be planned in advance. Initial questions should be (a) clearly related to the stated purpose of the study, (b) likely to be answered with ease so that no ego threat arises, (c) phrased to show the respondent that the interviewer has knowledge about the subject of the study, and (d) conducive to the kind of free-flowing answers that the researcher hopes to receive in the interview rather than to flat, factual answers. (If you need background information on the respondent, it can be obtained later in the interview.) Questions that stress the respondent's feelings about or definition of a situation can be especially useful opening questions.

6. In contrast to survey research, questions should often be subject to multiple interpretations. Remember that the objective is to learn how *respondents* see the situation and what they feel is relevant.

7. Comments, as well as questions, can be used to evoke a response. A remark like, "that is not the way it is usually done," for example, can lead to revelations about how respondents believe things do work.

8. Always maintain eye contact when possible (unless interviewees seem uncomfortable with this), and make it clear that you are listening intently and sympathetically. Phrases like *I see* or *of course* or simply a thoughtful *yes* can serve to encourage respondents and keep them talking.

9. Remember that one of the chief rewards respondents get from granting in-depth interviews is the chance to "teach" someone who is knowledgeable about and genuinely interested in a subject of great importance to them. It can be important to let them realize that they are, in fact, helping and informing you.

10. It is generally best to appear to accept whatever comments respondents make. Do not appear to reject their opinions or challenge their statements of fact.

11. An exception to rule 10 occurs when respondents are reluctant to reveal information you feel sure they have. In that situation, it may be necessary to employ what is often referred to as the *Nadel technique* which was first popularized in S. F. Nadel, "The Interview Technique in Social Anthropology," in F. C. Bartlett et al., eds., *The Study of Society* (Kegan Paul, Trench, Trubner & Co., 1939. pp. 317–27). Here you play the role of critic or antagonist, questioning and challenging respondents' remarks in hopes of forcing them to reveal information in order to defend their views or prove a point.

12. Respondents who are reluctant to divulge information because they fear the way it may be used can sometimes be reassured by a reminder that the information will be kept confidential or that the researcher is really not in any position to affect the situation in any way.

13. Note-taking can be used as a tool to improve interviews. In elite interviewing (in contrast to survey interviewing, in which note taking should be kept inconspicuous), respondents can often be encouraged to give more information or stay on a given subject by the way an interviewer takes notes. Intense recording can serve as a cue that you find comments useful, and putting the pencil down altogether can signal that the respondent has ventured off the central topic. Because you have to take such extensive notes that it is probably impossible to be inconspicuous, you may as well use note-taking for all it is worth.

14. Always be sensitive to the interviewee's personality and personal style, and adapt your tactics to it. Some people are highly formal and others very casual. Some deal in ideas almost exclusively, and others tend to personalize everything. Some people are accustomed to interacting mainly with superiors, and others mainly with subordinates. You may be able to get more information by adopting one of these roles. Never enter an interview with a fixed idea of the style you will use, but decide what is necessary as you talk with the respondent.

15. Always review your interview notes as soon as possible after the interview to elaborate at points where you could get only an outline and to make comments about your interpretation of the interview. This may mean sitting in a cold parking lot or buying an unwanted cup of coffee in order to have a place to write, but it is important to trust to memory as little as possible.

16. Type up handwritten notes as soon as possible. Make several hard or electronic copies and store them in separate places to insure against loss.

Tape recorders are controversial tools in interviewing. Obviously they can help you avoid mistakes about what is actually said, and they can capture subtle facts about the *way* in which things are said. They can also help interviewers learn how they sound to respondents. This is useful because the way in which a question is asked can be an important consideration in interpreting a response. A drawback to taping interviews is that respondents are often inhibited by a tape recorder, because it denies them the chance of claiming that they have not made some remark if it later proves embarrassing. Sometimes they fear that technicians can edit the tape to make it appear as if they had said things they have not. Moreover, the mechanics of working the recorder can distract from the interview.

Researchers must decide about the use of recorders on the basis of the type of question they are investigating, the nature of the interviews they expect, and the character of the respondents. If the subject matter is highly sensitive or respondents are likely to be inhibited by recorders, the costs of using them probably outweigh the advantages. If lengthy, detailed, and technical interviews are necessary and specific facts are crucial to the study, recorders may be necessary.

If a recorder is used, the researcher should ask permission to use it and should place the device in full view of the respondent. Pretest the recorder to ensure that it is suitable for the kind of interview anticipated (sufficiently sensitive, simple to operate, able to play long enough tapes). *Never depend exclusively on a recorder.* It can malfunction and cause the loss of an irreplaceable interview. Always take written notes as well.

A final issue in elite interviewing is confidentiality. This can be more important with elite interviews than with surveys, because elites are often asked for information that, if revealed or misused, may have considerable public impact or personal consequences. If confidentiality is promised, and it generally must be, *researchers should make every reasonable effort to safeguard information.* This is often easier than in survey research, because large numbers of personnel are not generally required in elite studies, but interviewers can buy a little insurance by storing records in secure places and keeping the purpose of the study from becoming general knowledge, if possible. One threat to confidentiality occurs when a typist is used to type handwritten notes or transcribe taped interviews. If researchers absolutely cannot do this work themselves, they should both employ only dependable people to do it and conceal from the typist the identity of respondents when possible. Never make interview records available to people not involved in the project.

Specialized Interviewing

In some studies, political scientists do not want to obtain information from specific individuals, as in the case of elite interviewing, or from respondents who are representative of the general population, as in surveys, but need information from persons who are *representative or typical of some particular group*. This often calls for **specialized interviewing.**

A specialized interview is any interview in which the characteristics of respondents demand procedures different from those employed in standardized survey interviewing. Interviews with children, illiterate adults, prison inmates, homeless persons, non-English-speaking migrant workers, mental patients, and members of a religious cult are all examples.

Specialized versus Survey Interviewing   Specialized interviewing is called for when researchers cannot assume that they and their respondents share a *common vocabulary*. Words that researchers use frequently may not be understood by respondents. Similarly, respondents may use terms or slang with which the researcher is not familiar or may use conventional words in special ways the researcher does not understand. A second distinctive feature of specialized interviews is that interviewers often cannot assume that respondents can read or have the ability to follow a line of argument that would be expected of an average person in the culture. In addition, specialized interview situations often involve distinctive relationships between respondents and interviewers. Whereas ordinary respondents regard interviewers largely as equals who can be trusted to a degree and treated cordially, specialized subjects may view interviewers as authority figures or "outsiders" and may be hostile and suspicious. In these circumstances, communication can be difficult and the validity of responses can suffer.

All of these features of specialized interviews combine to create settings in which researchers cannot take communication for granted. Rather, interviewers have to carefully establish a basis for communication and then check to be sure that communication is occurring.

An Example   If we want to know the degree to which children consider the U.S. political system legitimate, we first need to define the concept of legitimacy and be sure that our young respondents know what we mean when we speak of the political system. Once we have verified their grasp of these concepts and have asked our central questions, we need to ask additional questions to determine whether the children's answers mean to them what we would expect the same answers to mean if they came from typical adults. One way to do this is first to give our child respondents examples of children acting in ways that suggest they accord either a high or a low level of legitimacy to some institution, then to ask our respondents to interpret the actions described as showing either high or low levels of respect for the political system, and then to tell us whether or not they would be likely to take these same actions. If children frequently misinterpret the fictitious actions or say they would take actions that are inconsistent with the level of legitimacy they have told us they accord the political system, we will not feel safe in assuming that they understand our questions or their answers in the same way we do.

Conclusion

Intensive interviewing techniques, like direct observation, offer access to information about the world that cannot be obtained through other methods. When properly conducted, these interviews can yield valuable insights leading to further research, help us more fully develop our theories of some phenomenon, and let us discover *why* things happened as they did to a greater degree than more "detached" methods can.

Like direct observation, however, they also place special demands on the abilities and discipline of the researcher(s). They should never be the only approach you use to answering a research question because you cannot be assured of access to the right people or of being able to validate the information you collect in this way in advance of actually doing the study. It is also important to be especially diligent in planning and training for your interviews, and careful to enlist the help of others in verifying your interpretations of the discussions.

As we advised at the end of Chapter 19, when you read research based on elite or specialized interviewing you will want to pay special attention to the details of the description of the methods used. This will be necessary if you are to accurately judge the degree to which bias might have been introduced into the findings by the unique challenges of intensive interviewing.

Intensive interviews can be an enormously rich source of data for social scientists. But they require the development of almost artistic skills to be effectively used. In developing this skill, no amount of reading about in-depth interviews can substitute for experience with them.

Summary Points

• Intensive interviewing can let us learn about events that only a few people know about and can be used to study people who are outside the norms of society.
• Intensive interviewing of "elites"—persons with unique knowledge—is as much an art as a science and has to be done in a manner appropriate to individual respondents and situations.
• Intensive interviewing of "special" respondents who are unlikely to respond to questions the same way as "average" citizens, requires great sensitivity and in-depth knowledge of the circumstances of the respondents.
• Ensuring the validity of conclusions drawn from elite and specialized interviewing poses special challenges that require both crosschecking of the researcher's reasoning and detailed reporting of observations so that others can draw their own conclusions.
• Research designs employing intensive interviewing must be far more flexible than most quantitative research designs and are aimed at developing theory and gaining unexpected knowledge rather than rigorous theory testing. In addition, the information produced by intensive interviewing methods is almost never quantitative and must be analyzed with techniques other than standard statistical analyses.

Suggested Readings and References

Two texts that explain intensive interviewing in detail are Steinar Kvale, *Interviews: An Introduction to Qualitative Research Interviewing* (Thousand Oaks, CA: Sage, 1996) and Tom Wengraf, *Qualitative Research Interviewing: Biographic Narrative and Semi-Structured Methods* (Thousand Oaks, CA: Sage, 2001). For an examination of the role of interviewing in the larger context of qualitative methodologies, see John Lofland and Lyn H. Lofland, *Analyzing Social Settings: A Guide to Qualitative Observation and Analysis,* 3rd ed. (Belmont, CA: Wadsworth, 1995).

Reference: Anthony Lewis Dexter, Elite and Specialized Interviewing (Evanston, IL: Northwestern University Press, 1970).

Research Exercises

1. State a research question that can be answered through elite interviewing. List the types of information you would need in order to answer the question, and identify either by name or by official position (for example, all federal district court judges in the eleven Southern states), the people you would expect to interview in gathering that information. Tell what steps you would take to ensure the validity of your conclusions. How would you check the accuracy of what respondents tell you?

2. (NOTE: Do not undertake this exercise without permission from your instructor.)

   a. State a research question dealing with the local government of your community or with decision making in your college that can be studied through elite interviewing. List the types of information you will be seeking and the specific persons you will have to interview to acquire that information.

   b. After the project has been approved by your instructor, arrange and conduct interviews with three of the persons you need to interview. (*Remember:* You need to tell these people that this is part of a class assignment, so do not set your sights too high. You may well be unable to see the mayor of a large city or the president of a large university. Also, to avoid embarrassing yourself and creating a poor opinion of students at your school, you should do enough background research to ask intelligent questions on the subject you have selected.)

   Type up the notes from the interviews along with all of your observations about the significance and interpretation of different remarks. Explain what you have learned about the subject from these interviews, state what else you need to know, and tell how you would proceed if you were going to carry the research further. Also identify any steps you feel could be used to verify the information gained in the three interviews.

Key Terms

Intensive interviewing
elite interviewing
scheduled interviews

unscheduled interviews
specialized interviewing

CHAPTER 22

Writing (and Reading) the Research Report

- When does the planning for the research report begin?
- What are the main components of a research report?

If the purpose of science is to discover or understand the world we live in, then the purpose of scientific writing must be to communicate our discoveries or understandings to others in as effective a manner as possible. Just as science, or social science, itself must be explicit, systematic, and controlled, the descriptions and assessments of scientific findings must be clear, complete, and—most especially—well organized. Because it often constitutes the first statement of discovery, and because it provides a primary means for developing a shared understanding, the research report is one of the most important, and potentially most effective, instruments of scientific communication.

Good research reports do not simply emerge, unassisted, from good research. Rather, the writing of a solid report requires every bit as much craftsmanship, and every bit as much practice, as any other stage of the research process. It requires the same planning, careful organization, clarity of thought and expression, and attention to detail that have been exercised all along the way. And while it is true that good research eases the writing of a good research report, it is equally true that a poorly written report can obscure the value of even the best research effort. After all, the research report is the *only* means we have to tell others of our work, and, conversely, it is the *only* means by which those others can learn what we have accomplished. If we fail to communicate fully and effectively, the value of our research itself is greatly lessened.

In general, considerations of style, organization, proper grammar and usage, and other elements of effective writing lie well beyond the scope of this book. There are, however, a number of practical concerns that have a particular bearing on the writing of the research report and that do deserve some comment. In this chapter we examine several of these very briefly and present an annotated example of research reporting to help illustrate applications. Although the chapter itself is oriented toward writing a research report, the points we present also provide a basis for the *critical reading* of research reports prepared by others.

The Plan

Planning a research report should begin at the earliest stages of the research process. Recall that the six steps of the research process are: (1) the selection of a topic, (2) the systematic examination of related literature, (3) the formulation of a theory and hypotheses, (4) the determination of what type of evidence is required and (5) how it is to be obtained, and (6) the decision about how the resulting data are to be analyzed. Each of these actions contributes in an important way to the writing of the research report, and each should be undertaken with that fact in mind. Indeed, one of the greatest dangers the beginning researcher can confront is the tendency to compartmentalize the work, to treat each stage in the research process as if it were virtually independent of every other stage. In point of fact, the reverse is true. No stage of research, from problem formulation to the reporting of results, stands alone. Not only is each stage dependent on every other stage, but each must also be carried out with the others in mind. We may speak of six stages of the research process, but we speak of only one unified *process*.

Nowhere is this interdependence of parts clearer than in the writing of a research report, for it is in that report that we must join the pieces of our work together. We must precisely state our concepts and definitions; demonstrate the linkage between concept and research; describe, summarize, and evaluate our procedures and results; and assess our findings as they relate back to our concepts. In reality, then, the planning of a research report is inseparable from the planning of the research itself, and the writing of a report is inseparable from the conduct of our inquiry.

The Structure

Because different subjects and different approaches to research can give rise to many different forms of research report, it is neither possible nor desirable to set forth hard-and-fast rules for the structure of these communications. We can, however, suggest the basic elements that should be present in any such report and point out the most commonly accepted way of organizing them. Those elements are (1) the introduction, (2) the statement of research methods, (3) the statement of findings, and (4) the conclusion.

The Introduction   The introduction to a research report should state clearly the theme or purpose of the research, the principal hypotheses (work that is primarily descriptive may not include hypotheses), and the rationale underlying both conducting the research and writing the report. Whenever possible, these elements should be integrated by a review of the relevant literature that brings to bear both the research and the theories of those who have worked on related problems in the past. The author may challenge or discount that literature but should be sure to cite it when appropriate and to state clearly the reasons for making certain judgments. In general, the purpose of the introduction is to set forth the *goals* of the work, to defend them, and to put them into what the author regards as the proper perspective.

It is at this point, too, that we alert readers to what we see as the major significance (the main contribution) of the research being reported. Only if the purpose of the work is stated clearly at the outset can readers judge the relevance to the central point of each argument or piece of data analysis presented. Surprise endings may be appropriate for short stories, but in a research report they only create extra work for readers.

The Methods   The methods section should answer several questions. What was the source of data for the research? How were data gathered? Was there a sample? How was it selected? How many cases were included? How were the principal variables operationalized? Did the study encounter any special problems or develop any special instruments (for example, a new scale for measuring a particular attitude or behavior) worthy of note? The object here is to make a complete and precise statement of the steps taken in performing the research. As we pointed out in the introductory chapters, one important benefit of science as a way of knowing is that the findings of science are replicable, that the scientific method provides a way for sharing and evaluating both knowledge and the way to knowledge. Only if we state explicitly what we have done during the undertaking of our research can the results of our work be judged fully and critically by others. *The statement of the method of our study is the component of the research report that contributes most directly to such sharing.* For that reason, it must be written with honesty, thoroughness, care, and precision.

The Findings   The presentation of findings may include tables, graphs, or charts that help to summarize the results of our work, together with statistical or other analyses that prove germane. Researchers may be tempted at this point in their writing to include every shred of evidence and every table or chart that they examined when analyzing the data. The result is often a presentation that overwhelms the reader with unedited facts, some of which may be only marginally useful. It amounts to something of a *laissez-faire* approach to writing: here are the facts—you decipher them however you wish. Remember that no one is better positioned than you to identify and assess the meaning of your research results. Indeed, it is an obligation of the researcher to present in as clear a manner as possible only those results that speak most pointedly to the issues at hand.

Two suggestions, one general and one more specific, may offer some guidance here. First, the presentation of findings should be organized so as to illustrate the principal variables, hypotheses, or arguments set forth in the introduction to the report. Results not relating directly and importantly to these foci should not be included. By keeping this in mind, the researcher not only can eliminate a great deal of trivia from the report but also can present those findings that are included in a logical and meaningful manner. Second, it is a general rule of thumb that any table, chart, or graph included in a research report should be accompanied by at least a page of text in which the points illustrated and their significance are discussed. If the researcher cannot generate enough points of discussion to fill a page, it is quite likely that the particular table, chart, or graph in question is not sufficiently important to warrant inclusion in the report.

We also should emphasize that the researcher should not be reluctant to report either unexpected results or "nonfindings." The fact that a hypothesis is not supported by one's data may be just as important and scientifically interesting as the fact that it is. Thus, the criterion for including or excluding a piece of evidence in writing a research report is not whether or not it shows anything or whether or not a piece of evidence shows what was predicted, but, rather, whether what it shows is of any importance or interest.

The Conclusion   Finally, a research report generally concludes with a summary of findings, a discussion of the relationships between those findings and the theory in which the research was grounded, and, in some cases, an evaluation of the method of the study. Have we found anything of significance? If so, why is it significant, and what does it tell us? If not, why not? Were our hypotheses simply incorrect, or did we make some error or encounter some problem in designing or carrying out our research that prevented us from finding supporting evidence? Where do we go from here? This section of the report is, in effect, retrospective toward both the research paper and the research process. It presents the researcher with an opportunity to place the work in proper perspective between past and future scientific effort.

The placement of these several elements can vary somewhat depending on the development of a particular research report, but all or most will usually be present. In fact, these components can serve as an outline or organizing basis for most research reports, and the beginning researcher should take some care to see that each component is represented where appropriate and also that the relationship among them in the body of the report is both straightforward and logical.

The Style

Research reports are not—nor should they be—written like best-selling novels. Unlike novelists, scientists often must communicate very complex technical information to a specialized audience in a relatively small space. But it does not follow that scientific writing must be stodgy and heavy-handed, nor so overburdened with jargon as to be virtually incomprehensible to all but a select few. A more appropriate mode is one in which readability is coequal with precision, and clarity with thoroughness. The following guidelines may help you to achieve these goals.

1. Work from an *outline*. Be sure the logic of your writing is clear to the reader.
2. Use words and phrases with which you are comfortable. Do not use big words just because they sound impressive. Use the word that most precisely defines your terms.
3. Reread, revise, and rewrite. Reading your work aloud to see if it sounds right can help to identify and smooth out obvious rough spots. First drafts are *never* final drafts.
4. Seek others' opinions when possible. Often researchers are so close to their subject that they cannot clearly see what is necessary to convey the information they want to communicate. Asking friends or colleagues who are likely to be familiar with your basic research method to read a draft of the report can alert you to errors that countless readings on your own will not reveal.
5. Do not overstate a point. For example, you will find very few exclamation points in scientific writing. Rhetoric and research should remain separate.
6. Be sure to differentiate between observations and opinion.

One additional element of style—the proper citation and documentation of source materials—deserves mention. Footnoting and documentation are not petty harassments or empty formalisms dreamed up by professors as a means of torturing students. They are essential to the academic enterprise. Documentation is ethically required as it keeps us intellectually honest by preventing the fabrication of convenient evidence. More importantly, it provides a basis on which others can judge the validity of our arguments. If we draw evidence from dependable sources or rely on the opinions of informed authorities in reaching our own conclusions, the persuasiveness of our argument is increased. Without proper documentation, readers cannot evaluate the merit of our conclusions except to the extent that they derive from abstract logic or from our own data.

If we use the ideas of others or cite facts they report, we must document this either with a bibliographic entry that includes a full description of the source and a parenthetical citation in the text (as this text uses) or a footnote that ties specific material in our paper to particular pages in the source document. Citations should be used *whenever* we borrow facts or ideas from another author. Not only direct quotations, but *any* data or ideas we draw from the work of others must be accompanied by references. Information on the form and placement of citations and construction of a bibliography is best obtained from a style manual, several of which are listed at the end of this chapter. Alternatively, we might adopt the citation style of a major journal, such as the *American Political Science Review* or the *Journal of Politics*. Consistent form and complete information are the keys to documenting a research report correctly.

The Title and Abstract

The title of a research report should be descriptive and complete, but it should not be overly detailed. It should give readers a good idea of what the report discusses, but not so good an idea that one need not read the paper. Compare, for example, the following alternative titles for the same research:

1. *Politics on the Day That Hell Freezes Over*
2. *Control over the Distribution of Scarce Resources at Such Time as the Temperature of Certain Regions Remains below 0° Celsius throughout the Month of July, as Measured on a Mercury Thermometer and through the Use of Pretested Survey Instruments, Including Guttman Scales, on a Small Population of Residents of Minot, North Dakota: An Experiment*
3. *The Effects of Climate on the Distribution of Political Resources*

Title 1 is short and to the point but not sufficiently descriptive to give the reader much idea of the article's content. Title 2 is so comprehensive as to be unwieldy. Only title 3 conveys the content of the report without undue attention to detail. The point is that the title should tell the reader the general topic of the report, but should not itself substitute for the sections of the report that deal with methods and findings.

Often, we find it useful to follow the title page of a report with an **abstract,** a brief statement, usually not more than 150 words and often no more than one or two sentences, in which we briefly summarize the contents of our report. The summary usually includes in barest outline a statement of what we have found, how we found it, and why it is important. Consider the following example:

ABSTRACT: The Effects of Climate on the Distribution of Political Resources
Using both temperature and survey data from a study of Minot, North Dakota, the author concludes that resource allocations vary systematically with changes in the weather. More particularly, the data suggest that the poor are more adequately cared for and the downtrodden raised higher on the proverbial cold day in July than at other times. This finding offers considerable support for the hypotheses of Marx, Weber, and others.

By giving readers a concise summary of the accompanying report, the abstract tells one whether the material is likely to be of sufficient interest to warrant a close reading and thereby obviates the need for an extended title.

Conclusion

One final question about research reports that often arises is that of length. How long should a report be? There is no simple answer to this question. Most journals in political science prefer manuscripts of some 25 to 30 pages typed and double-spaced. A master's thesis may run to 100 or 150 pages, and a doctoral dissertation may take up to several hundred. Student research reports may run anywhere from 10 to 50 pages, though 15 to 20 is probably more common.

It is important to remember that the scope of your research project determines the report's length. Thus, if your outline threatens to exceed the paper's page limit, then you need to more tightly constrain your research. Similarly, if from the outset you struggle to fill the outline, you may need to enlarge your research focus. Therefore, the material itself determines the length of the report. The argument should be adequately developed and the appropriate literature adequately reviewed. The method of the study should be fully expounded, and the results fully but judiciously reported. The conclusions should be both well developed and properly supported. Yet the length of each portion will vary from one report to the next. How long, then, should a research report be? As long as it needs to be to cover the subject, but brief enough to maintain interest.

Summary Points

• The groundwork for producing an effective research report begins at the initial stages of the research project, and should be part of the project.
• The four parts of a research report are: introduction, methods used, research findings, and the conclusion.

A Case in Point

The remainder of this chapter is devoted to an annotated example of a research report. The example illustrates most of the elements we have described, and it should suggest to you the ways in which these components can be combined to produce an informative research report. The source of this report is Craig Leonard Brians and Steven Greene, "Elections: Voter Support and Partisans' (Mis)Perceptions of Presidential Candidates' Abortion Views in 2000," *Presidential Studies Quarterly*, 34 (2004), pp. 412–419; reprinted by permission of the publisher.

Title

Elections: Voter Support and Partisans' (Mis)Perceptions of Presidential Candidates' Abortion Views in 2000*

CRAIG LEONARD BRIANS

STEVEN GREENE

Abstract

Although the 2000 Republican and Democratic national party platforms show the parties at opposite poles on abortion policy, Governor George W. Bush publicly supported a vaguely defined "culture of life," rather than the constitutional amendment barring abortion that was advocated by his party. In light of Bush's campaign strategy, this article uses national survey data to examine the accuracy of citizens' knowledge of the candidates' abortion policy positions. Interestingly, pro-choice Republican voters were much less likely to defect from their party in 2000 than in 1996, suggesting that the Bush campaign's efforts to avoid public opposition to his abortion position were successful.

Introduction

Statement of research assertion

In August of 2000, a self-avowed fundamentalist Christian who had publicly pledged to "do everything in my power to restrict abortion" earned the Republican presidential nomination in Philadelphia.[1] In an apparent attempt to diffuse this controversial issue, throughout the nomination and presidential campaign Governor George W. Bush obscured his abortion views and avoided discussing the topic. His official position is that abortion should be outlawed except in cases of rape, incest, or to save the life of the mother.

In a debate with Senator John McCain on *Larry King Live,* Governor Bush simultaneously maintained that he completely endorsed and agreed with the Republican Party platform (which calls for a constitutional amendment barring all abortions) and he supported the above-noted exceptions. Senator McCain apparently found it so frustrating to attempt to force Governor Bush to clarify these mutually exclusive positions that he eventually quit discussing abortion (Larry King Live 2000).

Source citation

The Bush campaign's efforts to obscure the candidate's abortion position reached their height during the first presidential debate when Bush refused to verify his previously stated plan to try to overturn the FDA's approval of the RU-486 abortion drug, saying he was only interested in doing whatever would protect women's health. He then linked his position on abortion to promoting a "culture of life," saying that while "abortions ought to be more rare in America," this culture would also lead to fighting laws that "allow doctors to take the lives of our seniors" and change the culture to discourage "youngsters who feel like they can take a neighbor's life with a gun" (Commission on Presidential Debates 2000). It would be difficult to find anyone who actively favors more abortions and more killing of older people and

---

* Authors' Note: The data used in this article were made available by the Inter-University Consortium for Political and Social Research. Neither the collector of the original data nor the consortium bears any responsibility for the analyses or interpretations presented here.
[1] Quoted in the October 22, 1994 *Dallas Morning News.*

neighbors by teenagers. In the same debate, Vice President Al Gore clearly stated his support for a woman's right to choose abortion and RU-486, although he said he did not favor late-term or partial birth abortions (Commission on Presidential Debates 2000).

Importance of topic

Citation to relevant outside data

Explanatory footnote

During the campaign, disguising the Republican Party's long-standing strong opposition to legal abortions could have advantaged Bush in several ways. First, only a small minority of Americans shares the Republican Party's official position—only 17 percent in the most recent Gallup poll (Gallup Organization and USA Today 2003). Publicly supporting an unpopular policy is not likely to increase one's broad-based general election support.[2] Second, even within the Republican Party, the abortion issue has generated tremendous conflict. The last several conventions have been characterized by a certain amount of rancor over abortion, although these disagreements are most visible when the platform is written before the convention. Third, Bush's campaign may have been trying to avoid having an abortion controversy attach itself to the candidate and increase the attention paid to this issue by voters.

Statement of research question

It seems reasonably clear that Bush attempted to obscure his abortion position to broaden his appeal to pro-choice voters, but on an issue as salient as abortion, how effective was this strategy? Was it, in fact, any more effective at preventing defection of pro-choice Republicans than Gore's clear statement of his abortion position was effective at preventing defection of pro-life Democrats? Because there are a roughly equal number of pro-life Democrats and pro-choice Republicans (Greene and Brians 2001), the most effective test may be to determine how many of each party's adherents defected in presidential voting. This comparison is facilitated by the fact that there are only small differences in the issue importance between those in the minority in either party—that is, pro-life Democrats or pro-choice Republicans (Greene and Brians 2001).

Rationale underlying approach to research

Review of literature

Those holding minority abortion policy views in a given political party may not defect and vote for the candidate closer to their view because the voters may not see the issue as that important, they may choose to ignore their party's and candidate's views on the issue, or they may not realize they do not hold the dominant view in the party. While candidates' actions and statements may facilitate each of these possibilities by making their issue position less obvious, voters who attribute their own position to their favored candidate—or at least "move" their favored candidate's attitudes closer to their own position—find it easier to vote for that candidate (Wilson and Gronke 2000; Krosnick 1990; Martinez 1988). The tendency of some voters to project policy positions onto candidates to rationalize their vote choice was empirically identified in the 1948 presidential election (Berelson, Lazarsfeld, and McPhee 1954, 219–223), the 1968 election (Brody and Page 1972; Page and Brody 1972), and the 1980 election (Wattenberg 1991, 111–116).[3]

Assessment of strengths and weakness of the design

Quantitatively testing an apparent campaign strategy, such as the obfuscation of an abortion policy position, poses serious challenges, because one cannot know what other outcomes might have occurred in the absence of the

---

[2] Although Al Gore's issue positions were closer to more voters, the vice president often seemed unable to communicate his shared ideas with voters during this campaign, leading to a widespread lack of accurate issue knowledge about the candidates in 2000 (Waldman and Jamieson 2003).
[3] While Reagan benefited from rationalizations that citizens used to vote against Carter in 1980, voters seemed more comfortable acknowledging their policy differences with Reagan in 1984 while still supporting him at the polls (Wattenberg 1991, 116).

Use of a control

strategy. On the one hand, Governor Bush would seem to be successful if he did not do worse than Vice President Gore at preventing defections by abortion opinion minorities in his party through projection. On the other hand, an identical outcome could suggest that Gore was more successful, because he achieved no worse defections without obfuscating his abortion position. Alternatively, if abortion has been a more contentious issue for Republicans, Bush simply holding his defections equal to Gore's may connote success. Ultimately, it is not possible to know for certain what voters would have done if Bush had more clearly stated his abortion stance. Still, it would be instructive to compare the 2000 election data to 1996, when the Democratic nominee held Gore's position, but the Republican presidential nominee had been identified as open to a pro-choice position. This was particularly highlighted when Senator Bob Dole chose pro-choice New York Representative Susan Molinari to be the 1996 Republican National Convention keynote speaker, and proposed including language that tolerated alternative points of view on abortion in the party platform. Thus, to gain perspective, at several points in the analysis, 2000 data will be compared and contrasted with the 1996 results.

Data

Method of study
Secondary analysis of data
Identification of the (independent and dependent) variables

Discussion of question wording

Coding procedure

Footnote specifying the coding rationale

We primarily use data from the 2000 National Election Studies (NES), as well as the 1996 NES, in order to assess the role that abortion played in the 2000 campaign. Our analyses rely principally on several key variables: respondent's position on abortion, respondent's placement of the presidential candidates on abortion, respondent's partisanship, and respondent's two-party vote choice. The analyses are conducted by placing respondents into four groups based upon their partisanship and abortion position: pro-choice Democrats, pro-life Democrats, pro-choice Republicans, and pro-life Republicans.

The standard NES abortion question ranges from 1 to 4, with 1 being "abortion should never be permitted," 2 stating that "abortion should be permitted in case of rape, incest, and threat to mother's life," 3 indicating that "only after the need for the abortion has clearly been established," and 4 holding that "by law, a woman should always be able to obtain an abortion as a matter of personal choice." Respondents place themselves, as well as each candidate, on this scale. In order to categorize our respondents, we place those who indicated that their own position was 1 or 2 as pro-life and those indicating 4 as pro-choice. Unfortunately, the "clear need" category proves so problematic that we choose not to group respondents based upon this belief.[4] As for the partisanship basis of our group categorizations, because we are interested in how the supporters of each party stand on abortion, leaners may reasonably be grouped with self-identified party supporters (Greene 2000). We use these four categories to analyze respondent vote choice and respondent placement of candidates' abortion position in both 1996 and 2000.

---

[4] When exploring how people with this attitude characterize "supporters of abortion" and "opponents of abortion" on the 1990 NES feeling thermometer measures, the mean values are close—45 and 55, respectively (on a 0 to 100 scale)—and the distribution of scores has large numbers at the extreme ends of both measures. This group seems to contain persons holding a range of moderate and situational abortion views, making it impossible to accurately place them into either a pro-life or pro-choice category.

Data Analysis

Restatement of research purpose and cases and time periods

Our analyses examine general voting patterns depending upon abortion attitudes and partisanship and evaluate more specific tests of the possibility that voters projected their own attitudes onto candidates. Although our main focus is the 2000 election, we include 1996 data as well, to provide a relative baseline for the 2000 candidates' performance. The primary goal of these analyses is to determine which candidate benefited most from his

Democrats Only

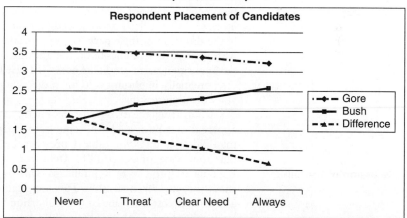

Republicans Only

Graphic presentation

Figure 1   Presidential Candidates' Abortion Position as Rated by Voters Depending upon Citizen Abortion Position

SOURCE: 2000 National Election Study.

NOTE: The x-axis represents respondents' positions on when abortion should be legal, and the y-axis tracks respondents' perceptions of each candidate's abortion view. On the x-axis, never means "by law, abortion should never be permitted," threat indicates that "the law should permit abortion only in case of rape, incest, or when the woman's life is in danger," clear need means that "abortion should be permitted only after the need for the abortion has clearly been established," and always indicates that "by law, a woman should always be able to obtain an abortion as a matter of personal choice."

Table 1

Vote Percent by Partisanship and Abortion Attitude in 1996 and 2000

	1996		2000	
	Dole	**Clinton**	**Bush**	**Gore**
Pro-choice Democrats	5	95	7	93
	(15)	(266)	(22)	(273)
Pro-life Democrats	8	92	15	85
	(13)	(156)	(26)	(148)
Pro-choice Republicans	71	29	82	18
	(93)	(38)	(118)	(26)
Pro-life Republicans	92	8	96	4
	(217)	(18)	(226)	(10)

SOURCE: 1996 and 2000 National Election Studies.
NOTE: The numbers in parentheses are cell frequencies.

Table

Presentation of the results

Discussion of the graphic presentation

Discussion of the table

campaign's approach to abortion policy: whether it was Gore's more plainly stated position, or Bush's less clear abortion position. The secondary and related goal is to assess the relative impact of projection for the candidacies of Bush and Gore.

The initial examination of projection on the abortion issue indicates similar levels of misperception about both candidates by both Republicans and Democrats, regardless of abortion attitude. In Figure 1, we see that as Democrats become more liberal on abortion, the distance they see between Bush and Gore on the issue increases dramatically. Likewise, as Republicans become more conservative on abortion, the distance between Gore and Bush increases in a similarly pronounced fashion. In general, as respondents move in the direction of their party's core position, they are not only more in line with their party's candidate on the abortion issue but are more distant from the opposition party candidate as well. These figures thus further demonstrate the potentially important role for projection of abortion positions to play in voter decision making.

Comparing the two-party vote with partisans' abortion stances, it is apparent that Bush held the Republican Party together much better in 2000 than did Dole in 1996. Table 1 presents the percentage of voters in each of our four categories (pro-life Democrat, pro-choice Democrat, pro-life Republican, pro-choice Republican) who voted for each of the major party candidates in 1996 and 2000. This cross-tabulation of the two-party vote by a four-level combined measure of abortion stance and partisanship demonstrates that the GOP lost substantially more pro-choice Republican votes (29 versus 18 percent) in 1996 as opposed to 2000, and even saw 8 percent of the pro-life Republicans defect in 1996. On the other hand, even though Gore held onto pro-choice Democratic votes at a rate almost equal to Clinton (93 versus 95 percent), he lost 15 percent of pro-life Democrats, in contrast to only 8 percent for Clinton. Thus, even though the Democratic Party appeared to have an absolute advantage on the abortion issue in 2000, its position was weakened relative to 1996.

Given the political salience and personal importance attached to the abortion issue, one might ask why there are not more defections in vote choice, especially among pro-life Democrats. Tables 2A and 2B present analyses

Table 2a
Projection of Abortion Attitudes on 2000 Presidential Candidates

	Pro-choice Democrat	Pro-life Democrat	Pro-choice Republican	Pro-life Republican
Abortion rating for Gore	3.56	2.76	3.34	3.54
Abortion rating for Bush	2.02	2.30	2.70	2.07
Respondent-Gore abortion distance	0.48	1.12	0.78	1.84
Respondent-Bush abortion distance	2.07	0.76	1.43	1.22

SOURCE: 2000 National Election Study.
NOTE: Gore's and Bush's abortion positions were rated by respondents on a scale ranging from 1 to 4, with 1 barring all legal abortions and 4 leaving the choice entirely to the woman. Respondent-Gore and Respondent-Bush distance shows the relative distance between the respondent's own abortion placement and where he placed Bush and where he placed Gore. The lower this number, the closer the respondent's own abortion position is to the candidate's perceived position.

Table 2b
Projection of Abortion Attitudes on 1996 Presidential Candidates

	Pro-choice Democrat	Pro-life Democrat	Pro-choice Republican	Pro-life Republican
Abortion rating for Clinton	3.56	2.76	3.26	3.59
Abortion rating for Dole	1.99	2.26	2.45	2.12
Respondent-Clinton abortion distance	0.44	1.12	0.74	1.86
Respondent-Dole abortion distance	2.00	0.94	1.55	0.47

SOURCE: 1996 National Election Study.
NOTE: Clinton's and Dole's abortion positions were rated by respondents on a 1 to 4 abortion scale, where 1 bars all legal abortions and 4 leaves the choice entirely to the woman.

Table

demonstrating the high levels of projection taking place on the abortion issue. The projection on abortion is most evident in the pro-life Democrats' ratings of Gore and Clinton and pro-choice Republicans' ratings of Bush and Dole. One can clearly see that these groups are, in fact, dramatic outliers. Pro-life Democrats place Gore at 2.76, when objectively, his true position would have to be close to 4. Likewise, pro-choice Republicans place Bush at 2.70, when his actual position could objectively not be considered more than 2—which is almost exactly where the other groups placed him. The results follow a very similar pattern in 1996. The notable difference is that Bush is seen as more pro-choice, 2.70, by pro-choice Republicans, than is Dole, 2.46, who was actually the more liberal of the two on abortion. At least relative to Dole, Bush's strategy on abortion was clearly more effective.

Discussion of the table

Assessment of the correspondence between predictions based on theory and actual observations

Additionally, Tables 2a and 2b provide strong evidence as to why the Democratic candidates are more effective at holding their party's minority abortion position voters. In both 1996 and 2000, pro-life Democrats saw themselves as 1.12 away from the Democratic candidate. In contrast, Bush was seen as 1.43 away from pro-choice Republicans. In sum, the results in Tables 2a and 2b suggest that Democratic candidates benefit from projection on the abortion issue more than Republicans. Crucially, in 2000's razor-thin outcome, Bush was much more successful in keeping pro-choice Republicans loyal, clearly in part from a campaign that allowed very substantial projection of their own abortion issue position onto him.[5]

Conclusion

This study indicates that campaigns may be able to influence voters' level of misinformation about candidates' issue positions. These preliminary results suggest that Governor Bush was more successful in obscuring his, and his party's, abortion policy position among voters in 2000, than was Senator Dole in 1996. Vice President Gore's more straightforward approach may have cost him some support, when compared to President Bill Clinton in 1996.

The salience of abortion will most likely only increase in upcoming elections. With recent controversies over "partial-birth" abortion and anticipation already building over what are likely to be among the most contentious Supreme Court appointments ever made—largely due to concerns over the continued legality of abortion—the ability of presidential candidates to strategically campaign on the abortion issue and take advantage of voter's predilections toward projection will become even more important. The Democrats seem to have an advantage on the issue, for the time being, but Bush's 2000 performance suggests that this advantage can be dramatically diminished.

Some may be concerned by this article's findings and the potential for future manipulation of public opinion by campaigns. Clearly, the degree to which candidates will be able to increase voters' misperceptions of their issue stances in the 2004 presidential election largely depends upon the news media's attention to the campaign. The substantially greater care most campaigns have used in preparing and documenting their advertising following the intense press attention to ads in the 1988 campaign demonstrates that candidates can regulate their own behavior when they know that the watchdogs are on duty. Thus, it is reasonable to conclude that if the press closely watches the candidates in 2004, the projection seen among voters in 2000 is less likely to be repeated.

References

Berelson, Bernard, Paul F. Lazarsfeld, and William N. McPhee. 1954. *Voting: A Study of Opinion Formation in a Presidential Campaign*. Chicago: University of Chicago Press.

Brody, Richard A., and Benjamin I. Page. 1972. "Comment: The Assessment of Policy Voting." *American Political Science Review* 66 (June): 450–458.

Commission on Presidential Debates. 2000. *General Election Presidential Debates, October 3*. University of Massachusetts, Boston. Available from http://www.debates.org/pages/debhis2000.html.

---

[5] In an analysis not reported here, we found that abortion is not the only issue where Governor Bush benefited from voter projection in 2000. More voters projected their government spending views onto Bush in 2000 than had done the same with Dole in 1996.

Gallup Organization and *USA Today.* 2003. October 24–26, 2003. *National Survey of 1006 Adults.* Storrs, CT: Roper Center at the University of Connecticut.

Greene, Steven. 2000. "The Psychological Sources of Partisan-leaning Independence." *American Politics Quarterly* 28 (October): 511–537.

Greene, Steven, and Craig Leonard Brians. 2001. "Elite Versus Popular Views on Abortion within American Political Parties." Paper prepared for presentation at the Annual Meeting of the Midwest Political Science Association, April 19–22, Chicago.

Krosnick, Jon A. 1990. "Americans' Perceptions of Presidential Candidates: A Test of the Projection Hypothesis." *Journal of Social Issues* 46 (Summer): 159–182.

Larry King Live. 2000. GOP Debate with Senator John McCain and Governor George W. Bush. *CNN,* February 15.

Martinez, Michael D. 1988. "Political Involvement and the Projection Process." *Political Behavior* 10 (Spring): 151–167.

Page, Benjamin I., and Richard A. Brody. 1972. "Policy Voting and the Electoral Process: The Vietnam War Issue." *American Political Science Review* 66 (September): 979–995.

Waldman, Paul, and Kathleen Hall Jamieson. 2003. "Rhetorical Convergence and Issue Knowledge in the 2000 Presidential Election." *Presidential Studies Quarterly* 33 (March): 145–163.

Wattenberg, Martin P. 1991. *The Rise of Candidate-Centered Politics.* Cambridge, MA: Harvard University Press.

Wilson, J. Matthew, and Paul Gronke. 2000. "Concordance and Projection in Citizen Perceptions of Congressional Roll-Call voting." *Legislative Studies Quarterly* 25 (August): 445–467.

Suggested Readings and References

A book that addresses all facets encountered in writing political analyses is Diane E. Schmidt, *Writing in Political Science: A Practical Guide,* 3rd ed. (New York: Pearson Longman, 2005). For excellent suggestions on ways to improve your writing style, see William Strunk, Jr., with E. B. White, *The Elements of Style,* 4th ed. (Boston: Allyn and Bacon, 2000). *Bartlett's Roget's Thesaurus* (Boston: Little Brown, 1996) can contribute much to the clarity and variety of your presentation and can, on occasion, offer direction for reducing your reliance on jargon. For guidance on the proper form and placement of footnotes and bibliography, consult *The Style Manual for Political Science,* rev. ed. (Washington, DC: American Political Science Association, 2001); Kate L. Turabian, *A Manual for Writers of Term Papers, Theses, and Dissertations,* 6th ed. (Chicago: University of Chicago: Press, 1996).

The best place to find sample research reports is in the journals of political science and related disciplines described in Chapter 3. Excerpts from articles that illustrate many of the principles of research discussed in this text are found in Marcus E. Ethridge, *The Political Research Experience: Readings and Analysis,* 3rd ed. (Armonk, NY: M.E Sharpe, 2002).

Examples of the APSA reference and citation format are available at the author's Web site www.psci.vt.edu/brians/.

Research Exercises

1. Read and *outline* three research articles in political science journals. Decide whether all the necessary elements of a research report are present in each case.

2. Read and *evaluate* the writing of three research articles in political science journals. Pay attention both to the method of the study and to the structure of the research report.

3. Read and *abstract* three research articles in political science journals. Where possible, compare your abstract with that prepared by the author of the article (which you should not read until you have finished your abstract).

Key Term

abstract

CHAPTER 23

Overview

We have now presented the basic information you need to plan and execute a complete research project. In Figure 5.6 in Chapter 5 we provided an overview of the research process. We have explored the components of that process at length in the remainder of the text. In this closing chapter we review the research process as an integrated whole. We stress the ways in which the steps you have seen separated by chapter boundaries are, in practice, interwoven and interdependent. Our purpose is to facilitate your attacking research questions with a full understanding of the research process rather than a disjointed focus on each stage as it is reached. The value of an integrated understanding, of course, is that *many research problems can be avoided if the researcher is aware of the implications of decisions made at one stage of a project for subsequent stages.*

Developing Hypotheses, Measures, and a Research Design

Research begins with a research question that asks why things are as we observe them to be. We are generally seeking an explanation for observed events. The place to start looking for this explanation is in the social science literature pertaining to our general subject. If we are fortunate, a literature search will turn up a ready-made explanation in the form of a theory that others have developed to explain events like the one that interests us. More often, however, we have to use the literature more creatively to *devise* the best explanation we can, given existing information about the subject. The remainder of the research process is then devoted to testing this explanation to see how much it adds to our understanding of the events in question.

Stating Hypotheses   The first step in this testing is to state some hypotheses that logic tells us must be accurate if our proposed answer to the research question is valid. These hypotheses serve several key functions. In the first place, they identify the units of analysis that must be observed if we are to assess our explanation. Second, they isolate the variables for which we must devise indicators. Finally, hypotheses suggest ways in which our observations must be organized in order to provide useful evidence of the validity of our explanation. In stating hypotheses we must always ask whether we can actually observe the stated relationship. Can we locate the necessary data, or do we have the resources required to collect them for ourselves? It is essential that researchers select hypotheses that can be adequately tested with the time, skills, and resources available to them. To do otherwise is to ensure failure.

Operationalizing Hypotheses   Next, the variables identified in the hypotheses must be operationalized so that we can obtain measures to compare in reaching a conclusion about the accuracy of our predictions. In selecting operationalizations or measurement procedures, we must be acutely sensitive to the resources required to apply them. If we don't have the necessary time, money, or cooperation of subjects, we cannot use the measuring procedure. In addition, we have to ask whether we are altering the meaning of any of the concepts included in our explanation when we let the results of any given measuring procedure represent them in our research. Though validity can often be assessed in data analysis, the question of validity must be faced well in advance of data collection, for no amount of clever data analysis can make an invalid measure useful.

Choosing Measurements   When creating measures, we must already be thinking ahead to the data analysis stage of the research. Researchers should examine their hypotheses to determine exactly what mathematical and statistical comparisons will be necessary to test their accuracy. They must then be sure that the measuring procedures they have selected will yield data suitable for those procedures. A central consideration here is the fit between the level of measurement obtained from a given operationalization and the level of measurement required by the statistical procedures that will be used to test the hypotheses. Those who plan to use a measure of association that requires ordinal-level measurement must be certain that their measuring process yields at least ordinal data. A second consideration here is the similarity between the distribution of the values obtained with a measurement procedure and the distribution assumed by the statistical procedures that will be applied. Those who plan to use a test of statistical significance requiring a normal distribution to be valid should be certain their measuring procedure does not preclude obtaining a near normal distribution.

Selecting a Research Design   The next step is the development of a research design to guide the application of our measuring procedures. The central purpose of a research design is to ensure that we can feel confident that any relationships we observe are the result of the processes described in our explanation and not of some other set of processes. Research designs provide this confidence by allowing us to rule out alternative rival hypotheses. A good research design, then, begins with a review of the literature. That review (along with logical analysis of situations) can suggest the major alternative rival hypotheses that must be ruled out before we can place confidence in our central explanation of observed events.

Research designs are developed by (1) identifying the comparisons that must be made in order to test a hypothesis, (2) deciding what observations must be made (of whom or what, in what order, by what means, under what conditions) before those comparisons can be made, (3) anticipating all results that might be obtained from making the comparisons (no relationship, a positive relationship, a negative relationship, and so forth), (4) identifying the major alternative rival hypotheses that can explain each possible result, and (5) organizing a set of observations that will allow the additional comparisons necessary to test the validity of the most important of these alternative rival hypotheses as explanations of whatever results are observed.

Choosing Data Analysis   It is essential that we know what statistical analyses we want to perform when we develop a research design, for it is the design that determines what data will be available for analysis. For example, if we anticipate controlling for many variables in the data analysis stage, we must be certain that our research design will yield enough cases to allow for such a complex breakdown of the sample. If we want to hold party affiliation constant by examining measures of association between two key variables for members of each party separately, we must include enough members of each party for computation of valid measures of association and must plan to obtain information on subjects' party affiliation. If we plan to use time-series analysis in a study employing aggregate data, we must be sure that data on values of our independent variable come from a period prior to the time at which data on the dependent variable are collected if we have theoretical reasons to believe that there is a lag in the impact of the IV on the DV.

In the design of research, as in the selection of hypotheses and the devising of measures, it is essential that we ask whether we are setting ourselves too ambitious a task. The best research design in the world is useless if the researcher lacks the resources to execute it. One must give careful consideration to the costs and logistics of data collection in designing research projects.

Data Collection and Analysis

As we have presented the research process, data collection and analysis are carried out in order to test hypotheses. We have discussed the primary rules to be observed in using various methods of data collection and analysis and, in Chapter 2, described the process of reasoning from empirical results to theory, thereby completing the research circle. There is no need to repeat those discussions here. We would, however, like to make two points that may not have come through our sequential presentation as clearly as they should.

Using Multiple Methods   The first point is that although we have presented the various data collection techniques separately, they need not be kept separate in the research process. In fact, there are very good reasons for *mixing* methods of data collection in a study. In the first place, different methods can serve different purposes. Researchers may, for example, use focus groups to determine the breadth and nature of people's concerns about a set of political issues, then use survey research to estimate the *distribution* of those same views among the general population. In addition, it is often useful to employ a variety of methods in the data collection stage of a study because of the added confidence *multiple methods of measurement* can give us in the validity of results, as discussed in Chapters 5 and 11. For example, in studying variations in the quality of public services among a city's neighborhoods, one will find it useful to confirm assessments of service quality obtained from survey research by means of aggregate data, official records, interviews with public officials, and the judgments of trained observers. If all these methods of measurement produce a similar ranking of neighborhoods, researchers can feel quite confident that they have accurately measured service quality.

Figure 23.1
Checklist

A CHECKLIST FOR EVALUATING EMPIRICAL RESEARCH

☐ 1. Is the research question clearly stated? Do we know what the objectives of the research are so that we can assess the overall project? Is the research clearly related to some larger political issue or problem? Is this an important subject to study?

☐ 2. Are the units of analysis clearly identified, correctly chosen, and consistently used throughout the project?

☐ 3. Are the concepts employed in the research clearly specified and adequately developed? Do the concepts have identifiable referents?

☐ 4. Is it clear what explanations are being tested? If a theory is used, is it logically correct? Do the concepts have identifiable empirical referents?

☐ 5. Is the theory or explanation consistent with existing literature on the subject? Is there evidence of a thorough literature review? Is the relationship of this research to prior research and larger political issues made clear?

☐ 6. Are hypotheses to be tested identified clearly and stated correctly? Do they logically follow from the explanation or theory being examined? Are they empirically testable?

☐ 7. If more than one hypothesis is being tested, are the relationships between them specified? Are all hypotheses clearly related to the theory, and their role in testing it made explicit?

☐ 8. Are the variables under investigation clearly identified and their status (independent, dependent, intervening, antecedent) specified in the hypotheses?

☐ 9. Are variables that might be expected to modify predicted relationships included in the study? (For example, can we expect relationships to hold for both men and women, or, in both industrialized and nonindustrialized nations?)

☐ 10. Are operationalizations of concepts stated clearly and measurement procedures specified in sufficient detail that others can replicate them? Have others used these operationalizations?

☐ 11. Are the measures likely to be valid and reliable? Are tests of validity and reliability anticipated? Are threats to validity and reliability recognized and provisions made to control them?

☐ 12. Is the research design clearly stated and appropriate for testing the hypotheses being examined? Are major alternative rival hypotheses recognized and provision made in the research design for examining these hypotheses as alternative explanations? Will the design provide a logically sound basis for causal inferences?

☐ 13. Is the population of interest to the researcher identified clearly? Is the sample used representative of that population? If not, does the researcher recognize the limitations this places on how results can be generalized? Are sampling procedures adequately described?

☐ 14. Is the data collection technique employed (survey research, content analysis, and so forth) appropriate to the study given its units of analysis and the type of information being sought? Are all procedural rules observed that pertain to the particular method of data collection?

☐ 15. Is the data collection fully described? Are outside primary data sources fully identified so others can locate them?

☐ 16. Are coding systems that might affect measurement (such as collapsing various income groups into broad categories or treating certain types of responses as supportive or nonsupportive) fully described and justified?

☐ 17. Is the construction of any indices or scales fully described? Do these summary measures preserve the meaning of the concepts? Do they seem to be unidimensional (to reflect a single underlying concept or pattern)?

(continued)

Figure 23.1
Checklist *(continued)*

A CHECKLIST FOR EVALUATING EMPIRICAL RESEARCH

☐ 18. Have instruments been pretested?

☐ 19. Have efforts been made to verify results? (For example, have follow-up calls been made to survey respondents, or have alternative sources of aggregate data been sought?)

☐ 20. In presenting the data, are the tables and figures appropriate for illustrating the point they are intended to make? Are they fully discussed in the text and their central significance pointed out? Do they represent the results accurately?

☐ 21. Are the tables and figures clearly and completely labeled so that they can be easily interpreted?

☐ 22. Are the interpretations of the tables and figures offered correct, or do they suggest a misreading of the data?

☐ 23. Are appropriate descriptive statistics (such as mean and standard deviation) used to summarize the data and supplement tables and figures?

☐ 24. In examining relationships between variables, do the researchers provide evidence of the strength, direction, form, and significance of relationships?

☐ 25. Do the researchers explore the possible effects of antecedent, intervening, and suppressor variables? Do they attempt to control these effects in the data analysis?

☐ 26. Are all statistics used appropriate for the level at which variables are measured, and are they suited to the purpose for which they are used?

☐ 27. Do the data conform to the assumptions (random sampling, normal distribution, and so forth) involved in legitimate application of the statistics used? Have the researchers investigated the degree to which their data fit these assumptions?

☐ 28. Are measures of statistical significance applied only where appropriate and correctly interpreted? Have the researchers avoided confusing statistical significance with substantive significance?

☐ 29. Are major alternative rival hypotheses statistically explored and the results both reported and correctly interpreted?

☐ 30. Is each piece of data analysis clearly related to the major conclusions drawn from the study? Are the interpretations consistent with the data and with the theory or explanation being tested?

☐ 31. Does the research report:

☐   a. contain a precise statement of the purpose of the study?

☐   b. review enough of the relevant literature to demonstrate the contribution of this study?

☐   c. adequately describe the research design, data, and methods used?

☐   d. follow a clear and appropriate organization in presenting findings?

☐   e. state conclusions clearly?

☐ 32. Are the conclusions reached actually warranted by the data presented and the research design used? Does the study make the kind of contribution to the literature the authors claim it does, or have the authors generalized too far beyond the limits of their research?

☐ 33. Have the authors been sensitive to ethical issues raised by the research? Have they satisfactorily resolved these issues?

Exploring Your Topic   A second point is that empirical research can be exploratory in nature. Rather than using it to test hypotheses derived from explanations, we can use it to provide data to be used in devising explanations in the first place. Each research project generally raises new questions, suggests new explanations, and leads to new research. If you look back at Figure 5.6, you will see a shortcut from *generalization of observed relationships* to *hypotheses* and back to *data analysis*. This shortcut is the result of applying inductive logic in data analysis. It can be an important step in empirical inquiry, for it suggests new data analyses that can allow researchers to refine and elaborate explanations in ways they did not anticipate when designing a project or, even without collecting new data, to test explanations they did not anticipate.

A Checklist for Judging Research

In an evaluation of others' research or in the design of your own, it is often helpful to step back from the details of each stage and try to get an overview of the research, asking whether it meets certain general but clearly stated requirements of sound empirical inquiry. To facilitate your doing this, we have provided, in Figure 23.1, a list of things to look for. The questions are listed in approximately the sequence in which you might expect to encounter different problems in a report of research or in the execution of a project. The rules suggested by these questions are broad, and a project that "checks out" on all these items may still contain subtle or highly technical errors. Nonetheless, if you can answer "yes" to each of the questions in the figure, the research being assessed is probably free of any error that this book has prepared you to identify and exhibits the basics of sound research.

In using the checklist, be aware of three cautions. First, not all questions will apply to any one research project. Exploratory research, for example, will not be designed to test hypotheses, and research based on elite interviews will probably not require a random sample. Second, the questions refer to technical rather than substantive aspects of research. A researcher may do everything correctly and still be investigating a trivial subject. *Valuable research is that which is both technically correct and substantively important.* In judging research, ask whether its proper execution will add useful knowledge to our attempts to understand significant political events. Sometimes, lower levels of technical sophistication are justified by the complexity and magnitude of an important subject. On the whole, the project that adds a little to our knowledge of an important subject is more valuable than a project that adds a lot to our knowledge of a trivial matter. Third, few projects can be free of limitations. For instance, it may be impossible to obtain a representative sample of an entire large population within the resource limits of a given study. It may be necessary to sample only one subgroup (as when a study of American political behavior is conducted with a sample from one city only). Such limitations become errors only when the researcher fails to recognize them and modify accordingly the conclusions drawn from the study.

The checklist can be used to assess others' research as well as to evaluate your own. As a research exercise, you may want to locate an article reporting the results of a research project and evaluate it using the checklist in Figure 23.1, identifying any errors you may find and explaining why they are errors. We have presented the table in a way that makes it easy to photocopy for repeated use.

Researching Ethically   The last set of standards included in Figure 23.1 for judging research is of a different character from the technical considerations listed there. Research must also be judged for its conformity to ethical standards. What constitutes an ethical or unethical practice is often a matter of personal judgment by researchers, and standards can vary widely. Some generally accepted standards of ethical conduct have evolved in all social science disciplines. We present examples in Appendix B. Practicing political scientists must be aware of these professional standards and sensitive to the ethical issues raised by specific research situations.

Throughout this volume we have emphasized the necessity of a strong commitment to ethical research. The questions in Figure 23.1 and the professional guidelines in Appendix B should offer concrete means to answer the myriad of ethical issues that are raised in research, ranging from the necessity of protecting research subjects from harm, to presenting analyses that fairly represent the underlying data.

Conclusion

Armed only with the information contained in this book, you could successfully carry out a very wide range of empirical investigations. You should recognize, however, that this text has only scratched the surface of the huge subject of empirical political research. The dozens of other books listed in our suggestions for further reading should convince you that there is much more to be said and much you cannot learn from this book.

In the process of research, you may discover the importance of the things you do *not* know. Even if you carefully and properly follow every guideline and rule presented in this text, you may find yourself either (1) unable to complete some research projects or (2) producing a set of research results that more experienced social scientists recognize as seriously flawed because you have made errors we did not warn you against. If you follow the suggestions presented in the first five chapters, you should make very few errors in stating hypotheses, operationalizing concepts, searching the literature, or devising a research design. Our chapters on sampling and data management probably provide less complete guides, however, because those processes are both more technical and more closely tied to the situations encountered in individual research projects. Similarly, we have been able to offer you a less than complete guide to the various data collection and data analysis techniques because of the scope and technical nature of these subjects, and you are well-advised to study them further before claiming expertise in empirical analysis. The suggestions for further reading at the ends of chapters provide good *starting places* for acquiring genuine expertise.

We have provided a sound foundation on which you can build your competence as a political scientist. We hope you find that task as exciting and rewarding as we have and that in the future you will agree that getting there was half the fun.

APPENDIX A

Statistical Tables

Table A.1
Random digits

10097	32533	76520	13586	34673	54876	80959	09117	39292	74945
37542	04805	64894	74296	24805	24037	20636	10402	00822	91665
08422	68953	19645	09303	23209	02560	15953	34764	35080	33606
99019	02529	09376	70715	38311	31165	88676	74397	04436	27659
12807	99970	80157	36147	64032	36653	98951	16877	12171	76833
66065	74717	34072	76850	36697	36170	65813	39885	11199	29170
31060	10805	45571	82406	35303	42614	86799	07439	23403	09732
85269	77602	02051	65692	68665	74818	73053	85247	18623	88579
63573	32135	05325	47048	90553	57548	28468	28709	83491	25624
73796	45753	03529	64778	35808	34282	60935	20344	35273	88435
98520	17767	14905	68607	22109	40558	60970	93433	50500	73998
11805	05431	39808	27732	50725	68248	29405	24201	52775	67851
83452	99634	06288	98083	13746	70078	18475	40610	68711	77817
88685	40200	86507	58401	36766	67951	90364	76493	29609	11062
99594	67348	87517	64969	91826	08928	93785	61368	23478	34113
65481	17674	17468	50950	58047	76974	73039	57186	40218	16544
80124	35635	17727	08015	45318	22374	21115	78253	14385	53763
74350	99817	77402	77214	43236	00201	45521	64237	96286	02655
69916	26803	66252	29148	36936	87203	76621	13990	94400	56418
09893	20505	14225	68514	46427	56788	96297	78822	54382	14598
91499	14523	68479	27686	46162	83554	94750	89923	37089	20048
80336	94598	26490	36858	70297	34135	53140	33340	42050	82341
44104	81949	85157	47954	32979	26575	57600	40881	22222	06413
12550	73742	11100	02040	12860	74697	96644	89439	28707	25815
63606	49329	16505	34484	40219	52563	43651	77082	07207	31790
61196	90446	26457	47774	51924	33729	65394	59593	42582	60527
5474	45266	95270	79953	59367	83848	82396	10118	33211	59466
94557	28573	67897	54387	54622	44431	91190	42592	92927	45973
42481	16213	97344	08721	16868	48767	03071	12059	25701	46670
23523	78317	73208	89837	68935	91416	26252	29663	05522	82562
04493	52494	75246	33824	45826	51025	61962	79335	65337	12472
00549	97654	64501	88159	96119	63896	54692	82391	23287	29529
35963	15307	26898	09354	33351	35462	77974	50024	90103	39333
59808	08391	45427	26842	83609	49700	13021	24892	78565	20106
46058	85236	01390	92286	77281	44077	93910	83647	70617	42941

Table A.1
Random digits
(continued)

32179	00597	87379	25241	05567	07007	86743	17157	85394	11838
69234	61406	20117	45204	15956	60000	18743	92423	97118	96338
19565	41430	01758	75379	40419	21585	66674	36806	84962	85207
45155	14938	19476	07246	43667	94543	59047	90033	20826	69541
94864	31994	36168	10851	81553	34888	01540	35456	05014	51176
98086	24826	45240	28404	44999	08896	39094	73407	35441	31880
33185	16232	41941	50949	89435	48581	88695	41994	37548	73043
80951	00406	96382	70774	20151	23387	25016	25298	94624	61171
79752	49140	71961	28296	69861	02591	74852	20539	00387	59579
18633	32537	98145	06571	31010	24674	05455	61427	77938	91936
74029	43902	77557	32270	97790	17119	52527	58021	80814	51748
54178	45611	80993	37143	05335	12969	56127	19255	36040	90324
11664	49883	52079	84827	59381	71539	09973	33440	88461	23356
48324	77928	31249	64710	02295	36870	32307	57546	15020	09994
69074	94138	87637	91976	35584	04401	10518	21615	01848	76938

Source: The RAND Corporation. *A Million Random Digits with 100,000 Normal Deviates* (New York: Free Press, 1966), p. 1. Reprinted with permission.

Table A.2
Sample size for sampling attributes at specified levels of precision (in percent with a 95% confidence interval, p = 0.5)*

Population Size	Sample Size for Precision of					
	±1%	±2%	±3%	±4%	±5%	±10%
500	†	†	†	†	222	83
1,000	†	†	†	385	286	91
1,500	†	†	638	441	316	94
2,000	†	†	714	476	333	95
2,500	†	1,250	769	500	345	96
3,000	†	1,364	811	517	353	97
3,500	†	1,458	843	530	359	97
4,000	†	1,538	870	541	364	98
4,500	†	1,607	891	549	367	98
5,000	†	1,667	909	556	370	98
6,000	†	1,765	938	566	375	98
7,000	†	1,842	959	574	378	99
8,000	†	1,905	976	580	381	99
9,000	†	1,957	989	584	383	99
10,000	5,000	2,000	1,000	588	385	99
15,000	6,000	2,143	1,034	600	390	99
20,000	6,667	2,222	1,053	606	392	100
25,000	7,143	2,273	1,064	610	394	100
50,000	8,333	2,381	1,087	617	397	100
100,000	9,091	2,439	1,099	621	398	100
⟶ ∞	10,000	2,500	1,111	625	400	100

SOURCE: Taro Yamane, *Elementary Sampling Theory* (Englewood Cliffs, NJ: Prentice Hall, 1967), p. 398. Adapted and reprinted with permission of the publisher.

* Proportion of units in the sample possessing the characteristic being measured; for other values of p, the required sample size will be smaller.

† In these cases, 50% of the universe in the sample will give more than the required accuracy. Since the formal distribution is a poor approximation of the hypergeometrical distribution when *n* is more than 50% of *N*, the formula used in this calculation does not apply.

Table A.3
Sample size for sampling attributes at specified levels of precision (in percent with a 99.7% confidence interval, p = 0.5)*

Population Size	Sample Size for Precision of				
	±1%	±2%	±3%	±4%	±5%
500	†	†	†	†	†
1,000	†	†	†	†	474
1,500	†	†	†	726	563
2,000	†	†	†	826	621
2,500	†	†	†	900	662
3,000	†	†	1,364	958	692
3,500	†	†	1,458	1,003	716
4,000	†	†	1,539	1,041	735
4,500	†	†	1,607	1,071	750
5,000	†	†	1,667	1,098	763
6,000	†	2,903	1,765	1,139	783
7,000	†	3,119	1,842	1,171	798
8,000	†	3,303	1,905	1,196	809
9,000	†	3,462	1,957	1,216	818
10,000	†	3,600	2,000	1,233	826
15,000	†	4,091	2,143	1,286	849
20,000	†	4,390	2,222	1,314	861
25,000	11,842	4,592	2,273	1,331	869
50,000	15,517	5,056	2,381	1,368	884
100,000	18,367	5,325	2,439	1,387	892
$\longrightarrow \chi$	22,500	5,625	2,500	1,406	900

SOURCE: Taro Yamane, *Elementary Sampling Theory* (Englewood Cliffs, NJ: Prentice Hall, 1967), p. 399. Adapted and reprinted with permission of the publisher.

* Proportion of units in the sample possessing the characteristic being measured; for other values of p, the required sample size will be smaller.

† In these cases 50% of the universe in the sample will give more than the required accuracy. Since the formal distribution is a poor approximation of the hypergeometrical distribution when *n* is more than 50% of *N*, the formula used in this calculation does not apply.

Table A.4
Distribution of χ^2

df	.05	.01	.001	df	.05	.01	.001
1	3.841	6.635	10.827	26	38.885	45.642	54.052
2	5.991	9.210	13.815	27	40.113	46.963	55.476
3	7.815	11.345	16.266	28	41.337	48.278	56.893
4	9.488	13.277	18.467	29	42.557	49.588	58.302
5	11.070	15.086	20.515	30	43.773	50.892	59.703
6	12.592	16.812	22.457	32	46.194	53.486	62.487
7	14.067	18.475	24.322	34	48.602	56.061	65.247
8	15.507	20.090	26.125	36	50.999	58.619	67.985
9	16.919	21.666	27.877	38	53.384	61.162	70.703
10	18.307	23.209	29.588	40	55.759	63.691	73.402
11	19.675	24.725	31.264	42	58.124	66.206	76.084
12	21.026	26.217	32.909	44	60.481	68.710	78.750
13	22.362	27.688	34.528	46	62.830	71.201	81.400
14	23.685	29.141	36.123	48	65.171	73.683	84.037
15	24.996	30.578	37.697	50	67.505	76.154	86.661
16	26.296	32.000	39.252	52	69.832	78.616	89.272
17	27.587	33.409	40.790	54	72.153	81.069	91.872
18	28.869	34.805	42.312	56	74.468	83.513	94.461
19	30.144	36.191	43.820	58	76.778	85.950	97.039
20	31.410	37.566	45.315	60	79.082	88.379	99.607
21	32.671	38.932	46.797	62	81.381	90.802	102.166
22	33.924	40.289	48.268	64	83.675	93.217	104.716
23	35.172	41.638	49.728	66	85.965	95.626	107.258
24	36.415	42.980	51.179	68	88.250	98.028	109.791
25	37.652	44.314	52.620	70	90.531	100.425	112.317

SOURCE: From Table IV of Ronald A. Fisher and Frank Yates, *Statistical Tables for Biological, Agricultural and Medical Research,* 6th ed., published by Longman Group, Ltd., London (previously published by Oliver & Boyd, Edinburgh). Reprinted with permission of the authors and the publisher.

Note: For odd values of n between 30 and 70, the mean of the tabular values for $df - 1$ and $df + 1$ may be taken. For larger values of n, the expression $\sqrt{2x^2} - \sqrt{2df - 1}$ may be used as a normal deviate with unit variance, remembering that the probability for x^2 corresponds with that of a single tail of the normal curve.

Table A.5
Values of the correlation coefficient for different levels of significance

df	.1	.05	.01	.001	df	.1	.05	.01	.001
1	.98769	.99692	.999877	.9999988	16	.4000	.4683	.5897	.7084
2	.90000	.95000	.990000	.99900	17	.3887	.4555	.5751	.6932
3	.8054	.878	.9587	.99116	18	.3783	.4438	.5614	.6787
4	.7293	.8114	.91720	.97406	19	.3687	.4329	.5487	.6652
5	.6694	.7545	.8745	.95274	20	.3598	.4227	.5368	.6524
6	.6215	.7067	.8343	.92493	25	.3233	.3809	.4869	.5974
7	.5822	.6664	.7977	.8982	30	.2960	.3494	.4487	.5541
8	.5494	.6319	.7646	.8721	35	.2746	.3246	.4182	.5189
9	.5214	.6021	.7348	.8471	40	.2573	.3044	.3932	.4896
10	.4973	.5760	.7079	.8233	45	.2428	.2875	.3721	.4648
11	.4762	.5529	.6835	.8010	50	.2306	.2732	.3541	.4433
12	.4575	.5324	.6614	.7800	60	.2108	.2500	.3248	.4078
13	.4409	.5139	.6411	.7603	70	.1954	.2319	.3017	.3799
14	.4259	.497	.6226	.7420	80	.1829	.2172	.2830	.3568
15	.4124	.482	.6055	.7246	90	.1726	.2050	.2673	.3375
					100	.1638	.1946	.2540	.3211

SOURCE: From Table VII of Ronald A. Fisher and Frank Yates, *Statistical Tables for Biological, Agricultural and Medical Research*, 6th ed., published by Longman Group, Ltd., London (previously published by Oliver & Boyd, Edinburgh). Reprinted with permission of the authors and the publishers.

Table A.6
Portions of area under the normal curve
(continued on next page)

(A) z	(B) Area between mean and z	(C) Area beyond z	(A) z	(B) Area between mean and z	(C) Area beyond z	(A) z	(B) Area between mean and z	(C) Area beyond z
0.00	.0000	.5000	0.40	.1554	.3446	0.80	.2881	.2119
0.01	.0040	.4960	0.41	.1591	.3409	0.81	.2910	.2090
0.02	.0080	.4920	0.42	.1628	.3372	0.82	.2936	.2061
0.03	.0120	.4880	0.43	.1664	.3336	0.83	.2967	.2033
0.04	.0160	.4840	0.44	.1700	.3300	0.84	.2995	.2005
0.05	.0199	.4801	0.45	.1736	.3264	0.85	.3023	.1977
0.06	.0239	.4761	0.46	.1772	.3228	0.86	.3051	.1949
0.07	.0279	.4721	0.47	.1808	.3192	0.87	.3078	.1922
0.08	.0319	.4681	0.48	.1844	.3156	0.88	.3106	.1894
0.09	.0359	.4641	0.49	.1879	.3121	0.89	.3133	.1867
0.10	.0398	.4602	0.50	.1915	.3085	0.90	.3159	.1841
0.11	.0438	.4562	0.51	.1950	.3050	0.91	.3186	.1814
0.12	.0478	.4522	0.52	.1985	.3015	0.92	.3212	.1788
0.13	.0517	.4483	0.53	.2019	.2981	0.93	.3238	.1788
0.14	.0557	.4443	0.54	.2054	.2946	0.94	.3264	.1736
0.15	.0596	.4404	0.55	.2088	.2912	0.95	.3289	.1711
0.16	.0636	.4364	0.56	.2123	.2877	0.96	.3315	.1685
0.17	.0675	.4325	0.57	.2157	.2843	0.97	.3340	.1660
0.18	.0714	.4286	0.58	.2190	.2810	0.98	.3365	.1635
0.19	.0753	.4247	0.59	.2224	.2776	0.99	.3389	.1611
0.20	.0793	.4207	0.60	.2257	.2743	1.00	.3413	.1587
0.21	.0832	.4168	0.61	.2291	.2709	1.01	.3438	.1562
0.22	.0871	.4129	0.62	.2324	.2676	1.02	.3461	.1539
0.23	.0910	.4090	0.63	.2357	.2643	1.03	.3485	.1515
0.24	.0948	.4052	0.64	.2389	.2611	1.04	.3508	.1492
0.25	.0987	.4013	0.65	.2422	.2578	1.05	.3531	.1469
0.26	.1026	.3974	0.66	.2454	.2546	1.06	.3554	.1446
0.27	.1064	.3936	0.67	.2486	.2514	1.07	.3577	.1423
0.28	.1103	.3897	0.68	.2517	.2483	1.08	.3599	.1401
0.29	.1141	.3859	0.69	.2549	.2451	1.09	.3621	.1379
0.30	.1179	.3821	0.70	.2580	.2420	1.10	.3643	.1357
0.31	.1217	.3783	0.71	.2611	.2389	1.11	.3665	.1335
0.32	.1255	.3745	0.72	.2642	.2358	1.12	.3686	.1314
0.33	.1293	.3707	0.73	.2673	.2327	1.13	.3708	.1292
0.34	.1331	.3669	0.74	.2704	.2296	1.14	.3729	.1271
0.35	.1368	.3632	0.75	.2734	.2266	1.15	.3748	.1251
0.36	.1406	.3594	0.76	.2764	.2236	1.16	.3770	.1230
0.37	.1443	.3557	0.77	.2794	.2206	1.17	.3790	.1210
0.38	.1480	.3520	0.78	.2823	.2177	1.18	.3810	.1190
0.39	.1517	.3483	0.79	.2852	.2148	1.19	.3830	.1170

Table A.6
Portions of area under the normal curve
(continued)

(A) z	(B) Area between mean and z	(C) Area beyond z	(A) z	(B) Area between mean and z	(C) Area beyond z	(A) z	(B) Area between mean and z	(C) Area beyond z
1.20	.3849	.1151	1.60	.4452	.0548	2.00	.4772	.0228
1.21	.3869	.1131	1.61	.4463	.0537	2.01	.4778	.0222
1.22	.3888	.1112	1.62	.4474	.0526	2.02	.4783	.0217
1.23	.3907	.1093	1.63	.4484	.0516	2.03	.4788	.0212
1.24	.3925	.1075	1.64	.4495	.0505	2.04	.4793	.0207
1.25	.3944	.1056	1.65	.4505	.0495	2.05	.4798	.0202
1.26	.3962	.1038	1.66	.4515	.0485	2.06	.4803	.0197
1.27	.3980	.1020	1.67	.4525	.0475	2.07	.4808	.0192
1.28	.3997	.1003	1.68	.4535	.0465	2.08	.4812	.0188
1.29	.4015	.0985	1.69	.4545	.0455	2.09	.4817	.0183
1.30	.4032	.0968	1.70	.4554	.0446	2.10	.4821	.0179
1.31	.4049	.0951	1.71	.4564	.0436	2.11	.4826	.0174
1.32	.4066	.0934	1.72	.4573	.0427	2.12	.4830	.0170
1.33	.4082	.0918	1.73	.4582	.0418	2.13	.4834	.0166
1.34	.4099	.0901	1.74	.4591	.0409	2.14	.4838	.0162
1.35	.4115	.0885	1.75	.4599	.0401	2.15	.4842	.0158
1.36	.4131	.0869	1.76	.4608	.0392	2.16	.4846	.0154
1.37	.4147	.0853	1.77	.4616	.0384	2.17	.4850	.0150
1.38	.4162	.0838	1.78	.4625	.0375	2.18	.4854	.0146
1.39	.4177	.0823	1.79	.4633	.0367	2.19	.4857	.0143
1.40	.4192	.0808	1.80	.4641	.0359	2.20	.4861	.0139
1.41	.4207	.0793	1.81	.4649	.0351	2.21	.4864	.0136
1.42	.4222	.0778	1.82	.4656	.0344	2.22	.4868	.0132
1.43	.4236	.0764	1.83	.4664	.0336	2.23	.4871	.0129
1.44	.4251	.0749	1.84	.4671	.0329	2.24	.4875	.0125
1.45	.4265	.0735	1.85	.4678	.0322	2.25	.4878	.0122
1.46	.4279	.0721	1.86	.4686	.0314	2.26	.4881	.0119
1.47	.4292	.0708	1.87	.4693	.0307	2.27	.4884	.0116
1.48	.4306	.0694	1.88	.4699	.0301	2.28	.4887	.0113
1.49	.4319	.0681	1.89	.4706	.0294	2.29	.4890	.0110
1.50	.4332	.0668	1.90	.4713	.0287	2.30	.4893	.0107
1.51	.4345	.0655	1.91	.4719	.0281	2.31	.4896	.0104
1.52	.4357	.0643	1.92	.4726	.0274	2.32	.4898	.0102
1.53	.4370	.0630	1.93	.4732	.0268	2.33	.4901	.0099
1.54	.4382	.0618	1.94	.4738	.0262	2.34	.4904	.0096
1.55	.4394	.0606	1.95	.4744	.0256	2.35	.4906	.0094
1.56	.4406	.0594	1.96	.4750	.0250	2.36	.4909	.0091
1.57	.4418	.0582	1.97	.4556	.0244	2.37	.4911	.0089
1.58	.4429	.0571	1.98	.4761	.0239	2.38	.4913	.0087
1.59	.4441	.0559	1.99	.4767	.0233	2.39	.4916	.0084

Table A.6

Portions of area under the normal curve
(continued)

(A) z	(B) Area between mean and z	(C) Area beyond z	(A) z	(B) Area between mean and z	(C) Area beyond z	(A) z	(B) Area between mean and z	(C) Area beyond z
2.40	.4918	.0082	2.75	.4970	.0030	3.05	.4989	.0011
2.41	.4920	.0080	2.76	.4971	.0029	3.06	.4989	.0011
2.42	.4922	.0078	2.77	.4972	.0028	3.07	.4989	.0011
2.43	.4925	.0075	2.78	.4973	.0027	3.08	.4990	.0010
2.44	.4927	.0073	2.79	.4974	.0026	3.09	.4990	.0010
2.45	.4929	.0071	2.80	.4974	.0026	3.10	.4990	.0010
2.46	.4931	.0069	2.81	.4975	.0025	3.11	.4991	.0009
2.47	.4932	.0068	2.82	.4976	.0024	3.12	.4991	.0009
2.48	.4934	.0066	2.83	.4977	.0023	3.13	.4991	.0009
2.49	.4936	.0064	2.84	.4977	.0023	3.14	.4992	.0008
2.50	.4938	.0062	2.85	.4978	.0022	3.15	.4992	.0008
2.51	.4940	.0060	2.86	.4979	.0021	3.16	.4992	.0008
2.52	.4941	.0059	2.87	.4979	.0021	3.17	.4992	.0008
2.53	.4943	.0057	2.88	.4980	.0020	3.18	.4993	.0007
2.54	.4945	.0055	2.89	.4981	.0019	3.19	.4993	.0007
2.55	.4946	.0054	2.90	.4981	.0019	3.20	.4993	.0007
2.56	.4948	.0052	2.91	.4982	.0018	3.21	.4993	.0007
2.57	.4949	.0051	2.92	.4982	.0018	3.22	.4994	.0006
2.58	.4951	.0049	2.93	.4983	.0017	3.23	.4994	.0006
2.59	.4952	.0048	2.94	.7984	.0016	3.24	.4994	.0006
2.60	.4953	.0047	2.95	.4984	.0016	3.25	.4994	.0006
2.61	.4955	.0045	2.96	.4985	.0015	3.30	.4995	.0005
2.62	.4956	.0044	2.97	.4985	.0015	3.35	.4996	.0004
2.63	.4957	.0043	2.98	.4986	.0014	3.40	.4997	.0003
2.64	.4959	.0041	2.99	.4986	.0014	3.45	.4997	.0003
2.65	.4960	.0040	3.00	.4987	.0013	3.50	.4998	.0002
2.66	.4961	.0039	3.01	.4987	.0013	3.60	.4998	.0002
2.67	.4962	.0038	3.02	.4987	.0013	3.70	.4999	.0001
2.68	.4963	.0037	3.03	.4988	.0012	3.80	.4999	.0001
2.69	.4964	.0036	3.04	.4988	.0012	3.90	.49995	.00005
						4.00	.49997	.00003
2.70	.4965	.0035						
2.71	.4966	.0034						
2.72	.4967	.0033						
2.73	.4968	.0032						
2.74	.4969	.0031						

SOURCE: Richard P. Runyon and Audrey Haber, *Fundamentals of Behavioral Statistics*, 3d ed. (Reading, MA: Addison-Wesley, 1976), pp. 378–79.

APPENDIX B

Ethical Standards in Empirical Research

American Political Science Association

The American Political Science Association has adopted a set of "Principles of Professional Conduct." The following rules are excerpted from the section on ethical research practices.[1]

---

1. Openness concerning material support of research is a basic principle of scholarship. . . .

3. In applying for research funds, the individual researcher should:

   3.1 clearly state the reasons for applying for support and not resort to stratagems of ambiguity to make the research more acceptable to a funding agency;

   3.2 indicate clearly the actual amount of time the researcher personally plans to spend on the research;

   3.3 indicate other sources of support of the research, if any; and

   3.4 refuse to accept terms and conditions that the researcher believes will undermine his or her freedom and integrity as a scholar.

4. In conducting research so supported, the individual bears sole responsibility for the procedures, methods, and content of research. The researcher:

   4.1 must avoid any deception or misrepresentation concerning his or her personal involvement or the involvement of respondents or subjects, and must avoid use of research as a cover for intelligence work or for partisan political purposes;

   4.2 must refrain from using his or her professional status to obtain data and research materials for purposes other than scholarship;

   4.3 with respect to research abroad, should not concurrently accept any additional support from agencies of the government for purposes that cannot be disclosed;

---

[1] Reproduced with the permission of the American Political Science Association. The full text of "A Guide To Professional Ethics in Political Science" is available online at www.apsanet.org/pubs/ethics.cfm.

4.4 should carefully comply with the time, reporting, accounting, and other requirements set forth in the project instrument, and cooperate with institutional grant administrators in meeting these requirements; and

4.5 should avoid commingling project funds with personal funds, or funds of one project with those of another.

5. With respect to any public scholarly activity including publication of the results of research, the individual researcher:

5.1 bears sole responsibility for publication;

5.2 should disclose all relevant sources of financial support;

5.3 should indicate any condition imposed by financial sponsors or others on research publication, or other scholarly activities; and

5.4 should conscientiously acknowledge any assistance received in conducting research.

5.5 Authors are obliged to reveal the bases of any of their statements that are challenged specifically, except where confidentiality is involved.

6. Scholars have an ethical obligation to make a full and complete disclosure of all nonconfidential sources involved in their research so that their work can be tested or replicated.

6.1 As citizens they have an obligation to cooperate with grand juries, other law enforcement agencies, and institutional officials.

6.2 Conversely, scholars also have a professional duty not to divulge the identity of confidential sources of information or data developed in the course of research, whether to governmental or nongovernmental officials or bodies, even though in the present state of American law they run the risk of suffering an applicable penalty.

6.3 Scholars must, however, exercise appropriate restraint in making claims as to the confidential nature of their sources, and resolve all reasonable doubts in favor of full disclosure.

7. Political scientists, like all scholars, are expected to practice intellectual honesty and to uphold the scholarly standards of their discipline.

7.1 Plagiarism, the deliberate appropriation of the work of others represented as one's own, not only may constitute a violation of the civil law but represents a serious breach of professional ethics.

American Association for Public Opinion Research

The American Association for Public Opinion Research has adopted the following Code of Professional Ethics and Practices.[2]

---

[2] *Code of Professional Ethics and Practices,* courtesy of the American Association for Public Opinion Research.

I. Principles of professional practice in the conduct of our work

   A. We shall exercise due care in developing research designs and survey instruments, and in collecting, processing, and analyzing data, taking all reasonable steps to assure the reliability and validity of results.

      1. We shall recommend and employ only those tools of analysis which . . . are well suited to the research problem at hand.

      2. We shall not select research tools and methods of analysis because of their capacity to yield misleading conclusions.

      3. We shall not knowingly make interpretations of research results, nor shall we tacitly permit interpretations that are inconsistent with the data available.

      4. We shall not knowingly imply that interpretations should be accorded greater confidence than the data actually warrant.

   B. We shall describe our methods and findings accurately and in appropriate detail in all research reports, adhering to the standards for minimal disclosure specified in Section III below. . . .

II. Principles of professional responsibility in our dealings with people

   A. The public

      1. If we become aware of the appearance in public of serious distortions of our research, we shall publicly disclose what is required to correct these distortions. . . .

   D. The respondent

      1. We shall strive to avoid the use of practices or methods that may harm, humiliate, or seriously mislead survey respondents.

      2. Unless the respondent waives confidentiality for specified uses, we shall hold as privileged and confidential all information that might identify a respondent with his or her responses. We shall also not disclose or use the names of respondents for nonresearch purposes unless the respondents grant us permission to do so.

III. Standard for minimal disclosure

      1. Who sponsored the survey, and who conducted it.

      2. The exact wording of questions asked, including the text of any preceding instruction or explanation to the interviewer or respondent that might reasonably be expected to affect the response.

      3. A definition of the population under study, and a description of the sampling frame used to identify this population.

      4. A description of the sample selection procedure, giving a clear indication of the method by which the respondents were selected by the researcher, or whether the respondents were entirely self-selected.

      5. Size of sample and, if applicable, completion rates and information on eligibility criteria and screening procedures.

6. A discussion of the precision of the findings, including, if appropriate, estimates of sampling error, and a description of any weighting or estimating procedures used.

7. Which results are based on parts of the sample, rather than on the total sample.

8. Method, location, and dates of data collection.

Glossary

Abstract. a brief statement summarizing the contents of a report

Additive index. a measure created by combining indicators of different aspects of the same concept

Aggregate data. data pertaining to groups of cases or to collectivities

Alternative rival hypothesis. an alternative explanation for obtained results that logically cannot be accurate if the initial hypothesis is accurate

Antecedent variable. a variable that causes variation in the variable that, for purposes of a given hypothesis, is regarded as the independent variable

Applied research. research the primary purpose of which is to examine or resolve particular policy problems

Areal group. a group defined by residence within a particular geographic area

Association. a relationship in which two (or more) variables covary

Assumption. (also *axiom* or *postulate*) an abstract assertion about relationships that serves as a foundation for theoretical reasoning but is not subject to empirical test

Bar chart. a graphic device in which bars are used to represent observations

Basic research. research the primary purpose of which is to develop or test a scientific theory

Beta weight or **beta coefficient.** a standardized partial regression coefficient used to compare the relative effects of independent variables on a dependent variable

Bibliographic sources. systematic listings of publications organized to assist in literature reviews

Bibliography. a compilation of books, articles, and other materials on a given topic

Bilateral bar chart. a two-directional graphic device in which bars are used to represent variation above or below some norm

Bivariate statistics. statistics summarizing the relationship between two variables

Boolean operators. words such as *and, or,* or *not* that provide linkages among concepts during a computerized literature search

Causal model. a model that graphically specifies a set of relationships between concepts or variables such that change in one or more precedes and gives rise to change in another

Causal relationship. a relationship in which change in one or more concepts or variables leads to or "forces" changes in one or more other concepts or variables

Central tendency (measure of). device for determining the value or score that best represents a set of cases on a given variable

Chi-square (χ^2). a test of the statistical significance of the association between two nominal variables

Closed-ended questions. questions that force respondents to choose an answer from a limited number of options

Cluster sampling. *see* **multistage random area sample**

Codebook. a listing of variables and values indicating how they are coded in a study

Coder. a person who assigns scores to cases or responses, usually with reference to content analysis coded in a study

Codes. numbers assigned to represent different values on variables for purposes of data analysis

Coding. the process of assigning numerical values to represent values on variables

Coding sheet. a structured form for recording data

Coefficient of association. a measure of the degree and direction of association between two variables

Coefficient of determination (R^2). the multiple regression coefficient tells how much of the variance in the values on a dependent variable is "explained" by variance in a *set* of independent variables

Cohort study. a study based on repeated surveys of a specific group (for example, persons born in a given year) at different points in time

Collectively exhaustive. a characteristic of measures by which all cases can be assigned to at least one category

Computer-assisted telephone interviewing (CATI). interviewing using computer display of instrument, usually includes continual calculation of summary statistics

Concept. a word or phrase that symbolizes some idea or phenomenon

Concurrent validation. the characteristic of a measure that allows accurate sorting of cases on the basis of related concurrent traits

Confidence interval. an indicator of the accuracy with which a population parameter can be predicted from a sample statistic stated in terms of the range of values above or below the sample statistic the population parameter is likely to fall

Confidence level. an indicator of the likelihood that a sample is representative stated in terms of the probability that a sample statistic is within a given confidence interval of a population parameter

Construct validity. the characteristic of a measure by which it behaves as we would expect on the basis of theory

Content analysis. a technique used in the study of communication-related materials and behaviors

Contingency question. a filtering device used in survey research to ascertain the appropriateness of asking a subsequent question

Control. in experimental design, to limit the factors influencing a variable under observation; in data analysis, to hold the values of one variable constant while examining the relationship(s) between two or more other variables

Control group. subjects in an experiment not exposed to the independent variable (experimental event)

Controlled time-series design. a research design that uses control groups to assess the impact of an event

Controlling. holding constant the effect of one variable on the relationship between two other variables in order to obtain an accurate measure of that relationship

Convergent validity. a characteristic whereby several measures of a common concept provide essentially the same result

Correlation coefficient (r). the coefficient of association between two interval variables measuring the closeness of fit of data points around the regression line

Covariational relationship. a relationship in which two or more concepts or variables tend to change together for unspecified reasons

Cross-sectional survey. a survey that compares data from different cases at a single point in time

Crosstabulation. a tabular presentation summarizing the relationship(s) between two or more variables

Data. observations of or information about reality arising from the research process

Data archives. collections of the results of previous research

Data specifications. detailed descriptions of the data that are to be recorded for each case and variable

Data transformation. modification of data to meet the requirements of a particular analysis technique

Deduction. reasoning that moves from abstract statements about general relationships to concrete statements about specific behaviors

Degrees of freedom (df). the number of cells in a table or points along a regression line that may be entered without being determined by prior entries

Demographic group. a group defined by some personal characteristic(s) of its members

Dependent variable. a variable whose value changes in response to changes in the value of some other variable

Descriptive research. research concerned primarily with measuring some aspect of reality for its own sake rather than with developing or testing some theory

Direct observation. a technique used primarily in the study of group norms and behaviors

Discriminant validation. a characteristic whereby a measure is valid for one concept alone as opposed to several concepts

Dispersion (measure of). an indicator of variation around the measure of central tendency, that is, an indicator of its representativeness

Ecological fallacy. the improper use of aggregate data to draw conclusions about the characteristics of individual cases or groups

Elite interviewing. gathering data through interviews designed to tap the unique knowledge of the respondents

Empirical. pertaining to or characterized by observations or descriptions of reality

Empirically grounded. a type of theory that is based on induction from actual observation

Empirical referent. an observable object or event that corresponds to a concept

Enumerative table. a simple tabular listing of research data

Equivalent measures. indicators that measure the same phenomena in more than one system

Experimental design. a research strategy in which the relationship between a given stimulus, event, or other variable and some observable behavior is isolated

Experimental group. subjects exposed to the independent variable (experimental stimulus)

Explanatory research. research that uses observations of reality to test hypotheses and to help identify or develop an understanding of patterns of behavior in the context of a theory

Exploratory research. research designed to discover factors that should be included in theorizing and research on a subject

Ex post facto **experiment.** a research design in which experimental controls are simulated in data analysis

External validity. see also generalizability, pertains to the degree to which a given study relates to other populations

Face validity. a characteristic of a measure that gives it intuitive appeal

Field experiment. a partial application of experimental design in a real-world setting, as distinct from a laboratory

Field notes. written records made during direct observation

Focus group. a small group used for in-depth study of a subject through directed discussion

Frequency distribution. an ordered count of the number of cases that take on each value of a variable

Frequency distribution control. a procedure by which experimental and control groups can be made equivalent by selection of combinations of subjects with comparable aggregate characteristics

Galton's problem. the task of testing for the effects of diffusion in comparative research

Gamma (G). a coefficient of association between two ordinal variables

Generalizability. the characteristic that permits the results of research on a limited set of cases to be extended to the population from which those cases are drawn

Going native. the situation in which a researcher involved in participant observation adopts the values and mind-set of those being observed and loses objectivity

Guide. a set of instructions to guide a moderator in conducting a focus group

Guttman scaling. a method of scale creation that provides internal criteria for determining the degree to which a set of items exhibit unidimensionality (measure a single concept)

Histogram. a bar chart showing the distribution of values on a variable

Homogeneity. the degree to which members of a given population are like one another

Hypothesis. a statement predicting the relationship(s) between variables

Independent variable. a variable whose own value changes influence the value of some other variable

In-depth interviewing. a technique for gathering information by interviewing subjects at length while being highly flexible in the structure and content of the questions asked in order to discover unexpected facts

Index construction. combining two or more related indicators into a single, more comprehensive indicator

Indicator. a specific measure of a variable

Indirect causation. the phenomenon by which one variable exerts causal influence on another only by changing the value of other variables that directly affect it

Induction. reasoning that generalizes from what has been observed to what has not—that is, in which an abstract theory is developed from concrete evidence

Inference. reasoning from either observation or a logical system to reach conclusions not already apparent

In-person interview. a survey interview in which the interviewer questions the respondent face-to-face

Instrument. a device or procedure used for taking a measurement

Instrumentation. the specification of steps to take in making observations; the creation of measurement devices

Intercoder reliability. agreement in the values assigned to the same or similar cases by independent observers

Internal validity. a form of construct validity evaluating if the measures are accurately evaluating the theoretical concepts

Interobserver reliability. the degree to which two or more individuals agree on the details of an event they have observed as part of a research project

Interval measurement. measurement that classifies and rank orders cases so that the distance between cases is known by using a standard unit of measurement

Intervening variable. a variable that influences the effect of an independent variable on a dependent variable

Interview schedule. the questionnaire used with in-person interviews

Judgmental sample. a sample in which specific cases are purposely selected

Key. the explanation of symbols used in a graphic presentation

Key word or **key phrase.** a word or phrase that is meaningfully related to a given concept, used for bibliographic search

Lambda (λ). a coefficient of association between two nominal variables

Level of measurement. the amount of information provided by a set of instruments

Likert scaling. a method of scale creation based on asking respondents to report the degree to which they agree or disagree with a series of statements selected to represent a trait

Line graph. a graphic device using lines to connect points representing observations so as to suggest trends or other relationships

Linear relationship. a relationship between two variables that can be graphically represented as a straight line

Longitudinal survey. a survey that compares the attributes or behaviors of a given set of cases at different points in time

Mail surveys. surveys conducted by mailing questionnaires to respondents and asking that they complete and return them

Marginals. the frequency distribution as it appears in the row and column totals of a contingency table

Mean. a measure of central tendency for interval variables

Measurement. the application of an instrument to count or in some other way quantify observations of reality

Measurement error. inaccuracies in the observation of reality; differences between reality and recorded observations of it

Measurement theory. a statement of why one expects values on an indicator to change when the value of the variable it represents changes

Median. a measure of central tendency for ordinal variables

Method effect. any misleading impact of the particular method used to study a subject on the results of that study

Mode. a measure of central tendency for nominal variables

Model. a simplified representation of reality

Model specification. the process of selecting the variables to be included in a regression model and specifying their relationship to one another

Moderator. the person who directs discussion in a focus group and reports on its results

Most-different-systems design. a strategy for comparative research in which characteristics that differ between units of analysis can be ruled out as explanations for others that are shared

Most-similar-systems design. a strategy for comparative research that focuses on units of analysis that are very similar, on the theory that shared characteristics can be held constant when differences between the units are examined

Multicollinearity. the condition in which one or more of the independent variables in a regression equation are perfect linear functions of one or more other independent variables in the equation

Multidimensional. having several facets or elements

Multiple causation. the common situation in the social sciences in which an effect is the result of more than one cause

Multiple indicators. more than one measure of the same variable, especially useful for enhancing the validity of indicators

Multiple regression. a statistical procedure for examining the relationship among a dependent variable and several independent variables

Multiple regression equation. the mathematical equation that represents the conceptual process described by a regression model and is used as a basis for multiple regression analysis

Multiplicative index. a single measure constructed from a combination of measures of different but related concepts

Multistage random area sample. a sample in which geographic units or their analogs rather than individuals are selected for analysis

Multivariate analysis. any statistical analysis examining the relationship between *more than two* variables simultaneously

Multivariate statistics. statistics relating to the relationships among more than two variables

Mutually exclusive. characteristic of measures by which a given case can be assigned to only one category

Negative relationship. the relationship said to exist when corresponding values on two variables change in *opposite* directions

Nominal measurement. measurement that merely classifies cases without regard to rank or distances between cases

Nonexperimental studies. studies in which there is no research design to provide a logical basis for causal inference

Nonrecursive. the term describing a causal model in which at least one variable influences another variable that occurs earlier in the model

Normal distribution. a distribution that is unimodal and symmetrical, with the peak at the center, and in which the mode, median, and mean take on the same value

Normative. pertaining to or characterized by preferences or value judgments

Observation. in science, the application of an instrument to assign values to cases on indicators

Observation point. the time of observation or measurement

Observation schedule. a form facilitating systematic recording of data observations

Obtrusive measure. a measurement that is evident to the research subjects

Obtrusive research. research employing obtrusive measures.

Open-ended questions. questions that allow respondents to answer in their own words

Operational definition. set of observations that represent abstract concepts

Operationalization. the process of designating sets of observations to represent abstract concepts

Ordinal measurement. measurement that classifies and ranks cases without regard to the distance between them

Pair-comparison scaling. a technique employed in content analysis to measure the intensity of evaluative statements

Panel study. a study that employs the same group of subjects for a series of observations at different points in time

Parameter. any characteristic of a population, as distinct from a characteristic of a sample

Parsimony. the presentation of material in as efficient a manner as possible; simplicity in a theory

Partial regression coefficient. a statistic that indicates the effect of an independent variable on a dependent variable when the effects of all other variables in a model are controlled

Participant observation. a form of direct observation in which the researcher becomes more or less actively involved in the behaviors of the group that is being studied

Path analysis. a statistical technique for assessing the relative influence of variables in a causal model

Periodical indexes. systematic listings of journals and other periodicals used in literature reviews

Pie chart. a graphic device in which sectored circles are used to represent observations

Pilot study. a small-scale trial of measures and procedures used to identify in advance any weaknesses in the research plan or instrumentation

Population. a set of cases about which one wishes to draw some conclusions

Positive relationship. the relationship said to exist when corresponding values on two variables change in the same direction

Posttest. in an experiment, a measurement taken after the introduction of the experimental event

Pragmatic validation. the process of determining the pragmatic (practical) validity of an indicator

Pragmatic validity. the validity of an indicator as a measure of a concept that is demonstrated by the ability to use it to predict the values of indicators of other concepts

Precision matching. a procedure by which experimental and control groups may be made equivalent through the selection of comparable individuals

Predictive validity. a characteristic of a measure that allows the accurate prediction of future events

Pretest. in an experiment, a measurement taken before the introduction of the experimental event

Proposition. a statement of the relationship between concepts that is logically derived from the assumptions of a theory; a component of a theory

Q-sort. a technique employed in content analysis to measure the intensity of evaluative statements

Qualitative. research based on the researcher's informed understanding of the events under study and not involving statistical comparisons of cases

Qualitative methods. research strategies designed to gather qualitative information, usually in narrative form, in order to describe or understand people and events in their natural setting

Quantile. a measure of position within a distribution

Quantile range. a measure of dispersion for ordinal variables

Quantitative. research based on statistical comparisons of the characteristics of the numerical measurement representing cases being studied

Quasi-experimental design. research in which data analysis techniques or data-gathering strategies are used to approximate the degree of control associated with experimental research

Question branching. ordering survey questions based on responses to earlier questions

Question format. the technique by which survey questions are presented and answered

Questionnaire. a survey instrument intended for use in mailed or self-administered surveys

Quota sample. a sample in which cases are selected to fill a predesignated distribution of attributes

Random errors. nonsystematic measurement errors that render indicators invalid and unreliable as measures of a concept

Randomization. a procedure for selecting cases for study (or for obtaining equivalence in experiments) in which each case in a population, and every combination of cases of a given size, has an equal chance of selection

Random sample. a sample in which cases are selected from a population in accordance with the principle of randomization

Raw data. the product of unstandardized or otherwise unprocessed observations

Reactivity. the circumstance in which persons under study modify their behavior in reaction to the research itself

Recording form. the form used to transfer aggregate data from a source document to machine-readable form

Recursive. the term describing a causal model in which no variable influences any variable that occurs before it in the model and thus contains no "feedback"

Regression line. the line that best summarizes the distribution of data points on a scatter diagram and the slope of which characterizes the relationship in units of change between two internal variables

Regression toward the mean. the natural tendency for extreme values to move toward more typical values over time

Reliability. the consistency with which a measuring instrument allows assignment of values to cases

Representativeness. the degree to which a relatively small number of cases resemble the larger number of cases from which they are drawn

Representative sample. a sample in which all major traits of the population being sampled are present in the same proportion as in the population itself

Research design. the plan of a study that organizes observations in such a way as to establish a sound logical basis for causal inference

Research question. a question identifying the basic information we are seeking in a research project

Respondents. persons who respond to an interview or questionnaire

Sample. a small group of cases drawn from and used to represent some larger group

Sampling error. differences between the attributes of a sample and those of the population from which the sample is drawn

Scale. a series of indicators that can be ordered so as to rank cases according to the degree to which they manifest a concept

Scale score. a single measure of how much a subject has of a given attribute measured by a scale

Scaling. the process of combining several indicators of a given concept into a single complex indicator of that concept

Scatter plot. a graphic summary of the distribution of cases on two variables, using dots to represent observations

Scheduled interviews. elite or specialized interviews that are guided by an interview schedule specifying the questions to be asked

Scientific research. a method of testing theories and hypotheses by applying certain rules of analysis to the observation and interpretation of reality under strictly delineated circumstances

Screening interview. an interview conducted to select participants for a focus group

Secondary analysis. analysis of data that have been gathered previously, usually by another researcher

Segmented bar chart. a graphic display of data with bars divided into segments to show the distribution of a second characteristic in the population represented by the bar

Solomon two-control-group research design. a variation on the classic experimental design intended to allow researchers to identify any *test effect* present in the experiment

Solomon three-control-group research design. a variation on the classic experimental design intended to allow researchers to identify any influence of *maturation* on the results of an experiment

Specialized interviewing. interviews with respondents who require nonstandard procedures to ensure communication

Spurious relationship. a relationship in which two variables covary but only because of chance or because of the action of some other variable

Standard deviation (s). the measure of dispersion for interval variables

Standarized measures. indicators adjusted so as to allow valid comparisons among units of different sizes in the analysis of aggregate data

Standard score (z). the measure of location in an interval distribution based on standard deviation units about the mean

Standard score of gamma (Z_G). a test of the statistical significance of an association between two ordinal variables

Statistical significance. the likelihood that an association noted between two variables, based on analysis of a sample, might have occurred by chance and might not exist in the larger population

Statistics. numbers that summarize either the distributions of values on or the relationships between or among variables; in sampling, the characteristics of a sample that correspond to the parameters of a population

Stimulus. the independent variable in an experiment

Stratified sampling. a procedure in which subgroups are selected on the basis of one or more shared characteristics and then sampled separately

Structural content analysis. analysis focusing on the format of a communication

Structured observation. direct observation using a prepared schedule or protocol to record data

Subjects. persons who are being studied in a research project

Substantive content analysis. analysis focusing on the meaning of a communication

Summative indicator. a measure of group characteristics created by combining the individual characteristics of group members

Survey research. a technique used in the study of individual attitudes, attributes, or behaviors

Syntality indicator. a measure of some quality or characteristic of a group as a whole

Systematic errors. measurement errors that affect all applications of an instrument and render indicators invalid as measures of a concept

Systematic random sample. a sample in which cases are drawn from a master list by random selection of the first case and application of a selection interval for choosing subsequent cases

Telephone surveys. surveys in which interviews are conducted over the telephone

Test effect. any difference in the pretest and posttest scores of a subject due exclusively to a response to the pretest

Theoretical import. the degree to which a concept plays an important part in a conceptual explanation of an event

Theorizing. the process of stating conceptual explanations for real-world events by asserting systems of relationships among concepts

Theory. a possible explanation for events, often a set of logically related assumptions and propositions

Theory elaboration. the result of theory testing that refines a theory rather than confirming or refuting the theory

Theory testing. an effort to demonstrate the utility of a theory through research

Thurston scaling. a technique of scale construction in which some members of the group being studied are asked to act as "judges" to assign values to items to be used in a scale in order to increase its validity as a measure of some underlying concept

Time-series analysis. a data analysis technique based on regression that seeks to establish causal relationships through temporal ordering

Time-series design. a research design that seeks to establish causal relationships through analysis across time

Trend study. analysis based on a comparison of the same general population (such as persons of voting age in a certain state) at different times

Unit of analysis. the smallest component or element about which generalizations are to be made

Univariate statistics. statistics relating to or describing one variable

Unobtrusive research or **measure.** a measurement that intentionally avoids influencing the behavior of research subjects

Unscheduled. free-form, without a specific format or instrument; said of interviews, observations, etc.

Unscheduled interviews. elite or specialized interviews that are *not* guided by an interview schedule listing questions to be asked

Unstructured observation. direct observation using notes but not a prepared schedule or protocol, to record data

Validation. the process of assessing the degree to which an indicator accurately reflects the concept it is intended to measure

Validity. the extent to which measures correspond to the concepts they are intended to reflect

Value. the characteristic or score of a particular case on a given variable

Variable. a characteristic that takes on different values from one case to another or, for a given case, from one time to another

Variation ratio. the measure of dispersion for nominal variables

Weight. to alter the relative importance of items in an index or cases in a sample; the differential value assigned to a particular item or case to accomplish this

Weighted index. an index in which scores on one variable have been standardized by reference to scores on some other variable in order to facilitate valid comparison of index scores for different cases

Working hypothesis. a statement predicting a relationship between indicators

Index

A

Abstract concepts, 19–21
  quantification of, 60–61
  variables and, 61–65
Abstract of research report, 370–371, 372
Accuracy, aggregate data and, 185–188
  of multivariate model specification, 294
  sample size and, 121–124
Activities of survey research, 128–129
Additive index, 190
Adequacy of research design, 92–93
Administration of measuring instrument, 74–75
After-only design, 99
Aggregate data, 183–202
  for cross-national studies, 213–214
All-channel network, 223–224
Alternative form method, 75
Alternative rival hypotheses, 29
  explanatory surveys and, 129
  field experiments and, 98–99
  and other hypotheses, 93
  randomization and, 98
  research design and, 87–93
  survey questions and, 131
Ambiguous questions, 134
American Association for Public Opinion
    Research (AAPOR), code of ethics,
    399–401
American Political Science Association (APSA),
    ethical guidelines, 398–399
American Political Science Review, 3, 46, 292,
    370
American Statistical Index, 194
America Votes, 194
Analysis of data, 9–11
  in direct observation, 324–325
  from focus groups, 350–351

and measurement errors, 75
  multivariate, 291–306
  preparation for, 230–231
  presentation of, 375–378
  of survey research, 129, 151
  units of. *See* Unit of
Analysis of variance, 305
Antecedent variables, 27
Applied research, 4, 344–345
Appropriate codes, 232–235, 239
  measures, 75
  operational definitions, 151
  qualities for secondary analysis, 151
  research techniques, 7
Areal groups, 184
Argumentativeness in interview questions, 135
Assistant moderator, for focus groups, 348
Assistants, structured direct observations by,
    326–327
Association between variables, 268–306
  measures of, 268–269
  interval variables, 282–288
  nominal variables, 275–279
  ordinal variables, 279–281
Association, coefficient of, 269–272
Assumptions, 16–18, 20
  hypotheses and, 28
  for regression procedure, 295
Asymmetrical matrix, 220–221
Attitudes, defined, 127
Attrition from sample, panel studies, 131
Audience for reports of focus groups, 351–352
Author search, defined, 42
Average, 261
Axes of graphs, 245–246
  of scatterplots, 282–283
Axioms. *See* Assumptions